THE MILITARY
DECORATIONS OF
THE ROMAN ARMY

FOR MY PARENTS

THE MILITARY DECORATIONS OF THE ROMAN ARMY

VALERIE A. MAXFIELD

UNIVERSITY OF CALIFORNIA PRESS

BERKELEY AND LOS ANGELES

Printed in Great Britain

University of California Press
Berkeley and Los Angeles

ISBN 0-520-04499-1

Library of Congress Catalog Number: 81-7406

CONTENTS

LIST OF PLATES

LIST OF FIGURES

LIST OF TABLES

ACKNOWLEDGMENTS

The Author and Publishers wish to thank the following copyright holders for permission to reproduce the photographic plates appearing in this book:

Staatliche Museen, Berlin, 15a, 15b; Rheinisches Landesmuseum, Bonn, 2a, 9a, 10a, 11c, 12b, 14c, 15a; Trustees of the British Museum, 1a–i; Museo Romano, Brescia, photos by courtesy of Professor Albino Garzetti from the collection of the Unione Accademia Nazionale for the preparation of the fascicule *Brixia* of the *Inscriptiones Italiae*, 6c, 14b; Foto-Hartmann, copyright Vindonissa Museum, Brugg, 9b; Foto E. Shulz, Basel, copyright Vindonissa Museum, Brugg, 6a; Rheinisches Bildarchiv, Cologne, 2c; Peter Connolly, 3a, 3b, 4a, 4b, 5c, 5d, 8b, 16b; National Museum of Antiquities of Scotland, Edinburgh, 16a; Museo Nazionale Atestino, Este, 13c; Istuti Culturali ed Artistici della Città di Forli, 7b; Istanbul Arkeoloji Muzeleri, 5a, 5b; Landesmuseum für Kärnten, Klagenfurt, 13a; Ch. Koukouli-Chrysanthuki, Kavalla Museum, 8a; Mittelrheinisches Landesmuseum, Mainz, 11a, 14a; Archaeological Museum, Ptuj, 10b; Deutsches Arhäologisches Instituts, Rome, 12a; Jean Sampson, 6b; Archeološki Muzej, Split, 11b; Andrew Stewart, 7a; Soprintendenza Archeologica della Toscana, 8c; Musée National du Bardo, Tunis, 9c; Direzione dei Musei e Gallerie d'Arte, Verona, 2b; Städtisches Museum, Wiesbaden, 13b.

The figures were drawn by Seán Goddard. The following acknowledgments are due: Fig. 5: based on a drawing in *Année Épigraphique* 1891, 15 and photograph of a squeeze of the inscription in Steiner 1906. Stone lost. Fig. 7: drawn from photographs provided by Professor G. Alföldy. Fig. 10: drawn from photograph in *Epigraphaites Makedonias* I (1915), 28. Stone cannot be traced. Fig. 13: (a) is reproduced by permission of the Historical Archive of the City of Cologne from a drawing interleaved in a copy of J.W.C.A. von Hüpsch, *Epigrammatographie oder Sammlung von Inschriften der alteren mittleren und neueren Zeiten der Niederdeutschen Provinzen* (Cologne 1801); (b) is after J.M.

Schannat, *Eiflia Illustrata* (Cologne 1824–55), Vol. I, pt. I, Taf. X. Stone lost. Fig. 15: Based on illustration in Ianus Gruterus, *Inscriptionum Romanorum Corpus Absolutissimum* (1616), II.l, p. MXXX, no. 9. Stone lost. Fig. 17: Based on illustration in J.C. Bruce, *Lapidarium Septentrionale* (1870–5), 498. The stone is now in Carlisle Museum but much of it has been lost since Bruce's drawing was done.

EPIGRAPHIC CONVENTIONS

[ ]   square brackets indicate letters which are thought originally to have been in the text but which are now lost.

( )   round brackets indicate letters not on the original text but which have been restored to make clear the sense of the text.

Leg   a dot below a letter indicates that the reading of that letter is not completely certain.

For the explanation of bibliographical abbreviations, see the first page of the References, p. 273

PREFACE

The value attached by soldiers to a little bit of ribbon is such as to render any danger insignificant and any privation light if it can be attained.

Duke of Newcastle to Prince Albert, 20 January 1855

The growth and stability of the Roman world depended, to a large degree, on the continuing success of its armies. Emperors could rise and fall through the intervention of the military, by whom new territories were conquered, an extensive empire acquired, its frontiers guarded and external enemies repulsed. The remarkable success which the Roman army enjoyed over a lengthy period can be ascribed to its superior training, organization and equipment but also, as contemporary writers observed, to its discipline, to the importance which was attached to the judicious use of reward and punishment. No shirker, no coward, would go unpunished; no soldier who showed conspicuous gallantry would go unrewarded. It is the positive side of this treatment, the incentives to valour, which this book seeks to explore, tracing the development of formal military decorations, *dona militaria* (literally, military gifts) from their first appearance in the early Republic through to their final manifestations in the Byzantine empire in the sixth century AD. During this long period – a stretch of time roughly equivalent to that which divides us today from the England of the Saxons – many changes took place. The ways of rewarding soldiers evolved gradually over centuries of warfare, culminating in the first century AD in the development of a complex system of rank-related decorations functioning in a manner broadly comparable to that employed in the twentieth-century British army.

The evidence for these developments is often slight and capable of more than one interpretation: care has therefore been taken to examine both the nature of the evidence itself and the degree of confidence which can be placed in it and to present in some detail the basis on which conclusions have been reached, particularly on the obstinate but critical problem of the scales of award which operated during the hey-day of the Empire. I have attempted to answer those questions most commonly asked about Roman military decorations: what were they like, how were they won, who was eligible to win them, who got what, were they worn and if so how?

The last systematic study of the *dona militaria*, and the one which is still the standard work of reference on the subject, is an article by Paul Steiner which appeared in the *Bonner Jahrbücher* for 1906. While certain limited aspects of the subject have been examined since then, no overall reassessment has been made. The sheer increase in evidence, particularly in relation to the careers of soldiers who won decorations, has made such a reassessment long overdue.

It is my pleasure here to offer my sincerest thanks to the many people who have given me advice and practical assistance during the preparation of this book. I am indebted to the authorities of the National and Capitoline Museums in Rome, the Vatican Museum, the Museo Maffeiano, Verona and the Landesmuseum, Bonn for access to their stores and reserve collections and to numerous museum curators around the Roman empire who have cooperated in the provision of photographs. For hospitality I am grateful to the British School at Rome and the Römisch-Germanische Kommission des Deutschen archäologischen Instituts, Frankfurt, through its director, Professor Dr Hans Schönberger. The text figures were drawn by Seán Goddard and the final typescript produced by Judith Saywell, Hillary Tolley and Dawn Williams. I have profited much from discussions with many students of the Roman army who have been unstinting with their time and expertise: in particular Professor Eric Birley who first encouraged my interest in Roman military studies, Professors John Mann and Frank Walbank and Drs D.J. Breeze, J.S. Rainbird and Margaret Roxan. Professor Peter Wiseman and Dr Brian Dobson both very kindly read through an earlier draft of the text and made a number of suggestions which I have gratefully incorporated in the final version. I owe a particular debt to Brian Dobson who supervized my work as a research student at Durham and who has ever since been a source of invaluable advice, criticism and encouragement. The flaws that remain are mine alone.

Valerie A. Maxfield, UNIVERSITY OF EXETER

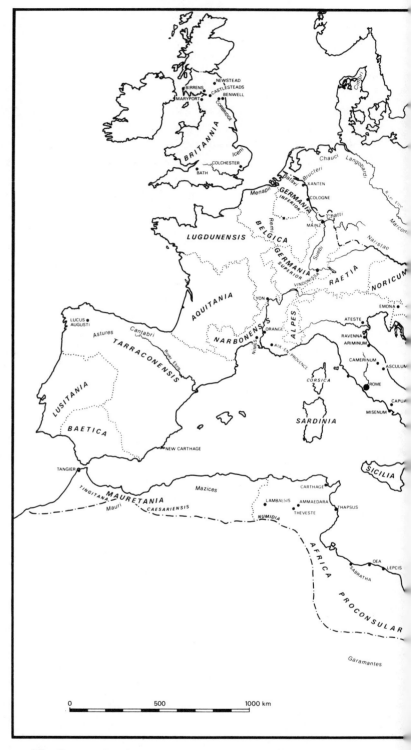

1 The Roman Empire

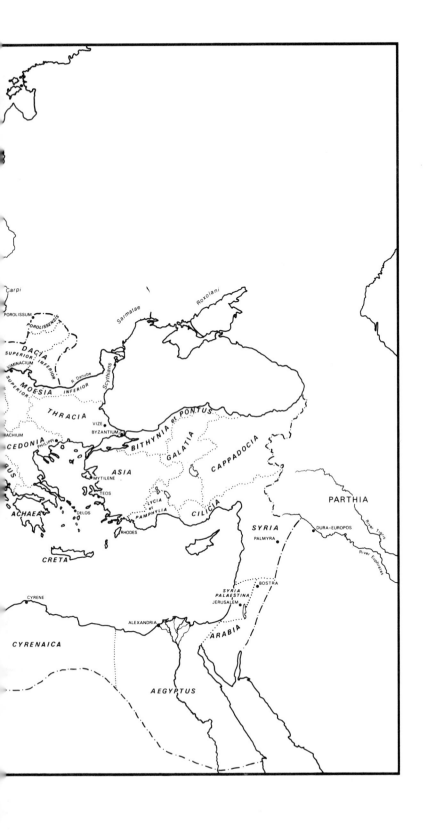

Carpi

POROLISSUM
POROLISSENSIS

DACIA
SUPERIOR. INFERIOR
UMINACIUM

MOESIA
SUPERIOR   INFERIOR

THRACIA

Sarmatae

Roxolani

Scythians

R. Danube

PONTUS

VIZE
BYZANTIUM

BITHYNIA et

CEDONIA
PHILIPPI

US

ACHAEA

CRETA

ASIA
MYTILENE

TEOS

DELOS

RHODES

GALATIA

CAPPADOCIA

LYCIA
et
PAMPHYLIA

CILICIA

SYRIA
PALMYRA

PARTHIA

River Tigris

DURA-EUROPOS

River Euphrates

CYRENE

ALEXANDRIA

SYRIA
PALAESTINA
JERUSALEM

BOSTRA

ARABIA

CYRENAICA

AEGYPTUS

CHAPTER I

THE MILITARY BACKGROUND

The first recorded example of Roman military decoration dates to the very early years of the Republic, to the middle of the fifth century BC. At the other end of the scale, award-giving on a regular basis came to an end in the early third century AD, though sporadic examples do occur to the very end of the Roman Empire in the West and into the Byzantine era. During this lengthy period the nature and organization of the Roman army changed radically if gradually, through slow evolution and periodic reform.

The biggest single factor which brought about change was the acquisition of overseas territory: the transition from a city state to an Empire which, at its greatest extent, was to stretch from Scotland in the north to the edges of the Sahara in the south, to the Euphrates, the Transylvanian Alps, the Rhine and beyond (fig. 1). The type of army fit to deal with military problems within the orbit of the Italian peninsula and the Mediterranean world was totally unsuited to cope with the conquest and, more important, the long-term occupation and protection of far-flung provinces. For this a full-time army composed of professional soldiers was required, capable of being maintained in the field for years on end. Such a professional standing army required a career structure with incentives to the potential recruit, the prospects of advancement in rank and status, and the security which came from adequate regular pay, good conditions of service and a gratuity on discharge sufficient to ease the transition back into civilian life. Likewise the expansion of Rome's military commitments led to a steady proliferation of permanent regular units requiring to be officered. This, together with the acquisition of overseas territories to be governed, necessitated changes in the structure and organiz-ation of command at its higher levels. The army of the late Empire was in many respects very different from the army of the early Republic from which it had ultimately evolved; and yet old traditions and habits of mind persisted.

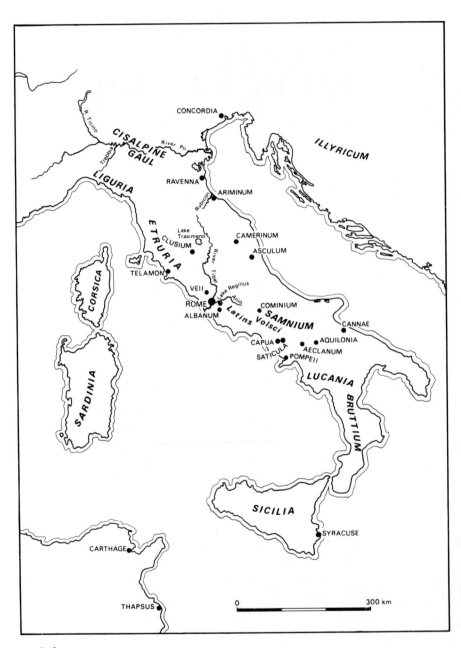

2   Italy

Generals and commanding officers

For the greater part of her history the armies of Rome were led by generals who were not full-time professional soldiers. Supreme command was vested in the leaders of the state, the magistrates whose mandate to rule, their *imperium*, encompassed authority in peace and in war. It was not until the military reforms of the Emperor Constantine in the early years of the fourth century AD that civil and military commands were finally separated, bringing to a logical conclusion the growing tendency towards specialization which had first appeared a century or so earlier.

With the expulsion of the last of the Etruscan kings in 510 BC (according to tradition) and the establishment of the Republic, the highest authority in the Roman state was vested in a pair of magistrates, *consuls*, who were elected annually and held power alternately. The purpose of sharing the power in this way was to prevent any one man from seizing and retaining authority. Each provided a check on the other. They were elected by an assembly of the people and were advised by the senate, a body composed of ex-magistrates. Having completed their year in power they were open to censure by the senate if their conduct had not been appropriate. In times of war the consuls commanded the army: a standard two-consular army was composed of four legions plus allies, each consul commanding on alternate days. The size of the army could be increased if the military situation required it. Such a system has obvious drawbacks, notably a lack of continuity of leadership not just within the consular year but from one year to the next, a factor of some significance should a single war extend over more than one campaigning season. One answer to the former problem was the appointment of a *dictator* who, singly, held supreme command. This expedient was limited to periods of particular crisis and was for the restricted period of six months only (that is, in effect, one campaigning season). The latter problem could be circumvented by allowing repeated tenure of the consulate or by allowing ex-consuls to retain their military authority as *proconsuls*. Further armies could be put into the field under the command of lesser magistrates, *praetors*, who again were subject to annual election and could retain their commands as *propraetors*. A basic praetorian army was half the size of a consular army as befitted their lower status. The third category of magistrate, the *quaestors*, whose responsibilities were essentially financial, could also be used to command extra legions. Their commands, however, were not independent, for they came under the authority of the appropriate consul or proconsul. The growing involvement of Rome in lengthy wars inside and outside Italy and the need to keep commanding officers out in the provinces led to the steadily increasing use of proconsuls, praetors and propraetors for military command.

Throughout the period of the Republic the individual legions were commanded by tribunes, *tribuni militum*. In the army of the mid-second

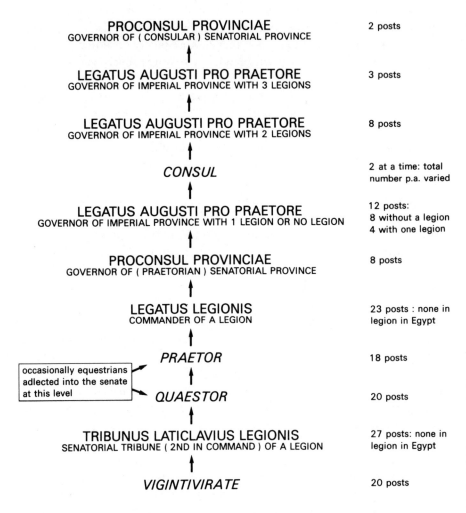

PROCONSUL PROVINCIAE
GOVERNOR OF (CONSULAR) SENATORIAL PROVINCE — 2 posts

↑

LEGATUS AUGUSTI PRO PRAETORE
GOVERNOR OF IMPERIAL PROVINCE WITH 3 LEGIONS — 3 posts

↑

LEGATUS AUGUSTI PRO PRAETORE
GOVERNOR OF IMPERIAL PROVINCE WITH 2 LEGIONS — 8 posts

↑

CONSUL — 2 at a time: total number p.a. varied

↑

LEGATUS AUGUSTI PRO PRAETORE
GOVERNOR OF IMPERIAL PROVINCE WITH 1 LEGION OR NO LEGION — 12 posts: 8 without a legion, 4 with one legion

↑

PROCONSUL PROVINCIAE
GOVERNOR OF (PRAETORIAN) SENATORIAL PROVINCE — 8 posts

↑

LEGATUS LEGIONIS
COMMANDER OF A LEGION — 23 posts : none in legion in Egypt

↑

PRAETOR — 18 posts

↑

occasionally equestrians adlected into the senate at this level

QUAESTOR — 20 posts

↑

TRIBUNUS LATICLAVIUS LEGIONIS
SENATORIAL TRIBUNE (2ND IN COMMAND) OF A LEGION — 27 posts: none in legion in Egypt

↑

VIGINTIVIRATE — 20 posts

3   Senatorial career ladder: mid-second century AD

22

century BC as described by Polybius there were six tribunes per legion, commanding in pairs for two-month periods at a time (the computation here clearly based on the concept of the six-month campaigning season linked to the principle of collegiality). Of the twenty-four tribunes required for the four-legion (two-consular) army, ten were senior, that is appointed from among those who had already seen ten years service, the remaining fourteen junior, with five to ten years service. Men of considerable experience, including ex-magistrates, could and did hold these posts. In terms of age and experience the military tribunes of the republican period were very different from their imperial counterparts. Not until the early years of the Principate did each individual legion acquire a single overall commander: when such a commander did come to be appointed he was known as the *legatus legionis*. *Legati*, who were members of the senate, had been used in a variety of capacities during the Republic, assistants to consuls, proconsuls and the like, commanding fleets, and under Caesar we find them being placed, on an *ad hoc* basis, over single legions, a legion plus detachments, or groups of legions. It is under Augustus that the *legatus legionis* emerges as an established legionary commander, drawn initially from among either the ex-quaestors or ex-praetors but, from the time of Vespasian, regularly from ex-praetors. The *tribuni* had by now become regularly subordinate to the legate.

During the early years of the Principate the career of the senator was given a much more structured form than it had hitherto known. The three magistracies of *quaestor, praetor* and *consul* remained at the core, the pair of consuls still supreme. In between these appointments there was a large selection of other posts which the senator might hold: some, such as curatorships of the Italian roads or care of the aqueducts and sewers, of civil importance, others of military concern. A senator who was not a patrician by birth and who hoped to make a success of a political career, rising to the consulate, had to pull his weight in the service of the emperor (fig. 3). After an initial appointment in the *vigintivirate* (a board of twenty minor magistrates) the aspiring candidate would commonly serve as a military tribune. Of the six traditional tribunates only one was reserved to potential senators, the other five being held by equestrians (below p. 24). The tribune who was destined for a career in the senate was known as the *tribunus laticlavius* (after the broad purple stripe down his tunic contrasting with the narrow stripe of the equestrian tribune, the *tribunus angusticlavius*). The importance of the tribunate, especially of the five equestrian tribunates, within the legions had clearly declined from the position it had previously held, though this process had already begun in the last century of the Republic. The laticlave tribunate was held by a potential legate and its holder was indeed second-in-command of the legion: but it was now an initial army appointment occupied by a man with minimal experience of civil administration and no military experience. The laticlave tribune was a legionary legate in training.

The five equestrian tribunes were responsible for matters of a largely administrative nature: their tasks included hearing complaints, punishing offenders, checking on supplies, keeping the key to the gates and inspecting the sick. The senatorial tribune entered the senate as a *quaestor*, a magistracy which could either keep him in Rome or send him out to the provinces as quaestor to a governor. Tenure of the next magistracy, that of *praetor* (a minimum of five years later and at no less than thirty years of age) qualified him for service as a legionary legate followed by the governorship of a province with no legions in it or with just one legion. In such one-legion provinces the governor served as joint legionary legate and governor. The consulate (minimum age thirty-three for a patrician and normally forty-two for a plebeian) then gave access to command in the provinces containing two or more legions or in one of the two prestige provinces of Asia and Africa. The patricians who held the early consulate are very unlikely to have been employed in the emperor's service.

Most important in military terms were the so-called 'imperial provinces', that is the provinces under the control of, and whose governorships were in the gift of, the Emperor. In 27 BC Octavian (Augustus), having eliminated the other two members of the second triumvirate (M. Lepidus and M. Antonius), formally 'restored the Republic'. The senate remained, the traditional magistracies remained but bereft of effective power because Augustus himself retained control of nearly all the legions. He chose for himself a *provincia*, a sphere of influence or province, which consisted of Gaul, Spain and Syria. Illyricum was subsequently added. In precisely these areas lay the Empire's military problems, here lay the bulk of the legions. Augustus ruled these areas with the powers of a proconsul but he clearly could not directly govern them himself: he therefore appointed deputies, legates, to act on his behalf. Their power had to be less than his, so their authority was that of a *propraetor*: hence they bore the title *legatus Augusti pro praetore*. The provinces remaining under direct senatorial control were governed by proconsuls. All, with the exception of Asia and Africa, were ex-praetors: Asia and Africa fell to ex-consuls. Such new provinces as were subsequently created (for example the Germanies, Britain, Dacia) went to the emperor.

One of the imperial provinces, that of Egypt, was of such significance that the emperor would allow no senator to enter it. Egypt was the major supplier of Rome's grain and whoever held Egypt held the key to power. As a result, the highest positions in the province were held by equestrians, members of the lesser aristocracy. Its governor, the *praefectus Aegypti*, was one of the highest-ranking equestrian officials, indeed initially *the* highest, though later out-ranked only by the prefect who commanded the emperor's bodyguard, the *praefectus praetorio* (fig. 4). Its legions lacked both legate and senatorial tribune, command being in the hands of a *primipilaris* (below p. 31).

Egypt was not the only province to be governed by an equestrian instead of a senator, though in the case of the others the reason lay in their relative unimportance rather than in their supreme importance. The provinces in question are those such as Alpes Maritimae which entirely lacked troops, the Mauretanias which contained no legion, though they held a substantial auxiliary garrison, or Raetia and Noricum which held auxiliaries but (until the creation of *II* and *III Italica* by Marcus Aurelius) no legion. From the early third century onwards the number of equestrian appointments increased. Septimius Severus (193–211) created the province of Mesopotamia, putting it under an equestrian prefect. The two legions in the province, *I* and *III Parthica*, raised by Severus for his eastern wars, were commanded by *primipilares*, as was *II Parthica* which, on its return from the east, was based in Italy, at Albanum near Rome. Gallienus (253–268) greatly extended the use of *praefecti* in legionary command, indicating a trend towards the use of men more experienced in military than in civil administration, a trend which reached its logical conclusion in the early years of the fourth century with the divorce of civil and military responsibilities and the breakdown of the traditional pattern of advancement.

During the Republic the consuls or, abnormally, dictators, conducted Rome's wars. During the Principate armies were commonly led into the field by the Emperor himself or by a designated member of the imperial family. In the absence of an imperial presence a senator of appropriate seniority and experience would be briefed for the task: this might be the governor of a province adjacent to the area of campaigning or, in the case of wars involving the conquest and acquisition of new territory, a man transferred from elsewhere. For example, for the conquest of Britain the expeditionary force of four legions plus auxiliaries was led by an ex-consul, Aulus Plautius, who was appointed to the task direct from the governorship of the imperial consular province of Pannonia. When the emperor Claudius joined the invading army late in the first campaigning season, Plautius will have handed over command to him. When Claudius departed just sixteen days later, Plautius resumed command. He became the first governor of the new province. Subsequent governors continued to play this dual role, governing the province as it existed and endeavouring to extend its bounds. No emperor campaigned again in Britain until the early years of the third century, when Severus and his sons fought against the Caledonii and Maeatae. Wars there certainly were during this period, but each was conducted by the governor of the day in his capacity as military commander. However, such generals as Plautius and his successors were regarded as fighting simply as deputies for the emperors: the ultimate honours bestowed on such occasions, the triumphs, fell to the emperors themselves and not to their substitutes. Wars connected with the senatorial provinces were conducted by the appropriate proconsul, the consuls themselves having lost all responsibility for fighting. Given the distribution of provinces between the

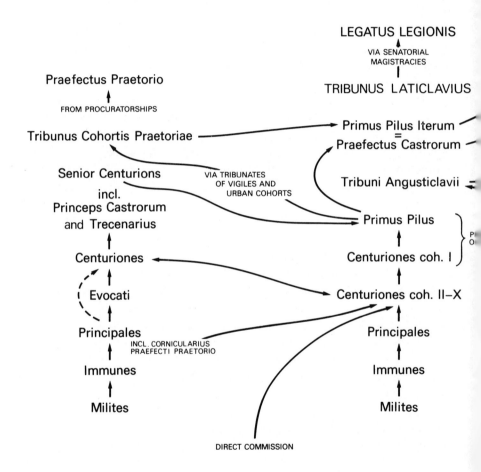

PRAETORIAN GUARD

LEGIONS

4 Army promotion patterns: mid-second century AD

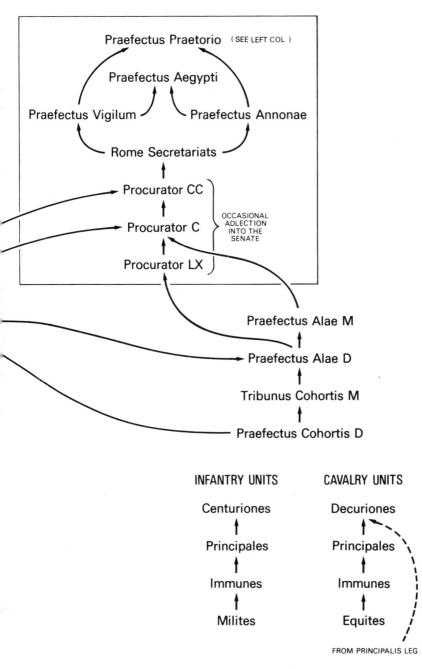

emperor and the senate such encounters were comparatively rare, though we do find successive proconsuls of Africa conducting a prolonged campaign against the rebel Numidian Tacfarinas in the early years of the first century AD.

The legion

The Roman legion, which remained until the late Empire the backbone of the army was, in origin, the Roman citizenry in arms. According to the practice which existed in the mid-second century BC, men were liable for military service between the ages of seventeen and forty-six; if called upon they were obliged to serve. Initially the legions were recruited completely afresh each year, and the citizen could be called up for a normal maximum of sixteen years. This scheme evolved at a time when Rome was fighting her wars close to home, so that at the end of the summer campaigning season the armies could disperse to their homes for the winter. As long as sporadic warfare within Italy was all that was in question, there was no need to establish the practice of full-time military service. However, hostile encounters with other peoples around the Mediterranean seaboard, which came about naturally as a result of Rome's expansion into peninsular Italy, and the subsequent acquisition of overseas territories, changed things. Troops had to be stationed for lengthy periods away from home, a fact which gradually undermined the practice of the annual levy – though this was still necessary for producing the recruits to bring existing legions up to strength, replacing those who had died in service and providing substitutes for the men who had fulfilled their statutory maximum term of service.

The principles of annual recruitment and discontinuous military service meant that there was no concept of a military career structure as such, with a natural progression upwards from one post to another. There were in fact very few different posts through which to progress. There were the centurions in charge of the individual centuries into which the legion was divided: each centurion had a deputy, an *optio*. The centuries were grouped in pairs, or maniples, and two standard bearers, *signiferi*, were appointed to carry the standard (or *signum*) of each maniple. According to the system described by Polybius the centurions were selected by the tribunes from among the mass of men already picked out for service. These centurions then chose the *optiones* and *signiferi*. The first centurion to be chosen by the tribunes was the most senior, the *primus pilus*. Selection for any one of these posts at one annual levy did not guarantee selection to the same grade on a subsequent occasion. Hence a man could be, in effect, demoted, a potential source of discord. Such a case is indeed recorded by Livy who tells of an episode in 171 BC during the third Macedonian war when the tribunes enrolling the four legions were faced with twenty-three men all of whom had served previously as *primus pilus*. One of the men eventually appointed, Spurius Ligustinus, cited a very distinguished record. His twenty-two years of service included four previous appointments as *primus pilus* and extensive campaigning experience during which he had won military decorations on no less than thirty-four separate occasions. This man was appointed to a rank comparable to that in which he had served before and so presumably were three others: nineteen unsuccessful candidates had to settle for less. Similar situations, if in not quite so extreme a form, must have been enacted time and again during the conduct of the levies. It represented a practice which was incompatible with the trend towards the maintenance of standing armies.

This steady move towards continuous, rather than intermittent, military service and permanent legions led to the units acquiring individual identities and the numbers with which they appear, for example, in Caesar's account of his wars in Gaul in the middle of the first century BC. Eventually the majority also took names as well as numbers, names which might, for example, commemorate the emperor under whom they were raised (*II* and *III Augusta* and *II Traiana*), a place where they had served (*IX Hispana*) or the circumstance which led to their creation (*I, II* and *III Parthica* raised on the occasion of Severus' Parthian war).

Certain military reforms had been instituted some fifty years before the Caesarian campaigns by the senator C. Marius. In 107 BC Marius was appointed consul and given command of the Roman army fighting in Africa against the Numidian leader Jugurtha. Military service in Africa, and particularly in so unrewarding a campaign against a particularly intransigent enemy, was not popular. In order to facilitate recruiting Marius dropped the existing property qualification, which had in any case been gradually diminishing, but which had hitherto exempted the poor and landless from liability to serve. Volunteers, not conscripts, from among the urban proletariat were for the first time admitted into the Roman army, a significant move towards the creation of a professional army. The landless could not live off the income from their property and their enrolment thus necessitated the making of proper financial provision in the form of adequate pay and pensions for the troops. Until the time of the emperor Augustus, the burden of arranging for the provision of discharge grants in the form of money or land rested on the shoulders of the individual general. In AD 6 Augustus established a military pay-chest, the *aerarium militare*, to provide the necessary finance, the money being raised through regular taxation.

Soldiers' pay is said by Livy to have been introduced by Camillus at the time of the siege of Veii in 396 BC, when the army had to be kept in the field beyond the normal summer season and into the winter months. The only figures we have for the pay of the soldier of the mid-Republic are those given us by Polybius who quotes Greek currency. According to him the ordinary soldier received two obols a day, the centurion four (equivalent to five and ten *asses* in Roman currency). There is no evidence to suggest that Marius altered this sum and not until the time of Caesar do we hear of a pay rise, the sum then being doubled. More than a century elapsed before the next pay rise under Domitian, and another century before the next under Severus. Thereafter the gathering rate of inflation led to a quick further increase under Caracalla and eventually resulted in increasing dependence on payment in kind, in grain rather than in cash.

While the Marian reforms caused one significant change in the pattern of recruitment to the legion, another came about as a result of the Social War of 91–88. The basic criterion for eligibility for service in a legion was Roman citizenship, that is citizenship of the city state of Rome. Such citizenship was enjoyed by the inhabitants of the *urbs Roma* itself and also by the people living in the Roman colonies, established initially in Italy and later overseas (for example Ostia, traditionally the first Roman colony, or Narbonne, founded in 118 BC: the majority of those overseas were founded from the time of Caesar onwards). Other Italian cities allied to Rome were under a treaty obligation to provide troops, but these were enrolled in the *alae* not in the legions (see below, Allies and Auxiliaries). In 91 the allies went to war with Rome over the question of citizenship; the war resulted in the enfranchisement initially of the communities who had remained loyal to Rome but subsequently of the whole of Italy. Hence the potential recruiting ground for the legions was considerably extended, that for the allied *alae* totally subverted. As further territory outside Italy came under Roman control so more colonies were established. One relatively cheap and easy way of providing for discharged soldiers was to give them land instead of money, and so veteran colonies were set up first within Italy and later throughout the Empire. These provincial colonies were commonly founded on the sites of abandoned legionary fortresses, that is on land which the army had already appropriated. In Britain, for example, Colchester (Colonia Victricensis or Camulodunum) was established in AD 49 on the site of the fortress of *XX Valeria* after the legion had moved on westwards, while in Lower Germany the double legionary fortress at Cologne was replaced by a colony, the Colonia Claudia Ara Agrippinensium, subsequent to the transfer in AD 35 of the two legions in residence, *I Germanica* and *XX Valeria* to Bonn and Neuss respectively. Such veteran settlements went on being established as long as the Empire kept expanding and whole legions were on the move from site to site: here among the sons of soldiers was a potential source of legionary recruits not in Rome, not even in Italy but out in the provinces where the legions had come to be permanently based. The grant of Roman citizenship to discharged auxiliary soldiers and their children, put on a regular basis by Claudius, provided yet another pool of provincial recruits for the legions, while the extension of the citizenship by Caracalla in AD 212 to all free-born *peregrini* (that is the non-Roman citizens within the Empire) opened it up even further.

All this caused considerable shifts of emphasis in the legionary recruiting pattern. Marius' reforms had caused a social shift. The Social war opened up the whole of Italy and until the middle years of the first century AD Italians predominated in the legions. As a result of the Marian reforms recruitment became largely voluntary (although conscription remained important at periods of major wars when large armies were required), and service in the provinces far from the Mediterranean homeland did not retain its appeal for the Italians. By the latter part of the first century AD more provincials than Italians were serving in the Roman legions, with the proportion of provincials steadily increasing. Only when new legions were raised was Italy the prime recruiting ground: this was not a case of military conservatism but a sheer practicality to avoid upsetting the flow of provincial recruits to the existing legions.

The long-term result of the Marian reforms was that military service became a career instead of an inconvenient interruption to civilian life. The sixteen-year liability for service was regularized at sixteen plus four *sub vexillo*, as part of a veteran reserve: this was lengthened in AD 5 to twenty plus five. Progress as far as centurion and *primus pilus* had, as we have seen, long been possible on an *ad hoc* and temporary basis. During the early Empire, and particularly under Augustus, steps were taken to lengthen this career ladder. In practice many men did still retire after serving as *primus pilus* for there were relatively few posts available for them to move on to: however, the primipilate was no longer the theoretical ceiling beyond which they could not advance. The considerable skills and experience acquired by these men was, in a professional army, not to be wasted. *Primipilares* (ex *primi pili*) came to be employed in a number of capacities, inside the legion as *praefectus castrorum* (prefect of the camp) subordinate only to the legionary legate and senatorial tribune, or outside it as tribunes of the Rome cohorts (below), as commanders of the fleets, as equestrian governors and in a host of other posts up to the heights of the command of the emperor's bodyguard as *praefectus praetorio* (fig. 14).

Below the centurionate specialist posts proliferated. The *signiferi* were joined by the *aquilifer* who carried the eagle, the symbol of the legion adopted at the time of Marius, and the *imaginifer* who bore a portrait (or *imago*) of the emperor. The more senior officers all had staffs of general clerks (*beneficiarii*) and adjutants (*cornicularii*) in numbers according to their rank: these posts would be filled by the more literate and numerate of the troops. Craftsmen too were needed, specialists in building, tent-making, the construction and maintenance of artillery, armour and weaponry in general, doctors, vete-rinary surgeons and a host of others. In order to accommodate and reward the acquisition of special skills a pay structure developed whereby a soldier could proceed from basic pay to basic pay with exemption from fatigues (*immunis*), to pay and a half (*sesquiplicarius*) to double pay (*duplicarius*). Thence

31

promotion was into the centurionate and beyond.

The career structures outlined in fig. 4 were largely complete by the time of Vespasian (69–79) and remained essentially the same until the latter part of the third century AD.

Allies and auxiliaries

When Republican Rome went to war the armies which she put into the field were very considerably strengthened by troops provided by her allies. The allies were obliged to raise an army to match in size that of Rome. The allied units were organized in a manner similar to Roman legions but were known as *alae*, literally wings, from the position which they occupied on the flanks in line of battle. Each *ala* was commanded by six officers, the equivalents of the tribunes of the legions but called prefects of the allies, *praefecti sociorum*. Half of these officers were selected by the consuls from among the Roman citizenry, the other half were provided by the allies themselves.

While the number of infantry in each *ala* was equal to the number in the legion, the number of cavalry was considerably superior, 900 horsemen compared with the Roman 300. In this sense the contribution of the allies to the army was of particular significance, for they greatly strengthened an arm in which Rome itself was weak. Indeed the figure of 300 cavalrymen per legion given by Polybius for the army of the mid-Republic did not continue to hold good. The legionary cavalry element had disappeared by the first century BC, though a small contingent (120) was attached to the legion during the Empire.

The allies were organized in a manner similar to the legionaries, and they fought in like manner. They were not discriminated against to the same extent as were the auxiliaries of the imperial army. With the extension of the Roman franchise to the whole of Italy which resulted from the Social War, the basic distinction between legions and *alae* promptly disappeared. Those who had hitherto enrolled in the *alae* were now eligible for the legions. The Italian allies disappeared and with them a substantial body of cavalry. The army which Rome could now put into the field consisted exclusively of heavy infantry fighting with javelin (*pilum*) and short sword (*gladius*): even the lightly armed skirmishers described by Polybius had disappeared by the first century BC. All other types of troops had to be provided by sources outside the Italian peninsula. This practice was not entirely new, for non-Roman or non-Italian troops had long been employed in the service of Rome either as mercenaries or as the result of treaty arrangements. Such sources of men now became all the more important, leading eventually to the development of regular *auxilia* (literally 'helping' troops) which took on a steadily increasing role both in offensive warfare and in the defence of the Empire. The employment of such troops was initially on an *ad hoc* basis. These men were organized and fought in manners traditional to the areas whence they came and were led either by *praefecti* appointed by Rome or by their own native leaders. For example, during his campaign against the Bellovaci of northern Gaul, Caesar employed a large number of cavalry provided by the nearby tribe of the Remi (area of modern Rheims). These Remi were led by the chief magistrate of the tribe, Vertiscus, who despite advancing years insisted on taking part in the fight. In addition to cavalry and infantry provided by pro-Roman Gallic tribes, Caesar employed slingers from the Balearic islands, archers from Crete, Numidian horsemen, Germans, and Syrians.

In time many of the areas which had provided military assistance of this type became permanent settled provinces of the Roman Empire. The men of these areas, not being Roman citizens, were not eligible for entry into the legions, but they were clearly a valuable source of potential recruits able to provide a variety of the fighting skills in which Rome itself was defective. Hence there developed under Augustus the *auxilia*, firstly units of cavalry (*alae* – not to be confused with the allied *alae* which comprised infantry and cavalry) and, a little later, units of infantry (*cohortes*) the organization of which was modelled, not surprisingly, on the organization of the legion, commanded by Roman officers, *praefecti* and *tribuni*, and recruited from among the *peregrini*. These auxiliary units were commonly named after the areas where they were raised, using an ethnic or tribal designation. Tribal names are borne, for example, by the *alae* and *cohortes Batavorum*, raised in the area of the Batavian tribe in what is now Holland, or by the units of *Astures* from north-west Spain. Ethnic names are used by, among others, units of Gauls, Spaniards, Britons and Dacians, *alae* and *cohortes Gallorum, Hispanorum, Britannorum* and *Dacorum*; or both tribal and ethnic might be combined as with the *alae Hispanorum Asturum*. In the early days of the auxiliary cavalry, individual units were often identified by the name of their commanding officer. In time this was institutionalized and a number of units retained the name of one particular (and presumably in some way significant) past commander: an example is the *ala Gallorum Indiana*, named after Iulius Indus, a philo-Roman Gallic leader of the tribe of the Treveri (in the area of modern Trier) or the *ala Gallorum Petriana*, named after T. Pomponius Petra, an early first-century equestrian officer. Both of these *alae* were of Gauls, and the fact that far the greater proportion of these early cavalry units were drawn from Gaul and Spain meant that ethnic titles alone were of little help in distinguishing individual units: hence the need for personalized titles.

The origins of the recruits to the *auxilia* are as far flung as the Empire itself, and there must have been an interesting racial mix in many of the units. Once a unit had been sent away from the area where it was originally raised it would start to recruit locally – a considerably more convenient and economical practice than having constantly to transfer new recruits half way across the empire. Thus it could happen that a unit raised in Spain and designated

Hispanorum might contain not a single Spaniard within a quarter century or so of its creation. The main reason for moving units was, of course, the exigencies of warfare and the shifting pattern of military control. For example one of the large concentrations of troops in the early part of the first century AD was in the Rhineland: many of these units shifted eastwards in the latter part of that century and the early part of the next when the major theatre of war transferred to the Danube with the campaigning against Decebalus and his Dacians. Troops might also have to be moved for security reasons. There is an obvious danger in leaving a unit stationed in the area where it was originally raised, in cases of internal insurrection. For example, many of the Rhineland units turned against Rome and joined in the rebellion of the Batavian Civilis in AD 69: with the suppression of the rebellion these troops were promptly transferred elsewhere. However, with the practice of local recruiting any unit would, in time, identify with the area where it was stationed, regardless of the area where it was originally raised.

Another of the effects of local recruitment will have been to reinforce standardization and the loss of regional characteristics. An exception to this general rule occurs in the case of certain specialist units. The Syrian archers, for example, retained their traditional weapon and continued to recruit from Syria in order to maintain their particular excellence.

The auxiliaries employed by Caesar were organized into units of various sizes, but once they became fully integrated into the Roman army their size was standardized. Initially all were given an establishment strength modelled on that of the legionary cohort. Each cavalry *ala* was divided into sixteen troops (*turmae*) thirty-two men strong, each troop commanded by a decurion; the infantry cohorts were composed of six centuries, each eighty men strong and each century commanded by a centurion. There were also units of infantry with a cavalry element attached (*cohortes equitatae*), composed of six infantry centuries plus four cavalry *turmae*. During the reign of Vespasian there first appears a larger size of each type of auxiliary unit – twenty-four troops, ten cohorts, and ten cohorts plus eight cavalry troops respectively. These new units were described as milliary cohorts and *alae* (though this number does not mean that they were *literally* 1,000 strong), in response to which the old-size units were designated quingenary. Some of the milliary units were entirely new formations, others were created by enlarging existing quingenary units.

When these auxiliary units were first integrated into the Roman military structure they were commanded by whatever officer happened to be available, future senator, equestrian, *primipilaris* or centurion. However, as the units themselves became regularized so the career patterns of the different categories of officer were given a distinct order. As we have already seen, the career structure of the *primipilaris* as developed by the middle of the first century AD had no place for auxiliary command: by this date auxiliary command had become the sole preserve of the equestrian. The established sequence of posts is indicated on fig. 4. There were three basic steps, or four from the time of Hadrian. In ascending order these were prefect of a quingenary cohort, tribune of a milliary cohort (or equestrian tribune in a legion), prefect of a cavalry *ala*, quingenary or milliary. Hadrian's contribution to the development of the career was to turn the command of a milliary *ala* into a further step on the ladder – beyond, instead of as an alternative to, the quingenary command. Centurions and *primipilares* now appear as auxiliary commanders only in a stop-gap capacity. For example, if an equestrian officer died during his term of service a centurion might be sent from the nearest legion to 'hold the fort' until a replacement could be sent.

Service in the *auxilia* was open to all free-born inhabitants of the empire. Twenty-five years became the normal term, a figure commonly exceeded up to and including the Trajanic period, rarely thereafter, and on completion of service the auxiliary soldier would be rewarded with Roman citizenship for himself and his children (below, p. 227). Since the sons of soldiers provided a ready pool of recruits for the army, and since it would be natural for a son to wish to serve in the same unit as that in which his father had served, the result was gradually to blur the distinction between legions and *auxilia* as being between citizen and non-citizen units. This particular distinction was totally eliminated in 212 when Caracalla promulgated the *Constitutio Antoniniana* giving Roman citizenship to all free-born inhabitants of the empire.

The auxiliary cavalry enjoyed a rather higher status than did the infantry and received more pay: indeed it is possible that they were paid as much as were legionaries, and while transfer from legion to cohort was unknown transfer from legion to *ala* did occasionally occur. The cohorts were certainly regarded as second-class units. Their soldiers were less well paid than the legionaries, equipped with armour of a poorer quality and not so highly trained: they were expected to reach a somewhat lower level of competence. However, from taking an essentially supportive role to the legions in the early days of their existence, the auxiliaries became of steadily increasing importance. For example, the one set-piece battle fought by Agricola during his conquest of Scotland, the battle of Mons Graupius, was won by his auxiliaries without recourse to the legions. The auxiliaries had been put in first: the legions were not needed. Moreover, it was the auxiliary cavalry who mopped up after the battle, doing the job for which they were particularly suited, hunting down the fleeing survivors. The auxiliaries also took on the basic responsibility for patrolling and controlling the frontiers of the empire, doing what was essentially a policing job, dealing with minor incursions as well as taking part in the major excursions beyond the frontier lines.

A further category of non–citizen unit should perhaps be mentioned here: that is the *numerus*. The *numeri* retained what the *auxilia* lost when they became 'established', that is their flexibility in size, organization, equipment and fighting style. *Numeri* were irregular units with no set establishment strength, used both in warfare – they appear, for example, fighting alongside legionaries and auxiliaries on Trajan's Column – or on frontier policing duties. The Moorish horsemen (*Mauri equites*) who rode and fought bareback and the Swiss spearmen (*Raeti Gaesati*) are examples of *numeri*.

The Praetorian Guard

The establishment of a permanent praetorian guard was the work of Augustus: its *raison d'être* was basically to serve as a bodyguard to the emperor. Such a guard was not a concept new to the Roman army for the generals of the Republic were often accompanied by a body of troops to whom the name *cohors praetoria* was attached. These republican *cohortes praetoriae* did not form a permanent corps but were simply drawn on an *ad hoc* basis during campaigning from among the most trustworthy of the available troops. Augustus' guard was put on a permanent footing. It consisted of nine cohorts each under the command of a tribune and, from 2 BC, under the overall charge of two (later one) prefects. The post of *praefectus praetorio* was a singularly influential one, being based in Rome and with ready access to the person of the emperor: it became the apogee of the *primipilaris* or equestrian career (fig. 4). The tribunes who commanded the individual cohorts (the exact number and establishment strength of which was changed from time to time) were drawn from among the *primipilares*, while the centurions were chosen from among those who had risen through the ranks of the guard itself or from members of the equestrian order who had opted to enter military service at the level of centurion instead of as commanding officer in the *auxilia*. While a soldier from the ranks of the guard could obtain a legionary centurionate it was not possible for a man from the legions to hold a praetorian centurionate, discrimination which stemmed from the rather élite status of the guard. Praetorians, like legionaries, were recruited from Roman citizens but, in normal circumstances, almost exclusively from Italians or from the most Romanized of the provinces. Service in the guard was a most acceptable alternative to service in the legions for those Italians who were attracted to a military life but not to a military life in the provinces. The term of service was only sixteen years as compared with the twenty-five of the legions (twelve when the legions served sixteen), with the soldiers picked out as being worthy of a centurionate being retained, *evocati*, until an opening was available for them (though not all *evocati* were destined to become centurions). The pay was higher than that in the legions as were the other perquisites of the job and the conditions, with barracks in the capital, considerably more attractive. Indeed the sense of grievance among the mutineers on the Danube in AD 14 was aggravated by their comparison of the pay and conditions of the legions, enduring hard winters, quartered among savages, in sight of the enemy, with those of the guardsmen in Rome, considerably better paid, serving for a shorter term and serving it in Rome. Under Augustus the guard was split between Rome itself and other towns in the vicinity: those stationed in Rome were scattered about the city. In AD 23 Tiberius brought the cohorts all together in a barracks on the north-east side of Rome, the *castra praetoria*.

Being based in Rome, at the heart of the empire and close to the emperor, the guard and especially its officers had a significant part to play in imperial politics, while in its role as bodyguard it accompanied the emperor on campaign in the provinces, thereby participating in most of the major wars throughout the length and breadth of the empire. Both these circumstances provided the opportunities for its members to win military distinction. It was its significance in internal power politics which led to periodic deviations in the normal recruiting pattern and ultimately to its disbandment. For example, in AD 69, the year of the four emperors, the guard which had supported Otho was disbanded by Vitellius who substituted men from the Rhine legions which had been instrumental in raising him to the imperial purple: he also increased the size of the guard. Again at the end of the second century Septimius Severus, who also came to the throne through civil war, disbanded the existing guard which had sparked off the war by the murder of Pertinax in 193, and recruited his own from among the soldiers of the frontier legions. Finally in 306, the guard supported Maxentius' unsuccessful claim for Empire – a fact which led the successful contender, Constantine, to disband it in 312.

Equites singulares Augusti

A cavalry element in the guard was created by the establishment of the *equites singulares Augusti* whose members were drawn from the *auxilia*. They were commanded by a praetorian tribune and, in common with other cavalry establishments, were organized into troops, each commanded by a decurion. They were stationed, like the praetorians, in Rome.

Urban cohorts

The three urban cohorts which were stationed in Rome, sharing the *castra praetoria* with the guard, functioned as an urban police force. They were created by Augustus at the same time as he established the praetorian guard and were numbered consecutively with the guard, x, xi and xii following on from the i to ix of the guard. Each cohort was commanded by a tribune and all were under the charge of the *praefectus urbi* (the city prefect). They played no part in campaigning outside Italy. In addition to the three cohorts established by Augustus at Rome there were subsequently created further units, stationed elsewhere in Italy (there was, for a short while, one at Ostia and one at Pozzuoli) and two permanently stationed from the time of Vespasian outside

Italy, *cohors I Flavia urbana* at Lyon where there was an imperial mint, *cohors XIII* at Carthage. The tribunates of these two units outside Italy were virtually independent unit commands, coming under the overall jurisdiction of the governor in whose province they lay, Gallia Lugdunensis and Africa Proconsularis respectively. Like the cohorts in Rome, they functioned as city police but were also available to operate elsewhere inside or even outside their province. It is thus that the *cohors XIII urbana* enters the present study, for in the later first century it was transferred for a period away from Africa, operating as part of Domitian's campaigning army on the Rhine and Danube frontiers. The tribunes who commanded the urban cohorts away from Rome appear to have held their post for about three years (a period comparable to the duration of a normal auxiliary command), whereas the posts in Rome lasted just one year for the gifted. *Primipilares* were used in these tribunates, men of exceptional calibre being appointed to I and XIII, the cohorts outside Rome, to which they were promoted direct from the primipilate, moving therefrom straight to the procuratorships. (Compare on fig. 4 the route taken by the men who went to the urban cohorts in Rome.)

The vigiles

The *vigiles*, the Roman fire brigade, were a paramilitary organization with a command structure integrated into the equestrian/primipilaris/centurion career (fig. 4). There were seven cohorts, each with responsibility for fire prevention and control in two of the fourteen regions into which Rome was divided. Each cohort was commanded by a tribune (a *primipilaris*) under the overall jurisdiction of the *praefectus vigilum*. The centurions were drawn not from the ranks of the *vigiles* but from ex-praetorians. Since their job was combating fires in Rome and they functioned as soldiers only in Rome's domestic upheavals, the *vigiles* do not feature in the record of soldiers winning military decorations.

The fleets

Not until the first century BC did Rome maintain anything like a standing navy: prior to this date fleets had been raised and ships built as and when required. Naval warfare does not, overall, figure large in Rome's military history though on occasions the fleet had an important role to play. The power and eminence of Carthage rested on the commercial contacts which she maintained through her control of the Mediterranean. Carthaginian influence in Sicily was a potential menace to Roman interests in Italy and in order to eliminate this threat it was necessary for Rome to break the Carthaginian command at sea. Hence Rome must have a navy. In 241 BC the Roman navy decisively defeated the Carthaginian off the Egadi Islands (off the western tip of Sicily) so bringing to a successful conclusion the first Punic war. Rome occupied Sicily. She now had control of the western Mediterranean and dictated a general naval disarmament. When, from time to time, a battle fleet was required, Rome depended heavily on her eastern allies to provide the ships and crews. In 167, following the battle of Pydna and the successful conclusion of the Third Macedonian war, Rome punished one of these erstwhile allies, Rhodes, for what she considered to be equivocal behaviour during that war. Rhodes lost its recent acquisitions on the mainland of Asia, while its trading pre-eminence in the Aegean was destroyed by the creation of Delos as a free port. The Rhodians became so impoverished that they were no longer able to maintain their war fleet: the effect of this was to allow the rise of a serious pirate menace which ultimately threatened not only maritime trade and Rome's vital supply lines but the very lives and property of those who lived or had business along the coast. In 67 BC an extraordinary command was conferred on Gnaeus Pompeius (Pompey the Great), giving him authority over the Mediterranean and Black Seas and the coastline as far as eighty kilometres inland, with power to appoint legates and to raise the necessary fleet and army. Pompey's rigorous campaign restored Roman authority over the Mediterranean and hereafter a standing navy was maintained.

Sea power also had a significant part to play in the civil wars which brought to an end the period of the Republic. In 31 BC Octavian (later Augustus) defeated M. Antonius at the battle of Actium. From the ships which survived the battle the best were chosen to form the nuclei of the imperial fleets. One fleet was stationed at Forum Iulii (Fréjus) on the Mediterranean coast of Gaul from 31 BC until it had become redundant and was disbanded in AD 69. Two fleets were permanently based on Italy, the Ravenna fleet on the Adriatic at the mouth of the river Po and the Misene fleet at Misenum on the Bay of Naples. Two further Mediterranean fleets were subsequently added: the *classis Alexandrina* based at Alexandria at one of the mouths of the Nile Delta and another further east in Syria, the *classis Syriaca*.

With the expansion of the Empire to embrace within its limits a number of other major seas and rivers further fleets were created: the *classis Pontica* was based on the Black Sea, the *classis Britannica* on the Channel with bases at Boulogne and in south-east Britain, the *classis Germanica* on the lower Rhine, and the *classis Pannonica* and the *classis Moesica* on the upper and lower Danube, respectively. The major functions of those fleets were connected with transportation and with general policing duties. In times of war they were used for the movement of men and supplies and the general support of land-based troops.

The battle fleets of the Republic had operated under the command of the appropriate magistrate or pro-magistrate. The individual fleets of the Principate, on the other hand, were commanded by equestrian prefects of varying grade. The whole structure was based on the familiar army structure, each individual ship being the marine equivalent of the century. The crews, part seamen, part marines were composed of free men (not slaves), *peregrini* like the auxiliaries. The term of service was twenty-six years, and an unblemished record was rewarded with Roman citizenship. The marines were trained and served as soldiers, able to participate if necessary in battles on land. Indeed two legions, *I* and *II Adiutrix*, were formed from fleet personnel. In AD 68 Nero raised *I Adiutrix* from men in the Misene fleet and in the following year marines from the Ravenna fleet defected to Vespasian, forming the unit which in AD 70 was turned into a full legitimate legion, *II Adiutrix*. In stressful times such as those of the civil war when considerable numbers of troops were needed, men from the fleets will have been welcome additions to the army, needing considerably less training than completely raw recruits.

The army of the late empire

The late third and fourth centuries witnessed considerable and radical changes in the nature of the army and the organization of command. Senators were ousted from positions of military responsibility and the notion of the indivisibility of command, civil and military, finally collapsed. This was the logical conclusion of a process which we have already seen occurring as early as the reign of Severus, with the appointment of equestrians and *primipilares* to posts previously reserved for senators. Under Diocletian senators were relieved of responsibility in the frontier provinces, those which contained large numbers of troops; these were transferred to the charge of an equestrian governor with the title of *praeses*. A few years later during the reign of Constantine, the frontier units were removed from the authority of the *praesides* and placed under the command of *duces* whose areas of command were not necessarily co-terminous with the civil provinces. They could command troops stationed in more than one province – a logical step from the military point of view as it allowed for the creation of more unified frontier commands. Separate careers were now followed by civil governors and military commanders.

The nature of the commands changed too. The basic distinction between citizen and non-citizen troops no longer applies: the division which takes its place is that between static frontier troops and mobile field armies. Once the empire had ceased to expand the army had settled down to a largely defensive policing role. No longer were units regularly moved around the empire. Inertia set in. When reinforcements were needed in one particular area it became an increasingly common practice to sent not entire units but detachments which were intended to return to the parent unit when the particular emergency was past. As early as the late second and early third centuries, Septimius Severus, campaigning in Parthia and in Britain, reinforced his armies with detachments from the Rhine and Danube legions.

These were *ad hoc* field armies, raised for a specific purpose and disbanded when that purpose was achieved. The increasing stress on the frontiers of the empire which characterised the second half of the third century led the essentially conservative Diocletian to increase the numbers of troops stationed on the periphery of the empire, adding to the frontier commands a new (and higher) grade of troops later referred to collectively as *ripenses* (this name applies literally to troops stationed along river banks, *ripae*, such as those along the Rhine and Danube frontiers but was used also of the mobile troops sent to non-riverine frontier areas such as Britain). Constantine took a more radical approach to the problem, not only dividing civil and military command but also creating permanent mobile field armies separate from the commands of the frontier *duces*. The first of these field armies was attached to the person of the emperor, the Augustus, and his deputies, Caesars: hence the name given to them, *comitatenses*, a word deriving from the *comitatus*, the emperor's travelling court. This central field army had two heads, the *magister peditum* and the *magister equitum* (the masters of foot and horse), positions of very considerable influence indeed. The *magister peditum* Stilicho was the effective power behind the throne of Honorius to whom he had been guardian. A later development was that of regional field armies not attached to the emperors: in the west one was based on Trier, in the east on Antioch. These regional field armies were commanded by *magistri militum*. Finally, in the latter part of the fourth century, and probably as a result of action by Stilicho, there was a proliferation of small field armies, mobile, but operating over more restricted areas than the major regional armies.

Thus the basic distinction at the end of the fourth century is between, on the one hand, static frontier armies (the old frontier troops plus the *ripenses*) known generically as *limitanei* (troops on a *limes* or frontier) and commanded by *duces*, and on the other mobile field armies known, whether or not they were attached to the emperor, as *comitatenses* and (with the exception of the small regional armies) commanded by *magistri*. Military service was no longer voluntary but hereditary and no longer particularly attractive: self-mutilation to avoid 'call-up' was not uncommon. The armies were on the defensive and while military reforms such as those of Constantine may have postponed the end they could not evert it. In 476 Romulus Augustulus was deposed – the last Roman emperor in the west.

CHAPTER II

THE NATURE OF THE EVIDENCE AND ITS PROBLEMS

There are three main categories of evidence for Roman military decorations: literary sources, inscriptions on stone (and occasionally on metal) and sculpture. Paradoxical as it may at first appear, archaeological evidence in the form of the decorations themselves is of relatively little importance; the reasons for this will become apparent. The evidence is altogether very patchy. The great majority of the inscriptions relate to the first and second centuries AD; a handful belong to the first century BC. There are none of an earlier date and very few that are any later. The sculptural evidence has a similar bias, but with a particular concentration in the Augustan period. The reason is connected with generous donatives given by the emperor to his troops after the upheavals of the Civil War, which allowed their heirs to erect fine decorated tombstones in their honour. The literary material, however, is predominantly of an early date, with slightly over two thirds of the references relating to the republican period.

The types of information provided by these three sources are complementary and do not greatly overlap. The value of the sculptural evidence is limited largely to what it can tell us of the physical appearance of the decorations. The inscriptions are concerned exclusively with specific awards either to individual named soldiers or to complete units, while the literary evidence, though it also includes a number of specific cases of award, is of paramount importance for what it tells us of the mechanics of the system of award: how, when, why, by whose authority and to whom decorations were given. Doubtless there existed in the Roman period a written code of practice relating to the presentation of awards for gallantry; such a code would be necessary for the efficient and equitable running of the system, but none such has survived, nor any of the rolls of honour which must have been maintained at Rome, nor the soldiers' individual files which would have recorded all details of their military career including any distinctions gained in the field.

Failing specific and direct information of this sort the rules and regulations behind the awards have to be discerned from the individual cases pieced together to see if any pattern emerges; the ceremonies must be reconstructed from the passing references of the historians. The picture which emerges will therefore be only a partial one for it is based on partial evidence. Many of the conclusions which will be put forward about the development and functioning of the system of military reward are based on negative rather than on positive evidence and must therefore be regarded as far from definitive – no more than one way of interpreting the material available.

Literary sources

The written sources pertinent to this study range in date of composition from the work of Caecilius Statius in the first quarter of the second century BC to that of the Greek historian Procopius in the middle of the sixth century AD. The chronological range of the relevant subject matter extends from the early years of the fifth century BC when Rome was involved in fighting against her neighbours within Italy to the middle of the sixth century AD and the attempt by the Byzantine Empire to win back Italy from the Ostrogoths. The source material is very uneven in quality, its reliability depending on both the aims and methods of the individual writers as well as on their competence to deal with military matters.

Some of the authors in question, for example Livy and Cassius Dio, were writing histories of Rome from its foundation. Hence much of what they wrote was of people, events and institutions entirely outside their own experience, necessitating heavy and often not very critical use of annalistic tradition. Livy, who was at work in the Augustan period (he was in his mid-seventies when he died in AD 17), was entirely inexperienced in military matters and had little knowledge of early Roman institutions. Two centuries later Dio covered much of the same ground as that covered by Livy (whose work provided one of his sources) but added on a further 200 years of history which had elapsed since Livy's time. Dio was reasonably at home with the events and personalities of the Empire but was ignorant of republican conditions. The danger with this sort of writing is that anachronisms will creep in and that circumstances surrounding the basic facts and events will be coloured and distorted in the light of later ideas and practices. This problem becomes particularly acute when trying to trace the development of an institution such as *dona militaria*. By the time Livy was writing the system had reached a maturity which it certainly did not have in the early years of the Republic and there is no objective criterion against which to measure the observations which he and those of his own and later generations make about military decorations in their earliest manifestations.

The problem may be illustrated by the case of Lucius Siccius Dentatus, a renowned and perhaps legendary warrior of the mid-fifth century BC, whom tradition credits with an amazing collection of military decorations. Whether or not the man ever really existed is impossible to say with certainty. The fullest account of the career and decorations of Dentatus is given by the Augustan historian Dionysius of Halicarnassus, in the form of a speech which Dentatus supposedly gave to an assembly of the Roman populace in 453 BC.[1] Details are given of posts held by Dentatus, including commands over cohorts and over whole legions, of some of the exploits which he performed and of the decorations he won, totalling 1 *corona obsidionalis* 14 *coronae civicae*, 3 *coronae murales*, 8 *coronae aureae*, 83 *torques*, 160 *armillae*, 18 *hastae* and 25 *phalerae*. The speech is clearly a fictitious one: it contains references to posts which, as far as we know, never existed, and its wealth of detail must therefore be viewed with deep suspicion. Dionysius is the only source to attempt to give details of the career and the deeds of valour: a further seven writers refer to the case of Dentatus but the concern of all of them is limited to the wounds, decorations and spoils, none of them making any attempt to put them in context.[2] The earliest record known to have existed dates to four centuries after the events concerned: it appeared in the pages of Varro, but in a part of that work which does not survive in the original, being referred to only in the work of Fulgentius, a fifth-century African bishop. Varro is our only known republican source for the story of Dentatus which is next recorded by the Augustan writers Dionysius of Halicarnassus and Verrius Flaccus whose *Libri de significatu verborum* have survived in an epitome by the second-century writer Pompeius Festus, itself epitomized in the eighth century AD by Paulus Diaconus. Two writers of the first century AD repeat the story, Valerius Maximus and the Elder Pliny, and it is recorded in the mid-second-century *Noctes Atticae* of Aulus Gellius and the third-century *Collectanea Rerum Memorabilium* of Solinus who is known to have drawn heavily on the work of Pliny. Finally the fourth-century historian Ammianus Marcellinus alludes briefly to the plurality of crowns. Gellius almost certainly shared a common source with Flaccus, or else drew on Flaccus himself, for of the seven known sources for Dentatus only these two plus Ammianus call him Sicinius the rest use the form Siccius and these two writers alone note that he was known as the Roman Achilles. Elsewhere in the *Noctes Atticae* Gellius does in fact acknowledge the use of the work of Flaccus though he does not do so in this particular context.

Dionysius of Halicarnassus alone stands as witness for the career and daring exploits of Dentatus: we do not know the source of his information or whether it is, in part at least, a piece of historical embroidery designed to bring alive an otherwise shadowy central figure. It is rather surprising that Livy makes no mention whatever of the man and that none of the other sources who do refer to him have anything to say on his distinguished career. All the sources are in broad agreement over the detail of his military awards and yet the list is out of place in a fifth-century context. It is, for example, highly doubtful whether specific crowns for saving the lives of Roman citizens and for being the first to scale an enemy wall had developed as early as this. The whole thing is suspiciously anachronistic: it is most unfortunate that the story can be traced back no further than the mid-first century BC: one can only speculate on how and why the story arose.[3]

For the middle years of the Republic we are on much firmer ground with the work of Polybius. Polybius' Universal History is much more limited in scope chronologically than are the works of Dio and Livy: it covers the period 220–145 BC and was written fairly soon after the events described (Polybius lived, *c.* 203–120 BC). Polybius' history provides us with one of the few straightforward factual accounts of *dona militaria*. In Book VI the author turned aside from his main narrative to discourse upon the constitution of Rome, and in a section on the Roman military system he wrote of 'methods of encouraging young soldiers to face danger'. The theme is the judicious use of reward and punishment and it deals in clear and specific terms with military decorations and the circumstances under which they were awarded. The value of the narrative is enhanced by the fact that Polybius was writing from his own experience. He had as a young man, after the Third Macedonian war, been interned in Rome and here he came under the protection of Aemilius Paullus at whose home he stayed. He struck up a friendship with Paullus' younger son, later to become, by adoption, Publius Scipio Aemilianus, on whom he was in attendance during the Third Punic war, witnessing the destruction of Carthage in 146 BC. He thus acquired wide military and political experience on top of a good liberal education and had, moreover, intimate knowledge of many of the events and personalities of whom he wrote. His detailed observations on military decorations can therefore be accepted as basically sound and used with some confidence as evidence for the practices of his own day and perhaps shortly before.

Another historian who wrote from first-hand knowledge of his subject matter and with complete familiarity with military affairs was of course C. Iulius Caesar, whose accounts of the Gallic and Civil Wars give an excellent picture of the day-to-day workings of an army in the field. Unlike Polybius, Caesar does not devote a section to a specific discussion of how he rewarded his soldiers; instead he shows us such a system at work in his passing references to the decorations, money prizes and promotion bestowed on his men at the end of a successful campaign. There is no reason to doubt the veracity of his observations on these matters. While bias may have crept into certain other aspects of the narrative, with Caesar's desire to enhance his own successes and to minimize his failures, there would be little point in the distortion of such incidental references to soldiers' rewards. The same is broadly true of what we learn of *dona* from biographies. Generally the allusions to decorations are no more than passing references and so are unlikely to share in the general bias which the biographer might have for or against the individual who forms his subject matter. Thus, although the thoroughly biased and anecdotal approach of Suetonius inspires no confidence in his judgements, it does not invalidate his basic material. He may, for example, be scathing in his assessment of the Emperor Claudius and his campaigns in Britain but, despite the facetious tone in which he records the incidents, he provides some valuable and interesting sidelights on the subject of decorations.

More precise evidence on the nature, significance and origins of the decorations is provided by the encyclopaedic works of writers such as Aulus Gellius and the Elder Pliny. Gellius' *Noctes Atticae* were written about the middle of the second century AD and comprise a discussion of points of law, grammar, literary criticism, biography, history and antiquities. Gellius is deemed to be a conscientious and accurate scholar: he sometimes quotes the sources of his information – by no means a normal practice in his day – and these sources include extracts from writers whose works are otherwise unknown. The important section in the present context is that 'On military crowns', in which he carefully describes eight different types of crown, their appearance and how they were won and gives the names and exploits of some of those known to have been awarded them.[4] It is unfortunate that here Gellius does not tell us the source of his information. Military crowns are also the subject of two substantial sections in Pliny's *Naturalis Historia*.[5] Like Gellius, Pliny discusses the nature and origins of the crowns and gives some actual examples of award. The narratives of the two writers are broadly in agreement. The career of Pliny (AD 23–79) included equestrian military service as prefect of a cavalry regiment in Germany, so he can be assumed to have had first-hand knowledge of the theory if not of the practice of the system of military award as it operated in his own day. His narrative however is concerned with historic instances rather than current practices, and there is clearly a strong reliance on tradition as he traces the crowns back to their origins, actual or mythical. The information provided by Pliny and Gellius on crowns is complemented by material from the etymologies of Varro, Verrius Flaccus and Isidor of Seville who provide fragments of evidence on the nature and origin of types of decoration other than crowns.

None of the surviving technical military treatises has anything substantial to say on the subject of rewards. They are completely outside the scope of the works on castrametation and tactics by pseudo-Hyginus and Arrian respectively and receive just one rather oblique reference in the *de Re Militari* of the fourth-century writer Vegetius. The only one of these works which devotes a section to the subject of reward and punishment is the book on 'The General' by Onasander. Written sometime between 49 and 59 AD (it was dedicated to Quintus Veranius, consul in 49, who died in Britain in 59), the book deals with general ethical and military principles which will lead to success in arms. It is of an untechnical nature, talking in terms of broad principles which could apply to any army at any time, despite the fact that Onasander claimed in his introduction that 'all the principles are taken from authentic exploits and battles especially of the Romans'. One aspect of the commander's duty is the upholding of morale by rewarding the brave: Onasander enunciates the principle but takes it no further, making no attempt to relate it to the particular case of the Roman army.

One exceedingly important source of evidence for many matters concerning the Roman army are the military papyri which have survived in the dry conditions of the eastern parts of the Empire, notably in Egypt and Syria. Not a single reference to *dona* survives in any of these. This loss is particularly acute because the official military documents, drawn up by army staff for use by the army, form a very effective record of personnel and routine. Nor do the unofficial military papyri, for example letters written by and to soldiers, contain even a passing reference to *dona*. The failure in this respect of the material from Dura Europos on the Euphrates is almost certainly in part at least due to its date: it belongs to the third century when military decorations appear no longer to have been given on a regular basis.

The range of written material which provides some sort of evidence on *dona militaria* is wide, it includes the works of historians, biographers, orators, poets, satirists, etymologists and encyclopaedists. Between them they provide a remarkably consistent picture of the development and operation of the system of military reward, the origin and nature of the decorations, who was eligible to be decorated and in what ways the awards might be won. We see the system as it was meant to work and how it might be abused. The biggest single problem which the literary material throws up (apart from those arising from its frequent lack of precision) is that of anachronism – as seen in the case of Dentatus. Undoubtedly some of the practices of the republican period were still in operation virtually unchanged in the Empire; for example the ceremony of award as described by Polybius is paralleled in many details by that of Josephus some two centuries later and both these writers probably in this context were working from their own experience.[6] However, it is equally clear that many aspects of the system did undergo considerable change and development so that any writer who is dealing with a period well outside his own knowledge and experience must be used with considerable caution.

Inscriptions

Inscriptions form the single largest source of evidence for military decorations during the period of the Empire. Although literary material is still available for the Principate it is generally poorer in quantity and quality than it is for the Republic. Also the inscriptions provide a rather different type of information from most of the literary material. The bulk of the inscriptions deal with specific examples of soldiers and units who have been decorated; they tell us virtually nothing of the mechanics of the system and the ceremonies involved and rarely do they mention the nature of the deeds performed. What they do give are the names, ranks and units of the soldiers decorated and details of the awards received. The awarding emperor is frequently named as also is the campaign involved. From the information provided by a large number of specific individual cases it is possible to build up a broader picture of how the system worked during the Empire, which awards went to which ranks, how the system changed over time and how the individuality of the various emperors asserted itself.

Tombstones and honorific inscriptions provide the bulk of the material, for their concern was to record, in terms as fulsome as possible, the lives of those whom they were set up to commemorate. Dedicatory inscriptions on altars also provide some information, though generally rather less detail, for the emphasis here is on the deity rather than the dedicator. The soldier making such a dedication commonly gives his name, current rank and unit, and perhaps highest honours won, but rarely does he give the career details which appear, often at great length, on tombstones.

Although the practice of setting up inscriptions to honour the dead or the living was one which spread over almost the whole social scale, the quality and quantity of information given is heavily weighted towards the top end of the economic and social ladder. The reason for this is readily apparent. The cutting of monumental inscriptions was a skilled job and the stone-mason would have charged accordingly; the more competent the mason the higher the fee he could command, the longer and more verbose the text the greater the cost. A legionary centurion of the Principate earned more than sixteen times as much as did a common soldier, a camp prefect two-and-a-half times as much again. An equestrian officer at the height of his military career had a salary comparable to that of the camp prefect but only half that which a ducenarian procurator could command.[7] Modern parallels are virtually meaningless, so suffice it to say that in the later first century AD while a simple *miles* was earning a mere 1,200 sesterces per annum a ducenarian procurator received 200,000. The effect of this on potential spending power needs no emphasizing.

Military service was something for a man to be proud of and so it was invariably referred to in some way on a soldier's tombstone. It could be done in the tersest possible way with the single word veteran or by referring only to the highest post held without any detail of the steps by which that rank had been reached or even of the unit or units involved. However, even when only the barest of details are given the winning of military decorations is extremely likely to be included for it formed a highlight in a career and was an honour of which relatively few men could boast. Hence references to *dona* occur in the tersest of inscriptions even if only in the briefest of forms, as for example the two letters *d.d.* for *donis donatus*, ('having been decorated'). At the opposite extreme the career may be given in the fullest of details, all posts listed, units named and occasionally even the provinces served in; the decorations may be listed in full, associated with the post in which they were won, the campaign involved and the emperor who awarded them. The majority of cases fall between these two extremes. There are however few proven cases of inscriptions set up in honour of retired or serving soldiers who are known to have received military decorations which fail to refer to the *dona* in one form or another. One such case which can be proved is that of P. Cominius Clemens. Clemens undertook equestrian military service, commanding three auxiliary units, and being decorated during the second of these commands, before going on to hold a series of procuratorial posts. Three inscriptions were set up in his honour by the cities of Concordia and Aquileia of which he was patron: one of these inscriptions mentions his decorations, two do not. But what has happened in these two cases is not simply that the *dona* have dropped out but that the whole of the military part of the career has been summarized in the words *omnibus equestribus militiis functo*, ('having served at all the equestrian military levels'). This example illustrates one of the problems in using the inscriptions. While the relatively poor might not be able to afford to record the career in full, the richer and more powerful who have attained positions of honour and influence might not deem it worthwhile to specify the lower posts held, particularly if, as in Clemens' case, more than one inscription has been set up in any one place.[8] This tendency is not seen only in the case of the higher officers. Inscriptions relating to centurions, for example, commonly give no post lower than that of centurion, so that if *dona* are recorded it is difficult to know at what stage in the career they were won, particularly if no mention is made of the unit or the campaign involved.

The fact that *dona* are something out of the ordinary, the highspot in a career, has disadvantages as well as advantages. In a full career record they may be divorced from the context to which they belong. Instead of being mentioned in order beside the post in which they were won, they are transferred to the beginning or the end of the text in order, presumably, to give them greater emphasis. This happens frequently with equestrian careers. The decorations are listed at the end of the military part of the career, dividing the army commands from any ensuing civilian posts held. The immediate inference in these cases is that the *dona* belong to the last military post held, which may or may not be the case. It is only by consideration of the known movements of the units served in and the area where the campaigning took place that it is possible to match the *dona* with the post in which they were won.

The epigraphic material considered so far has all been dealing with single individual cases of decoration. Another type of material is that relating to groups of individuals, *laterculi* or lists of soldiers serving at a particular time in a particular unit. On three such lists – one recording soldiers discharged in AD 195 from legion *VII Claudia* at Viminacium in Moesia Superior, another relating to members of legion *II Parthica* at Albanum in central Italy and a third listing men recruited to the praetorian guard in Rome between 153 and 156 – a proportion of the men are designated with the letters *d.d.* before or after their name.[9] It is probable, though incapable of proof, that these men are *donis donati* and if so these lists provide some useful statistical material on proportions of men decorated at any one time.

In addition to awarding decorations to individuals the Romans went in for the practice of bestowing honours on a whole unit. This is particularly important in the case of the *auxilia*, the non-citizen units, whose members were, generally speaking, not eligible to receive decorations as individuals (see Chapter VI). The honours bestowed on units are reflected in the units' titles as recorded on inscriptions of all sorts. One particularly valuable source of evidence for these block awards are the military diplomas or certificates of privileges which were given to the auxiliaries normally on completion of service, though until the time of Trajan they were sometimes given to soldiers who were still serving.[10] The normal practice from the time of Claudius onwards was for auxiliaries to be granted Roman citizenship and the right of *conubium* (the right to contract a legal marriage with a non-Roman woman) at the end of their twenty-five-year period of service. Each soldier given this grant received a document to prove his enhanced status, and each of these military diplomas as well as naming the man to whom it was being awarded listed all the units which had men receiving their privileges on the same occasion. These are official military documents and assign to the units their correct official designation, often, though by no means invariably, incorporating into their names the honorific titles which they have been granted in recognition of distinguished conduct on the battlefield. Their value as evidence for unit titles is all the greater because they are very precisely dated, not only to the year but to the day and month. Sometimes these diplomas record abnormal grants made to a unit as a reward for valour, for example citizenship before completion of the statutory twenty-five years, or discharge with full privileges before the normal period of service has elapsed.

Sculpture

One thing which neither the literature nor the epigraphy can do adequately is to convey to us what the decorations actually looked like. Verbal descriptions of many of the decorations do exist but they lack the precision and immediacy of visual representations. The majority of the decorations are, however, depicted in some form or another, either in relief sculpture or as coin types; the importance of this sort of evidence is emphasized by the fact that we can do no more than guess at the appearance of the siege crown which is described but nowhere depicted, and of the *corniculum* which is nowhere either described or depicted. Moreover the literary material gives no indication whatever of the variety of design which existed even within a single type of military decoration: there was clearly no absolutely stereotyped form which each award had to take. To take one example, the *armilla* (armlet) is variously depicted as a broad flat band, a narrow twisted band, as a complete ring or as penannular with either plain or animal-head terminals. The only variation indicated by the literature is that sometimes they were made of gold, sometimes of silver (below, p. 89).

The sculptural representations of the decorations sometimes show just the awards themselves but occasionally they show these awards being worn. Two particularly fine examples of this are the tombstones of Marcus Caelius and Sertorius Festus (pl. 2a and 2b). This latter method of representation is particularly useful as the literature has nothing to say on this subject. Commonsense would indicate that the crown was worn on the head and the *armilla* on the arm; but it would also lead one to suppose that the *torques* (neck-ring) was worn around the neck. It was not. This is certainly how the Celt wore it but the Roman soldier had an altogether different method of displaying it. The way in which medals were worn is also indicated by the sculpture.

It is tacitly assumed in the foregoing that these sculptures provide an accurate representation of the decorations. Such an assumption requires justification. The decorations themselves cannot provide a cross-check because there are so few of them surviving and even these few can be identified as military decorations rather than as other types of ornament only by reference to the sculptures (below, p. 54). Many of the tombstones which carry the reliefs will have been the products of Roman military sculptors: this is particularly true in the case of tombstones commissioned by comrades of the deceased and set up in the graveyards of the forts and fortresses where they had served. Such sculptors can be confidently assumed to have had good first-hand knowledge of the artefacts which they were depicting, and they will have been working for knowledgeable and critical patrons. In matters such as helmets and body-armour where there is more readily identifiable surviving material to provide a cross-check, these military tombstones have been shown to be reasonably accurate in what they represent.[11] The tombstones set up in the home towns of retired soldiers are more likely to be the products of civilian craftsmen less familiar with the military uniforms and other paraphernalia which they were called upon to depict. However, in the case of the larger cities, of the veteran colonies and particularly of Rome itself where there was a permanent military presence in the form of the praetorian and urban cohorts, there were in all probability sculptors who specialized in commissions of a military nature. Even sculptors who had no personal knowledge of military dress could be given examples of actual uniforms and decorations to work from or could acquire the necessary illustrations on which to model their work. A sculptor doing reliefs of this sort could not afford to rely on artistic imagination: his work was intended to be seen by the public at least some of whom would be well informed. Reasonable accuracy would be essential.

The triumphal monuments set up in Rome and elsewhere in the Empire provide disappointingly little evidence on military decorations. Neither Trajan's Column which shows scenes from the campaigns of that Emperor in Dacia in 101–2 and 105–6, nor the Marcus Column which records events in the wars of Marcus and Verus in Germany in 166–175, shows any awards. This is perhaps surprising, for although the bulk of the scenes concern the army on active campaigning – marching to war, building camps, fighting the enemy and so on, contexts in which they clearly would not wear their decorations – we know from literary sources that award-giving ceremonies were held during campaign and did not always await the triumph which concluded the war. In his commentary on Trajan's Column Cichorius considered the possibility that one scene did show an award-giving ceremony.[12] This relief (pl. 16b) depicts the emperor seated with one of his officers and two other persons standing behind him. An auxiliary soldier bows before the emperor, taking his outstretched hand while five more auxiliaries observe the scene from the front, two more embrace one another and a ninth walks away from the emperor with something, though it is unclear what, slung over his left shoulder. No gifts appear to be changing hands, no decorations are in sight – which is not surprising as there is strong negative evidence that at this period auxiliaries did not usually receive military decorations.

Apart from one or two coin types nearly all the visual representations of *dona* appear on tombstones. The major exception is in the context of honours awarded to units as a whole. When this happened the honour appears to have been commemorated by attaching a token of this award to the unit's standards. Such decorated standards frequently appear on military sculpture such as the columns of Trajan and Marcus and other monuments such as the Arch of the Argentarii and a slab now used as the side of an altar in the Church of San Marcello in the Via del Corso, both in Rome. When decorations appear on tombstones they are sometimes depicted as well as being mentioned in the text, while sometimes the reliefs are the only evidence there is that the men being commemorated had won decorations. While it can be accepted without doubt that the man whose tombstone depicts decorations had won something at least, it should not be assumed automatically that the scale of the award is identical with that depicted. What is shown might represent no more than a token of what had actually been won, either because a soldier's heirs could not afford the work involved in depicting the full complement or, in the case of a particularly large collection, because the size of the stone was a limiting factor. In three out of the four cases where *dona* are recorded in both text and sculpture the two do not tally. Sextus Vibius Cocceianus set up a very fine stone in honour of his patron, Sextus Vibius Gallus. Two sides of this freestanding monument depict the *dona* won by Gallus, a third shows the scene of a horseman, presumably Gallus, riding down a Dacian warrior. The bi-lingual text on the face of the stone records that Gallus won, over the course of his military career, a total of six *coronae*, five *hastae*, two *vexilla, torques, armillae* and *phalerae*. The *dona* depicted include the full total of *coronae, hastae* and *vexilla* but omit the lesser awards entirely (pl. 5).[13] There are almost certainly grave omissions in the case of Tiberius Claudius Maximus, a soldier of the late first to early second century AD whose great claim to fame is that he slew the Dacian king Decebalus.[14] Maximus was decorated on three separate occasions, during the Dacian wars of Domitian and Trajan and finally in Trajan's Parthian war. The decorations are referred to but not enumerated in the text, while the sum total depicted is two *torques* and two *armillae* (pl. 8a); this cannot possibly represent a combination of three separate awards. The bottom of the stone is broken away and Speidel has suggested that further decorations were shown on the missing portion. However the extant portion is already almost three times as tall as it is wide (2.64 m high by 0.90 m wide at the base tapering slightly towards the top), so it is unlikely that more than the few remaining lines of text have been lost. Perhaps the *dona* depicted represent what was awarded on each occasion, perhaps they are no more than a token designed to draw the attention of the onlooker to the fact that the man commemorated had been decorated.

While the texts of Gallus and Maximus indicate larger awards than are actually shown that of Lucius Antonius Quadratus does the opposite (pl. 14b); the text mentions *torques* and *armillae*, the sculpture shows two *torques*, two *armillae* and two very stylized sets of *phalerae*.[15] Only in the case of Titurnius Quartio are the single *torques* and multiple *armillae* of the text accurately reflected in the one *torques* and two *armillae* of the sculpture (pl. 9c).[16] This lack of precise correlation between text and sculpture in those cases where it can be checked (whether deliberate as in the examples of Gallus and Maximus or inadvertent as is probably the case with Antonius Quadratus) counsels caution in using sculpture as evidence for scale of decoration where there is no such check.

Archaeological evidence

There are, throughout the whole of the Roman Empire, very few well authenticated examples of military decorations. The reasons for this lie firstly in the problems of survival and secondly in the problem of identification. If the literary and epigraphic evidence for *dona* is to be taken at its face value (and there is no apparent reason why it should not) the materials from which many of the decorations were made were silver and gold. Texts and inscriptions are in agreement over this. The intrinsic value of the decorations, taken together with their sentimental value, would ensure that they were not casually lost or mislaid: indeed the very size of the major awards would prevent this. A passage from the *Histories* of Tacitus points to what may well have been the ultimate fate of large numbers of decorations in times of financial crisis.[17] It tells how some of the supporters of Vitellius at Cologne in AD 69, not having money to give to help finance the war, were urged to part with their valuables including their *phalerae* (which could mean horse-trappings, but in this context more likely medals). Another allusion to the melting down of military decorations appears in the pages of the Elder Pliny: 'if only Fabricius who forbade gallant generals to possess more than a dish and a salt-cellar of silver would see how nowadays the rewards of valour are made from the utensils of luxury or else are broken up to make them.'[18]

Of the wide range of decorations known, not one military crown of any type has been identified, nor a *vexillum* nor a *hasta pura*. A few examples of the minor awards have come to light but in many cases their interpretation as military decorations rather than merely as personal ornaments is in some doubt. If it is correct as is argued below (p. 60) that certain of these minor awards were derived from personal ornaments it is not particularly surprising that they should be virtually indistinguishable from them, the more so because, as is clear from the sculptural evidence, there was no one stereotyped design for the *dona*. This problem of interpretation is illustrated by the case of the Benwell *torques*. A rather inelegant bronze *torques* came to light during the excavation of the Roman fort of Benwell on Hadrian's Wall; its excavators, F.G. Simpson and I.A. Richmond, suggested that it was a military decoration won by one of the soldiers serving in the Wall garrison.[19] One of the basic reasons for this conclusion was the fact that the object was found in a Roman fort. A reassessment of the evidence, starting from the basic premise that an auxiliary soldier was not generally eligible to win *dona*, leads to the conclusion that it is rather more likely to have been a native *torques* which could easily have found its way into a Roman military establishment as plunder, by trade or as the personal possession of one of the auxiliaries, the bulk of whom would, after all, be native Celts.[20]

The commonest type of decoration to be found is the *phalera*. The problem of interpretation here arises from the fact that *phalerae* were used for purposes other than military award; they served for example as horse-trappings and these trappings are not always readily distinguishable from military decorations – both are ornate metal discs designed to be attached to leather straps. Only in cases such as that of the Lauersfort *phalerae* where a complete set was found in close proximity to a legionary fortress (Vetera bei Xanten in Lower Germany) can we be confident that we are dealing with genuine *dona militaria* (the Lauersfort *phalerae* are discussed on p. 94f.). For these reasons very little use will be made of putative examples of *dona*. It is unfortunate that at present more confidence cannot be put in this material, but at the moment it is the literary and epigraphic and sculptural evidence which must be used to clarify the archaeological material and not the reverse.

CHAPTER III

THE ORIGIN AND DEVELOPMENT OF DONA MILITARIA

The scheme of Roman military awards which had developed by the first half of the second century AD was of a complexity and sophistication paralleled only in comparatively modern armies. In its final form the system comprised some ten different basic awards which were given in a variety of different formalised combinations. The exact nature of these combinations depended largely on the rank of the recipient but with sufficient flexibility to allow for the recognition of individual merit. Such a scheme is a far cry from the situation in the early republican period with its *ad hoc* methods of reward, in which the nature of the deed rather than the status of the doer determined the composition of the award, and different again from the late Empire when the formalised system had broken down to be replaced by something akin to the *ad hoc* situation of the Republic.

The reasons which lie behind the need to devise a satisfactory system of reward are readily apparent: they are those which apply to any army of any age. To fight is what the Roman soldier was trained to do; penalties for failure in the execution of his military duties, for cowardice in the face of the enemy, for desertion of his post, were fearful. But stern punishment must be counterbalanced by fair reward. Public and tangible recognition of conspicuous gallantry, whether in the form of extra pay or rations, promotion, booty or symbolic decorations, will always be one of the devices by which a wise general can help to keep up the morale of his troops and spur them on to extra endeavour. As Polybius observed, by acknowledging and rewarding acts of outstanding bravery, by making those who performed them famous not only in the army but in their own home towns, the Romans stirred up rivalry in the field; soldiers were incited to emulate the conduct of their peers. No wonder, he says that the wars in which the Romans engage end so successfully when they pay such attention to reward and punishment in the army. Precisely the same sentiment is echoed about a century and a half later by Onasander in his treatise on 'The General'. 'Whenever honour is paid to the brave and punishment of the cowardly is not neglected then an army must have fair expectation.'[1]

The development of ordered schemes of award parallels the developments which were taking place in the composition and organisation of the army itself. The army evolved from a part-time body of citizen-soldiers into a full-time professional force with a rigid hierarchy and structure of command. So it became necessary to organize the giving of rewards so that they reflected the differing roles which were played at the different levels within the army. Clearly the military prowess exhibited by the officer with a large number of units under his command is of a very different kind from that displayed by the soldier whose courage and fighting ability are tested in the mêlée of the battlefield. The decoration designed to reward the soldier who is the first to enter an enemy camp or city can in no practical sense be won by the general who masterminded the assault, unless he elects to lead his men into battle. Opinions in the Roman world varied as to the advisability of a general exposing himself to the danger of being killed in action, the short-term morale-boosting effect upon the soldiers of seeing their commander fighting alongside them in line of battle, sharing their dangers and their triumphs, being weighed against the longer-term consideration of the devastating effect which the death of the commander would have both upon the morale of the soldiers and upon the whole conduct of the rest of the campaign. Onasander is clear and unequivocal in his views. 'Even if in battle (the general) shows that he is not to be outdone in valour, he can aid his army far less by fighting than he can harm it if he should be killed, since the knowledge of a general is far more important than his physical strength. Even a common soldier can perform a great deed of bravery, but no-one except the general can, by his wisdom, plan a greater one.'[2] Polybius adopts the same standpoint, praising Scipio for the care which he takes to ensure his own safety in battle.[3]

Military rewards in both the Republic and the Principate took a variety of different forms. The routing of an enemy army, the taking of a city or camp would yield plentiful spoils which the general might grant in part or whole to his troops, either in the form of the plunder itself or of gifts of money raised from the sale of the plunder. Rations could be supplemented, additional pay given, or promotion to a higher rank bring with it both extra pay and prestige. Such rewards bestowed immediate practical benefits on the soldiers who won them: not so the *dona militaria*, the decorations which acknowledged in a more symbolic fashion the valour of those to whom they were awarded. True, these decorations might be made of precious metals – and we know that originally the majority of them were fashioned from gold and silver and continued, in theory if not in practice, to be so – but their true value lay more in what they represented than in the weight of bullion from which they were made. A crown of gold would clearly have been a valuable asset but an asset which generally would not have been realised except in times of dire necessity. The significance which the *dona militaria* had for the Roman soldier can be assumed to be that which the Victoria Cross, the Distinguished Service Order and other decorations have for the modern British soldier. The preeminence of the symbolic over the intrinsic value of the decoration is neatly illustrated in an anecdote which Valerius Maximus relates. During campaigning in Africa in 47 BC Scipio distributed *dona* to those who had distinguished themselves in the field, but refused to award gold *armillae* (armlets) to a certain cavalryman nominated by the legate Titus Labienus because he was an ex-slave. Thereupon Labienus gave the cavalryman a gift of some gold which had been taken from the Gauls. ' "All you have there", said Scipio, "is a present from a rich man." At these words the soldier, confused, lowered his eyes and threw the gold at Labienus' feet. But when he heard Scipio say "The general gives you silver *armillae*" he was filled with joy. There is not a man so low that he is not affected by the sweetness of glory.'[4] This stress on the symbolic value of *dona* is reflected in the fact that the two highest awards which could be won, the *corona obsidionalis* and the *corona civica*, are the only two which, from the very beginning, were made of materials of no intrinsic value whatever, the *corona civica* being made from oak-leaves, the *corona obsidionalis* from grass or whatever vegetation grew in the place where the award-winning deed was performed (below, pp. 67 and 70).

The practice of allowing soldiers to keep some of the booty which they had plundered was widely used in the pre-Imperial period as an incentive to recruitment and a means of rewarding the army in general and those who had distinguished themselves in particular. The practice continued to a lesser extent into the Principate. The victor in a battle acquired complete control over the defeated enemy and his property: it was up to the victorious general to dispose of these spoils as he thought fit and in accordance with customary practice. 'Conditions were dictated to those who had been vanquished in war, for when everything had been surrendered to the one who was the stronger in arms he had the absolute right to say what they might retain and of what they were to be deprived.'[5] For example, an enemy city which gave itself up with little or no resistance would generally receive better terms than one which had put up a strong defence, costly in time and lives. Sulla's siege of Aeculanum in the territory of the Hirpini was prolonged because the inhabitants tried to play for time, hoping for relief from the neighbouring Lucani. When the city fell it was plundered, as Appian tells us, because it had not delivered itself up voluntarily. Sulla spared the other towns that gave themselves up.[6]

Much of the plunder might be retained by the state and sold to defray the costs of campaigning; some would be offered to the gods, and variable proportions bestowed upon the general and upon the army, particularly upon those who had distinguished themselves in battle. One of the problems which arose with the distribution of plunder was its fair allocation to all who had claims on it – the state which launched and financed the campaign, the general who led it and the soldiers who fought in it. An army which thought itself ill rewarded was a very considerable potential menace.

A good account of the allocation of spoils comes in the account by Dionysius of Halicarnassus of an episode in the struggle between Rome and the Etruscan town of Veii in 475 BC. The Romans under Lucius Aemilius had defeated a force of Veieans who had fled their camp. 'On the following day the consul rewarded with the most magnificent presents those who had distinguished themselves in battle and gave to the soldiers all the beasts of burden and slaves that had been left behind in the camp together with the tents which were full of many valuables. And the Roman army found itself in greater opulence than after any former battle for the Tyrrhenians (Etruscans) were a people of dainty and expensive tastes both at home and in the field, carrying about with them, besides the necessities, costly and artistic articles of all kinds designed for pleasure and luxury.'[7] Many years later during campaigning in Cilicia in the early 50s BC the then governor, Cicero, gave an equally generous allocation of booty to his soldiers when he allowed them to keep everything but the horses.[8]

Generous disposal of the spoils of war was one effective way which the commander had of ingratiating himself with his men and ensuring their loyalty and support; and yet it could work to his disadvantage as well as to his advantage. Towards the end of the prolonged campaigning of the Mithridatic Wars Lucullus' soldiers became demoralized when they saw Pompey's men being richly rewarded when they were not: 'If our campaigns are never to come to an end, do we not reserve what is left of our bodies and our lives for a general in whose eyes the wealth of the soldiers is the fairest honour.'[9] On an earlier occasion in the same war Mithridates had been allowed to escape because of the acquisitiveness of Lucullus' troops. Both Plutarch and Appian record the episode in 71 BC when Mithridates' army had been routed and the king was fleeing. His pursuers, on the point of capturing him, cut open the pack saddle of a mule and found it to be full of gold, which fell out. So busy were they gathering up these riches that they allowed Mithridates to escape and hence the war to drag on.[10] In marked contrast to these two episodes is the gesture made by Marius' soldiers after the battle of Aquae Sextiae (Aix-en-Provence) in 102 BC. According to Plutarch 'the Romans pursued (the enemy) and either slew or took alive over a hundred thousand of them, besides making themselves masters of their tents, waggons and property all of which, with the exception of what was pilfered, was given to Marius by vote of the soldiers'.[11]

The weapons and personal ornaments taken from an enemy slain in single combat would often be awarded to the soldier involved and of particular significance in this context were the *spolia opima*, the spoils taken from the enemy commander. Traditionally there were three categories of *spolia opima* – *prima, secunda* and *tertia* – though none of the ancient sources which mention this classification (said to have originated with a *Lex Numae*) make clear what is meant by it.[12] The most likely explanation is that the category of *spolia* depended on the rank of the person who won it, *spolia opima prima* being captured by the supreme commander, *secunda* by an officer of lesser rank and *tertia* by an ordinary soldier (see below p. 104 for a dispute over the right to *spolia opima prima*). These spoils were given as offerings to the gods, *spolia opima prima* to Jupiter Feretrius, *secunda* to Mars and *tertia* to Quirinus. The one explanation given by an ancient author of the meaning of the threefold classification of *spolia opima* is clearly incorrect. Servius suggests that the three categories apply to the three known winners, Romulus, Cornelius Cossus and M. Claudius Marcellus; this cannot be so for each of these dedicated his spoils to Jupiter Feretrius.[13]

Evidence for the *spolia opima* belongs almost exclusively to the regal and republican periods but the equivalent of the *spolia opima secunda* (though not called by this name) is attested during the Principate. An inscription commemorating the long and distinguished military career of M. Valerius Maximianus, whose service extended over the reigns of Marcus, Verus and Commodus, records that he killed a king of the Naristae (a Germanic tribe) called Valao and that he was publicly praised by Marcus and rewarded with a horse, *phalerae* (in this context probably horse-trappings rather than medals) and arms (*ab imp. Antonino Aug. coram laudato et equo et phaleris et armis donato quod manu sua ducem Naristarum Valaonem interemisset*).[14]

Spolia, other than those deposited in the temples, would be hung up in the house of the man to whom they had been awarded: 'in their homes they hang up the spoils they won in the most conspicuous places, looking upon them as tokens and evidences of their valour'.[15] The prestige and honour attached to the acquisition of these *spolia* was such that on the occasion of a review of the composition of the Roman senate in 216 BC the categories of citizen deemed worthy of consideration for admission were, in addition to those who had served in minor magistracies, the men who had spoils of the enemy affixed to their houses or had received the *corona civica*.[16]

With the growing size and complexity of the Roman empire and the changing nature of the army itself, the use of booty as a means of rewarding soldiers appears to have dwindled somewhat. The full-time professional soldier paid by the state and given land or a money grant on retirement was very different from the citizen-soldier of the regal and early republican periods. The upkeep of a vast army and central bureaucracy required large sums of money which could be very satisfactorily augmented by the plunder from a successful war. Moreover the responsibilities of the Emperor were so extensive and geographically so widespread that he dared not hazard the development of a situation in which he was plunged into a war of aggression because of the army's thirst for plunder. One way this could be achieved was by making special payments to the troops on occasions other than victories and triumphs. This was done in the form of donatives, though it is clear from the literature of the Empire that donatives never completely supplanted booty: they simply took the pressure off the spoils of warfare as the one major source of a soldier's perks. A successful campaign continued to yield a rich harvest for the army, and this was certainly so in the case of the army which fought under the command of Vespasian and Titus in the Jewish War. 'So glutted with plunder were the troops one and all that throughout Syria the standard of gold was depreciated to half its former value.' And yet more was to come. In a victory ceremony performed after the capitulation of Jerusalem Titus 'further assigned to them out of the spoils silver and gold and raiments and other booty in abundance'.[17] Spoils were still around in plenty. What does appear to have been abandoned in favour of the donative was the money payment made to the soldiers on the occasion of the triumph. The donatives of the Principate were not associated with triumphs or even necessarily with campaigning. They were commonly paid by emperors on their accession, but were also given on other auspicious or inauspicious occasions, as for example the donative given by Claudius to mark the entry of Nero into public life or by Nero after the detection of the conspiracy of Piso when it was clearly necessary for the emperor to assure himself of the loyalty of his troops. The amount paid to each soldier was dependent on his position on the pay-scale. This association of size of grant with rank was nothing new, for the gifts of money made to the soldiers of the Republic at the time of the triumphs were founded on this principle. Livy for example records a series of triumphs celebrated in the early to middle years of the second century BC, at which centurions received twice and cavalrymen three times as much as was given to the infantrymen.[18] Donatives were given only to citizen troops and not to auxiliaries (except sometimes to the *cohortes civium Romanorum*), a type of discrimination which was exercised also in the distribution of the *dona militaria* (below, p. 121). The gifts made by the general to his troops on the occasion of his triumph were true rewards for their bravery: the donatives which descended from and supplanted such gifts, having been dissociated from the exploits of the battlefield, are little more than rewards for past loyalty and bribes for the future.

A second practice which appears to have descended, in part at least, from the taking and redistribution of booty was that of awarding *dona militaria*. The form taken by several of these decorations is derived from the personal belongings of the enemies whom Rome had encountered in the field. Included in the various lists of spoils plundered by the Roman armies, in addition to such things as tents, waggons, horses, clothing and precious metals are personal ornaments such as *armillae* (armlets) and *torques* (neck-rings). The Romans considered adornments of this kind to be effeminate and yet they included both these types of ornament in the *dona* awarded to soldiers. In his etymology, Isidor of Seville includes *torques* in a section on feminine ornaments, while of *armillae* he writes that they are suitable for men in that they are given to soldiers to mark their valour.[19] While the Greco-Roman world looked upon these ornaments as effeminate they were worn by both men and women among the barbarian peoples with whom it came into contact. Both *torques* and *armillae* figure frequently in the personal attire of Rome's enemies, are often referred to in literature, appear in painting and sculpture and are found with burials. The seizing of these ornaments as spoils is the most likely channel by which they entered into the repertoire of Roman military decorations. This link is neatly illustrated in the case of the Manlian *gens* whose *cognomen* '*Torquatus*' is said to have been bestowed upon the family when Titus Manlius stripped a *torques* from the neck of a Gaul whom he had slain (below, p. 87). A link between spoils and decorations can also be suggested in the case of *phalerae* and of the *corniculum*, though here other origins are possible.

While some of Rome's military decorations have a barbarian ancestry others spring from her classical heritage. The practice of giving various types of crowns is no doubt based on Greek usage. The Greeks used crowns extensively as a festive and a funeral decoration, as an acknowledgement of public service, as prizes at poetic and athletic competitions and as a reward for wisdom and for valour. These crowns were sometimes of leaves, as for example the olive crowns awarded to Eurybiades and Themistocles by the Lacaedemonians, or of precious metals, as in the case of the gold crowns given by Alexander to those who had distinguished themselves by their bravery and by Ctesiphon to Demosthenes in acknowledgement of his public services.[20] The Romans adopted the practice and developed it to a considerable degree, designing a whole range of different types of crown to reward the individual exploits performed on the battlefield.

The third main source of inspiration for military decorations was provided by the arms and equipment of the Romans themselves, specifically the *hasta* (spear) and the *vexillum* (flag). Thus by the closing years of the first century BC a wide range of military decorations was available to be won:

Corona obsidionalis	siege crown
Corona civica	civic crown
Corona navalis/classica/rostrata	naval crown
Corona muralis	mural crown
Corona vallaris	rampart crown
Corona aurea	gold crown
Hasta pura	ceremonial spear
Vexillum	flag/banner
Torques	neck-ring
Armilla	armlet
Phalera	medal/horse-trapping
Patella	shallow dish (?)
Corniculum	small horn (?)

In addition there were the triumphal crowns worn by those participating in a triumphal procession and, from the early years of the Principate, the triumphal ornaments awarded to a successful general not of the imperial family, in lieu of a triumph.

The earliest commentator to give any details about Roman military decorations is Polybius.[21] His list of awards comprises by no means all those mentioned above. He mentions a spear ($\gamma\alpha\tilde{\iota}\sigma\sigma\varsigma$ the equivalent of the *hasta*), medallions or horse-trappings ($\phi\alpha\lambda\alpha\rho\alpha$: the equivalent of *phalerae*), a small dish or disc ($\phi\iota\dot{\alpha}\lambda\eta$: the equivalent of the *patella*) and crowns ($\sigma\tau\epsilon\phi\alpha\nu\sigma\iota$). He notes only two types of crown, that awarded to the first man over an enemy wall and that given to the man who saves the life of a Roman citizen, the equivalents of the *corona muralis* and *corona civica*. He does not, however, call them by these specific names, and since Polybius is a writer whom we can trust on military matters, his failure to use the names by which the crowns are known to later writers may well indicate that these names had not yet been acquired. The only other relevant author of a comparably early date, Caecilius Statius, likewise does not call the *corona civica* by this name but refers to it as *iligna corona*, a crown of oak.[22] Civic and mural crowns are certainly attested, and by these specific names, in the pre-Polybian period, but in all cases the source of evidence is some time later and the writers in question may have been using anachronistically the names familiar to them from their own day. If the system of award evolved slowly and pragmatically rather than having been devised as a whole, it is to be expected that its scope will have extended as time went on and that more decorations will have been added and their names gradually emerged.

The practice which developed during the Republic was one in which the nature of the deed determined the reward received. Merit was rewarded with little regard for rank. Some of the decorations were, as we have seen, designed to reward a particular feat of arms, hence the *corona muralis* for the first man over the wall of an enemy city, the *corona vallaris* for the first man over the rampart of an enemy camp. All the crowns with the exception of the *corona aurea* were tied in this way to a specific exploit, but of course many of the deeds which merited recognition were much less easy to categorize. Hence others of the decorations were of a more general nature and some may indeed have changed their usage over time, as appears to have been the case with the spear. According to Polybius it was originally awarded to a man who wounded or slew an enemy in a single combat which had been entered into voluntarily. By the time he was writing the practice had changed so that the man who slew an enemy received a $\phi\iota\dot{\alpha}\lambda\eta$ (*patella*) if in the infantry, $\phi\alpha\lambda\alpha\rho\alpha$ (*phalerae*) if in the cavalry. From what we know of the circumstances in which these awards subsequently came to be won, these conditions no longer applied. It is unfortunate that, in the examples which we have of the *hasta* being awarded, the sources are in general very unspecific about the nature of the deed which had been performed. Detail is equally scarce in the case of the other types of award. The *vexillum*, for example, is known to have been awarded to a commanding officer in a naval battle (it was awarded to Agrippa for his role at Actium in 31 BC) as well as in encounters on land (the second Punic War and the Jugurthine War).[23] No further information is available on the precise circumstances.

From the time of their inception until the early years of the Principate merit was the most significant factor in the allocation of military decorations. The more valuable and prestigious awards were not reserved for the rich and powerful: a simple footsoldier was in theory as eligible for the major awards as were his commanding officers. Gaius Laelius was admiral in command of a fleet when he won a gold crown at the siege of New Carthage in 210 BC; but on the same occasion mural crowns – also made of gold – were won by a centurion, Quintus Trebellius, and a sailor, Sextus Digitius.[24] After the capture of Aquilonia *armillae* and *torques* were awarded to four centurions and also to a maniple of *hastati*. (*Hastati* were soldiers in the prime of life who formed the front line when the army was drawn up in battle array.) A couple of other officers also won *armillae* on this same occasion.[25] In many cases the rank of the individual at the time he was decorated is not indicated, but the phrases which occur again and again are that the awards are being made to each according to his valour and his merit: *virtus atque opera in ea pugna* ('his valour and his deeds in that battle'); *virtutis causa* '(because of his valour'); *ut meritum* ('according to merit').[26]

By the third quarter of the first century AD this had changed and there had developed a scheme whereby rank determined to a large extent the composition of any reward received: merit was no longer the overriding criterion. Such a structured system of reward developed as a natural corollary of what had become a sharply stratified military society. The principle is far from being unique to the Roman army: it is enshrined for example in the system of reward used in the British forces today. The Distinguished Service Order can be won only by commissioned army officers; the Military Medal is reserved to warrant officers, non-commissioned officers and men in the ranks. An officer or warrant officer in the Royal Air Force is eligible for a Distinguished Flying Cross, a non-commissioned officer or man in the ranks, the Distinguished Flying Medal. These distinctions grew up from the very earliest days of modern medals. And even before this, when no statutory method of reward existed, the *ad hoc* provisions which were made based themselves on this same principle. For example, the sailors who fought with Nelson at the Battle of the Nile in 1798 were rewarded privately, gold, silver, gilt bronze and bronze medals being distributed to all participants to each according to his rank, from gold for the admirals and ships' captains to bronze for the ordinary seamen and marines. Another parallel between the Roman and the modern British practice is worthy of note: just as the Victoria Cross is today and has since its inception been rewarded irrespective of rank, so the Roman army maintained the *corona civica* as a decoration to be competed for on equal terms by all.

The Roman system never became completely static: what appears in general to have developed was an overall framework, a series of guidelines rather than rigid rules. A number of the underlying principles can be detected. For example the *hasta pura* was not normally awarded to a soldier below the rank of senior centurion, only senators and equestrians could win a *vexillum* and only consulars could receive a *corona navalis*. With the exception of the *corona civica*, the crowns lost all connection with the deeds which they were originally designed to commemorate: no naval encounter was necessary for an ex-consul to win a *corona navalis*, no capture of town or camp for a centurion to receive a *corona muralis* or *vallaris*. What did survive virtually unchanged was the form taken by the decorations and their relative significance. For example the *corona aurea* was the most frequently awarded crown in the republican period (no doubt because of its lack of a precise designation) and it becomes the least of the crowns in the imperial scheme. Conversely the *corona navalis* was rarely awarded in the republican period and it develops into the most select of the imperial crowns, awarded only to those who had held the consulate. The system which developed during the Principate, while thus reserving particular awards for particular ranks and laying down broad principles as to how many of each type of decoration any one soldier might receive, never became totally rigid. Individual emperors could and did vary it according to their own predilictions. Hadrian for example was notably parsimonious in the awards he granted to his officers, while Marcus and Verus were more generous than most to centurions. Even within a single reign it is possible to see sufficient variations in the composition of the awards made to any one grade of soldier to justify the belief that rank never became the sole criterion and that degrees of individual merit were being noted and suitably recompensed.

But when did this shift of emphasis from merit to rank take place? Signs of it are clearly visible in the later years of the Republic. For example, the standard award in the Principate for a soldier below the rank of centurion (or *evocatus* in the case of the praetorian guard) was *torques, armillae* and *phalerae*; one or other of the awards might be omitted but in the majority of cases all three appear together. The earliest example of this combination takes us well back into the Republic, to 89 BC and the period of the Social War when Pompeius Strabo rewarded some Spanish cavalrymen in the *turma Salluitana* with Roman citizenship, double rations and *dona* including *torques armillae* and *phalerae*.[27] This is followed in the period of Caesar's Gallic Wars by the case of Caius Canuleius who was killed in Gaul while serving as *evocatus* in legion VII.[28] Some time during his years of service Canuleius had been awarded *torques, armillae* and *phalerae* and a *corona aurea*, precisely the same combination of decorations as later became characteristic of the praetorian *evocatus* (below, p. 210). These two examples are both attested by inscriptions and therefore give considerably more detail of rank and composition of award than do the majority of the literary references. But the literature too hints at this same tendency towards standard combinations of awards, specifically in the case of those decorations which are not tied to a particular type of exploit. Despite the fact that any rank could win any award, there is singularly little evidence in the literature of the Republic for senior officers winning minor awards. Another republican practice which foreshadows that of the Empire is the way in which gifts of money were made to soldiers at the time of a triumph, the size of the gift depending on the rank of the recipient (above, p. 60). Similarly the three categories of the *spolia opima* are distinguished by the rank of the adversaries involved. Hence the practices of the imperial period represent no sudden and revolutionary departure from established tradition, but rather the culmination of tendencies already at work, tendencies which were bound to be accentuated with the development of clearly defined ladders of promotion within the army structure, emphasizing differences of rank and status.

That the earlier practices persisted into the reign of Augustus is suggested by a passage in Suetonius' life of Augustus.[29] Talking about the ways in which Augustus rewarded valour in the field the biographer notes that he gave *coronae murales* and *vallares* as sparingly as possible, but that he gave them 'without favouritism and even to the common soldiers' (*sine ambitione ac saepe etiam caligatis*). Leaving aside the case of the *corona civica* which appears never to have lost its original significance and was certainly never integrated into imperial schemes of award, the latest example of a decoration being given irrespective of rank is that of M. Helvius Rufus. It was while taking part in the campaign against Tacfarinas in north Africa in AD 18 that Rufus was decorated by the provincial governor with a *torques* and a *hasta*, for saving the life of a Roman citizen, the latest case of a *hasta* being awarded to anyone of lower rank than senior centurion – Rufus was a common soldier, *miles gregarius*, at the time.[30] The fact that Apronius, the governor, did choose to give him the *hasta* as opposed to some other decoration is of considerable interest. The saving of a Roman life would normally have merited the *corona civica*, and indeed Tacitus goes on to narrate how Tiberius, regretting that the governor had not awarded the crown, added it himself. Why therefore did Apronius choose a *hasta*? Could it be connected with the fact with which Polybius acquaints us, that the *hasta* was originally awarded to a soldier who voluntarily and deliberately engaged in single combat and slew an enemy, just as might well have occurred in saving the life of a fellow-citizen?

Subsequent to this episode a *corona navalis* was awarded in connection with a naval exploit, but the circumstances are somewhat out of the ordinary, so the award cannot count as a true case of the survival of the traditional practice. Suetonius records how, after the invasion of Britain in AD 43, Claudius had set up over the gable of his residence on the Palatine Hill in Rome two crowns, a *corona civica* and a *corona navalis*, the latter to commemorate the crossing and conquest of *Oceanus*, the sea that surrounded the 'known' world and separated Britain from the provinces of Gaul.[31] Such a gesture is well in keeping with the antiquarian tendencies of the emperor Claudius.

The period from Augustus to Vespasian is the era of experiment and change as far as *dona militaria* are concerned, just as it is in various other fields. There are few attested cases of the survival of traditional practice and yet the set combinations of award which can be seen *par excellence* under Domitian and Trajan have not yet fully evolved. There is as yet little order in the senatorial decorations, while the equestrian awards, at the opposite extreme, appear completely inflexible, reflecting neither the nature of the exploit nor the rank of the recipient – the result no doubt of the fact that the equestrian career itself was only now developing into a set pattern. Only the decorations received by the centurions and the men in the ranks quickly took on the form they maintained throughout the Principate, but then, as has already been seen, their awards were becoming fairly standardized within the later years of the Republic.

It has been suggested that towards the end of the republican period the *dona* began to lose their significance in the eyes of the soldiers, who no longer prized them as highly as had their predecessors.[32] But neither the literature of the period nor the subsequent history of *dona* bears this out. The crucial passage comes from Plutarch's life of Q. Sertorius which recounts how Sertorius, serving as a commanding officer during the Social War of 90–88 BC, lost an eye through a wound received in battle. Sertorius, far from being ashamed of his disfigurement, prized it as a permanent and visible record of his bravery which, unlike military decorations, he carried around with him always.[33] Is he here denigrating the *torques, hastae* and *coronae* which he won or merely making the point that a man does not wear his military decorations all the time? A facial disfigurement he does, and it cannot be hidden. This passage, far from suggesting that the decorations were deemed of little value, can be construed as indicating that *dona* were still regarded at this time as effective evidence of valour: they were just less obvious and less permanent than that other evidence of valour, the loss of an eye. If the practice of awarding *dona militaria* had lost its value, it is doubtful whether it would have survived and developed for as long as it did. *Dona* were still being awarded at the end of the second century AD and perhaps early in the third. The system came to an end, or was altered beyond all recognition, only when the basis of recruitment was so changed as to subvert one of the fundamental principles around which the system was built – the distinction between citizen and non-citizen unit (below, p. 253). Thus at their end as in their origins and development *dona militaria* are responding to the conditions of their time, not changing as a result of sudden doctrinaire policy decisions but being adapted piecemeal to serve the changing needs of an evolving military system.

CHAPTER IV

THE DECORATIONS

Corona obsidionalis

Pre-eminent among Roman military decorations was the *corona obsidionalis*, the siege crown. This crown was awarded to the man responsible for raising a siege and thereby saving the lives of numerous people, of a whole army or township. It was conferred by the rescued upon their rescuer and was of entirely token value; unlike the lesser crowns it was not made of gold or silver but of grass or whatever vegetation grew upon the site where the besieged had been held. The reason is symbolic: 'for in old times it was the most solemn token of defeat for the conquered to present grass to their conquerors, for to do so meant that they withdrew from their land, from the very soil that nurtured them and even from means of burial'. The material from which the crown was made provides the alternative name by which it was sometimes known, *corona graminea* or crown of grass: 'no crown indeed has been a higher honour than the crown of grass among the rewards for glorious deeds given by the sovereign people, lords of the earth'.[1]

According to Pliny, who discusses it at some length, the siege crown was the first military crown to be introduced: this statement is incapable of verification though there is no particular reason to doubt it. The form of the crown is simple and unsophisticated and it is easy to imagine how it may have evolved from a spontaneous token gesture on the part of the inhabitants of a beleagured town or of an army which had given up hope of survival. In such a way might the rescued have demonstrated their gratitude to their rescuer, handing to him, just as according to Pliny they would have to their conqueror, the plant life which symbolized the very soil to which they belonged.

The siege crown was evidently the hardest of all the decorations to win; rarely would the necessary circumstances of siege have arisen, and more rarely still would it have been possible to extricate the situation in such a way as to justify the award. Hence it is not surprising to find that the fabulous collection of *dona* won by L. Siccius Dentatus which comprised a total of twenty-six crowns (in addition to other types of award) included only one *corona*

67

obsidionalis. Pliny lists just six recipients known to him to have received the award and states that nobody else up to his time had done so. The evidence of other authors is consistent with Pliny, for although some duplicate the names given by him none add any new ones.

The type of exploit for which a *corona obsidionalis* might be won is well illustrated by Livy's narrative of the way in which P. Decius Mus saved an army from destruction.[2] The episode in question belongs to the first Samnite war in which, we are told, Decius was serving as a tribune under the consul A. Cornelius. Cornelius, marching into Samnite territory, led his army into a deep defile through a forest near Saticula. Not until he had penetrated well into the defile did he realise that the enemy was posted on the heights above him; he had walked straight into an ambush. Decius, with a large legionary detachment, observed that one hill overlooking the enemy camp had been left unguarded. This he succeeded in taking, unobserved by the enemy, who were so nonplussed on observing what had happened that Cornelius and the remaining part of the army were able to withdraw safely to more favourable ground. Decius and the troops he had with him were now cut off from the main body of the army but under cover of night they succeeded in escaping from their hilltop position, crossing over the enemy's position and rejoining the consul. There ensued a victorious battle against the Samnite army. For his part in this exploit Decius received gifts of oxen, a gold crown and two siege crowns: one of these siege crowns was bestowed upon him by the legions whom he had saved, the other by the detachment who had taken part in the capture of the hilltop and who, in turn, had been rescued from the trap in which they lay by the courage and astuteness of their tribune.[3]

Given the circumstances in which it had to be earned, this crown is unlikely ever to have been won by a man in the ranks; only an officer with some overall responsibility for a military detachment if not for an entire army, is likely ever to have been in a position to fulfil the necessary conditions. The lowest-ranking soldier known to have been awarded it was a senior centurion, the *primus pilus* Cn. Petreius. The legion in which he was serving in the war against the Cimbri in 101 BC had been cut off by the enemy and when the tribune in command balked at the idea of breaking through the enemy camp Petreius promptly killed him and led his men to safety.[4] A rather different type of exploit is illustrated by the case of Fabius Maximus who, by his 'Fabian' tactics, eventually succeeded in saving Rome and Italy from the menace of Hannibal in the second Punic War: in recognition of his services he was presented with the crown by the senate and people of Rome, the highest honour perhaps to which any commander could aspire, recognition as saviour of a whole state.[5]

The first attested example of the *corona obsidionalis* is that attributed to Siccius Dentatus, the crown being won in unknown circumstances in the sixth century BC. The last occasion on which it is known to have been earned in traditional fashion belongs to the latter years of the Republic when it was awarded to Sulla during his service as legate at Nola during the Marsian campaign of the Social War, 91–88 BC. Thereafter it appears just once in the account of an episode in Julian's Persian War.[6] On this occasion the siege crown was awarded 'to those who had fought valiantly' during the relief of the siege of Maiozamalcha in AD 363. The association with a siege has been retained but the true conditions for the winning of a siege crown have not been fulfilled; this suggests an attempt to revive an ancient but evidently misunderstood custom. It is uncertain quite when the award originally lapsed, though there is reason to believe that it had gone out of use before the end of the Republic, for the siege crown plays no part whatever in the award schemes of the Empire.

One of the unfortunate results of the failure of the award to survive into the Principate is that there is great uncertainty as to its physical form. The only clue to its appearance is given by the verbal descriptions of it as having been woven from grass or other vegetation. No representations survive either on coins or in sculpture unless the otherwise unidentifiable crown belonging to C. Vibius Macer is an *obsidionalis*. This crown (fig. 5) bears little resemblance to any other known form of crown; it could conceivably be a *corona aurea*, but a rather oddly executed one.[7]

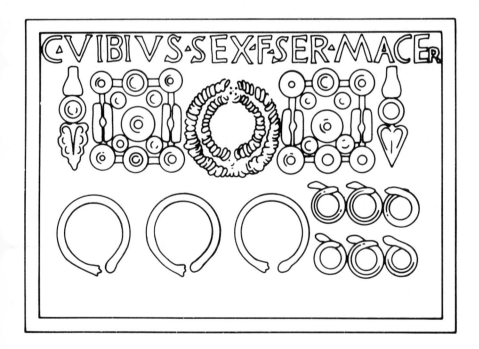

5   C. Vibius Macer

Corona civica

The *corona civica* or civic crown was regarded by the Romans as second in importance only to the siege crown, which it resembled in that it too was of purely symbolic value. Stringent conditions were laid down concerning the awarding of this crown and they are set out in some detail by Aulus Gellius and by Pliny.[8] The narratives of the two authors agree in all important particulars, though the latter gives much the fuller account. The *corona civica* was awarded to the man who, in battle, saved the life of a Roman citizen and for the rest of the day held the place where the exploit had occurred. Furthermore, the person whose life had been saved had freely to admit this fact, witnesses to the event being of no value in establishing the deed if the rescued himself failed to acknowledge it. The honour attached to the award was as great whether the man rescued was a general or a simple private, and it is evident from Pliny's testimony that very great prestige accompanied the decoration. Once a man had received the civic crown he could wear it for the rest of his life; when he appeared at the games he had the right to sit by the senators who would rise at his entrance. In commemoration of his award M. Helvius Rufus who, according to Tacitus,[9] won the crown during campaigning in Africa in AD 18, took the surname 'Civica'. We learn this from the chance survival of an inscription set up in his honour in Italy.[10] Apart from conferring status the award also conveyed more practical benefits in that the recipient, his father and paternal grandfather were exempted from all public duties. It might also be the passport to social advancement. Livy records an occasion when the composition of the senate was being reviewed and gaps in its membership being filled; among those considered worthy for consideration were those who had received the civic crown.[11]

Although the regulations governing the award were stringent, discretion appears to have been used over their application. For example there was one case in which the emperor Tiberius was asked to adjudicate over a question of eligibility. A soldier had saved a Roman citizen in battle and killed two of the enemy, but he had failed to hold his ground and was thus technically ineligible for the award. Tiberius however ruled in favour of the soldier, saying that the place in which the rescue had been effected must have been perilous indeed if even so valiant a soldier could not hold it.[12]

The earliest reference to a *corona civica*, in this case called a crown of oak, *corona iligna*, comes in a passage of Caecilius Statius who wrote in the early part of the second century BC: unfortunately the passage is fragmentary and the context lost.[13] Polybius describes a crown to which he gives no specific name but which must clearly be a *corona civica*;[14] the conditions under which it was won vary in some respects from those later described by Pliny, but the essentials are the same. Polybius speaks of a crown which can be given by any citizen or ally to the man who saves his life: if not made freely the award was made under compulsion. Herein lie two discrepancies between the narratives of Pliny and Polybius, the use of compulsion and the inclusion in the terms of reference of the ally or non-Roman citizen. Polybius adds that for the rest of his life the rescued had to reverence the rescuer as a father. This father-son relationship between rescued and rescuer is mentioned also by Cicero when speaking specifically of the *corona civica*, noting the reluctance of men to take on the great burden of being under the same obligation to a stranger that they owe to a parent.[15] Such an obligation would have been no extra burden to one of those reputed to have earned (though not to have received) a *corona civica*; this is Scipio Africanus whom tradition credits with saving the life of his father.[16] According to Pliny he was offered the crown but turned it down. The episode took place in northern Italy in an encounter with Hannibal on the Ticinus in 218 BC. The general, Scipio's father, was wounded and cut off by the enemy until saved by the intervention of his son, then a youth in his late teens, who was in command of a detachment of cavalry. An alternative version of this story attributes the rescue of the Elder Scipio to a Ligurian slave. This version is related by Livy, who gives as his source the rhetorician and historian Coelius Antipater: this may have been an attempt to detract from Scipio's glory. Livy himself states his preference for the version 'most authorities have handed down and tradition has established' – that is the version which gives credit to the son. Polybius, who attributes the deed to the son, is of course an admirer of the Scipios, but he drew his information on this point from Gaius Laelius who personally knew and served under Scipio Africanus: his testimony is therefore to be preferred.[17]

The *corona civica* never lost its original significance through being incorporated into set imperial schemes of *dona*. The reason perhaps lies in the fact that this crown, being of no monetary value, was worth nothing beyond what it symbolized; the same is of course true of the *corona obsidionalis*, the only other republican crown which played no part in imperial schemes. Indeed the *corona civica* continued to be awarded in its traditional manner at least into the mid-first century AD. In AD 48, it was awarded to M. Ostorius Scapula, son of the then governor of Britain, during the revolt of the Iceni (though no detail is given of his exploit),[18] and was still available to be won some fourteen years later when Corbulo, governor of Syria, marched into Armenia to go to the assistance of Caesennius Paetus who was hard pressed by the Parthians. Corbulo exhorted his men with the hope of winning civic crowns for the saving of many citizen lives, the lives indeed of almost two whole legions.[19]

With the exception of the dubious cases recorded in the untrustworthy Augustan History lives of Probus and Aurelian the very latest reference to a *corona civica* appears on an inscription set up in honour of one C. Didius Saturninus who, as a centurion, received from the emperors Severus and Caracalla *corona aurea civica*. It has been suggested that this is an entirely new type of crown, a civic crown made of gold, first introduced by Severus.[20] If this is so it is not only the first but also the last attested reference to it. The whole practice of giving *dona* was on the wane by the early third century and it is most unlikely that a new award would be devised at this time. Further, any new award would hardly have been given the same name as another highly coveted decoration, the memory and tradition of which were still very much alive at the time in question. The decoration of Didius Saturninus can best be explained as comprising two crowns, a *corona aurea* and a *corona civica* of traditional type (see further below, p. 199). This, the last attested case of the award, is also the only one known to have been made since the time of Claudius, for Tacitus does not tell us if any of Corbulo's men did actually succeed in winning one. Two reasons may be adduced for this lack of evidence. One is the absence of good literary sources for much of this period, for most of what we know about civic crowns even during the Principate comes from literary rather than epigraphic evidence. The second is the fact that much of the fighting of the late first and second centuries took place on the frontiers of the Empire and was conducted by auxiliary troops who, as non-citizens, were not eligible for the award.

The civic crown, apart from being a highly coveted military decoration, was also adopted as an imperial emblem. Dio records that the Senate granted to Augustus the right to hang the crown over his residence to symbolize his being victor over his enemies and saviour of the citizens; this same honour was duly entered in the *Res Gestae divi Augusti*, a summary record of the deeds of Augustus, which is remarkably preserved in a copy inscribed on the walls of the temple of Rome and Augustus at Ancyra (in Asia Minor), the so-called Monumentum Ancyranum.[21] Subsequently other emperors were awarded this same privilege though Tiberius is said to have refused it. The emblem frequently appears on coins (pl. 1e), accompanied by the legend *ob cives servatos*.[22]

The form taken by the *corona civica* is very well attested (fig. 6): the description given by our literary sources is wholly consistent with the pictorial evidence provided by both coins and sculpture. It was made of oak leaves and is sometimes known as the *corona quercea* from *quercus*, the generic name for the oak. The clearest sculptural representation of the civic crown appears on the cenotaph of M. Caelius from Vetera (pl. 2a), which shows Caelius resplendent in his military decorations which include a crown of oak leaves with the acorns attached. Similarly a fragmentary relief from Cologne, depicting military equipment and decorations (pl. 2c), shows a crown formed of leaves whose shape is less well shown than those on the Caelius stone but which clearly have acorns interspersed among them. The top of the relief is broken away so that the front of the crown is missing but the back is shown, demonstrating how the two ends are tied together with a ribbon looped into a bow with long loose flowing strings. The crown worn by Q. Sertorius Festus

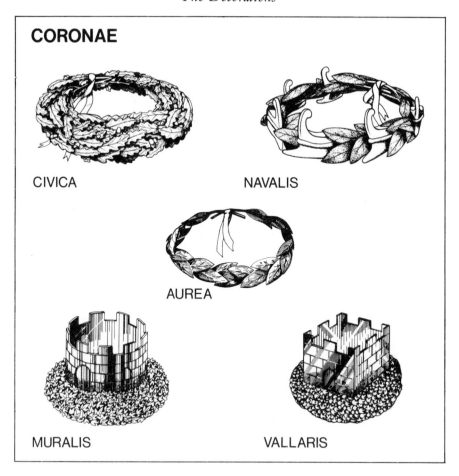

CORONAE

CIVICA

NAVALIS

AUREA

MURALIS

VALLARIS

6   Coronae

(pl. 2b) may also be a *corona civica* though in this case, despite the generally very high standard of the sculpture, the leaf formation is not at all clearly shown. The civic crowns which appear as imperial emblems on coins do not always include acorns: the reason may lie simply in the problems of executing such an intricate design in so small a space.

Another very fine representation of a *corona civica* is embossed in high relief on the crown of a cavalry sports helmet from Thrace (pl. 3a).[23] This helmet of silvered bronze comes from the grave of a Thracian chieftan at Vize in Turkey: it predates the creation of the Roman province of Thracia in AD 45. The skull is covered with short wavy hair, encircled on the crown by a very naturalistic wreath of interwoven oak leaves and acorns. A small rosette is set at the front of the wreath where the opposing sides come together. The cheek-pieces of the helmet are decorated with winged victories and *tropaea* (trophies). Cavalry sports helmets, of which this is a particularly fine specimen, were worn by the Roman auxiliary cavalry when taking part in their elaborate equestrian exercises, the *hippika gymnasia*. Arrian, describing these exercises, indicated that only the officers and more accomplished horsemen wore these helmets and face-masks which were commonly decorated with scenes and motifs from classical history and mythology.[24] The appearance of a civic crown on a cavalry helmet in no way indicates the winning of the crown by the man who wore the helmet – this man was simply playing a part. The participants in the *hippika gymnasia* appear to have re-enacted scenes from classical tradition: Arrian speaks of the horsemen dividing into opposing teams, and the presence of female as well as male masks among the surviving equipment suggests that one of the battles played out was that between the Greeks and Amazons. Whatever significance the civic crown has in this context relates not to the person wearing the helmet thus adorned but to the figure whom he is intended to represent. The same is true of the *corona muralis* which adorns the Ribchester helmet and the other types of wreath which are embossed on, for example, the Newstead and Straubing helmets.[25]

The reason for the use of oak leaves for the civic crown is obscure. Plutarch puts forward three possibilities, the first of which is a down-to-earth practical one and far the most likely:[26] he suggests simply that it was easy to find an abundance of oak anywhere on campaign. The prevalence of the oak at this period thoughout western Europe is well attested. Plutarch's other two possibilities take us into the realms of mythology. The oak is sacred to Jupiter and Juno who are regarded as guardians of the city and hence is fittingly bestowed on one who has saved the life of a Roman citizen. Finally he suggests that it may derive from the fact that the Arcadians, early colonists of Rome were called acorn-eaters in an oracle of Apollo. The development of military decorations appears in general to have been strictly pragmatic; and so it might be conjectured that a type of foliage chosen originally as a matter of convenience later acquired the traditions which imbued it with a certain magico-religious significance.

Corona navalis, classica or rostrata

The naval crown has its origin, as its name implies, in the battles which Rome fought against her seaborne enemies. It is included among those crowns which, according to Pliny were instituted later than the *corona obsidionalis*.[27] The reason in this case is not far to seek. It was not until the time of the Punic Wars that Rome became involved with a naval power and was forced to fight battles in an environment generally alien and uncongenial to her, that is at sea. Thus the earliest possible date for the inception of the naval crown is the mid-third century BC and the first Punic war. There is, however, no reference to this crown in Polybius' discourse on military awards and it is not mentioned until considerably later: the earliest reference to it belongs to the late Republic. Only one certain case of its award is attested for the whole of the period up to and including Augustus, that is the award to Marcus Agrippa who commanded a fleet in the war against Sextus Pompeius in 36 BC. It was the belief of both Seneca and Dio that Agrippa was the only person ever to have won the naval crown, while Livy thought that he was the first person to gain the award.[28] Thus the statement by Pliny that Marcus Varro was given the honour in 67 BC by Pompey the Great, as a result of his involvement in the war against the pirates who infested the Mediterranean, is thrown into some doubt. Indeed it has been suggested that Pliny is muddling the names of the sources for, and the personalities involved in, the various sea battles.[29] This is possible, though there is in theory no reason why Varro should not have received the decoration with which Pliny credits him. Despite the leaning towards scholarship which exhibited itself in his early years, he did not opt entirely out of public life and the responsibilities which his rank carried with it. When Pompey the Great launched his campaign against the pirates, Varro was numbered among the twenty-five commanders who were put in charge of fleets which were to patrol the Mediterranean. Such a post would have provided plenty of scope for winning a naval crown. Thus, despite the contrary testimony of Seneca, Livy and Dio, Varro must be regarded as a serious candidate for the distinction. The rarity with which this type of award is attested when compared with other types is hardly surprising in view of the comparative infrequency of naval battles.

The name of the naval crown appears in three variant forms – *corona navalis, corona classica* and *corona rostrata* – and this has led scholars in the past to suggest that more than one type of crown is in question. Their hypothesis would appear to draw strength from the fact that, while the one certain and one probable case of award were to a naval commander, the descriptions of the *corona navalis* given in the works of both Aulus Gellius and Pompeius Festus relate to a crown awarded to the first man to board an enemy ship in a sea battle – hardly the fleet commander.[30] Could there then be two distinct types – the *corona navalis* awarded in the way described, the *corona rostrata* reserved for the commander? Such an hypothesis is not borne out by the evidence. Pliny, in Book 16, describes the crowns of both Varro and Agrippa as *rostratae*, but in Book 7 calls that of Varro a *corona navalis*. Livy describes Agrippa's crown as *navalis* as does Seneca, while Velleius Paterculus calls it a *corona classica*.[31] In the literature which we have, the three terms would thus appear interchangeable, applying to an award which could be won in either of two different ways; and if any difference of title had once differentiated the categories, this difference had been lost by the late Republic.

The naval crown survived into the Principate as part of the set of awards made to an officer of consular rank, irrespective of the nature of the encounter in which he may have been involved (below, p. 146). Any connection which it had originally had with the sea is lost. The naval origin of the crown was last stressed in AD 44 when the emperor Claudius set up a *corona navalis*, along with a *corona civica* on the gable of his palace, in commemoration of his victory over Oceanus in his crossing to Britain.[32] During the Principate the *corona navalis* was reserved to the consular: no-one of lower rank is known to have received the award. It is the one type of crown which was omitted from the *dona* of the praetorian prefect, which, in all other respects, were identical to those of the consular. It was no doubt because of its rarity value in the Republic that it became characteristic of the highest ranking award in the Principate when it is referred to without distinction as either *navalis* or *classica*, though never *rostrata*.

The appearance of the crown is hinted at by the use of the name *corona rostrata*: it was a crown decorated with the beaks, or *rostra*, of ships (fig. 6) and was made, originally at least, of gold.[33] The best pictorial evidence for it appears on coins. Two Augustan coin types show slightly variant forms of a crown of leaves, probably laurel, interspersed with stylised ships beaks and prows. Two of these beaks meet over the brow and two more are attached to either side of the crown (pl. 1a, b). A similar crown is illustrated on an *as* of Agrippa, the one certain recipient of the award. The coin in question (pl. 1c) bears on its obverse the head of Agrippa wearing the *corona navalis* together with the legend *M. Agrippa L. f. cos III*. The production of this coin began during the reign of Gaius (Caligula) and probably continued under Claudius.[34] It may be no coincidence that this pictorial allusion to naval victory was put into circulation at a time when one emperor was perhaps planning, and another certainly undertook, a campaign *trans Oceanum*.[35] A beaked device, similar to that on the naval crown, appears occasionally on military standards. A relief, now in the church of San Marcello in Rome, illustrates three standards, the central of which is decorated towards its base with a ship's prow (pl. 4a).

Corona muralis

The earliest surviving reference to a mural crown is contained in a passage of Polybius which refers to a gold crown being awarded to the first man to mount the wall at the assault of an enemy city. Although the crown is not given a specific name, the allusion is clearly to the same award as that which Aulus Gellius is describing when he says: 'a *corona muralis* is that which is given by the commander to the man who is first to mount the wall and enter by force into the enemy town'.[36]

It is unlikely that the crown was awarded very frequently, for few can have been the first to scale an enemy wall and have lived to enjoy the distinction which their courage had earned. And yet the desire to win this reward served as a spur to greater effort in battle. A unique example of a disputed claim to a military decoration involves the *corona muralis*; a legionary centurion and a sailor both put forward a claim to having been the first to scale the wall in the siege of New Carthage during the campaigns of Scipio Africanus in Spain.[37] So hotly were the claims disputed that there was a threat of mutiny, with the soldiers and sailors on the verge of coming to blows. Scipio appointed three arbiters to decide the question and the equitable result was that mural crowns were bestowed on both for having climbed simultaneously to the wall top. Livy graphically described the problems and dangers of mounting the assault on well-defended city walls, and it was not until the second attempt that the attack succeeded: inspired to prove their courage in the sight of their commander, 'the men dashed on in the face of wounds and missiles, and neither walls nor armed men standing on them can restrain them from vying with one another in the attempt to climb'. Another recipient of the *corona muralis* was the adopted grandson of Scipio Africanus, Scipio Aemilianus, who also won it in Spain.

It is clear from these two examples that the *corona muralis* was awarded regardless of rank and status and it would appear that this remained true right down to the time of Augustus, if we are to believe the testimony of Suetonius when he tells us that Augustus awarded mural crowns rarely and with due regard to merit, and that private soldiers sometimes won them.[38]

The first specific example of the award of a *corona muralis* in the Principate dates to the reign of Gaius when it appears as part of the award made to Anicius Maximus, then serving as *praefectus castrorum*. By this time it had apparently lost its traditional meaning; it had come to form part of the collection of decorations given to the senatorial commander; it figures also among the combinations of awards made to equestrians and is occasionally awarded to the centurion. However the infrequency with which the centurion received the *corona muralis* as compared with the *vallaris* perhaps reflects the difficulty with which it was traditionally won and the rarity with which it is attested in the Republic. No soldier below the rank of centurion was eligible for this crown in the Principate.

Aulus Gellius describes the crown as being made of gold and ornamented with representations of the battlements of a wall (fig. 6). Such a crown is depicted with great clarity of detail on the side of an inscription set up in honour of Sex. Vibius Gallus, a *primipilaris*, who amassed an impressive collection of decorations during a career which spanned the Rhine and Danube campaigns of Domitian and Trajan. A relief on the back of the stone shows a cavalryman riding down a Dacian, while on either side are sculpted the major part of the *dona* which are listed in the bilingual (Greek and Latin) text (pl. 5a, b). In order that there should be no doubt whatever what is being shown, the name of each decoration is engraved beside the representation of it. The mural crown is circular in contour; from a cushion-like base it rises up in the form of a wall, the individual stones of which are shown, a gate and windows. The top is crenellated just as Gellius' description states. Mural crowns are both recorded and illustrated on an inscription in honour of Ti. Claudius Iunianus (fig. 7) while one is shown on the tombstone of Sulpicius Celsus (pl. 5c); here the surviving text gives no indication that Celsus had won decorations and it is only on the evidence of the sculpture that we are able to identify his awards.

7   Tiberius Claudius Iunianus

The front part of a *corona muralis* – more like a coronet than a crown – appears across the brow of the mask part of the Ribchester sports helmet. This crown is considerably smaller and neater than those indicated by all the sculptural representations, being only about one centimetre high. The 'wall' is broken centrally by a double portalled gate with round headed arches, and at either side by single gates: three projecting semi-circular bastions, each with three round-headed windows and a conical roof, are interposed between each set of gates.[39]

Corona vallaris

The *corona vallaris* was the counterpart of the *corona muralis* but awarded in the context of the storming of an enemy camp rather than of a town. It was given to the man first over the rampart or *vallum* – hence its name. An alternative name given to it by Gellius and Festus is *corona castrensis* ('camp crown');[40] they are certainly alluding to the same type of crown as the *vallaris* for the description of the manner in which it was won is identical. The *corona vallaris* may have been a fairly late innovation, though the reason for this supposition is based on negative rather than positive evidence. Polybius does not discuss it in his discourse on the rewarding of soldiers in a passage where he does refer to the crown which became known as the *corona muralis*. It is possible that at this date the one type of crown served the two purposes, for as has been said Polybius does not give it a specific name. Nor is a *corona vallaris* included in the lengthy list of *dona* reputed to have been won by Siccius Dentatus; the only other crown which is lacking in this collection is the *navalis* which he would have had little opportunity to win. Indeed not one single recipient of the *corona vallaris* is known by name for the whole of the republican period.

Just three references relate to a *corona vallaris* in a republican context and all belong to the third century. Livy writes of soldiers who took part in the triumph of Papirius wearing *coronae vallares* (293 BC) and later, with reference to Hannibal's army which would meet Scipio's troops in Africa, that many of the soldiers had won *coronae murales* and *vallares*.[41] If taken literally this means that the Carthaginian army had a system of military decorations similar to that of the Romans (which is doubtful) or that it included soldiers who had previously fought in a Roman army. More likely, Livy's statement was merely a device to give force to the point that the enemy included brave warriors who, we are told, had slain Roman praetors, generals and consuls and captured Roman towns, and who had they been fighting for instead of against Rome might well have won crowns for their exploits. Such an interpretation is hardly good evidence for the existence of the *corona vallaris* at the date of the encounter in question, 202 BC. The third allusion to this type of crown in the Republic is provided by Valerius Maximus who was writing in the Tiberian period. During an assembly held on the day following the capture of a camp of the Bruttii and Lucani in 283 BC an appeal went out for the man who had been first to break into the camp to come forward and claim his reward, a *corona vallaris*. The appeal met with no response and those present were led to conclude that the god Mars himself had come to their aid.[42] The vagueness of these three references is such that none can be used with any confidence as good evidence for the existence of the *corona vallaris* at as early a period as that in question, the third century BC.

During the Principate the *corona vallaris* was a fairly common form of award. It lost its original significance, was included among combinations of awards given for valorous deeds of a less specific nature and was no longer awarded regardless of rank. Its scope was the same as that of the *corona muralis*, appearing invariably among the awards made to the consular, being available to the equestrian and also to the centurion who was the lowest ranking soldier now eligible for it. The relative importance of the *muralis* and the *vallaris* is perhaps reflected in the fact that the *vallaris* is awarded far more frequently to the centurion than was the *muralis*, which must have gained in prestige through its rarity value.

The *corona vallaris* was made of gold and ornamented with a rampart (*insigne valli*: fig. 6).[43] The clearest sculptural representation is on the stone set up in honour of Sex. Vibius Gallus (pl. 5b) where its form is very similar to that of the *muralis*; the only distinction between the two types is that where the *muralis* has rounded contours the *vallaris* is square (though the cushion on which it sits is rounded, no doubt for facility and comfort of wearing). The distinction between the two types probably springs from the regular rectangular planning of the Roman military camp contrasted with the irregular shape of the circuit of a city's walls: such a rectangular camp can hardly have been inspired by the outlines of the native earthworks which Rome besieged. The construction of the rampart of the *corona vallaris* appears to be regularly coursed masonry but the intention was probably to convey the impression of turfwork: a similar confusion arises, for example, on Trajan's Column where the appearance of men cutting and carrying as well as building with the material leaves no doubt that it is turf which is portrayed (pl. 3b).[44]

Corona aurea

Gold crowns without any more specific designation were used to reward gallantry of a type not covered by the other crowns of more limited application. For example, T. Manlius and M. Valerius serving as tribunes both received the *corona aurea* for fighting and slaying an enemy in single combat, in both cases Gauls, the former in 361 BC, the latter in 348. Sp. Nautius earned his gold crown by leading a cavalry charge against a Samnite force, Sp. Papirius for fighting well in a cavalry encounter and a night pursuit of the Samnites as they attempted a secret flight from Aquilonia.[45] During this same last battle four unnamed centurions with a maniple of *hastati* received the crown for capturing the gate and wall of Aquilonia. As well as illustrating the range of deeds deemed worthy of the gold crown, these examples also make the point that there was no limit put on the rank of the recipient; here we have men in the ranks, centurions and tribunes, while in 210 at the siege of New Carthage G. Laelius, serving as admiral of the fleet, was rewarded with the same type of decoration.[46]

The legendary Siccius Dentatus was credited with a total of eight; one of these was awarded in an encounter of which we have some detail. 'I was then twenty-seven years of age and in rank I was still under a centurion. When a severe battle occurred (during the war against the Volsci in 485 BC) and a rout, the commander of the cohort had fallen and the standards were in the hands of the enemy, I alone exposing myself on behalf of all recovered the standards of the cohort, repulsed the enemy and was clearly the one who saved the centurions from incurring everlasting disgrace which would have rendered the rest of their lives more bitter than death, as they themselves acknowledged by crowning me with a gold crown.' The historical veracity of this tale must, however, be viewed with some suspicion. As we have already seen, of all the writers who record the career of Dentatus only one, Dionysius of Halicarnassus, embroiders the bare facts of the man's legendary bravery with such detail of the exploits he performed.[47]

This, the simplest of the military crowns, was probably also the earliest. The examples quoted all belong to the third century BC or earlier, though all are related by authors writing, with hindsight, many years after the events with which they were concerned. Polybius, writing in the mid-second century, is the earliest reliable source and he refers to a crown of gold given to the first man to mount the wall at the assault of an enemy city. Here, it would seem, is the clue to the development of crowns as decorations. Simple gold crowns, adopted from the Greeks and Etruscans, were originally used to reward various types of deed; only with the passage of time did the various discreet types of crown emerge, each type adapted for a specific purpose which is reflected in its form as well as its name with the *corona aurea* remaining as a general, all-purpose type of decoration.

Because of its lack of a precise meaning the *corona aurea* was easily assimilated into the imperial schemes of *dona*, where it was clearly considered to be the lowest of the four types of crown commonly awarded. It was the *corona aurea* which was received by the *evocatus*, almost but not quite a centurion (below, p. 210). Occasionally it was received by the centurion instead of the *vallaris* or *muralis* and it formed part of the various combinations awarded to the equestrian and senatorial officers.

There is no verbal description of the *corona aurea* but its appearance is indicated by the specific evidence of the Gallus stone (fig. 6 and pl. 5a): a wreath of leaves, fashioned presumably in gold, was tied at the back with ribbons with long trailing strings. The form of the leaf appears to be that of the laurel. Similar crowns appear on a number of tombstones, notably those of C. Allius Oriens and C. Purtisius Atinas (pl. 6a and 7b).

Vexillum

It is not clear when the *vexillum*, or flag, first came to be used as a military decoration. It is attested rarely in the literature of the republican period, is not included in Polybius' list of awards and is one of very few types not reputed to have been won by Siccius Dentatus. The first convincing reference to it dates to 107 BC when the *vexillum* is included among the *dona* which C. Marius claims to have won.[48] Sallust was writing within sixty years of the event which he is describing and he is dealing with a specific well-known figure. This is not however the very earliest allusion to the *vexillum* being given as a military award. The earliest example comes from the *Punica* of Silius Italicus, though it is just possible that Italicus is here being anachronistic, for, while the second Punic War dates to the late third century BC, the work was written towards the end of the first century AD.[49]

The paucity of evidence about the *vexillum* leaves us in the dark as to the original conditions laid down concerning its award, how it could be won and who was eligible to win it. The context of Marius' award is unknown but cannot have been in a naval battle – which is the case with the other well-attested award during the Republic, when in 31 BC Agrippa was awarded a blue *vexillum* in recognition of his naval victory over Antony at the battle of Actium.[50] Both these examples refer to officers, but this may be of no significance as such figures are always better documented than are their subordinates. A total of one specific and two vague allusions provides an insufficient basis for speculation as to the original conditions of award.

In the Principate the *vexillum* became one of the standard decorations for officers, though its earliest datable appearance in this context is Neronian. It is not attested among the *dona* of either equestrians or senators for the period up to and including Claudius though the evidence for the decorations of this period, for the equestrians at least, is relatively plentiful. At no time during the Empire does the *vexillum* appear to have been awarded to an officer of lesser rank than *praefectus castrorum*; it is possible that a *primus pilus* was also eligible to win one but positive evidence is lacking (below, p. 204). Neither a man in the ranks nor lesser centurion enjoyed sufficient seniority to win what had evidently become a prestige award.

The *vexillum* as a form of decoration was an exact replica of the *vexillum* carried as a standard by both legionaries and auxiliaries. Its appearance was that of an ordinary flag, square or rectangular in shape, sometimes with a fringe along the bottom, and slung from a horizontal cross-bar attached to a shaft (fig. 8). The *vexillum* awarded to Agrippa was described as *caeruleum*, blue, and the implication here is either that it was painted or, more likely, it was made of some coloured fabric as was the normal flag. The one example of a Roman *vexillum* which has survived is made of linen dyed scarlet and decorated in gold, with a scarlet fringe across the bottom: it is 500mm square.[51]

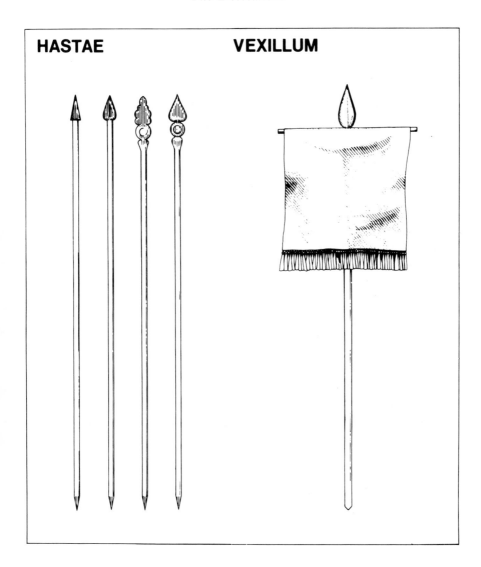

8 Hastae and vexillum

Subsequently the *vexillum* acquired, in common with other types of *dona*, more than just a token value. When Titus awarded decorations to his men after the siege of Jerusalem he gave silver *vexilla*, and this is consistent with the evidence of inscriptions, four of which describe the material of which *vexilla* were made and all of which give silver. One of these inscriptions is Flavian in date, one is Trajanic, one is Antonine and the fourth is undated.[52] Two *vexilla* appear on the Gallus stone (pl. 5a, b) and are the only certain representations of the *vexillum* as a military decoration. The stone set up in honour of Sulpicius

Celsus depicts a *vexillum* but it is, from its context, more likely to be a standard than a decoration for it appears side by side with a praetorian *signum* on the opposite end of the stone from the undoubted decorations, a *corona muralis* and a *torques* (pl. 5d).

Two inscriptions of the Antonine period record a decoration named as a *vexillum obsidionale*, in both cases awarded by the emperor Marcus to a praetorian prefect. The *primipilaris*, Bassaeus Rufus, won *dona* including four *vexilla obsidionalia* in the German war of AD 166–175 while the equestrian, Furius Victorinus, won the same decorations in the Parthian war of AD 162–166.[53] The significance of the epithet *obsidionale* in this context is obscure, these being not just the only two examples of its use but also the only two cases from any period of the *dona* of a praetorian prefect. It seems unlikely that anything other than the normal *vexillum* is intended; the scale of award is comparable to that of the consular, omitting only the *corona navalis*. It is unfortunate that on all the inscriptions recording consular *dona* of the Antonine period the reference to the *vexilla* is fragmentary: it is therefore impossible to compare the award made to the prefects with those of the ex-consul. Both the texts which refer to *vexilla obsidionalia* come from Rome (as also do the four fragmentary inscriptions recording consular *dona*) and it may be that this description of them is no more than a regional quirk. Such a quirk must however reflect reality: could it be that *vexillum obsidionale* was the correct full designation of the decoration, so called to distinguish it from the ordinary *vexillum* or standard? It would not normally be necessary to give the full title as it would be readily apparent from the context whether a military decoration or a standard was meant; only if being pedantic might one have the whole thing written out in full – and it is notable that all the honours won by both Rufus and Victorinus were written out very fully. The allusion to *obsidio*, a siege, can have had no more reality at this date than the naval element in the *corona navalis*; it was doubtless no more than a convenient military epithet, adopted perhaps from the now defunct *corona obsidionalis*.

Hasta pura

The earliest reference to the use of the spear as a formal military award is by Polybius who states that it was given to the man who had wounded an enemy not in the heat of battle or at the storming of a city but only when single combat had been entered into voluntarily, in circumstances in which danger could, if desired, have been avoided.[54] A cavalryman who slew and stripped an enemy had originally also been awarded a spear but this was later changed to *phalerae*. How long these conditions remained in force it is impossible to say. The only occasion on which any detail of the exploit leading to the award of the *hasta* is given dates, not to the Republic, but to the early years of the Principate. During the campaigning in Africa against the rebel Tacfarinas,

Helvius Rufus, a *miles gregarius* ('a man in the ranks') saved the life of a Roman citizen; the proconsul of Africa, Apronius, presented him with a *torques* and a *hasta* and the emperor Tiberius later added a *corona civica*.[55] In saving the life of the citizen Rufus may well have fulfilled the conditions as specified by Polybius, and this may be the reason why he, a mere *miles*, won a *hasta pura*. The case of Helvius Rufus is unique. He is the only man in the ranks known to have won the *hasta* during the Principate, for it appears very early on to have become restricted to those of the rank of senior centurion and above. Just one specific case of award is known between the time of Polybius and that of Helvius Rufus. In 107 BC Marius, addressing the people of Rome after he had been appointed to command in Numidia during the Jugurthine war, includes *hastae* among the decorations of which he boasts, but unfortunately no details are given as to the circumstances of award.[56]

There have, over the years, been some differences of opinion as to the nature of the *hasta pura* and the meaning of its name. The confusion arises from the definition of the award given by Varro – *pura hasta id est sine ferro* – that it was, literally, 'without iron'.[57] Varro's definition has been construed as indicating a spear without a head, and in support of this interpretation have been adduced two coins of M. Arrius Secundus on which are depicted spears which appear, from their context, to be military decorations (pl. 1f, g). However, the belief that the spears on these coins had blunted ends arose from a disfigurement of the types in an inaccurate drawing.[58] The spear as it appears on the *denarius* does not have a very competently executed point, but the same is not true on the *aureus* where the spear has a well-defined triangular point at its end. The coin evidence does not support the view that the *hasta pura* was a spear without a head; on the contrary. The term which Polybius uses for the *hasta* as a military decoration is not δόρυ the literal Greek translation and that which commonly appears in inscriptions of the Principate, but γαῖσος *gaesum*. The *gaesum* is the name of the Celtic throwing spear, a traditional weapon which continued to be used by Celtic peoples well into the Principate; it gives its name, for example, to the unit of *Raeti Gaesati*, the Raetian spearmen. The *gaesum* was certainly made of iron – the Greek lexicographer, Hesychios, describes it as being made entirely of iron – and it is notable that Polybius used the term *gaesum* on occasions when speaking of the weapon known in Latin as the *pilum*, the legionary's javelin which had a small iron head forged in one piece with an iron shank fastened to a wooden butt. There is no doubt that the *gaesum* of Polybius had a head, and in the absence of good evidence to the contrary it seems better to identify this award with the *hasta pura* rather than to regard them as two distinct types of decoration.

Good evidence for the appearance of the *hasta pura* comes from sculpture of the first and second centuries AD (fig. 8). The Gallus stone (pl. 5a) shows five spears, labelled *hastae purae*, δόρυ καθαρόν; the heads of these spears are small and triangular, like the heads of throwing spears. These contrast with the small leaf-shaped heads shown on the two spears of C. Purtisius Atinas, on an inscription of pre-Claudian date (pl. 7b). Another early stone, probably Augustan, is that of C. Vibius Macer; this shows a set of decorations including two spears with leaf-shaped heads: one of the heads is plain, the other lobate (fig. 5). These two spear-heads are considerably larger than those shown on the Atinas and Gallus stones; only the heads of the spears are shown, giving no indication of the length of the shafts. The sculptural renderings of the *hasta pura* suggest that in size it was overall perhaps slightly smaller than the ordinary spear, but not significantly so. The head varied somewhat in size, while the shaft may have been a little shorter. Against this evidence there is the testimony of Josephus who, describing the awards made after the successful siege of Jerusalem, speaks of δόρατα μικρά, small spears.[59] It is commonly assumed from this passage that the decorations were only miniatures (the word is applied to the *vexilla* as well as the *hastae*): however the reading μικρά is in some doubt; an alternative version renders it μακρά, giving us a *long* spear.[60] Hence, bearing in mind the pictorial evidence, it seems best to regard the *hasta pura* as a more or less full-sized replica of a weapon.

If the conventional rendering of *hasta pura* as 'headless spear' must be eschewed, as clearly it must, what should replace it? *Pura* in this context may well imply ritual purity – a weapon never used to shed blood in battle, but a purely honorific one. The spear had a particular significance among the Romans as it did among the Etruscans as an expression of power – *hasta summa armorum et imperii est*[61] – and it was an important weapon of the early Roman soldier. It would therefore have a considerable symbolic value as a decoration, a symbolic or honorific spear. Polybius' use of the term γαῖσος may give some further indication of the origin of the use of the spear as a decoration. It was a common practice for barbarian personal effects to be adopted as military awards, a practice originating no doubt from their capture as booty. The *gaesum* is specifically a Celtic spear used against the Romans and no doubt often taken as booty. What therefore could be more normal than that, as Polybius records, a spear should be awarded to a man who slew an adversary in single combat.

The original award was, perhaps, an actual weapon. In time it came to be an honorary one. The material from which it was made is very rarely specified: there is one literary and one epigraphic reference. The spears awarded by Titus after the siege of Jerusalem were of gold; that which Severus and Caracalla gave to C. Didius Saturninus was of silver.[62] There is insufficient evidence either to prove or disprove Alföldi's hypothesis that the metal varied according to the rank of the recipient.

Torques

Many of the barbarian peoples with whom Rome came into contact during her years of expansion, for example the Persians, Scythians and Celts, wore the *torques* or neck-ring as a personal ornament or symbol of rank. The evidence for this has been fully rehearsed elsewhere and need not be repeated here.[63] It is no doubt through contact with these peoples that Rome adopted the practice of giving the *torques* as a military decoration, for the ornament had hitherto played no significant part in the classical world except in so far as the term was used of a woman's necklace. A formal award was created in the form of the barbarian ornament which must on many occasions have been stripped as booty from the neck of a slain foe. Just such an occurrence is adduced by Livy in explanation of the *cognomen* Torquatus borne by the Manlian family.[64] During the Gallic uprising of 361 BC the Gauls and Romans confronted one another at the crossing of the Via Salaria over the river Anio, just to the north of Rome: the forces were evenly matched so that neither could claim mastery of the bridge. The stalemate was broken when a Gaul of extraordinary size challenged the bravest man among the Romans to single combat. Titus Manlius volunteered, slew the Gallic champion and 'to the body of his fallen foe he offered no other indignity than to despoil it of one thing – a chain which, spattered with blood, he cast around his own neck . . . amidst the rude banter thrown out by the soldiers in a kind of verse was heard the appellation of "Torquatus" '. And so Torquatus was adopted as the family surname and the *torques* as the family symbol, appearing for example on a coin issued when L. Manlius Torquatus was *triumvir monetalis* (pl. 1h).

The adoption of the *torques* as a military decoration must be assumed therefore to follow some years after the Romans first encountered it: Polybius in his list of awards makes no mention of it however though his work contains, in other contexts, references to the *torques* taken as booty from Gallic adversaries. It may be inferred from this that the *torques* had not yet been taken up as a formal decoration, though such an inference, in the absence of any supporting evidence, must remain speculative. Apart from the eighty-three *torques* attributed to Siccius Dentatus the earliest attested example of the award belongs to the year 89 BC: the evidence comes from an inscription. A bronze plaque set up in Rome records the grant of Roman citizenship and *dona militaria* to the *turma Salluitana*, a troop of Spanish cavalry; among the decorations listed is the *torques*.[65]

There is no indication of the specific conditions, if there were any, which governed the award of the *torques*, nor of any restriction on the rank or status of the recipient. It had been the men of the *turma Salluitana* who had received the award; it was the commanding officer of the *turma Cassiana* to whom Caesar awarded a *torques* after the defeat of Sextus Pompeius in 45 BC, the men in the unit on this occasion receiving their reward in the form of extra pay.[66]

During the Principate the *torques* was regarded as one of the lesser decorations, and formed part of the combination of awards given to men of the rank of centurion and below. It was never again won by more senior officers. It is well attested from the time of Augustus onwards, continuing in use as long as the practice of giving decorations continued. Besides being given to individuals, the *torques* could also be awarded to a unit as a whole – here the republican case of the *turma Salluitana* makes an interesting analogy; units so honoured took the title *torquata*, perhaps decorating their standard with a *torques* as a visual indication of the distinction they had won (below, p. 220).

The Roman soldier did not wear his *torques* in traditional barbarian fashion around the neck. They were normally, though not invariably, awarded in pairs and those reliefs which show the *torques* being worn suggest that they were attached to the cuirass on either side just below the collar bones. The device for attaching them is shown most clearly on the relief of M. Caelius (pl. 2a) where the *torques* are slung on loops of leather or fabric which appear to curve inwards as though going around the back of the neck. The relief of Cn. Musius (pl. 11a) is rather more stylized but suggests that here the *torques* are fastened to the shoulder pieces of the harness which also carries the *phalerae*.

There was no single standard pattern for the military *torques* (just as appears to have been true with the *hasta*) and although some of the apparent differences between the plain and the elaborate ones may be no more than a question of the ability of the artist faithfully to reproduce the decoration, it is nevertheless clear that several different designs were being employed (fig. 9). Some were formed of twisted bands of metal while others were plain bands which might, as in the case of Musius' *torques*, be decorated on the surface (pl. 11a). The ends of some swelled out into zoomorphic terminals, while one particularly fine example ended in rosettes behind which were attached the hook and eye fastening which joined the ends together (pl. 7b). Most of the *torques* were penannular with no apparent device for fastening: since the *torques* were not worn around the neck there was no need to secure the ends together. A few of the reliefs appear to indicate complete rings, which would clearly have been impossible in a *torques* worn around the neck but is credible in the Roman context. The existence of more than one type of *torques* is also hinted at in the written evidence. The decoration won by C. Iulius Aetor was called a *torques maior* from which one might infer the existence of a *torques minor* though none such is actually attested.[67] Quite what is meant by this is not clear, perhaps one of the more elaborate types, or perhaps the reference is to the material of which it was fashioned. Both gold and silver were certainly used. Pliny distinguishes between the silver *torques* of the citizen and the gold one given to non-citizens, though this distinction is of doubtful validity.[68] For the major part of the Principate at least there is no evidence that non-citizens were eligible to receive decorations though things may well have been different in the Republic, and the author of the *de Bello Hispaniensi* records the award of five gold *torques* to the (citizen) prefect of the *turma Cassiana*. Similarly the *torques* to which Josephus refers are of gold.[69]

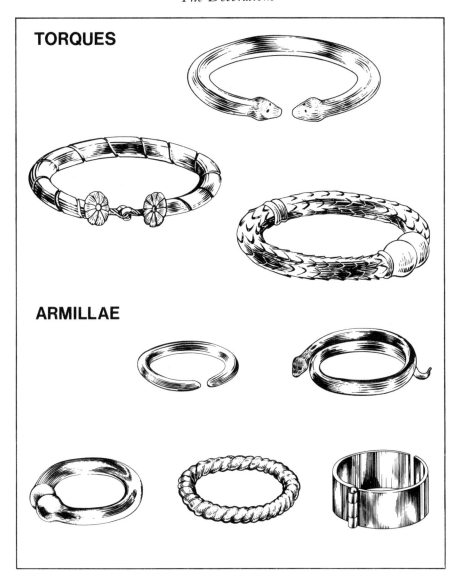

TORQUES

ARMILLAE

9 Torques and armillae

Armilla

The wearing of bracelets by men in the Roman world was thought of as a sign of effeminacy, for bracelets were regarded as female adornment: this is clearly implied by Suetonius when he describes the mode of dress adopted by Gaius who, ignoring both fashion and male convention, wore an elaborate gem encrusted cloak, a long-sleeved tunic and bracelets.[70] However bracelets or *armillae* awarded as military decorations were an exception to the general rule. Such bracelets were suitable for men, having been won by force of arms (*armillae autem proprie virorum sunt, conlatae victoriae causa militibus ab armorum virtute*).[71] The adoption of the *armilla* as a military award is a case analogous to that of the *torques*, for *armillae* were worn by both men and women of the tribes against whom Rome fought in her years of expansion. For example, according to Livy the Sabines decorated their left arms with heavy gold bracelets, while Xenophon describes some Persian nobles who were 'necklaces around their necks and bracelets on their arms'.[72] Polybius, describing the Celts (Gaesati) who invaded Etruria and engaged the Romans at the battle of Telamon in 225 BC, tells us that all the warriors in the leading ranks were richly adorned with gold *torques* and *armillae*.[73] The appearance and gestures of these warriors, we are told, dismayed the Romans who nevertheless were spurred on by the prospect of all the spoils which would be theirs when they won.[74]

There are few literary allusions to the awarding of *armillae* as military decorations in the republican period. Pliny informs us briefly that *armillae* were given only to citizen soldiers. Following the destruction of Aquilonia and Cominium during the war against the Samnites in 293 BC military decorations were distributed to those who had distinguished themselves: Sp. Nautius who had led a charge against the enemy, who far outnumbered the men he had with him, received *armillae* of gold in addition to a gold crown. The same award was made to his nephew Sp. Papirius who, with his cavalry had both fought well in line of battle and had harried the Samnites during their night time flight from Aquilonia, and also to four centurions and a maniple of *hastati* who had been the first to capture the gate and wall of Aquilonia. The cavalry received silver *armillae* in recognition of generally distinguished conduct.[75] The use of silver *armillae* as a rather lesser award than the gold is repeated in an episode narrated by Valerius Maximus in which a soldier, refused gold *armillae* because he was an ex-slave, was given silver ones instead (below, p. 128).

During the Principate *armillae*, in common with *torques*, were never awarded to an officer of higher rank than centurion. They were normally awarded in pairs and commonly, though not invariably, in combination with *torques* and *phalerae*, to men in the ranks and to junior officers. The grant of an *armilla* could also be made to an auxiliary unit, as is attested by the title *armillata* borne by the *ala Siliana*. The title is much rarer than that of *torquata*, there being, to date, just this one known example (below, p. 221). A final use for *armillae* in their guise as military awards is attested by Festus who noted that they were worn by triumphing generals: the name he gives them in this context is *calbei*.[76] This statement is incapable of verification for in none of the reliefs which depict triumphal processions are *armillae* shown.

The military *armilla*, was made to a variety of different designs (fig. 9).

Those worn by M. Caelius are broad, flat and apparently undecorated (though a design may have been painted on); the band is broken by what is either a hinge or a fastening (pl. 2a). Snake bracelets appear fairly commonly (Ti. Claudius Maximus, C. Purtisius Atinas and the unknown from Picenum pl. 7b, 8a and fig. 10), as do narrow bands, either twisted or plain, sometimes forming complete rings, sometimes penannular and terminating in knobs (pl. 2c, 6b, 10a, 14b). In many cases the *armillae* appear simply as smaller versions of the *torques*. Of the inscriptions of the imperial period which mention *armillae* only one specifies the metal from which it was made: in this case gold.

10   Tombstone of a soldier from Picenum

Phalerae

A *phalera* is a small disc, commonly of metal though sometimes of glass or paste, decorated to a greater or lesser degree, which was used in the ancient world for a variety of different purposes. Alföldi has already presented in some detail the case for the use of the *phalera* as a badge of rank of the equestrian *ordo*.[78] The term is also applied to the bosses which decorate and reinforce a helmet and to the pendant ornaments attached to a horse harness, the equivalent of horse brasses. For example, at the triumph which Claudius celebrated in honour of his victory in Britain, M. Crassus Frugi is described as riding an *equus phaleratus*.[79] Sets of these horse-trappings are frequently shown on the equestrian reliefs which often adorn cavalry tombstones; the *phalerae* worn by these horses are sometimes decorated with concentric circles in relief, sometimes with rosettes.[80] A very fine set of such trappings has been found at Doorwerth in Holland, another at Newstead near Melrose in Scotland, while single *phalerae* are commonly found on Roman military sites.[81] Another use for *phalerae* was as military decorations: Polybius is again the earliest source of evidence. He states that a man who had slain and stripped an enemy was rewarded with a *patella* ($\phi\iota\acute{\alpha}\lambda\eta$) if he was in the infantry, with *phalerae* ($\phi\alpha\lambda\alpha\rho\alpha$) if he was a cavalryman. It may be inferred from this distinction that the *phalerae* in question were horse-trappings, rather than, as they later became, trappings worn by the soldier himself. The literary references to *phalerae* during the Republic are too sparse and too vague to allow of any close determination of the date at which *phalerae* ceased to be the sole preserve of the mounted soldier. The earliest dated example of an infantryman winning *phalerae* is difficult to ascertain as so few early tombstones give much detail of the military career. A few cases of foot soldiers with *phalerae* belong to the period of the Spanish and Illyrican wars of Augustus (below, p. 216). However, by this date the conditions of award described by Polybius were, in general, no longer applicable. It was normal, during the Principate, for *phalerae* to be awarded to men of the rank of centurion and below, invariably in combination with other awards.

The *phalerae* were awarded in sets, commonly of nine, though Q. Sertorius Festus has only seven and M. Caelius five. The individual pieces within the set do not always bear the same design, and the designs themselves vary from the very plain to the very ornate. Some appear to be completely plain flat discs, though it is highly unlikely that they were actually quite so stark. In some cases the appearance may be due to inferior workmanship and in others, where the sculpture is otherwise competently executed, as for example that of C. Allius Oriens (pl. 6a), it may be suspected that the apparently flat and featureless *phalerae* once had detail painted in. A common form of *phalera* is that of a disc with a central boss and concentric raised circles: for example those of Cn. Musius and Q. Cornelius (pl. 11a, 13b). This type invariably appears in matching sets: not so the more highly decorated pieces where a combination of designs is the norm. Rosettes, lion-heads, bird-heads, heads of gods, goddesses and spirits of the underworld are common motifs (pl. 2a, 2b, 10a, 11b, 11c, 15). There is no apparent correlation between the rank of the recipient and the quality of the design.

Phalerae shown on reliefs are consistently circular in shape; the only possible exception to this is on the inscription which commemorates C. Vibius Macer (above, p. 69). On this drawing four of the pieces, one in each side of two sets of decorations, are sub-rectangular with a split down the middle (fig. 5). Surviving examples include lunate and kidney-shaped pieces.

The Decorations

Phalerae were worn, something like medals, on the chest. The individual pieces were attached to a harness of straps, no doubt of leather, which ran straight around and up and down the front of the chest, or else diagonally across it, or both, and continued over the shoulders and around the back where they would have been fastened, presumably with buckles (fig. 11). The

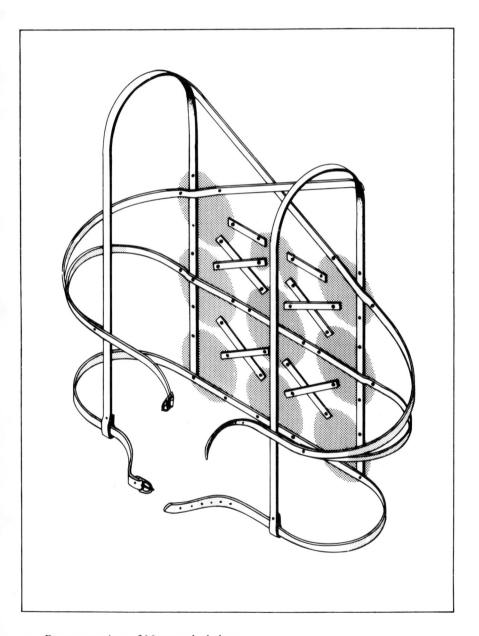

11   Reconstruction of Newstead phalerae

reliefs on the tombstones of M. Caelius, Cn. Musius and Q. Sertorius Festus show this harness being worn (pl. 2a, 2b, 11a), while that of M. Pompeius Asper and a fragmentary relief from Burnum in Dalmatia depict the harness without the wearer and so are able to show something of the straps which would have gone around the back (pl. 12a, 11b). The shoulders of the harness worn by M. Caelius are decorated with upstanding lions' heads while on that of Asper are bearded human heads. The function of these is obscure: they may be purely decorative or they may have had some practical purpose such as disguising fastenings, though it is difficult to see quite what.

Evidence as to how the *phalerae* were attached to the harness is provided by actual finds of decorations. One very fine set of *phalerae* came to light in 1858 in Germany, at Lauersfort near Krefeld not far from the legionary fortress of Vetera.[82] It consists of nine circular pieces decorated with heads of lions and mythological figures and one crescent-shaped piece bearing a double sphinx (pl. 15). They are made of silver-plated bronze and are in very high relief; the design and execution are classical and are of a very high standard of workmanship. The decorated plates are folded over flat bronze backing-plates on each of which is punched the name Medamus, presumably the owner of the set, the name being given in the genitive case. On just one piece another name, that of T. Flavius Festus, is punched on the face: the significance of this is unclear (but see below, p. 95). To each of the backing-plates are attached three small metal loops which must have served to fasten the pieces to the leather harness: the loops could have slipped through eyelets in the straps and been secured on the inside by split pins (as in fig. 12a). Alternatively they could have been sewn to the straps. A different method of fastening is suggested by

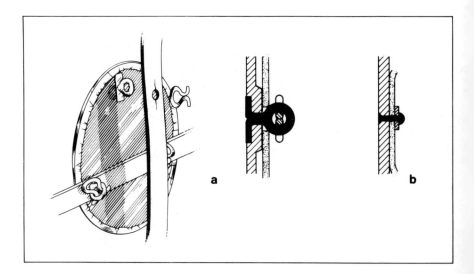

12   Methods of attaching phalerae to straps

the Newstead find; this comprises a set of nine bronze plates, eight circular and one kidney-shaped, which are almost certainly the backing-plates for *phalerae*, the decorated fronts of which are missing (pl. 16a).[83] Small holes have been pierced through these plates, and through each hole passes a bronze rivet secured at the back with a washer. These rivets will have secured the plates to the leathers of the harness (fig. 12b). Fig. 11 is an attempt to reconstruct the layout of the Newstead set of *phalerae*: the detailed positioning of the straps is hypothetical, but is based on the number and spacing of the rivet-holes on the backing plates. The owner of this set of awards was presumably the Dometius Atticus whose name is scratched on the back of each piece. The size of these bronze plates varies between a maximum of 115mm diameter and a minimum of 86mm. This compares closely with the Lauersfort pieces which average 108mm and vary from 105mm to 110mm.

As has been noted, the Lauersfort *phalerae* were made of bronze plated with silver. All the literary allusions to *phalerae* imply or state that they were made of precious metals, silver or gold. Indeed originally they probably were, but the substitution of plated bronze for the pure metals is hardly surprising. When Suetonius states that Augustus rewarded valour with *phalerae* and *torques* of silver and gold, it must remain uncertain whether or not the allusion is to pure metal. The inference that pure metals were still in use in AD 69 can be made from a passage in Tacitus' *Histories* which records how the soldiers at Cologne, who supported the claim of Vitellius for the imperial purple, instead of giving money to the cause, handed over their *phalerae* (by implication to be melted down to produce money); the *phalerae* in question were probably, in view of the context, military decorations.[84] The Lauersfort *phalerae* are by no means securely dated. The circumstances of their finding, during the digging of drainage ditches, means that they cannot be dated archaeologically by their stratigraphic relationship to dated levels. Roman legions were stationed at nearby Vetera from the Augustan period until the Frankish invasion of 276 (except for a gap of about ten years *c.*94–104), while a colony for legionary veterans was established there early in the Trajanic period.[85] Historically the most likely contexts for the decorations are the German campaigns of the Augustan, Tiberian and Flavian periods, with the earlier part of this date range to be preferred on an art-historical grounds.[86] However, this tentative typological dating of the artefacts themselves does not necessarily give the date of their deposition. Such fine objects will have had a long life. On the death of the soldier who won them they may well have been returned or sold back to his unit (this was common practice with standard military equipment) and later been re-used; this could explain the two different names, one of which it should be noted was a T. Flavius, a man whose citizenship, or whose forebear's citizenship, had very probably been awarded by a Flavian emperor. Such a name inscribed on the decoration would best fit the context of Domitian's or Vespasian's campaigns.

Patella or Phiale

The *patella* is one of the least well attested types of military decoration. There is only one reference to it and this dates to the year 89 BC when the *patella* was included among the awards won by the *turma Salluitana*. However the *patella* is probably the same type of decoration as that referred to by Polybius as the φιάλη, the *phiale*.[87] Both words, taken literally indicate a shallow dish or bowl. Polybius states that the *phiale* was awarded to an infantryman who slew and stripped an enemy, while a cavalryman would receive *phalerae*. Just as *phalerae* came to be awarded to infantry as well as cavalry, so apparently did both categories of soldier come to be eligible for *phialai* or *patellae*.

The shortage of evidence regarding this type of award leaves us in some doubt as to what it looked like. Jahn suggested that the decoration was some kind of ornament worn on the breast: he supported his argument with reference to a number of lines in the *Dionysiaca* of the epic poet Nonnus where dancing Bacchantes wear *phialai*.[88] However, in this context the wearing of drinking cups or, as Jahn would have it, ornaments derived from them, is hardly to be wondered at. Steiner followed Jahn in rejecting the idea that a small metal vessel would have been used as a military decoration. He too thought in terms of a medallion, suggesting that what was in question was some sort of miniature shield, a much more suitable award for a soldier.[89] The shields carried by the three main lines of infantry in Polybius' day were oval in shape, and small versions of these would have been significantly different from the circular *phalerae*. The skirmishers, on the other hand, carried circular shields as did, or had, certain of the enemies whom Rome had met in the field, the Samnites, the Macedonians, the Cathaginians and the Celtic cavalry. Since *phialai* and *patellae* were circular vessels the allusion ought to be to a circular shield.[90] However, miniature versions of such circular shields would have been virtually indistinguishable from *phalerae*. Steiner drew attention to the enigmatic Macer relief as possibly illustrating *phialai*, a fact which emphasizes the likely confusion, for what is shown on this relief could equally well be interpreted as two sets of *phalerae* (fig. 5). Would two such visually similar awards have co-existed? There is no problem in thinking they might, given the Polybian context: the one is awarded to a cavalryman the other to an infantryman, for performing the same deed. The cavalrymen of the *turma Salluitana*, however, received both *patellae* and *phalerae*, a fact which implies that either they are something distinct or that we are wrong to equate the *phiale* with the *patella*.

Since these attempts to explain away *phialai* and *patellae* as medallions rather than dishes are not totally satisfactory, it is worth considering whether they could have been, literally, small bowls or drinking-cups. Such vessels certainly were used as prizes for the victors in chariot races.[91] Such a context is not military, but neither were many of the early uses of crowns, while *armillae*,

PLATE 1

a   b   c   d

e   f   g   h   i

a   *Dupondius* of Augustus, depicting a *corona navalis* consisting of a wreath of laurel leaves interwoven with ships' beaks or *rostra* (BMCRE Augustus 721)

b   *Denarius* of Augustus, depicting a *corona navalis*: similar to 'a' but with the back tied together with a ribbon (BMCRE Augustus 669)

c   *As* of the period Gaius–Claudius. The obverse bears a head of Marcus Agrippa wearing a *corona navalis* (BMCRE Tiberius 161)

d   Reverse of an *aureus* of Augustus depicting Marcus Agrippa wearing a combined mural and naval crown, a *corona muralis* with a ship's beak at the front (BMCRE Augustus 110)

e   Obverse of an *aureus* of Augustus. The words *ob civis servatos* are encircled by a *corona civica*, a crown of oak leaves (BMCRE Augustus 314)

f – g   Coins produced under the moneyer M. Arrius Secundus, depicting a wreath, a *hasta pura* and a stylized set of *phalerae*. The allusion is perhaps to an act of valour performed by one of Secundus' ancestors; 'f' is an *aureus* (BMCRR Rome 4209), 'g' a *denarius* (BMCRR Rome 4210)

h   *Denarius* produced when Lucius Manlius Torquatus was moneyer (*IIIvir monetalis*), 65 BC. The *torques* which encircles the reverse is an allusion to the exploit of Titus Manlius in 361 BC (BMCRR Rome 3511)

i   *Denarius* of Augustus. Victory carries a round shield inscribed CL.V. (*clipeus virtutis*), an allusion to the award of a shield to Augustus (BMCRE Augustus 342)

PLATE 2

a

b

c

a   Marcus Caelius, centurion of legion XVIII, who died in the Varan disaster of AD 9. This cenotaph was set up at Vetera (Xanten). Caelius wears a *corona civica*, a set of embossed *phalerae*, two *torques*, and one *armilla* on each wrist

b   Quintus Sertorius, centurion of legion *XI Claudia* who died shortly after AD 42 and was buried at Verona. He wears a crown, probably a *corona aurea*, a set of *phalerae* and two *torques*

c   Part of a military relief from Cologne depicting a shield, a sword in a finely decorated scabbard and a set of military decorations, a *corona civica*, two *torques* and an *armilla*

PLATE 3

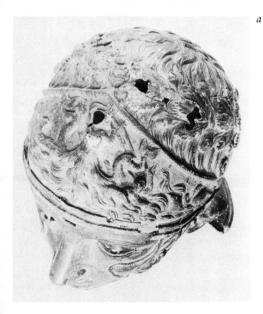

a

b

a   Roman parade helmet from
Vize in Thrace, where it was
found in the tomb of a Thracian
chieftain. It is made of bronze
and was originally silvered. The
crown of the helmet is decorated
with hair encircled by a *corona
civica*

b   Scene from Trajan's Column
showing legionaries building
with turf

PLATE 4

b

a

a   Relief from Rome depicting military standards decorated with *phalerae*, crescents, laurel wreaths, a mural crown and a ship's beak

b   Scene from Trajan's Column. To the left legionary standards, *signa* decorated with *phalerae*, an eagle and a flag. To the right praetorian standards decorated with images of the Imperial family and with crowns of various type

PLATE 5

a

b

a – b Scenes from the sides of an inscription set up at Amastris in Bithynia in honour of a man who was probably a native of the town, Sextus Vibius Gallus. The front bears a bilingual (Greek and Latin) text, the back a relief depicting a Roman cavalryman riding down two Dacians

a Left side: a *vexillum*, five *hastae purae*, a *corona aurea* and two *coronae vallares*

b Right side: a *vexillum* and three *coronae murales*

c

d

c – d Reliefs from either end of a stone set up in Rome in honour of Sulpicius Celsus

c Left side: above a cuirass with sword, a *corona muralis* and a *torques* with zoomorphic terminals

d Right side: a praetorian standard decorated with *phalera* and *corona muralis* and a *vexillum*

PLATE 6

a   b

c

a   C. Allius Oriens, a first-century legionary centurion, born at Dertona in northern Italy and buried at Vindonissa in modern Switzerland. His decorations comprise three *coronae aureae*, two *torques*, two *armillae* and a set of plain *phalerae*, perhaps originally with painted decoration

b   C. Gavius Celer, a centurion of legion *III Augusta* serving at Ammaedara in Africa Proconsularis. He won a *corona aurea*, two *torques* and two *armillae*. Flavian period

c   L. Leuconius Cilo, a veteran of legion *XXI Rapax*. He probably won his crown and two *armillae* campaigning in the Rhineland in the early first century AD

PLATE 7

a   A pair of reliefs now built into the façade of the church of the Panaghia
Gorgoepikoos in Athens. Each depicts a laurel wreath, two sets of decorated
phalerae and an annular object, perhaps a *torques*, perhaps another wreath

b   Decorated ends of the upper part of the funerary monument of C. Purtisius
Atinas, set up at Forli, north-west of Rimini. Left side: two *coronae aureae* and
two *hastae purae*; right side: two snake-like *armillae* and a fine twisted *torques*
with rosette terminals and a hook and eye fastening. Early first century AD

PLATE 8

a   b

c

a   Tombstone of Tiberius Claudius Maximus, captor of the Dacian king Decebalus, who won military decorations on three separate occasions during the Dacian and Parthian wars of Domitian and Trajan. His *dona* include two *torques* and two snake-like *armillae*. Above is a relief showing a Roman cavalryman riding down a Dacian chieftain.

b   Scene from Trajan's column, showing the capture of Decebalus

c   Tombstone of a praetorian soldier, L. Avaenius Paser. Below his military equipment (helmet, sword and dagger) are two *armillae* (or *torques*)

PLATE 9

a

b

c

a A. Volsonius Paulus, veteran of legion *I* (*Germanica*), who served in the German campaigns of the first half of the first century AD. His *dona* comprise two *torques*

b Tombstone of Caeno, an auxiliary centurion, serving with *cohors III Hispanorum* at Vindonissa. The *torques* depicted at the centre of the stone may be a military decoration

c C. Titurnius Quartio, a cavalryman in legion *III Gallica* in Syria, was decorated in the Parthian war of Marcus and Verus. His award comprises two plain *armillae* and a *torques* with zoomorphic terminals

PLATE 10

a   b

a   C. Marius, calvaryman in legion *I Germanica*, was born at Lucus Augusti in north-west Spain and died at Bonn. The figure on the tombstone wears one set of *phalerae*. Another ornate set is shown bottom right with two *armillae*, and a pair of *torques* appears at each top corner of the stone

b   M. Petronius Classicus, a native of central Italy, rose to the centurionate in legion *VIII Augusta* with which he served in Illyricum. His tombstone, now incomplete, depicts a centurion's vine-stick and helmet with transverse crest, a pair of greaves and a cuirass with two *torques* and at least five *phalerae*

PLATE 11

a   b
                    c

a   Cn. Musius, *aquilifer* in legion *XIIII Gemina*, was born at Veleia in northern Italy and died at Mainz. A harness over his cuirass carries a set of *phalerae* and two *torques*. He wears an *armilla* on his right wrist

b   Fragmentary remains of a door-type tombstone from Burnum in Dalmatia. The unknown recipient of the military decorations was evidently a centurion: the ribbons from two crowns are visible above the *torques*, *armillae* and *phalerae* and a centurion's vine-stick is depicted down the left side of the stone

c   Tombstone of Lucius from Bonn. Above the set of *phalerae* is one, probably originally two, *torques*

PLATE 12

a

b

a   Inscription and relief commemorating M. Pompeius Asper, directly commissioned centurion who rose to be prefect of the camp in legion *XX*. On either side of the stone is a praetorian standard, at the centre a legionary eagle – Asper served as centurion in both praetorian guard and legion. To the left a pair of greaves flanks a set of *torques*, *armillae* and *phalerae*; to the right is a hen-coop, an allusion to the post held by Asper's freedman, *pullarius*, keeper of the sacred chickens. From the area of Tusculum, south-east of Rome

b   Squeeze of an inscription (now lost) from Narona in Dalmatia. A pair of greaves flanks a set of military decorations, *torques*, *armillae* and *phalerae*. The soldier commemorated came from Ariminum, modern Rimini, and served in legion *XIII*

PLATE 13

b

c

a   Tombstone of the two Vettii brothers, cavalrymen in legion *VIII Augusta*. It is not clear which of them won the *torques*, *armillae* and *phalerae* illustrated. Early first century AD

b   Tombstone of Q. Cornelius, soldier in legion *XVI Germanica* at Mainz. Above the text a cuirass with a set of *phalerae*, two *torques* and, top centre, an *armilla*

c   L. Blattius Vetus, centurion of legion *IV Macedonica* in Spain: commemorated at Este in north-east Italy. Below a set of *phalerae* are two *armillae* or *torques*

PLATE 14

a

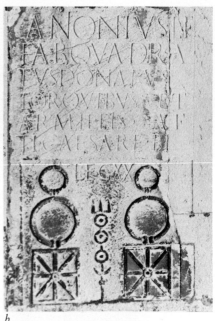

b

c

a L. Refidius Bassus, a native of Venafrum, centurion of legion *XVI* died aged 35 and was buried at Mainz. His *phalerae* (and other decorations now missing) were probably won in Germany

b L. Antonius Quadratus, a soldier in legion *XX*, was decorated twice by Tiberius Caesar. The text refers to *torques* and *armillae*, the relief shows two of each of these plus two stylized sets of *phalerae* and a legionary *signum*

c Unknown soldier who rose to the rank of centurion in legion *XIIII Gemina*. Buried at Boppard in upper Germany. A *torques* encircles each of the top outer *phalerae*

PLATE 15

a

b

a The Lauersfort *phalerae*. Note the name *T. Flavi Festi* punched into the side of the top left piece.

b Backing plates of two of the Lauersfort *phalerae*, showing loops for attachment to harness straps. The name *Medami*, presumably the owner, appears on each piece

PLATE 16

a

b

a   Newstead *phalerae:* bronze backing-plates and rivets for attaching to harness.
The name of the owner, Dometius Atticus, is scratched on each

b   Scene from Trajan's Column. An auxiliary soldier bows before Trajan

before being adopted as military awards for men, were thought of in the Roman world as being specifically women's ornaments. Elsewhere we do find a *patera*, a handled bowl rather like a saucepan, being given in a military context, awarded along with the trappings of a triumph to Masinissa of Numidia (below, p. 105). One archaeological find may be of some significance here. A fragment of a small decorated silver dish, 270mm in diameter, was found in association with the Lauersfort *phalerae*. It was decorated with an oak-leaf wreath and had punched on its surface the same name, T. Flavius Festus, as appeared on one of the *phalerae*. To identify this fragmentary vessel as a type of military decoration rare in the Republic and completely unattested in the Principate would be highly speculative, but it is on the other hand an identification which should not be lightly dismissed.

Clipeus

Round shields, *clipei* or *clupei*, were occasionally awarded as military prizes though they never became, in a regular sense, military decorations. Neither of the two army officers of the early Principate known to have received *clipei* received them from a normal awarding authority: both awards were made by subordinates to their officers. C. Iulius Macer, *evocatus* in the *Raeti Gaesati* some time in the Augustan or Tiberian period, was given a shield together with crowns of unspecified type and gold rings by his comrades, while the equestrian officer, Q. Cornelius Valerianus, received his (more than one but exact number unknown) along with crowns and statues from men of the units which he commanded: his career dates to the Claudian period.[92]

There is one particularly famous example of the use of the *clipeus* as an award, and that is the shield granted to Augustus by decree of the senate: this award accompanied that of the *corona civica* already discussed, and is recorded in the *Res Gestae*: '. . . a golden shield was placed in the Curia Julia: an inscription on the shield testified that the senate and the Roman people gave me this in recognition of my valour, clemency, justice and piety.' Illustrations of the shield, inscribed with the letters *CL. V.* (for *clipeus virtutis*) appear on coins of the period (eg. pl. 1i) and it is commemorated on a number of inscriptions.[93]

Corniculum

Probably the most obscure of all the military decorations is the *corniculum* or *cornuculum*. It is attested in just three (or possibly four) literary passages and in one inscription, that relating to the awards made to the *turma Salluitana*. The earliest recorded example appears in Livy who recounts how the consul Papirius Cursor gave silver *cornicula* and *armillae* to all the *equites* who had taken part in the siege and destruction of Aquilonia in the Samnite War, 293

BC.[94] Two awards belong to the closing years of the second and the early part of the first century BC. Lucius Orbilius Pupillus, the teacher and grammarian, is said by Suetonius to have won a *corniculum* in Macedonia, while the *de Viris Illustribus* records the same award made to M. Aemilius Scaurus in Spain.[95] All these certain records of the *corniculum* belong to the period of the Republic. In the comparatively plentiful epigraphic evidence of the Principate there is not a single reference to it, while the one possible literary passage which belongs to the period of Trajan's Parthian war is very fragmentary and of doubtful value.[96] The context is clearly military but the allusion is not necessarily to the *corniculum* as a decoration.

The apparent failure of the *corniculum* to survive into the imperial period has had one particularly unfortunate result; there is no way of knowing for certain what it was. There is no pictorial evidence for its appearance, and nowhere is it described. It is conceivable that isolated examples of the decoration itself may have survived but it would not be possible to recognize them for what they are in the absence of any norm against which to measure them. Thus the form taken by the award can only be assumed in the broadest terms from its name. The word *corniculum* would appear to be a dimunitive of *cornu*, a horn.[97] If this is so, it must be considered what place a 'little horn' has in a Roman military context. Firstly the classical heritage: one symbol of military prowess and excellence which the Romans inherited from the Greeks was that of the ram's head. The emblem of the ram, the leader of the flock and thus a symbol of leadership and supremacy, appears commonly from the archaic period onwards on helmets, swords, shields and other such items of equipment. This is amply attested by the evidence of sculpture, vase paintings and surviving artefacts.[98] From Greece the tradition passed to the Roman world where the emblem of the ram's head was used not only in the Greek east but in Rome itself. One of the Lauersfort *phalerae* depicts the head of Jupiter Ammon in its familiar form with ram's horns on either side of the head, while one of the *phalerae* depicted on the tombstone of an unknown soldier at Burnum is decorated with the head of a ram (pl. 11b). The ram was adopted as the badge of legion *I Minervia*, it being one of the animals frequently associated with the goddess Minerva. Here then is one possible connection with the *corniculum*.[99] Another likely source lies in Rome's Celtic heritage on which she drew, as has been shown, for such decorations as *torques* and *armillae*. The artefactual and sculptural evidence for Celtic armour provides plentiful examples of helmets decorated with horns, sometimes those of the ram, sometimes of the bull. The friezes of the Arc d'Orange illustrate several examples, while others are depicted in the reliefs on the Gundestrup cauldron.[100] The precise meaning of the horn in Celtic iconography is unclear but that it was very significant is beyond dispute: witness for example the widespread appearance of horned gods.[101] Which, if either, of these sources of inspiration lay behind the Roman adoption of the *corniculum* as a military decoration is not clear, but either is possible.

An alternative interpretation of the *corniculum* was put forward some years ago and must be considered here. Anita Büttner advanced the theory that *corniculum* is the diminutive not of *cornu* but of *cornus*, the cornelian cherry tree or, by synecdoche, a javelin made from the wood of the cherry. The *corniculum*, then, became a small javelin made of the hard wood of the cherry tree, and was equated with the *gaesum* which, according to Polybius, was awarded to the man who slew his enemy in single combat; this equation rests on the assumption that the *gaesum* was made of wood.[102] As has already been argued, the evidence is strongly in favour of its having been made of iron, and if this is so the case for the equation of *gaesum* and *corniculum* must collapse. Büttner's belief that the *corniculum* was a weapon was strengthened by a basic scepticism of the idea that the Romans would use horns as decorations – an unwarranted scepticism in view of the plentiful evidence that the form of Rome's military decorations drew heavily on the material culture, military and civilian, of her enemies and that among some at least of these enemies the horn had a particular significance.

The *corniculum* was in all probability a helmet decoration, though how or where it was fixed must remain a matter of speculation. This is consistent with the evidence of a passage which refers to a *corniculum* in a non-military context. Pliny in his Natural History, describes a man who used to hunt with ravens, and went down into the forests with them perched *corniculo umerisque* 'on his *corniculum* and his shoulders'.[103] The so-called plume tubes at the sides of helmets would provide one possible place of attachment, or it might have been fastened in some way in connection with the crest mounting.

It is possible that the term *cornicularius* by which the post of adjutant was known, was, in origin, a title applied to a soldier who had been awarded a *corniculum*. Certainly the two words would appear to have a common root though any further connection cannot be proved. An analogous case of the linking of such a title and a post or rank is supplied by Vegetius who names, among the *principales* of the *antiqua legio*, *torquati simplares* and *torquati duplares*. Similarly men who had earned double rations for their valour in the field were known as *duplicarii* (below, p. 238).

In addition to the awards commented on above the literature of the Republic provides numerous instances of a wide range of gifts being given by successful generals to their subordinate officers and men. Increased rations or pay figure frequently as do oxen – some of these destined to be slaughtered in sacrifices to the martial gods. A *patera* (a small handled bowl), *catelli* and *fibulae* (chains and brooches) are also attested, as are tunics. Many of these gifts will have originated in the booty taken from the enemy and there is little reason to doubt that here too lies the origin of many of those 'gifts' which became regularized and turned into *dona militaria* proper. Pliny, discoursing on the uses of gold, suggests that the first gold crown was awarded to the soldier chiefly responsible for the defeat of the Latins at Lake Regillus (*c.* 496 BC). The detail of the narrative is dubious but what is of particular significance is the suggestion that the crown was made of gold taken from captured booty.[104] The lavish bestowal of decorations fashioned from precious metals would have had to be funded from somewhere; the captured gold and silver could have provided the wherewithal. From such *ad hoc* beginnings developed a sophisticated system, a complex of awards designed to acknowledge particular exploits, and latterly a hierarchical system of rank-related decorations.

CHAPTER V

TRIUMPHS AND TRIUMPHAL ORNAMENTS

It is not the intention here to look in detail at the complex subject of the Roman triumph; such a study would be outside the scope of the present book.[1] However, a work on military decorations would not be complete without a brief consideration of the means of rewarding the highest military commanders, the generals who were themselves responsible for awarding *dona militaria* to their subordinate officers and men and who were thus, if the testimony of Suetonius is to be trusted, held ineligible to receive decorations themselves.[2]

The right to celebrate a triumph was the highest military honour which could be voted a successful general. The *triumphator* rode into Rome at the head of his army. Normally no army commander could bring his soldiers into the City, for he relinquished his command of them as soon as he left his *provincia*: for the day of the triumph therefore he held military *imperium* within the city of Rome itself.[3] The triumphal procession entered the City by the *Porta Triumphalis* and made its way up the *Via Sacra* to the Forum, and thence to the temple of Jupiter Capitolinus where white oxen were sacrificed to the god. Everyone in the procession wore a crown of laurel and carried a laurel-branch. There were trumpeters, harpists, pipers and incense bearers. All those who had gone to the war as secretaries, aides, armour-bearers and the like were present. The army would wear their military decorations and, as was the custom, joyfully shout obscenities about their supreme commander. Presents given to the *triumphator* by the allies, by the army and by friendly cities were displayed along with the wagon loads of spoils taken from the enemy. Josephus, describing the triumph celebrated by Vespasian and Titus over the Jews in AD 70, refers to the prominence given to the spoils captured in the temple at Jerusalem. These included the table of the shew-bread and the menorah, a seven-branched candlestick, and were clearly depicted on one of the triumphal scenes decorating one side of the passage through the Arch of Titus in Rome.[4] Tableaux were staged showing scenes of captured cities and various exploits from the war; boards were carried bearing the names of the peoples who had been defeated and brought under Roman domination. It was, for example, at his Pontic triumph that Julius Caesar is said by Suetonius to have displayed the famous slogan *'veni, vidi vici'* ('I came, I saw, I conquered'), in reference to the speed with which the war had been accomplished.[5] It was also customary for numbers of the captives to be paraded, particularly enemy kings and chiefs and their families. We know that the Arvernian chieftain Vercingetorix was kept in custody for six years so that he might be paraded through the streets of Rome in Caesar's Gallic triumph in 46 BC, paraded and then promptly put to death. As the procession reached the foot of the *clivus Capitolinus*, the steep slope up to the Capitol hill, the most eminent of the captives were taken away to be executed by strangulation.

The *triumphator* himself rode in a two-wheeled chariot pulled by four horses. He was dressed in a *tunica palmata* (a palm-embroidered tunic), a *toga picta* (a purple toga richly embroidered with gold stars): he wore a laurel crown, carried in one hand a laurel branch and in the other a *scipio eburneus*, an ivory sceptre surmounted by an eagle. His face was painted red. The politico-religious symbolism of the Roman triumph goes back to the time of the Kings and beyond that to Etruria, for the triumph appears to have been introduced to Rome at the time of the Etruscan kings. The king in his regalia, the *ornatus Iovis*, was the personification of the god Jupiter: the republican general dressed in what had been the regal garb took on the symbolism of king and of Jupiter.[6] He was an almost god-like figure, and the slave who rode in the chariot with him holding an enormous gold crown above his head reminded him from time to time *hominem te esse memento* ('remember thou art mortal').

In order to win a triumph a general must fulfil certain strict conditions. The victory had to be in a *iustum bellum*, a war against a worthy enemy not one of low character such as slaves or pirates or in civil strife; the war had to have been formally declared and to have been won by battle and bloodshed. A bloodless victory, however worthy this might be, was not deemed a suitable reason for a triumph, though it might be marked by an *ovatio* (below, p. 104). According to Valerius Maximus, Livy and Cicero five thousand of the enemy had to be slain to merit a full triumph.[7] Above all, the would-be *triumphator* had to have been fighting *auspiciis suis* ('under his own auspices') and to have held the highest *imperium*. Hence consuls and proconsuls appointed direct by the Senate could triumph but technically not those who held any command on their behalf, their *legati*. However, this rule was not always strictly adhered to particularly in the later years of the Republic. For example, two of Julius Caesar's lieutenants who had been with him in Spain, Q.Fabius Maximus and Q.Pedius, celebrated triumphs in 45 BC – they are recorded in the *Acta Triumphorum* for October and December respectively – although, as Dio explicitly states, they had only been Caesar's *legati* and had achieved no individual success.[8] Subsequently, it is implied by Dio, both Antony and Octavian used their influence to obtain triumphs for men who strictly speaking were not eligible for them, while both Dio and Suetonius indicate that Octavian, once he had gained supreme power as Augustus, bestowed triumphs quite lavishly upon his generals, not only on those who had fought and won in legitimate warfare but upon those who had simply been engaged in the restoration of law and order, the arrest of robbers and the settlement of faction-torn cities.[9] The triumph was clearly a useful means for rewarding loyal supporters.

The accession of Augustus and the establishment of the Principate raised a serious problem regarding the triumph. It was henceforth the emperor who held supreme *imperium*: governors of the imperial provinces only acted on his behalf as his *legati*: they had *imperium* but a lesser *imperium* and when they went to war they were fighting not under their own but under his auspices. Hence in these areas it was the emperor alone and those members of the imperial family who shared in his powers who now qualified for a triumph. The generals who campaigned on his behalf were held ineligible. In fact, as we have seen, Augustus did at first allow some of his generals to celebrate full triumphs (Suetonius mentions thirty), but apart from members of the imperial family the last person known to have done so was Cornelius Balbus, who, in 19 BC, celebrated a triumph over the Garamantes of the Fezzan in central north Africa.[10]

The theory behind the prohibition on governors of imperial provinces celebrating triumphs is presumably that enunciated by Velleius Paterculus in relation to the exploits performed by Marcus Lepidus in Dalmatia: had these exploits been won *propriis auspiciis* Lepidus would probably have received a triumph.[11] This theory does not, however, account for the failure of the proconsuls to continue to be eligible for triumphs. In AD 23 Junius Blaesus, proconsul of Africa, brought to a successful conclusion the long-drawn-out campaign against Tacfarinas. He was awarded not a full triumph but the insignia of a triumph which came to be the standard substitute. Tiberius did however permit Blaesus to be hailed *imperator* by his troops, an honour which had earlier been denied to Licinius Crassus. Blaesus was the last general to be granted this distinction.[12] Here perhaps lies a clue to the true reason behind the assumption of an imperial monopoly over the triumph. Had the emperors genuinely wished to extend the triumph to their *legati*, it is unlikely that tradition would have stopped them so doing: it had not earlier stopped Caesar, Antony or Octavian. Appeal to republican tradition could justify the denial of the triumph to propraetorian imperial *legati*; it could in no way justify the exclusion of proconsuls appointed by the senate to govern senatorial provinces. Technically their constitutional position was no different from that of the emperor. The reason is political and it lies in the delicate position of the emperor who had assumed, *ex officio*, the title *imperator*. Whether or not he ever won imperial salutations in the field as a victorious general, the emperor was saluted *imperator* on his accession. To permit successful generals not of the imperial family to be similarly saluted, to parade in triumph through the streets of Rome, to be hero-worshipped by the people, was to raise up dangerous rivals. The combination of military might and popularity was potentially threatening.

The need to exclude legitimate claimants from the right of celebrating triumphs put Augustus into a difficult situation – he who posed as the upholder of tradition. The delicacy of his position is nicely illustrated by the inconsistencies in his treatment of M. Licinius Crassus, his colleague in the consulate of 30 BC. In 29 Crassus was sent to Macedonia to campaign against the Bastarnae. He slew with his own hands the enemy king Deldo and claimed the right to dedicate his armour as *spolia opima* (above, p. 58) in the temple of Jupiter Feretrius. He was denied this right on the grounds that, although he led the expedition as proconsul of Macedonia, he was fighting under the auspices of Octavian. This denial was supported by the opportune discovery, during the restoration of the temple of Jupiter Feretrius which had begun three years earlier, of the spoils of Lars Tolumnius, king of the Veientes, which had been dedicated by A. Cornelius Cossus in 428 BC.[13] A tradition, repeated by Livy, said that Cossus was only military tribune when he dedicated the spoils (in which case the date would be 437 BC);[14] if this were so the same honour could not be denied Crassus. However, the inscription on the linen breast-plate of the *spolia*, still legible some four hundred years after its deposition, attested that Cossus was consul.[15] Hence Octavian who did not want a rival at this crucial juncture in his transition from *triumvir* to *princeps* was able legitimately to refuse Crassus' claim.[16] However, Crassus was allowed to celebrate a triumph (though not until 27 BC) which, if he was not fighting *auspiciis suis* – the ostensible reason for his being refused the *spolia opima* – he should not have done. He was, moreover, refused the title *imperator*, Octavian taking the imperial salutation for the victory.[17] As Syme has so cogently argued, the real danger to Octavian, particularly prior to 27 BC, came from the proconsuls, men with the power and prestige to foil his plans.[18] He could not allow one of them, Crassus, to rival – indeed to outshine – him in military glory by winning a distinction which had, throughout the history of Rome, fallen to but three men, Romulus, Cornelius Cossus and Claudius Marcellus. Thus the permission to dedicate the *spolia opima* to Jupiter Feretrius was denied to Crassus, although in common with other generals of the period he was allowed to triumph. A reward for military success was clearly called for, but not one so rare as to raise its recipient above Octavian himself. A triumph was granted, imperial salutation denied, and at this point Licinius Crassus disappears from history.[19]

Gradually the right to celebrate a triumph with or even without imperial salutation was taken away. Even the lesser triumph, the *ovatio*, became restricted to members of the imperial family. The *ovatio* had traditionally been awarded as something of a consolation prize when a full triumph was not merited, as for example when the war was against an unworthy enemy or had been won with little bloodshed. The general celebrating an ovation processed into the city on foot instead of in a chariot, to the sound of flutes instead of trumpets. In place of the laurel wreath of the triumph he wore a crown of myrtle 'for the flute is an instrument of peace and the myrtle is the plant of Aphrodite'.[20] An *ovatio* was last celebrated by a general not of the imperial family as late as AD 47, when Aulus Plautius who had led the expedition to Britain in AD 43 was granted one by Claudius – an emperor known for his unconventionality in such matters.[21] Claudius himself celebrated a triumph for the British victory.[22]

Some substitute reward had therefore to be found for the generals of the Principate. The device that was adopted was to award the regalia of the triumph, the *ornamenta* (or *insignia*) *triumphalia*, without the honour of the triumphal procession itself. The general was thus deprived of the opportunity to attract the adulation of the people as he rode in splendour through the streets of Rome. The idea was not entirely new. The insignia of the triumphing general had, for example, been presented by Publius Scipio to the Numidian king Masinissa in 203 BC. The context was the second Punic war. For largely dynastic reasons Masinissa came to support Rome in her opposition to Carthage to which his rival for the Numidian throne, Syphax, was allied. With the help of Masinissa Syphax was defeated and captured. Among the other captives was Sophonisba, wife of Syphax and daughter of the Carthaginian Hasdrubal. According to Livy, Masinissa fell in love with Sophonisba and married her and, in order to prevent her being humiliated and sent captive to Rome, he sent her poison.[23] It was at this juncture, according to Livy's narrative, that Scipio made the award to Masinissa, in order to console him in his grief, for fear of what he might otherwise do. The gift comprised a gold crown, a gold *patera*, curule chair, ivory sceptre, decorated toga and palm-embroidered tunic. Apart from the *patera* these are the trappings of the triumph. They are not called by Livy *ornamenta triumphalia* (this term is not formally applied to them until the time of the Principate) but it is implicit in the narrative that this is what they were. When he presented the gift '(Scipio) added this tribute, that there was no higher distinction among the Romans than the triumph, and that those who triumphed had no more magnificent array than that of which Masinissa alone of all foreigners was accounted worthy by the Roman people.' While the detail of Livy's account of the circumstances of the award may be questioned the basic fact of the case, that one of Rome's allies received triumphal decorations for military services, need not be doubted.

From the time of Augustus onwards (and particularly during the reign of Augustus himself) the *ornamenta triumphalia* were awarded quite commonly to victorious commanders. Suetonius informs us that Augustus voted triumphal regalia to more than thirty of his generals and quite a few of these can be identified.[24] The earliest case may have been that of M. Vipsanius Agrippa. In 14 BC Agrippa refused a full triumph for putting down rebellious tribes in the area of the Crimea because his mere presence had quelled the unrest. According to Dio 'as a result of this no-one else of his peers was permitted to do so any longer either, but they enjoyed merely the distinction of triumphal honours'.[25] It may be inferred from this that Agrippa himself received these triumphal honours, though Dio does not specifically state that he did. Indeed, according to Suetonius, it was Tiberius who first won *ornamenta triumphalia*, though he does not give the context.[26] Tiberius certainly won the *ornamenta* in 12 BC after Augustus had prohibited him from celebrating the triumph granted him by the Senate for his Pannonian campaign, but if Suetonius is correct in saying that he was the first to receive the *ornamenta*, he must also have won them on a previous occasion, prior to their award to Agrippa in AD 14. The context was perhaps the expedition to Armenia in 20 BC.[27]

The honour of receiving triumphal ornaments was confined largely to consular commanders as befits an award which was a substitute for a triumph. Claudius, however, is known to have made the award to officers of lesser status, though Dio's assertion that he did so on the occasion of the British triumph and 'most lavishly on other occasions on the slightest excuse' is no doubt an exaggeration.[28] Certainly two and probably all three of the known cases belong to the British campaign. Hosidius Geta is singled out for mention by Cassius Dio who, describing a disputed river crossing (normally assumed to be the crossing of the Medway), tells how battle was dragging on into the second day and the struggle was indecisive until Geta, narrowly escaping capture, turned the tables on the Britons so that they were soundly defeated. For his services he received triumphal ornaments though, as Dio comments, he had not yet been a consul.[29] It is uncertain what office was held by Geta at this time: he may have been a legionary legate or alternatively may have gone on the campaign as *comes* to the emperor. This latter hypothesis is suggested by the identification of Geta with the senator commemorated on an acephalous inscription from Histonium, the home town of the Hosidii. This unnamed senator whose triumphal ornaments are referred to on the extant portion of the text, held a post which has been restored to read [*leg. leg. . . . . . et comes divi*] *Claudi in Britannia*.[30]

The legate of legion *II Augusta*, the future emperor Vespasian, also received *ornamenta triumphalia* for his part in the British campaign when, as his biographer comments, 'he fought thirty battles, subjugated two warlike tribes, captured more than twenty *oppida* and the Isle of Wight'.[31] Suetonius, describing the triumph which Claudius celebrated over the Britons in AD 44, refers to the presence of generals who had won the triumphal regalia, though the only one mentioned by name is M. Crassus Frugi who, we are told, had also won the honour on a previous occasion.[32] If it was unusual for non-consulars to win *ornamenta triumphalia* it was certainly in keeping with the spirit of the age: it was for this same campaign that a general not of the imperial family was permitted to celebrate an *ovatio* (above, p. 105), a concession which was not repeated by later emperors. None of the commentators who refer to the triumphal ornaments awarded by Claudius to L. Iunius Silanus Torquatus indicate the circumstances in which they were won, but a good case has been made for assigning them to the British expedition when Claudius was so lavish with rewards to his followers.[33] Silanus was a young man at the time, and in any case never rose to higher office than that of praetor.

The conquest of Britain was to provide further opportunity for the winning of military honours. The governor Cn. Iulius Agricola received triumphal ornaments from Domitian at the end of his unusually long tenure of command during which he conducted several successful seasons of campaigning against the tribes of northern Britain, won one decisive battle and extended the bounds of the Empire to the gates of the Highlands. His son-in-law Tacitus informs us that he was given *ornamenta triumphalia*, the honour of a splendid statue and all the other substitutes for a triumph.[34]

The statue was a normal part of the triumphal honours. Augustus, for example, required that 'such victors (who celebrated triumphs) and all others who received triumphal honours should have their statues in bronze erected in the Forum'.[35] Such statues are recorded quite commonly in literature and epigraphy, the inscriptions which were fixed to the bases having in many cases survived while the statues to which they belonged have long since been destroyed. It is to such triumphal statues that Tacitus is alluding when he remarks that, although the Numidian chieftain Tacfarinas was still ravaging Africa, there were already three laurelled statues in the City – those of Furius Camillus. Lucius Apronius and Iunius Blaesus. Previous generals. he notes, did just as much as was necessary to win triumphal ornaments; they then let the enemy slip.[36]

Statues were also awarded in recognition of military excellence as rewards in their own right, distinct from the *ornamenta triumphalia*. Dio implies as much when he accuses Tiberius of giving statues or triumphal honours to various unworthy persons.[37] Abuse of the system of reward is also castigated by the younger Pliny who accuses the authorities of awarding what he terms *statuae triumphales* to men who had never taken part in a battle, seen a camp or heard a military trumpet. He explicitly excepts from this category the triumphal statue voted by the senate on the recommendation of the emperor Trajan to Vestricius Spurinna for his activities among the Bructeri.[38] The epithet 'triumphal' is earlier used by Tacitus of the statue which Otho bestowed upon M. Aponius Saturninus who had enjoyed military successes against the Roxolani when serving in AD 69 as governor of Moesia.[39] Gordon assumes from this that the statue is simply part of the triumphal honours as instituted by Augustus, though this need not necessarily be so, the term *triumphalis* in relation to the statue is not decisive. Tacitus elsewhere alludes to statues which clearly *are* part of the triumphal honours not as *statuae triumphales* but as *statuae laureatae*, while the remarkable collection of eight bronze and marble statues voted by the senate, at Nero's prompting, to L. Volusius Saturninus, and which *are* called *statuae triumfales* were awarded posthumously, not on the occasion of the award of triumphal ornaments.[40]

Statues on their own went on being awarded long after *ornamenta triumphalia* had ceased to be given. No case of *ornamenta* is recorded after the middle of the second century. The last-known example belongs to the very end of Hadrian's reign (or early in that of Pius) when Haterius Nepos won them, presumably for military services in the province of Pannonia Superior of which he was governor in the late 130s and early 140s.[41] Nepos took over the governorship, and with it command in the war against the Suebi, from L. Aelius Caesar (Hadrian's designated successor) who died in AD 138. The major wars of the later second century have produced no examples of triumphal ornaments. This lack is conceivably due to the fact that the Parthian and German wars, which gave ample opportunity for the winning of military distinction, were all attended by one or other member of the imperial family. While an emperor was present the provincial governors lost their supreme command over the army: the highest honours went to the emperor and his companions, and the honour which these companions frequently received was that of a statue.

The statues awarded to these *viri militares* were of various types, though the mechanics behind the award appear commonly to have been the same: they were voted by the senate but on the recommendation of the emperor and often at public expense. T. Pomponius Proculus Vitrasius Pollio was honoured by the senate at the instigation of Marcus and Commodus with two statues, one in military garb (*habitu militari*) the other in civilian attire (*habitu civili*), the former to be set up in Trajan's forum the latter in a porch, conjecturally restored as being that of the temple of the deified Pius.[42] Proculus was a senator who had served as *comes* variously of Verus, Marcus and Commodus during the two German wars, for both of which he was also awarded military decorations. The appointment as *comes* came towards the end of a distinguished career in which he had risen to the proconsulate of Asia and was to enjoy the distinction of a second consulate.

One statue – *habitu civili* – was also awarded to M. Pontius Laelianus Larcius Sabinus, another of the senators of consular status who accompanied the Antonine emperors to the first of the German wars and who had earlier gone with Verus to Parthia, where he had won military decorations. His statue was to be set up in the forum of Trajan which is where the inscription recording the honour was found.[43] But not only senators were distinguished in this way. M. Bassaeus Rufus, praetorian prefect under Marcus, Verus and Commodus, was honoured with a total of three different statues, two military in character, one civilian. A *statua armata* was set up in Trajan's forum, a *statua loricata* in a temple, conjecturally that of Mars Ultor, and a *statua civili amictu* again in a temple, perhaps that of the deified Pius. Rufus was a *primipilaris* who rose to the praetorian prefecture and in this capacity took part in the first of the two German wars, won military decorations and was honoured with consular ornaments. It was Marcus and Commodus, the same two emperors who awarded him the *dona*, who recommended to the senate that the three statues be erected in his honour.[44]

Bassaeus Rufus was almost certainly voted the statues during his lifetime: Pomponius Proculus definitely was, for he outlived Marcus, one of the instigators of the award.[45] M.Claudius Fronto, on the other hand, was honoured posthumously. Fronto died 'fighting bravely for the Republic' during the first of Marcus's German wars in which he served initially as imperial *comes* and later as governor of the provinces of Upper Moesia and Dacia. An armed statue was erected at public expense in the forum Traiani *quod post aliquot secunda proelia adversum Germanos et Iazyges ad postremum pro r[ei] p[ublicae] fortiter pugnans ceciderit.*[46]

Thus, by the time of the great wars of the later second century, the most that Rome's eminent and successful generals could hope for in the way of state recognition was military decorations and perhaps in addition a statue, initiated by the emperor, voted by the senate and paid for by the people. Commoners might use their military prowess to win their way into the ranks of the lesser aristocracy; the equestrian officers might hope to attain senatorial status (below, p. 241); but for the senators themselves the legitimate prizes to be won on the battlefield had been steadily eroded away. While the successful exercise of command as legionary legate and as governor continued to play a vital part in ensuring the rise of the senator to the consulate, for the men at the top – the generals who led Rome's armies into the field – the reward had gradually diminished from the heady heights of the triumph itself to the mere external trappings of the triumph: finally that too was taken away.

CHAPTER VI

THE AWARDING
OF DONA

Contexts in which dona were awarded

The military decorations of the Romans could be awarded wherever and
whenever their armies were engaged in battle. Although there is no direct
statement to this effect by any of the ancient authorities who refer to *dona*, it is
implicit in the various narratives that decorations could be awarded as a result
of internal as well as external strife (although there is evidence to suggest that
the former may not have been regarded as an altogether acceptable context).
The same strict regulations which, in theory at least, governed the granting of
a triumph to the victorious general do not seem to have been applied as
rigorously to the rewarding of that general's soldiers. A triumph could be
awarded only as the outcome of a legitimate war, formally declared against a
worthy opponent; a war against slaves or pirates would not merit a triumph
nor would a war brought to a swift and bloodless conclusion, nor civil strife
which brought sorrow to the Roman people.[1] Although the majority of
awards of *dona militaria* belong to external wars, there are also several
examples, both literary and epigraphic, of decorations being granted during
or after civil strife of some sort or other. It was, for example, during the
Servile War, the revolt led by the Thracian gladiator Spartacus between 73 and
71 BC, that the younger Cato was rewarded for his valour by the commander
of the Roman forces, L.Gellius Publicola.[2] Cato refused the honour on the
grounds that he had done nothing worthy of it, but the fact remains that an
internal commotion of this sort was deemed a suitable context for the
awarding of military decorations. The commander-in-chief of the Roman
forces, M.Licinius Crassus, received an *ovatio* (a minor triumph) on account of
this war.

There are also cases of *dona* being awarded in connection with the detection
and suppression of conspiracies against the state. According to Aulus Gellius a
proposal was put to the senate that Cicero should be awarded a *corona civica* for
his role in putting down the Catiline conspiracy: this crown, normally
awarded to a soldier who had saved the life of a Roman citizen in battle, was
evidently thought to be an appropriate acknowledgement of acts by which

Cicero saved the citizens of Rome from the likely consequences had the conspiracy been successful. The suppression of the conspiracy of Piso against Nero in AD 65 also resulted in the granting of military honours to those who had upheld the cause of the dynasty. Once Piso and his followers had been defeated Nero, 'as though intending to present a report on a war, summoned the senate and gave triumphal honours to Petronius Turpilianus, ex-consul, Cocceius Nerva, praetor-elect, and Tigellinus, praetorian prefect'.[3] The exact nature of their role in the suppression of the conspiracy is not known, though it is possible that they had been instrumental in discovering the plot.[4] The inscription which records the *ornamenta triumphalia* won by Nerva in connection with this conspiracy mentions neither the context for the award nor the name of the emperor involved: the same is true of the two known instances of *dona militaria* attributable to this same episode, those of the senator Nonius Asprenas and the freedman Epaphroditus.[5] The implication is clear: the *ornamenta* and the *dona* are in themselves things to be proud of and therefore are mentioned; the actual means of winning them, not in regular warfare, was something to be quietly suppressed – as indeed was the name of the emperor, Nero. Neither of the two recipients of the *dona* were military men. Nonius Asprenas held no military command during his career as a senator, so the circumstances of his decorations, though not stated, must be abnormal. Enough is known of his career to place the *dona* with some confidence. He is known to have been governor of Galatia in AD 69 and the decorations shortly precede this post: the conspiracy of Piso would provide a most suitable context for an award of unparalleled magnitude (below, p. 152). Similar considerations apply in the case of Epaphroditus. He was a freedman of Nero with no military connections and hence no opportunity to win decorations except in a civil context.

This failure to acknowledge the context to which decorations belong is repeated in the case of awards connected with the Civil War of AD 69. Vespasian was generous with the rewards which he gave to the officers who supported the Flavian cause. Some he rewarded by hastening the progress of their careers, promoting their advancement, where appropriate, through the senate; some he awarded *dona militaria*.

One noteworthy career of this period is that of Firmus who held the post of tribune of legion *IV Scythica* in the late 60s.[6] While holding this command he was appointed acting legate, not yet having been quaestor let alone praetor (below, p. 153), and subsequently awarded *dona militaria* and *ornamenta praetoricia*. These latter presumably constituted the honour of the praetorship – the trappings without the reality of the post which he was probably, in view of his previous speedy advancement, too young to hold. The *dona* and the *ornamenta* are not attributed to any campaign and it may be suspected that they stem from Firmus' political allegiance. The same is probably true of the decorations of L. Antistius Rusticus which were won when Rusticus was serving as tribune of legion *II Augusta* in Britain.[7] While the loyalties of the rest of the British legions wavered as the civil war progressed, *II Augusta* remained constant to Vespasian who had commanded it some twenty-five years previously during the conquest of Britain.[8] Rusticus' *dona* make better sense as a reward for loyalty than as decorations received in an otherwise unattested British campaign, particularly in view of the fact that they are linked with raising by Vespasian and Titus to praetorian rank and are of a scale out of keeping with the rank held by Rusticus in 69. The censorship of Vespasian and Titus in 73–4 was also the occasion for the award of a *hasta pura* to P. Glitius Gallus, who did not hold a single military post and can therefore have merited military decorations only in the pseudo-military context of support for the Flavian dynasty.[9] Licinius Mucianus, whom Firmus replaced as legate of *IV Scythica*, was also honoured by Vespasian and in his case too an attempt was apparently made to suppress the real reason for his reward: he was given *ornamenta triumphalia* 'with many fine words for his part in the civil war, though a campaign against the Sarmatians was given as the reason'.[10]

While it might be thought surprising that those who had championed the winning cause should be reticent in acknowledging the fact, it is not unnatural that those who had supported the losers should choose to keep quiet about their allegiance. Indeed the very fact that they were on the losing side explains why there are so few examples of people known to have been honoured in any way by the other, unsuccessful, claimants. One man who was is Sextus Caesius Propertianus, an equestrian officer.[11] After serving as prefect of a cohort, Propertianus went on to an angusticlave tribunate in legion *IV Macedonica* which was disbanded in AD 70. Subsequently he held procuratorial posts which, as Pflaum has pointed out, should not date earlier than the time of Vitellius. Hence the military service ought to belong to the civil war period and the decorations to have been awarded by Vitellius – an observation which ties in neatly with the fact that no reference is made to the campaign to which the recorded decorations belong nor to the emperor who awarded them. This is subtly different to what normally occurred in the case of *dona* awarded in a legitimate external war but by an emperor whose memory was subsequently damned. In such cases, inscriptions erected after the *damnatio memoriae* tend to give full emphasis to the record of the *dona* and the context to which they belong, but fail to name the awarding emperor, occasionally omitting all reference to him but commonly using the deliberately ambiguous phrase *ab imperatore*.

The civil wars of the later first century BC also resulted in the award of military decorations to members of the armies involved. Julius Caesar, for example, rewarded the centurion Scaeva with promotion and a gift of 200,000 sesterces and his unit with double pay, grain, clothing, rations and military decorations for their services to him at Dyrrhachium in 48 BC, while Agrippa received a naval crown in 36 BC after the battle in which he defeated Sextus

Pompeius and five years later in 31 BC won the right to fly a blue flag (*vexillum caeruleum*) for his role at the battle of Actium against Marcus Antonius.[12]

The repeated failure of the epigraphic material to acknowledge the campaign in which decorations were won, when that campaign was connected with internal strife or indeed when there was no 'campaign' as such, reinforces the impression that the only really acceptable context for decorations was regarded as 'honourable' external warfare. Indeed it has been suggested that from the time of Domitian onwards *dona* could be won only in those wars in which the Emperor himself participated and for which a triumph was celebrated.[13] Certainly by far the greater proportion of instances of decoration from the later first century AD onwards belong to campaigns of this sort. Domitian's and Trajan's campaigns against the Dacians, the Parthian wars of Trajan, of Marcus and Verus and of Severus, the German wars of Domitian and of Marcus, Verus and Commodus together account for a very large percentage of the known *dona*: but there remains a considerable number of cases of decorations awarded in wars in which the emperor did not participate and for which he did not celebrate a triumph. Nerva was old and infirm when he became emperor, and in the brief duration of his reign (AD 96–98) there is just one example of military decorations, awarded in a war against the Suebi in which Nerva took no active part. The war was actually prosecuted by Trajan, then governor of Upper Germany, and it was during the course of the campaign that Nerva adopted Trajan and appointed him Caesar. It is not possible to tell whether the decorations awarded to Q. Attius Priscus as equestrian legionary tribune date to before or after this adoption, that is whether or not there was at least a representative of the imperial house present in Germany at the time. However, in view of the fact that the *dona* were awarded by Nerva alone, and not by Nerva and Trajan together, it is probable that they predate the adoption.[14] Another emperor not known to have conducted his wars in person was Antoninus Pius. His biographer states that he carried out many wars through his legates and, although we do not know to which war the decorations won by the centurion Cestius Sabinus belong, be it against the Dacians, the Germans or the Moors, it cannot be one in which the emperor himself participated.[15] P. Aelius Romanus received his decorations for activities against the Mazices in Spain.[16] The awarding emperor is not specified but the man's name, indicating Roman citizenship granted to him or his father by P. Aelius Hadrianus (emperor from 117–138), suggests a context in the middle years of the second century. The Moorish campaigns of Pius provide a possible occasion, but rather more likely is the expedition in the 170s during the reign of Marcus Aurelius, an expedition in which the emperor did not take part: 'when the Moors laid waste nearly all of Spain the affair was successfully dealt with by his legates'.[17]

The only emperor known to have visited Britain in the last quarter of the first or first quarter of the second century AD is Hadrian who came over in 122 and, as his biographer put it, *multa correxit* ('corrected many things'). From the terms in which the visit is described it may be inferred that the emperor was not concerned with active campaigning: no war is mentioned at this time, while the decision to build a frontier wall implies that the fighting was over.[18] There is evidence for war in Britain in 117 when Hadrian succeeded to the throne (*Britanni teneri sub Romana dicione non poterant*) but this trouble, whatever its exact nature, had presumably been settled in the five years which elapsed between the accession and the visit to Britain. Thus the decorations won in Britain by C. Iulius Karus were not won in a war in which an emperor participated.[19] These decorations certainly date between the two extremes of 89 and 128 and most probably belong to the last years of the reign of Domitian. The war is given simply as *bello Brittanico* and the awarding emperor is not named, a fact which would be consistent with a Domitianic context.

These then are some of the examples of decorations won in campaigns in which an emperor is not known to have participated. Nor were triumphs celebrated at the conclusion of any of these actions, nor, as Suetonius tells us, at the end of Domitian's campaign against the Sarmatae,[20] for which decorations are known to have been awarded to at least three soldiers – the senator Bruttius Praesens, the centurion Aconius Statura and the *primipilaris* Velius Rufus.

Hence it is apparent that, whatever might have been the theoretical limitations surrounding the awarding of military decorations, in practice they were used to reward soldiers who had taken part in military encounters of all types, in major external wars, in relatively minor campaigns such as Nero's action against the Astures and also in civil strife.[21] The system was clearly being abused when decorations designed to reward valour in the field were being given to civilians such as Nonius Asprenas and Glitius Gallus who had seen no military service, or were being awarded in military contexts through to non-combatants. Claudius, for example, awarded his doctor, C. Stertinius Xenophon (who was later to be privy to the plot to poison him), a *hasta* and a *corona aurea* for services in the British War.[22] Xenophon, it is true, was serving on this occasion as a legionary tribune, but there seems little doubt that this appointment was purely nominal: it is the only military post in a purely civil career and was held simultaneously with an appointment as *praefectus fabrum*.[23] Xenophon's role in Britain was more that of court physician than of soldier.

Nor are these irregular uses of *dona* limited to the period of the Empire. According to Aulus Gellius, it had been in order to win popularity among his soldiers that Marcus Fulvius Nobilior (early second century BC) had awarded crowns for industry in building a rampart or digging a well.[24] It was presumably as a bribe that the corrupt senator Gaius Verres had given to his clerk a gold ring and to Quintus Rubrius a crown, *phalera* and *torques*. These gifts were brought to light during the prosecution of Verres launched by Cicero on behalf of the Sicilians whom Verres had exploited and oppressed during his governorship in 73–71 BC.[25] Perhaps the oddest recorded use or abuse of a military crown was to reward a soldier who slew an officer who was a homosexual and had attempted to seduce him.[26] It is Plutarch who tells the story of Caius Lusius, a nephew of Marius, who had a weakness for beautiful youths. He made advances towards one of his young subordinates, Trebonius, who drew a sword and killed him. Trebonius, brought to trial for murder, told exactly what had happened, how he had often resisted Lusius' advances, refusing to prostitute himself despite lucrative incentives to do so. Marius thereupon called for the crown of valour and awarded it to Trebonius for displaying such noble conduct at a time when it was necessary that such good examples should be set. It is clear from Polybius that in his day at least male prostitution was considered to be a serious breach of military discipline.[27] It was punished by the *fustuarium*, which amounted to a virtual death sentence – the condemned man was cudgeled or stoned by his fellow-soldiers and if he escaped with his life became a homeless exile.

Not surprisingly the vast majority of recorded decorations were awarded, as far as we know, for encounters from which Rome ultimately emerged as victor. Equal or greater valour might well be displayed by a soldier involved in a disaster, but his chances of surviving to enjoy the distinction he had earned would be diminished while the outcome of his bravery was not success but failure. The point is made explicitly by the elder Pliny in relation to Marcus Sergius, a soldier who had the misfortune to be involved in the series of defeats which Rome suffered during the second Punic war, between 218 and 216 when Hannibal invaded Italy. How many crowns, Pliny asks, might this brave man have won had he fought against any other foe but Hannibal: 'what civic crowns were given at the Trebia, at Ticinus or at Trasimene? What crown was earned at Cannae?' Rhetorical questions; the answer clearly implied was none or very few.[28] In fact Pliny himself records elsewhere that Scipio Africanus was awarded but refused the civic crown for saving the life of his father at the battle of the Trebia in which two-thirds of the Roman army was lost (above, p. 71).[29] The basic point remains valid: a brave warrior such as Sergius clearly was – despite the loss of a hand he went on to fight against Hannibal – could well be denied tangible recognition of his valour because he was unfortunate enough to see service at a time when the tide of Rome's military fortunes was at its lowest ebb.

Who awarded decorations?

GENERALS, EMPERORS AND PROVINCIAL GOVERNORS

During the Republic it was the victorious general commanding the armies, who presented military decorations to the troops. Polybius describes how, after a successful battle, the general calls an assembly of the troops, praises the men who had distinguished themselves by their bravery and distributes the awards.[30] What Polybius describes in theory is shown in practice time and again by a wide variety of writers. For example, after the successful siege of New Carthage (210 BC) the general, Scipio, addressed the troops and bestowed military decorations on those who had earned them, adjudicating in the case of a contested claim for the *corona muralis*, destined for the man first over the walls of the besieged city.[31] Nothing had changed when, about a century and a half later, a similar scene was enacted before the besieged town of Thapsus in Numidia in 46 BC.[32] Having sacrificed to the gods, Caesar held a parade of his soldiers: he congratulated the men, rewarded his entire force of veterans and presented awards for gallantry and conspicuous service.

The picture painted by the literary sources is borne out by the one relevant inscription, that recording the award of citizenship and *dona* to the *turma Salluitana*: the decorations were awarded by Cn. Pompeius (Strabo) *imperator*, and the ceremony of award took place *in castreis apud Asculum*, in the camp before the town of Asculum, the town where the war in question, the Social War, had begun in 91 BC with the assassination of the Romans present.[33]

The general, be he one of the consuls or someone appointed to act for him, was acting on behalf of the Roman senate which presumably had the ultimate word as to who could or could not be decorated. It was, for example, by decree of the senate that Marcus Marcellus was forbidden to bestow military decorations on the survivors of Cannae whom he wished to be allowed to join his army against the Carthaginians at Syracuse (below, p. 128). Normally it would be left to the discretion of the general himself to use those powers vested in him by the senate.

In theory nothing changed with the coming of the Principate. It was still the victorious general who was responsible for the distribution of awards, but in practice this was now almost invariably the emperor or a member of the imperial family: this is because it was the emperor who now possessed *imperium* in all the imperial provinces, and the provincial governors whom he appointed to administer the provinces on his behalf were only his legates with delegated authority. Hence any campaign which was carried out in or launched from an imperial province was held to be under the inspiration of, if not actually led in the field by, the emperor: thus it was he who retained the authority to award decorations, being in theory at least in the same position vis à vis the senate as had been the consular generals of the republican period. The reason is the same as that which now forbade the celebration of triumphs by any but proconsuls and members of the imperial family. There is some indication from the literary evidence that in practice in the early years of the Principate the emperors did allow certain of their generals some discretion in the matter of awarding decorations.[34] Augustus permitted those who had themselves celebrated triumphs to award *dona*, and as we have seen some Augustan generals were allowed a triumph. Tiberius allowed some generals of consular rank to use their own initiative in the matter, though the men in question here could have been operating in senatorial provinces where the constitutional position was in any case rather different. The epigraphic evidence for the entire imperial period is unanimous on the point that it was the emperor or a member of the imperial family who granted *dona*, whatever discretionary powers their agents may in theory have had. No inscription records a provincial governor granting *dona*: the vast majority of cases record the emperor as the awarding authority, while just a few name a member of the imperial family, for example Tiberius Caesar, stepson and heir to Augustus, and Germanicus Caesar, nephew of Tiberius.[35]

The situation in the senatorial provinces was rather different. Here it was the senate who appointed governors, proconsuls, to act on their behalf: the proconsular *imperium* gave these men the same rights in the matter of awarding *dona* as had been granted to their republican predecessors. There is just one example of this theory being put into practice and that was in the province of Africa Proconsularis when the soldier Helvius Rufus distinguished himself during an encounter with the rebel leader Tacfarinas and was awarded a *torques* and a *hasta* not by the emperor Tiberius but by the governor Apronius.[36] That no further examples of decorations awarded by proconsular governors are recorded could be due to the fact that their powers in this respect were eroded away in favour of the emperor. It is, however, much more likely to be a simple case of desuetude. The *imperium* of Augustus had extended over almost all those areas where legions were stationed. From the beginning of his principate the emperor held nearly all of the provinces of military importance: the legions on the Rhine were under the command of his legates and when the provinces of Germany were created they were added to his *provincia*. When the provinces on the Danube were formed, when Britain and Dacia were conquered all these came under imperial control. These were the areas where most of the fighting was done: this was where there were battle honours to be won. Indeed on one occasion when trouble did arise in a senatorial province, Hispania Ulterior Baetica, the area was temporarily taken under imperial control so that responsibility for any *dona* awarded as a result of the campaign would presumably have fallen to the emperor.[37] It is unfortunate that the one and only example of *dona* assignable to this campaign, those of P. Aelius Romanus, does not state who made the award.[38] One other case of decorations assignable to activities within a senatorial province is extant: this is the case of Valerius Festus, legate of legion *III Augusta*, who was instrumental in suppressing a revolt of the Garamantes who had invaded the area of Tripolitania in the eastern part of the province of Africa Proconsularis.[39] The award to Festus was made *ab imperatore* and not by the provincial governor. However, this case is complicated by two factors.

Firstly it belongs to the civil war period, and the generous scale of the award made to Festus suggests that it might have been in some way influenced by the man's rather dubious role in the politics of the year 69. Secondly the position of the commander of *III Augusta* was an odd one. He was an imperial appointee in a senatorial province, the *de facto* though not yet *de jure* governor of the frontier area of Numidia. As such he cannot be used as good evidence for the abrogation of responsibility for *dona* by senatorial governors. It is unlikely that the right of proconsuls to award *dona* was ever formally withdrawn: it probably withered away with disuse.

THE SENATE

The generals who led the armies into battle or under whose auspices the campaigning took place were responsible for the rewards given to their troops: they made these awards ultimately on behalf of the senate and people of Rome, but in the normal way of things they could act on their own initiative without recourse to the senate for ratification of what they were doing.[40] Who then rewarded these generals? The one authority to which they owed allegiance and from which they obtained their *imperium* was the senate: hence it was the senate which rewarded its agents.

As we have seen, the highest military honour which could be done a victorious general was to grant him a triumph, and this reward was in the hands of the senate. 'It is in (the senate's) power to celebrate with pomp and to magnify the successes of a general or on the other hand to obscure and belittle them.'[41] Any commander who had the authority to award *dona* was in a position to win a triumph or the ornaments of a triumph and these rather than conventional decorations were granted by the senate. On the other hand the substitutes for the triumph, the *ornamenta triumphalia*, were commonly awarded not by the senate but by the emperor, it being his legates who were in a position to win them. There were, however, occasions when the senate might choose to award the *ornamenta* instead of a full triumph. This might arise, for example, in the case of a general who, although technically eligible to triumph, had performed deeds not thought worthy of this supreme honour. Such was the case with the *ornamenta* voted by the senate to Claudius.[42] According to Suetonius, Claudius thought it beneath his dignity to accept this lesser honour and so decided to conquer Britain in order to win a full triumph – which in due course he did.

The only types of military decoration proper which a general might be in a position to win were those which were presented by the rescued to a rescuer, the *corona obsidionalis* and the *corona civica*; in this context we find the senate, acting on behalf of or alongside the Roman people, presenting such crowns to leaders who had performed deeds of significance to the whole state. For example, when Quintus Fabius was instrumental in saving the entire Roman state by his opposition to Hannibal (employing what have come to be known as 'Fabian' tactics) he was rewarded with a *corona obsidionalis*, voted him by unanimous decision of the senate and people of Rome: he had, as it were, saved the whole of Italy from a state of siege and so was being rewarded in traditional fashion by those whom he had rescued.[43] It was the senate also which granted, first to Julius Caesar, and subsequently to several of the emperors, the right to use the *corona civica*, the crown of oak leaves, as a symbol of imperial authority and clemency. As Dio wrote of Augustus, 'the right to place the laurel trees in front of the royal residence and to hang the crown of oak above them was voted him to symbolize that he was always victor over his enemies and the saviour of the citizens'.[44]

Certain extraordinary grants required the ratification of the senate. For example, when Octavian granted Marcus Agrippa a naval crown on the occasion of his victory over Sextus Pompeius in 36 BC, the award itself was in the gift of the general but the grant by which Agrippa was given the right to wear this crown on all those occasions when a triumphant general wore his laurel wreath required confirmation by a decree of the senate.[45]

ARMIES AND INDIVIDUALS

There were, of course two major types of decoration to which none of the normal rules regarding eligibility to award applied: the *corona obsidionalis* and the *corona civica*, for the whole idea of these, as originally conceived, was that they should be presented by the person or persons whose lives had been saved and not by those in authority. These crowns, the two most honourable of all the awards, were also the two least valuable in cash terms, a not insignificant fact in the case of the civic crown in particular for it would be presented by a single private individual possibly with minimal financial resources. The state, after all, could recoup the substantial sums expended on gold and silver decorations from the copious spoils of warfare. The idea behind the civic crown was that its award should be a free and spontaneous gesture in acknowledgement of a deliberate individual act of heroism; hence the need for the absence of any major financial constraint which might prejudice the rescued from making such a gesture. Though the decision to award the crown was in theory meant to be freely made, Polybius does note pressure should be brought to bear by the consuls on any man who failed to make the award of his own free will. Indeed it is clear from the literary evidence relating to the *corona civica* that, although the decoration itself survived well into the Principate, it did not survive as an award made by private individuals. Already by the time of the later Republic it had fallen to the general to make the award. The first example of this falls in the governorship of Marcus Thermus in Asia in 80 BC when Caesar, serving in his first military post as legate to the governor, saved the life of a fellow soldier during the storming of Mitylene.

Caesar received his *corona civica* not from the soldier but from the governor.[46] It was the emperor Tiberius who awarded Helvius Rufus the civic crown, regretting that the governor had not himself done so; there is no expectation of the fact that the man whose life had been saved should have made the award. On a later occasion Corbulo, exhorting his disheartened soldiers, urges them how honourable it would be to win a civic crown *imperatoria manu* – from the hand of the emperor: this clearly was now the expectation.[47] By contrast, the *corona obsidionalis* does not appear to have survived the Republic – it is last attested in the context of the Social War – and the conditions surrounding its award appear never to have altered.

It was also open to the army to make other awards and gifts to its individual members. Whether these awards were regarded as unofficial, or whether the army was deemed to be a properly constituted authority for the purpose is not clear, but they were certainly sufficiently acceptable to be recorded on tombstones. There are just three examples, all dating to the Julio-Claudian period. The earliest case is that of C. Iulius Macer who had served as *duplicarius* of the *ala Atectorigiana* and was recalled to serve with the *Raeti gaesati*. He was presented by his comrades with a shield, crowns and gold rings at a date which must be sometime before the law of Tiberius restricting the wearing of such rings.[48] Q. Cornelius Valerianus, an equestrian officer, commanded detachments of cavalry and infantry which were sent from Moesia into Thrace to take part in the war against Mithridates, king of Pontus, in AD 45. The units of the Moesian army honoured him with gifts which included statues, crowns and shields.[49] Finally, one Numenius, a freedman, was honoured by an army with at least one gold crown (and perhaps more, for the stone is fragmentary), and was publicly praised for reasons unknown.[50] This practice of the army presenting gifts to its own officers and men is not attested as such in the Republic; the nearest equivalent is the army of Marius voting to give all the booty to their commander and keep none themselves. The practice is attested for a very restricted period only and perhaps gave way to the procedure indicated in the case of Camulius Lavenus when the army voted him the honours which the emperor Hadrian awarded him.[51]

Who was eligible to win decorations?

One of the reasons for the success of the Roman army, stressed by many writers of the period, was the emphasis placed on equitable reward and punishment. For such inducements to work effectively it was necessary for everyone to be treated, and to be seen to be treated, fairly. But that is not to say that all groups were dealt with in the same way; they were not. There is considerable evidence for discrimination in the ways used to reward bravery in the field and there were several categories of soldier who were simply not eligible for *dona militaria*. With one notable exception (below, p. 128), no-one who distinguished himself in Rome's service went entirely unrecognized and unrewarded. As we have already seen, the generals who commanded the armies on campaign were excluded from receiving *dona*: instead they won the greater honour of a triumph or triumphal ornaments. At the opposite end of the scale the *auxilia* of the Principate were generally ineligible for individual decorations but they could be honoured *en bloc* as units, and receive Roman citizenship or early discharge. *Dona militaria* were awarded to the emperor's companions on campaign, his *comites*, to provincial governors, to the officers and men of the citizen units, to the officers of the non-citizen units and, in the period of the Republic, to the allies. On occasions, non-military personnel doing jobs related to the war effort (as for example those concerned with supplies) were rewarded with *dona*, while in times of crisis, of civil war, the list of those deemed eligible was even further extended (above, p. 110).

CITIZEN TROOPS

Among the citizen troops the legions are, not unnaturally, particularly well represented. As the basic instrument of Roman expansion they bulk large in the records of distinguished service. For the period of the Principate the élite praetorian cohorts, the emperor's bodyguard, also feature largely: they were based in Rome but accompanied the emperor on campaign, occasionally also going into the field when the emperor was not present. The urban cohorts as citizen units were clearly eligible for decorations but, since the bulk of their time was spent policing the cities in which they were stationed (four cohorts in Rome, one in Lyon and one in Carthage), they had little opportunity to distinguish themselves in battle. However, on occasions when they did send men into the field these men could be decorated. When *cohors XIII urbana* from Carthage sent a detachment to take part in the wars of Domitian across the Rhine and Danube, a centurion, Q. Vilanius Nepos, and a tribune, C. Velius Rufus, are known to have received *dona*.[52] Doubtless there were others whose career records do not survive. Another group of units with little scope for military awards was the *vigiles*, the Roman fire brigade which, though classed as part of the army, never took to the battle field. Despite the fact that their work doubtless involved them in heroic deeds, there is no evidence for any means of rewarding them.

AUXILIARIES AND ALLIES

There is strong negative evidence that for the greater part of the Principate only citizen soldiers were generally eligible to be decorated as individuals. The entire body of epigraphic evidence relating to *dona* includes only four certain and three possible examples of auxiliary soldiers. This fact cannot be without significance for tombstones of auxiliaries as a whole are relatively prolific, while the role which the *auxilia* played in the campaigns of the Empire became increasingly prominent as time went on. By the middle years of the second century AD it was they who bore the brunt of the fighting in the frontier wars, and the large number of prefects and tribunes commanding auxiliary units who were decorated during this period indicates the important part which they took in all the major wars. It is unthinkable that the men of the *auxilia* did not frequently perform deeds of valour sufficient to merit their being decorated: their failure to receive decorations must therefore be a matter of imperial policy. This policy appears to have been one of excluding from individual awards not auxiliaries as such but non-citizens – an exclusion which almost certainly operated from the time of Vespasian.

There is just one straightforward, uncontroversial example of a decorated non-citizen auxiliary soldier. This is the case of the cavalryman, Antiochus, whose peregrine status is not in doubt. Antiochus served with the *ala Parthorum et Araborum*, rising in ten years from the post of *eques* to *evocatus triplicarius*.[53] He was *donis donatus* in an unnamed campaign or campaigns – he was twice decorated – which must belong to the early part of the first century AD. His tombstone has been dated on stylistic grounds to the Tiberian period.[54] It was set up outside the fort of Mainz-Weisenau, a site which is thought to have been first occupied in the early years of the first century AD.[55] The presence of an *ala Parthorum et Araborum* at Mainz in the early to middle years of the first century is independently attested by the tombstone of a trooper of the unit who died there after thirty years service.[56] Antiochus' decorations could have been won during the German campaigns of the Julio-Claudian period or possibly at some earlier stage in the career. The movements of the unit prior to its appearance at Mainz are uncertain but both soldier and unit are of eastern origin. An *ala Parthorum*, quite possibly the same unit, is attested in Dalmatia in the early years of the first century AD by the tombstone of one of its decurions who died there at the age of twenty-six.[57] Further it may be recalled that the Parthian noble Ornaspades had fought under Tiberius in the Dalmatian war, acquiring Roman citizenship as a reward for his services, and this Parthian *ala* may have originated from the troops which he had with him on this occasion.[58]

Of the other three auxiliaries known definitely to have been decorated one certainly and two possibly were Roman citizens at the time of their award. The clearest case is that of Tiberius Claudius Maximus who started his military career in a legion, *VII Claudia*, before transferring to the post of *duplicarius* in an auxiliary cavalry unit, the *ala II Pannoniorum*.[59] He was decorated both before and after the transfer, and there is no doubt whatever that he was a Roman citizen who chose to serve in a non-citizen unit, presumably because he was an accomplished horseman. Less clear-cut are the cases of Rufinus and Capito. The broken (and now lost) tombstone commemorating the military career of Rufinus refers to only one post, that of decurion in the *ala Moesica*, and it was probably while serving with this unit that Rufinus won the decorations depicted but not mentioned on the stone (fig. 13).[60] It is distinctly possible, though not capable of proof, that Rufinus, like Maximus, began his military career in a legion, for his tombstone was erected by a friend and heir who was a legionary centurion. Transfers from legions to auxiliary units are not common, but they are not unknown, particularly when the move is from the ranks of the legion to the post of centurion or, more especially, decurion in the auxiliary unit.[61] Titus Flavius Capito retired as decurion of an *ala Pannoniorum*.[62] The man's *praenomen* and *nomen* indicate citizenship received in the Flavian period and it was during this same period that he was decorated – the award was made by Vespasian in an unnamed campaign. It was still common practice at this time for auxiliary soldiers to receive citizenship before discharge and this could well have happened in this particular example – in which case Capito could have been a Roman citizen at the time he was decorated. Unfortunately insufficient information is given on the tombstone for his career to be mapped in any detail.

a. b.

13 Tombstone of Rufinus (now lost. a. anon. b. after Schannat)

Then there are three questionable cases. Caeno, centurion of a *cohors Hispanorum*, was certainly a non-citizen: his single name leaves us in no doubt of this. What is less certain is the fact that he was decorated. The assumption that he was, rests on the interpretation placed on a circular object carved on his tombstone (pl. 9b), for no mention is made of *dona* in the text of the stone.[63] The problems involved in the interpretation of this object which has been thought to be either a crown or a *torques* are discussed further below (p. 201). The stone dates to the first century AD. It was found, broken, in a pit backfilled with rubbish dating to the third quarter of the first century: the date of erection of the tombstone is therefore likely to have been no later than the second quarter of the century.

A tombstone from Tipasa in Algeria provides another putative decorated auxiliaryman, a veteran of the *ala Britannica*.[64] The text reads . . . *Elius Publius veteranus militavit ala Britannica bis torquatus* . . . As written, the *bis torquatus* ('twice decorated with a torques') certainly describes the veteran, but the phrase follows the name of the unit not the soldier, exactly as it would if it were describing the unit. Could it be that whoever drafted the text or whoever cut it got his Latin wrong? Should it be amended to read *ala Britannica bis torquata*, the unit, not the soldier, twice decorated? The description of a soldier as *torquatus* at the date in question – the inscription belongs to the middle of the second century – is unparalleled; to describe a unit in this way is perfectly normal (below, p. 220). It is surely no coincidence that the *ala Britannica* is one of just four units known to have borne precisely this battle honour, *bis torquata*. An argument based on the assumption of a lapidical error cannot be conclusive, but the oddities of the text as given must throw doubt on the conventional interpretation. Finally among the epigraphic material there is an only partly decipherable text from north-west Spain which appears to record *dona* and commemorates a decurion with a problematical name (? Icascaen) of an unparalleled *ala I Gig* [. . . . .]. This decurion has been variously interpreted as being of peregrine status or as being a citizen, L(ucius) Cas(sius) Caen(icus).[65]

Literary evidence provides us with one further example, again not without its problems. The date is early first century AD. During Germanicus' punitive campaigns across the Rhine into Germany in AD 16 there was serving in the Roman army a brother of the enemy chief Arminius: 'that brother, Flavus by name, . . . was a conspicuous figure both from his loyalty and from the loss of an eye through a wound received some years before during Tiberius' period of command . . . (Arminius) asked his brother how he had acquired the disfigurement of his face. Having been told of the place and the battle he enquired what reward he had received. Flavus referred to his increased pay, *torques, corona* and other *dona militaria*. Arminius scoffed at the cheap rewards of servitude.'[66] Tacitus here gives no clue as to the status of Flavus nor to the post he held either in AD 16 or on the occasion of his winning the military decorations. He is called by the single name of the non-Roman and in the list of rewards he received no mention is made of citizenship: had he been thus honoured one might have expected Tacitus to mention the fact. However we learn later on in the *Annals* that Flavus' son, Italicus, was born in Rome, not as a hostage but as a citizen (*nec obsidem sed civem*)[67] and the likelihood is that Flavus himself received citizenship at some stage in his career as a reward for his faithful and distinguished service to Rome. Ritterling suggested that he received citizenship from Augustus, and at the time of the encounter with his brother in AD 16 was serving as prefect of the *ala Gallorum Flaviana*. Timpe, on the other hand, prefers to see him as a simple *miles*, promoted centurion on the occasion when he distinguished himself in battle and won decorations.[68] This status when decorated cannot be proved one way or the other.

In summary, then, we have one perfectly clear plus a small handful of possible examples of non-Roman citizens receiving military decorations. The case of Antiochus alone is, however, sufficient to show that on occasions it *was* possible for a non-citizen soldier of the Principate to win *dona*. But the paucity of evidence for decorated auxiliaries still requires explanation: what were these occasions? One fact which emerges is that all of our putative decorated non-citizens either certainly or possibly held junior officer appointments at the time they were honoured. This may be due to nothing other than the more comfortable financial position of better-paid soldiers – their heirs could afford to put up more wordy tombstones – or it may, as Holder has suggested, be a case of equality in the treatment meted out to all who held such posts.[69] Auxiliary centurionates and decurionates were not infrequently filled by Roman citizens transferred from the legions (cf. the case of Ti. Claudius Maximus); such men would be eligible to receive decorations so the same privilege had, in all fairness, to be extended to the non-citizens who would be serving beside them in positions of equal seniority. Another feature which the individuals under consideration have in common is date: all but the highly dubious case of Elius Publius belong to the pre- or early Flavian period. The mass of material relating to the wars of Domitian and Trajan includes not a single example. The date is significant for it coincides with the period at which a rather different type of award for auxiliaries first appears; this is the practice of honouring not individual members of a unit but the unit as a whole, either with Roman citizenship or with a military decoration, the *torques* or the *armilla* (below, p. 220). A switch to the use of communal awards might explain the apparent disappearance of individual ones.

This leaves one unexplained and as yet inexplicable anomaly. It has been shown that recruitment to the auxiliary units became increasingly localized as time went on and that the civil settlements which grew up outside forts provided a high percentage of the new recruits.[70] These settlements contained a large number of army veterans who, on their discharge, will have received Roman citizenship for themselves and their children. Hence an increasingly large proportion of the recruits to auxiliary units must already have been citizens at the time they joined up, and so were, in theory at least, eligible to win decorations. Some time in the 140s Antoninus Pius altered the citizenship grant to exclude sons already born to the retiring soldiers. Implicit in the wording of the grant as it appears on the new type of diplomas is the fact that some of the auxiliary soldiers were already Roman citizens; the grant of citizenship was made explicitly to those who did not already have it (*civitatem Romanam eorum qui non haberent dedit*). And yet there survives not a single example of a soldier recruited with citizen status direct to the *auxilia* receiving the military decorations for which one might have thought him eligible. The one post-Flavian citizen auxiliary whom we know to have been decorated, Ti. Claudius Maximus, was a transfer from a legion. In the second decade of the third century AD, by the *Constitutio Antoniniana* Caracalla granted citizenship to all free-born males. Henceforth all recruits to the *auxilia* would be citizens and it is surely no coincidence that this is precisely the time at which *dona* virtually ceased to be awarded (below, p. 248).

This discrimination against non-citizen soldiers did not apply only in the matter of decorations for neither did the auxiliaries profit from the donatives which the emperors periodically handed out to the legions and the praetorian guard. However the non-citizen soldiers enjoyed one grant which by its nature was denied to the citizen soldier, that is the grant of Roman citizenship. To be a non-Roman in a Roman world was to be discriminated against. To be a citizen was to enjoy the full protection of the law, it was to have status. Roman citizenship was granted as a matter of course to the auxiliary who served with an unblemished record for twenty-five years, but it could be acquired earlier by those serving in a unit which distinguished itself in battle (below, p. 227). There are also a few examples of soldiers receiving citizenship prior to discharge or the completion of the statutory twenty-five years service, on an individual not a collective basis.[71] The reason behind such awards is presumably connected with distinguished service, very possibly on the battlefield. It is perhaps strange that in the case of none of the individuals for whom individual grants of citizenship have been claimed is it made clear that anything out of the ordinary has occurred. No mention is made of the circumstances involved, nor is attention drawn to the fact that the citizenship grant is anything other than the normal. It may be inferred from the fact that Antoninus Pius restricted the scope of the citizenship grant that the prospect of becoming a Roman citizen was a positive incentive to enlistment.

The general ineligibility of the non-citizen for military decorations excludes not only the soldiers of the *alae* and cohorts discussed above but also the men of the fleet. The fleets played a not insignificant part in a number of campaigns where river or sea transport was required – for example during the activities of Iulius Agricola in northern Britain in the 80s – but any rewards meted out to them came in the form of block grants similar to those made to the auxilia, and not as individual awards.

No such discrimination appears to have operated during the Republic – the allies were treated in many respects much more like legionaries than were the auxiliaries – but neither did the practice of automatically granting Roman citizenship to time-expired auxiliaries. The picture is not so clear cut for the republican period because so few relevant inscriptions survive and the literary evidence is often imprecise in its designation of the troops who were receiving decorations. The rewarding of the allies appears to have been done in a rather *ad hoc* fashion, sometimes with grants of Roman citizenship, sometimes with *dona militaria*. According to Pliny the Roman authorities awarded gold *torques* to foreign soldiers but silver ones to Roman soldiers.[72] In its detail the evidence of this passage is questionable: it would be rather surprising if the allies were to have received decorations more valuable than those awarded to the Romans themselves, while the assertion that Romans received silver *torques* is at variance with the description of the eighty-three *torques* of Siccius Dentatus as of gold.[73] Likewise the *torques* referred to by Silius Italicus in the context of the second Punic war and those awarded by Caesar to a prefect of cavalry in the Spanish campaign were all of gold.[74] Though the detail of Pliny's statement is suspect, the basic inference that decorations could be given to allies as well as to citizens is consistent with the known honours afforded allied generals and their men. For example Massinissa, one time king of Numidia, was presented by Scipio with the ornaments of a triumph after he had collaborated with Rome against Syphax and the Numidians (above, p. 105); while Sosis of Syracuse and Moericus, a Spaniard, were wreathed with crowns of gold when they took part in the *ovatio* celebrated by Marcus Marcellus – a distinction which they earned by betraying the garrison of Syracuse and acting as guide to the attacking Roman forces.[75] Both were rewarded additionally with a grant of land and Roman citizenship.

This use of citizenship as a means of rewarding non-Roman troops recurs. For example Marius bestowed Roman citizenship on about a thousand men from the city of Camerinum in northern Italy for their conspicuous bravery in war, though in this instance the grant was held to be illegal.[76] In 89 BC the Spanish cavalrymen of the *turma Salluitana* were given Roman citizenship by the general Cn. Pompeius Strabo under whom they were fighting in the Social War.[77] This was a block grant to a whole unit and provides a forerunner for the practice which came to prevail during the Empire, though in this case the cavalrymen received citizenship plus *dona militaria*.

The quantity of evidence for the Republic on this point is not great, but what there is indicates an absence of the clear-cut distinction which came to exist during the Principate – a distinction which developed no doubt with the integration of the *auxilia* into the Roman army as a full-time regular force. While there are the few cases of individual auxiliaries, both citizen and non-citizen, receiving military decorations up to and including the Flavian period, there is only one known later example and that to an ex-legionary, a citizen soldier, Tiberius Claudius Maximus, decorated by Trajan in the Dacian and Parthian wars. It is surely no coincidence that all the certain or putative cases of decorated non-citizen auxiliaries occur before the first recorded example of the decoration, en bloc, of an auxiliary unit, and that there is no significant overlap with the practice of awarding Roman citizenship to entire units *honoris causa*.

THE COWARDLY

The one category of soldier whom we see in the Republican period being firmly excluded from receiving military decorations were those who had in the past acted in a cowardly manner unbecoming of Roman soldiers, and had so betrayed both their fellow-soldiers and the cause for which they were fighting. The case is unique. The prohibition was applied to those soldiers who had deserted their comrades at the disaster of the battle of Cannae in 216 BC when the Roman army had been routed by Hannibal's troops. Wishing to make amends for their disgrace, these men, who had been banished to Sicily till the war in Italy should end, begged to be allowed to fight against the Carthaginians in Syracuse. The proconsul, Marcus Marcellus, wrote a letter on their behalf to the senate, requesting that they be allowed to redeem themselves in this way. The senate decreed that it saw no reason why the welfare of the state should be entrusted to these men, but that if Marcellus thought differently he might act as he saw fit, on condition that none of the men be exempted from any of the burdens of military service, that none of them be allowed back into Italy as long as the enemy was still there, and that they should not be decorated for valour.[78] The only reward that these soldiers might expect was the opportunity to rehabilitate their characters in the eyes of their fellow-citizens by paticularly distinguished service and perhaps a glorious death.

FREEDMEN

Freedmen were not normally eligible for military service except in the fleets and the *vigiles*; hence their opportunities to win military decorations would have been strictly limited. There are, however, examples of freedmen being recruited in times of emergency as occurred during the Punic war and the Social war.[79] In these circumstances, with freedmen fighting in the field alongside the free-born, there is no apparent reason why the freedmen should not receive military decorations. There is one clear example of this during the civil war between Caesar and Pompey: the building up of two large armies put a severe strain on the usual sources of recruits, so it is no surprise to find a freedman in military service at this period. The record of decorations provides a nice case of discrimination. Metellus Scipio refused to give to a certain cavalryman the gold *armillae* for which he had been recommended 'in order not to lower the reward . . . by giving it to a man who had been a slave';[80] in the event he gave him silver *armillae* instead, a compromise between the need to reward a man who had shown outstanding bravery and the desire to maintain some distinction in the treatment meted out to *ingenui* and *liberti*. The status of the recipient was clearly regarded as being of some significance.

This is the one and only perfectly straightforward case of a freedman receiving *dona* for his services in the field. All the other references to freedmen with *dona* – and there are a further four – have irregularities of one sort or another: all belong to the period of the Principate. The earliest example relates to Posides the eunuch who according to Suetonius, was one of Claudius favourite freedmen.[81] He received a *hasta pura* on the occasion of the emperor's triumph over the Britons though there is no evidence as to what he did to merit the decoration. The Epaphroditus recorded on a fragmentary inscription from Rome, and who was awarded multiple *hastae* and *coronae* is doubtless to be equated with the Epaphroditus who was a freedman of Nero.[82] The occasion for the *dona* was almost certainly the Pisonian conspiracy when, as we have seen, other rewards were made for services of a political and not a military nature. One freedman was honoured by an army: this was Numenius, recorded on a fragmentary inscription from Rome. Since the text is incomplete it is not possible to tell whether Numenius had actually served in the army, which army it is that honoured him and for what reason.[83]

This absence of decorated freedman-soldiers reflects no doubt both the social stigma attached to the status of *libertus* and the limited military opportunities which they enjoyed. There was, however, a tendency towards using freedmen, many of whom were well educated, in the civil administration, and here they might hold posts of some military significance. Such was the case with L. Aurelius Nicomedes, a freedman of L. Aelius Caesar who rose to be *praefectus vehiculorum* with responsibility for provisioning the army of Marcus and Verus in Parthia.[84] His status was enhanced above that of the normal freedman by his elevation to the *ordo equester* at the time of Antoninus Pius. While holding the post of *praefectus vehiculorum* Nicomedes was decorated, though not on a generous scale: the awards he received were those appropriate to a military tribune or cavalry prefect rather than to a centenarian procurator. It is probable that Nicomedes' rather irregular path to advancement lies behind the paucity of the *dona* – slave to freedman, elevation to equestrian status and administrative appointments without prior military service. The problems raised by this career are discussed more fully below (p. 130); suffice it here to say that Pflaum's initial reaction to the career, that the *dona* were deliberately kept low to avoid jealousy, may well be the right one.[85] A freedman might occasionally win *dona* but apparently never on quite the same terms as the free-born.

PROCURATORS

The vast majority of imperial procurators would not have been in a position to win *dona militaria* in legitimate circumstances simply because they did not hold jobs which, in the normal course of things, involved them in any way with military activities. The concern of most of them was with civil administration, with financial matters in Rome, in Italy or in the provinces.

The most important exceptions to this generalization are the procurator-governors, prefects of fleets and the men (such as Nicomedes) charged with responsibility for provisioning the armies on campaign. It was presumably these categories, and particularly the first, whom Domaszewski had in mind when he stated that procurators were not eligible to win decorations because they did not possess *imperium*, that is the power to command, with authority over Roman citizens.[86] Domaszewski gave no reasons why he thought a procurator in particular required *imperium* in order to qualify for decorations, nor did he substantiate the proposition that the procurator-governor lacked *imperium*. Far the greater proportion of men who are known to have been decorated did not have *imperium*. Men of equally high status, for example the *comites* or companions of the emperor, certainly did not and yet they clearly were eligible to receive *dona*. Among the companions who accompanied Verus to Parthia was the ex-consul Marcus Claudius Fronto and he is known to have been awarded *dona* on a consular scale.[87] Subsequently he went with Marcus to Germany and was again decorated. There is no good reason to believe that either a governor or any other official for that matter required *imperium* in order to merit *dona*: he certainly required it to award *dona*, but that is a separate issue.

In his masterly study of the procurators Pflaum looked in some detail at the question of the military decorations of the procurator-governors.[88] Careful examination of the careers of two officers who had in the past been quoted as examples of decorated procurators showed that in both cases the awards belonged to an earlier stage in the career. The second set of decorations won by Velius Rufus dates, in all probability, to his tribunate in *cohors XIII urbana* which, despite being based in Carthage, is known from independent evidence to have moved north to take part in Domitian's Danubian wars, while the awards won by Besius Betuinianus relate to his equestrian *militiae*.[89] Hence we are left with no examples of decorated procurator-governors; but this is not to say that procurator-governors were not eligible to win decorations on the relatively few occasions when they were in a position to do so. As Pflaum goes on to argue, there is no reason why, for example, Marcus Antonius Iulianus, procurator of Judaea at the time of the Jewish war of Vespasian and Titus and a member of the counsel of war held by Titus before the siege of Jerusalem, should not as commander of auxiliary troops within the confines of his own province, fighting in a war led by the emperor, have been in a position to receive military distinction.

The issue of the relationship between *imperium* and *dona* has been raised again in connection with a procurator holding the post of *praefectus vehiculorum*. L. Aurelius Nicomedes, the freedman whose career has already been considered briefly above (p. 129), was appointed by Antoninus Pius to the post of *praefectus vehiculorum* which he continued to hold under Marcus and Verus, with additional responsibility for provisioning troops, presumably on the occasion of the Parthian war. In this capacity Nicomedes was awarded military decorations though on a rather paltry scale, receiving only a single *corona*, *hasta* and *vexillum*. The point at issue is why Nicomedes did not receive an award commensurate with the rank of centenarian procurator which he held at the time. In an early discussion of this career Pflaum argued that the reason lay in Nicomedes' humble origins: he was a freedman elevated to the *ordo equester* and given responsible administrative appointments without ever having held any qualifying equestrian military posts. The reward was kept low in order not to arouse jealousy on the part of those who had come up the hard way. Subsequently Pflaum recanted this opinion, suggesting that the decorations were not awarded to Nicomedes in his capacity as *praefectus vehiculorum* because the *praefectus vehiculorum* exercised no *imperium* and therefore was not eligible for decorations.[90] The award was made purely in connection with the *cura copiarum*, a responsibility normally held by an equestrian tribune, a rank to which the scale of decoration is entirely appropriate (below, p. 177).

In support of this contention Pflaum quoted the case of C. Caelius Martialis who served as equestrian tribune of legion *XIII Gemina* in Trajan's first Dacian war and continued in this same post but with additional responsibility for provisioning the army during the second Dacian campaign.[91] It is clear, however, from Pflaum's own list of officers given the care of the *annona* (corn supply) or the *copiae* (general supplies) during wartime, that the responsibility was not one invariably given to a man of a particular rank.[92] M. Rossius Vitulus, for example, had already served as prefect of a cavalry unit before being put in charge of the corn supply on the occasion of Septimius Severus' march on Rome in 193. Tiberius Claudius Candidus had served as military tribune before being appointed *praepositus copiarum* during the German war of Marcus and Commodus. However he, unlike Caelius Martialis, did not hold the two jobs together; nor did he have complete responsibility for the *copiae* for M. Aurelius Papirius Dionysius was in charge of the supplies until they reached the head of the via Flaminia at Rimini. Dionysius, like Nicomedes, held the post of *praefectus vehiculorum*, uniting with it charge for the *copiae*: *praef. vehic. a copiis per viam Flaminiam.*[93] Hence provisioning the armies in wartime was a job with variable responsibility which could be given as appropriate to a junior or a senior official. It would appear to be a job whose status was determined by the seniority of the person who performed it. A rough analogy would be the command of army detachments which could be given to an officer of a seniority appropriate to the exact composition of the detachment, and who, if decorated, would receive awards suitable to his rank.

Thus we return to the point that Nicomedes had the rank of centenarian procurator when he was given responsibility for military provisions. The fact that he was, as *praefectus vehiculorum* in charge of the imperial posting service was no doubt material to his being appointed to the *cura copiarum*:

responsibility for organising and moving supplies is a logical extension of his powers as prefect, not a job completely divorced from them. It is surely no coincidence that Dionysius too linked the prefecture with the *cura copiarum*. That the *praefectus vehiculorum* did not have *imperium* is immaterial: neither did a military tribune, a cavalry prefect or a *praepositus annonae*. It is thus inappropriate to say that Nicomedes received the *dona* due to a military tribune because he was performing a task commonly given to a tribune.

No procurator, be he a procurator-governor or a financial procurator, requires *imperium* to qualify for *dona* any more than does a common soldier, a centurion, a legionary legate or an imperial *comes*. The power to command is relevant where *dona* are being given, not where they are being received. There is no theoretical reason why a procurator performing an appropriate task should not receive military decorations for his services.

The distribution of awards

According to Plutarch, Pompey criticised Lucullus for his practice of distributing gifts and honours while his enemy was still alive, instead of waiting, as was more normal, until the war had been brought to a successful conclusion;[94] Pompey then went ahead and did the same thing himself. The inference from this passage, that the distribution of awards while a war was still in progress was abnormal, is not borne out by any other evidence. Two distinct occasions emerge for the distribution of awards: at the triumph celebrated at the conclusion of a war and on the battlefield immediately following a successful encounter with the enemy, even if that enemy is not as a result yet completely defeated. Hence it was possible for a soldier to be decorated on several occasions within the duration of a single war, the number of occasions being limited in theory only by the number of successful encounters in which that soldier took part. In practice, though two awards for a single campaign is the maximum attested, this is a fairly common occurrence. Vettius Valens and Pellartius Celer both received their first set of decorations while serving in the ranks of the praetorian guard, the one under Claudius in Britain, the other under Titus in Judaea; both subsequently became *evocatus* and by the end of the war in which he was participating each had been awarded a gold crown.[95] The eight *coronae*, eight *hastae* and eight *vexilla* received by M. Cornelius Nigrinus Curiatius Maternus while taking part in Domitian's campaigns on the Danube in the late 80s are most likely to represent two separate awards on the normal four-fold consular scale rather than a single very large award (below, p. 151);[96] the decorations all belong to the period when Nigrinus was serving as a governor of Moesia. M. Valerius Maximianus, on the other hand, had changed unit between his first and second award, though both clearly belong to the same campaign. He was prefect of a quingenary *ala* when he was distinguished with the award of *spolia opima*: no doubt partly because of this distinction he was promoted to the command of a milliary *ala* and in this post was again decorated, both awards belonging to the German war of Marcus and Verus.[97]

These epigraphic records of multiple decoration indicate that there was more than a single occasion when decorations could be distributed: the setting for these award-giving ceremonies is well illustrated in the literary sources. A common time and place for them was on the field of battle on the day of or immediately following a succcessful encounter. Polybius describes how, after a battle, the general called an assembly of the troops, brought forward those deemed to have displayed conspicuous valour, publicly praised them and distributed military awards. The practice does not appear to have changed very much, for the ceremony described by Polybius and which belongs to the middle years of the second century BC is the same in all particulars as that which Josephus describes as having taken place in AD 70 on the day following the capitulation of Jerusalem.[98] Titus called an assembly of the troops, bade the officers read out the name of every man who, in the course of the war, had performed any outstanding exploit, praised them before their colleagues and distributed *dona*. Livy, Caesar and Valerius Maximus all allude to numerous similar scenes.

Except in the cases of those soldiers who have been decorated on more than one occasion within a single war the epigraphic material is rarely sufficiently precise to indicate at what stage in a campaign decorations had been received, whether midway or at its end. However, a delay between the actual winning and the award of decorations is indicated in the case of Claudius Fronto.[99] Fronto was decorated for the part he played in the Parthian war of Marcus and Verus in which he served first as legate of *I Minervia*, a German legion which he took east with him for the campaign, and then as legate of a combined force of legionaries and auxiliaries. Fronto left the east before the completion of the war, for in 165 he was involved in recruiting for Marcus' two new legions, *II* and *III Italica* which were raised in Italy. Now Fronto held the rank of ex-praetor at the time he was fighting in Parthia, but the *dona* he received, four *coronae*, four *hastae* and four *vexilla* were those of an ex-consul: his decorations must therefore have been deferred to the end of the war, probably to the occasion of the triumph which was celebrated in 166, by which time Fronto had presumably been elevated to the consulate. The decorations of the senators are so standardized that it is singularly unlikely that service as a legate would otherwise merit the *dona* of a consular (below, p. 149).

Award-giving ceremonies at the conclusion of a campaign or at the triumph are again indicated by the literary sources. After his successful recovery of Pontus in 47 BC Caesar split up his army, ordering the sixth legion back to Italy to receive its rewards and honours (*praemia atque honores*): presumably military decorations are included here.[100] The young Augustus received *dona militaria* at Caesar's African triumph though he had not been old enough to take part in the campaign, while Posides the eunuch was awarded his *hasta pura* at Claudius' British triumph alongside soldiers who had served in the field.[101] In AD 12 Tiberius celebrated a triumph on the conclusion of his campaigns in Illyricum, and Velleius Paterculus records that his brother, Magius Celer Velleianus, received generous *dona* on the occasion of the triumph, this despite the fact that the celebration had had to be postponed because of affairs in Germany.[102]

Many of the campaigns for which *dona* were awarded did not end in a formal triumph, so these rewards must have been distributed on the battlefields following the individual encounters or at a ceremony held for that purpose at the conclusion of the war. Precisely what happened in the case of Trajan's Parthian war can only be a matter of speculation. The emperor died before the war had been formally brought to an end, though no further active campaigning took place after his death. All the inscriptions recording *dona* for the Parthian war indicate that they were given by Trajan: many of these decorations were doubtless given in the course of the war while Trajan was still alive. Some however were probably reserved to the occasion of the triumph, for a unique posthumous triumph was celebrated, and these too were considered as having been awarded by Trajan himself, having been won under his auspices and presented at his triumph despite the fact that Hadrian was then emperor. Awards presented on Trajan's behalf were regarded, according to the evidence of the inscriptions, as having been given by him. This is indicative of what no doubt often occurred, an emperor's deputy making the presentations on his behalf. In particular this must have happened on the occasion of those wars in which the emperor did not participate and for which no triumph was celebrated. It is possible of course that a special investiture was held in Rome on the conclusion of the campaign, but it is much more likely that the presentation of the decorations was made, not by the emperor himself, but by whoever had waged the war on his behalf and that it took place in the province from which the troops had come or in the area where the war had been waged.

Recommendation for decoration

Most of the evidence which we have about military awards relates to the culmination of the process, to the nature of the decorations themselves, to the men who won them and the circumstances in which they were won. Very little is said of the procedure by which recommendations were made as to who should be decorated, of who it was who assembled the information on the names, ranks and suggested awards of those who had performed outstanding acts of bravery. The one specific piece of evidence we have indicates a practice which was doubtless atypical, for it indicates a legionary soldier, T. Camulius Lavenus, being honoured by the emperor through the vote of his fellows (*ex volumtate imp. Hadriani Aug. torquibus et armillis aureis suffragio legionis honorat.*).[103] The case is unique as far as actual evidence goes, but it no doubt points to an acceptable practice whereby a deserving soldier whose valour had perhaps been overlooked by his superiors, could be recommended for decoration by his peers. A somewhat similar situation exists in the modern British army whereby the officers and men of a unit can vote Victoria Crosses to their comrades.[104]

When the general himself was present on the field of battle it would be possible for him to observe personally some of those worthy of receiving decorations. For example, at the encounter which brought to a conclusion the siege of Antonia, Titus' officers prevailed upon him to watch rather than participate in the battle: 'if Caesar were watching every man would fight to the death. Yielding to their arguments Caesar explained to the men that he was staying behind for one purpose only, to be judges of their exploits, so that no brave man should go unrewarded, no coward unpunished through not being seen, and to be an eye-witness of every deed, able as he was both to punish and reward.'[105] But the general could not be everywhere, see everything, and in order that all the men be treated equitably it would be necessary for each and every officer to observe and make recommendations on those under his command. Something similar is recorded by Caesar who, in the context of his campaign against Ariovistus in 58 BC, notes that he put *legati* and a *quaestor* in command of each legion so that they might be witness to every man's valour.[106] Scipio was evidently relying on the reports of his subordinates in the matter of who first scaled the wall of New Carthage when he decided to award the *corona muralis* to both claimants. He was, we are told, reliably informed that they had reached the top together.[107] In the case of decorations of this type awarded to the man first over a wall, or first over a rampart, the would-be recipients were called on to declare themselves rather than being nominated by those in authority. This fact is clear both from Livy's account of the disputed claim at New Carthage and also in Valerius Maximus' account of the ceremony following the capture of the camp of the Bruttii and Lucani at Thurium when no claimant came forward.[108] Participants in the encounter who were witnesses to the deed could be called upon to adjudicate, should any claim for the honour be challenged.

The one case of which we know of an officer recommending a soldier for award is that of the freedman soldier, whom T. Labienus recommended to Scipio as being worthy of receiving gold *armillae*. Scipio took his officer's advice but only in part, for, as we have seen, the soldier was given not gold but silver *armillae* in view of his status as freedman.[109]

No more specific evidence is available; the rest is conjecture. It is apparent from the several accounts of award-giving ceremonies that a list of potential recipients was prepared, giving the name and rank of the soldiers and the citations of their awards. The background information on each soldier concerned must have been provided by the secretariat of the unit to which he belonged, while the detail of the act of bravery which was being rewarded was perhaps supplied by whoever it was who witnessed it being done. A further recommendation would probably be made as to the suitable decoration or combination of decorations to be awarded, the basis for which must have been a written code of practice. It would then presumably be the general's task to chose from those cases put up to him just whom he would decorate, or to accept without question the recommendations of his advisors. It is clear from the evidence of the Principate that the emperors exercised considerable personal discretion in the matter of decorations.

There is good reason to believe that much care and attention was paid to maintaining a fair system of reward. The literary sources stress time and again that the morale of the army was maintained by the just application of reward and punishment – 'by rewarding good soldiers they avoid seeming harsh to the men they punish' and again 'no-one who had been prepared to put more into it than the next man should get less than his due'.[110] To live up to this, required strict parity of treatment and scrupulous care in the selection of those chosen to be publicly distinguished and raised above their colleagues. As with all such schemes it was open to abuse, though most of the evidence we have for this comes from abnormal periods of civil strife. Among all the complaints which, over the years, the army registered in its various ways against bad conditions, irregular or insufficient pay, unfair treatment in the matter of rewarding bravery in the field features not at all.

Proportion of soldiers decorated

The surviving evidence for the officers and men of the Roman army is so partial that it will never be possible to work out a reliable figure for the proportion of serving soldiers who received military decorations. One thing which is certain, however, is that *dona militaria* never became campaign medals simply designed to acknowledge the active participation of a soldier in a given campaign: the individual who wished to receive a decoration of any sort had to fight harder, better and more successfully than those around him.

The only basis for any statistical analysis are the surviving lists of soldiers serving in particular units. Three of these lists designate certain soldiers with the letters *d.d.*, presumed to indicate decorations received, *donis donatus*. The earliest of these lists relates to men recruited to the praetorian guard in Rome between 153 and 156 AD, who will have been discharged between 169 and 172 after their standard sixteen-year term of service. During this period they could have accompanied the emperor Verus on his Parthian campaign (162–166) and Marcus and Verus on the early part of the German war of 166–175. Members of the praetorian guard are known from individual career inscriptions to have been present and won *dona* on both these occasions.[111]

The list is incomplete but, of the sixty-nine men, the relevant part of whose name survives (the *d.d.* precedes the name), nine were decorated, that is about thirteen per cent. This is a considerably higher number than is attested on the stone from Kostolac near Viminacium in Moesia Superior, where legion *VII Claudia* was stationed in the later second century. In a list of men enrolled in the legion in 169 and discharged in 195 ten out of 150 men are designated *d.d.*, slightly under seven per cent. *VII Claudia* is not directly attested as having participated in any warfare at this time, but it is logical to assume that it fought in the German wars of Marcus, Verus and Commodus. The other legion of Moesia Superior, *IIII Flavia*, certainly did participate in the first German war at least.[112] Also the participation of *VII Claudia* in the second German war would provide a satisfactory context for the transfer of the centurion P. Aelius Romanus from *VII Claudia* to *III Augusta*, the legion stationed in Numidia, but which is known to have sent a detachment to the Danubian frontier in the 170s.[113] The third list, which is undated, is assumed from its findspot, Albanum south-east of Rome, to belong to legion *II Parthica* which was raised in about 197 in advance of Severus' second Parthian war. The text is fragmentary and few names survive, with just one soldier designated *d.d.*[114]

These lists indicate a far higher proportion of decorated men in the ranks than would be assumed from the individual career records. They may be atypical, but they do indicate the dangers of making statistical assumptions on the basis of the fragmentary evidence available. All that one can get with any confidence is an impression. One impression which comes over strongly is the far higher proportion of officers who were decorated. This is certainly due in part to a bias in the evidence, the weighting in the quality and quantity of detailed evidence towards the top end of the social scale, both because the historians were naturally interested in people of significance, and because the rich put up more and fuller inscriptions than did the poor. However, even taking into account the bias in the material officers clearly had a proportionately far higher chance of winning *dona* than did their subordinates. This is hardly surprising. The one commander-in-chief who planned the strategy successfully executed by an army of thousands, the legate who led a legion of five thousand, the prefect or tribune at the head of 500 or 1,000 auxiliaries – all these stood a high chance of winning decorations: success lay ultimately in the hands of the many but this in its turn depended on good organisation and inspired leadership. Centurions too figure largely in the rolls of honour: 'the highest form of personal courage is required rather in the leader at the lower level – he who has to plunge into the turmoil of the battlefield',[115] and this certainly applied in the case of the centurion. The point is brought home in Caesar's account of a battle against the Nervii in 57 BC when the Roman army suffered substantial losses.[116] Of the twelfth legion he wrote: 'all the centurions of the fourth cohort had been slain and a standard-bearer likewise and a standard was lost; almost all the centurions of the other cohorts were wounded or killed, among them the chief centurion, P. Sextius Baculus, bravest of men, who was overcome by many grievous wounds so that he could no longer hold himself upright.' This episode brings to mind Polybius' description of the qualities required of a centurion: 'they do not desire them so much to be men who will initiate attacks and open the battle, but men who will hold their ground when worsted and hard-pressed and be ready to die at their posts.'[117] The standard-bearers too were particularly vulnerable, being often called on to display courage above the ordinary. They headed the units into battle and if they faltered the army faltered. Witness for example the behaviour of the eagle-bearer of the tenth legion on the occasion of the invasion of Britain by Caesar in 55 BC.[118] The men were holding back for fear of the depth of the sea into which they had to plunge, when the standard-bearer cried out 'Leap down soldiers unless you wish to betray your eagle to the enemy; it shall be told that I at any rate did my duty to my country and my general'. So saying he jumped down from the ship, bearing the eagle towards the enemy. 'Then our troops exhorted one another not to allow so terrible a disgrace and leapt down from the ship of one accord.' It was courage such as this which frequently earned for the standard-bearer the *dona militaria*, earned them that is when the man survived. As the passage above indicates the mortality rate among these officers was high and the Romans do not appear to have awarded medals posthumously. The evidence regarding posthumous awards is entirely negative; there is no positive statement to the effect that the Romans honoured only their live and not their dead heroes, but neither is there any statement to the contrary nor any single case of a soldier who must have been decorated after death. There is no reason to believe that the fine decorations illustrated on the cenotaph of Marcus Caelius who died in the Varus disaster of AD 9 were awarded to him posthumously (pl. 2a). On the contrary, the circumstances of his death in one of the most ignominious defeats ever suffered by the Roman army preclude the award of decorations. The *dona* must belong to an earlier stage in his career.[119] It is notable that, of the two Canuleius brothers who fought for Caesar in Gaul, both serving in legion VII, only Caius who survived received military decorations. Quintus who was killed did not. To deny the possibility of posthumous awards is to accept an argument *ex silentio* with all its inherent weaknesses, but the total quantity of evidence on the whole question of *dona militaria* is such as to justify the belief that had such a practice existed it would have been reflected in some way in the available evidence.

Ignoring completely the literary evidence which too rarely gives details of rank, the proportions of officers and men decorated in the period from Caesar to Severus are as shown in Table A. The standard-bearers have been singled out from among the junior officers of the legion because they form the largest single category of *principalis* to receive *dona*. The total numbers are not large but the proportion, 20 per cent of the group, is significant. The single most

TABLE A   NUMBERS OF DECORATED SOLDIERS · BY RANK

RANK	DATE						TOTAL
	Julio-Cl	*Flavian*	*Nerva-Hadrian*	*Antonine*	*Severan*	*?*	
COMES	1	0	3	6	0	0	10
PROVINCIAL GOVERNOR	0	3	5	0	0	0	8
LEGION							
Leg. leg.	0	4	7	5	0	0	16
Trib. lat.	2	4	5	2	0	2	15
Praef. castr.	1	0	1	0	0	0	2
Trib. ang.	7	1	6	2	0	0	16
Primus pilus	4	0	1	0	0	0	5
Senior centurio	0	4	3	3	0	0	10
Centurio	3	12	9	2	0	3	29
Signif/aquilif	3	1	0	0	0	2	6
Miles	18	2	1	2	1	0	24
PRAETORIAN GUARD							
Praef. praet.	0	0	0	2	0	0	2
Trib. praet.	1	0	0	0	0	0	1
Senior centurio	0	0	1	0	1	1	3
Centurio	0	0	1	0	0	1	2
Evocatus	1	3	3	0	0	0	7
Signifer	0	0	0	0	0	0	0
Miles	2	2	5	2	0	2	13
URBAN COHORT							
Praef. urb.	0	0	0	0	0	0	0
Trib. urb.	1	2	0	0	0	0	3
Centurio urb.	0	3	0	0	0	0	3
Miles	0	0	0	0	0	0	0
AUXILIA							
Praef. alae M	0	0	0	2	0	0	2
Praef. alae D	2	1	4	2	0	0	9
Trib. coh. M	0	0	1	1	0	0	2
Praef. coh. D	2	3	3	1	0	0	9
Centurio/decurio	1	2	1	0	0	2	6
Miles aux.	1	0	1	0	0	0	2
VEXILLATIONS							
Praefecti & Senators	0	3	0	0	1	0	4
praepositi Equestrians	1	0	1	4	0	1	7
TOTAL	51	50	62	36	3	14	216

striking figure is the number of 'other ranks' decorated in the Julio-Claudian period, largely during the years of active campaigning under Augustus in Spain, Illyricum and Germany. There are a number of possible explanations. Firstly, there is the intensity of the fighting at this period, though this alone will not account for the disproportionate number of ordinary soldiers, for in overall terms roughly the same number of cases of decoration is known for the Flavian period and considerably more under Trajan and Hadrian. Another factor which must be taken into account is the result of the generous donatives received by the armies of Augustus. The tombstones of the soldiers who died at about this time are generally finer than those of later periods, often including sculptural detail. For example sixteen of the stones of Augustan legionaries show *dona* in relief (and in only two of these cases are they also referred to in the text) and this is twice as many as the whole of the post-Augustan examples put together. The unusually high quality of the evidence may therefore be creating something of a false impression, but even bearing this in mind the contrast is so great that there must be some other contributory factor. The reason may well lie in the fact that the Julio-Claudian period saw the final throes of the republican system of decoration. Standard combinations of award were only just being worked out and decoration was still tied to the individual and his particular exploit. It is hardly surprising that, once it was no longer necessary to leap over walls and ramparts and physically strike against the enemy in order to win awards, more of the senior officers were decorated for their part in directing operations and proportionately fewer awards went to those who carried out these directions in the field.

The number of occasions on which the imperial *comites* were decorated need occasion no surprise. These men had the eye and the ear of the emperor. The figure is dominated by the ex-consuls who acted as companions and no doubt also as military advisers to Marcus, Verus and Commodus during their campaigns against the Parthians and Germans in the 160s and 170s. The absence of provincial governors receiving decorations at this same period is probably no coincidence: it suggests that the *comites* were supplanting the governors in their military capacity in times of war, that, when the emperor was present as commander-in-chief, accompanied by men selected in part for their military expertise, the governor from whose province the campaign was being launched was not necessarily needed to help lead the army. The governor was, after all, only the emperor's deputy, in charge of the province during his necessary absence. When the emperor was present there was bound to be some significant change in the status of the governor and the extent of his *imperium*. The case of Severus in Britain is instructive. Severus came to Britain with his two sons, Caracalla and Geta, and according to the testimony of Herodian when preparations for the campaign were ready he and Caracalla advanced against the enemy while the younger son, Geta, was left behind in the province 'to see to the judicial and civil aspects of government', that is to carry on the governor's normal non-military tasks.[121]

The largest single category of decorated soldier is, predictably, that of the centurions, the backbone of the army, whose vital role in time of war has already been emphasized.

The wearing of decorations

The majority of modern decorations, military or civil, come in the form of medals and sashes which can be pinned to or worn over tunic or jacket on formal occasions. When he is not wearing the medal, the recipient may have the ribbon of the order sewn or pinned onto his uniform. Etiquette lays down when decorations shall or shall not be worn. Something similar existed in the Roman world, this much is clear. There were certain occasions both military and civil when it was appropriate for military decorations to be worn. But how did one 'wear' decorations which consisted of collections of full-sized crowns, spears and flags in addition to large medals, bracelets and neck-rings?

Little trouble arises over the common soldier wishing to display a single standard set of two *torques*, two *armillae* and *phalerae*. Several sculptures show how these were worn with uniform, one *armilla* on each wrist, the *phalerae* on a harness over the cuirass (above p. 93) and the *torques*, normally awarded in pairs, suspended one on either side of the harness at the top of the chest (pl. 2a, 2b, 11a). Such paraphernalia was however unsuited to wearing with tunic or toga so presumably was worn only when the soldier was in military uniform.

Problems multiply as soon as one deviates from this standard set which is pictorially so well represented. Though the three types of award – *torques*, *armillae* and *phalerae* – commonly appear in combination, one or other can be omitted. Omission of one of the *armillae* creates no difficulty (pl. 11a), but omission of one of the *torques* raises a crucial point. Was the single ring worn on one side of the chest or was it worn native-fashion around the neck? And what happened if *torques* were awarded but no *phalerae*? The pictorial evidence suggests that where both were given, the *torques* were attached to straps of the *phalera* harness; the one exception is the Caelius stone where the *torques* are slung from a length of fabric which appears to go around behind the neck, independent of the harness. They could presumably be worn thus when no *phalerae* were present. Full military uniform will presumably have included the helmet, but the soldier who had won a crown will have had to discard this on ceremonial occasions in order to wear his decoration. The crowns were clearly life-size and meant for wearing not just for display. Marcus Agrippa, for example, is shown wearing a *corona navalis*, Marcus Caelius a *corona civica*, Quintus Sertorius a *corona aurea* (pl. 1c, 2a, 2b). If a soldier had more than one crown he would doubtless have chosen to wear the most prestigious. This problem arises in the case of M. Caelius. If he was decorated as a centurion, as he probably was, he is likely to have received a crown, *muralis, vallaris* or *aurea*, in addition to his *torques*, *armillae* and *phalerae*. However, there is no way of knowing if in fact he did because his tombstone shows him wearing a *corona civica*, indicating that he had saved the life of a Roman citizen, a rarer and greater honour. The civic crown, being made of foliage, would have had to be woven anew every time it was required. One ingenious solution to the problem of multiple crowns is shown on a coin of Marcus Agrippa which shows him wearing a *corona muralis et navalis*, a mural crown with beaks at the front (pl. 1d).

But what was done on formal occasions with those decorations which could not be worn, the *hastae* and *vexilla* awarded to senior officers or the large collections of lesser awards which their subordinates might amass in the course of a long military career? The literary evidence on what was done with decorations is unspecific and not very helpful. Tacitus' description of the march of Vitellius' troops on Rome in AD 69 speaks of the soldiers as being resplendent with their arms and decorations (*armis donisque fulgentes*).[122] Military decorations were also worn on the occasion of the triumph. All who took part in the triumphal procession were wreathed in laurel while each man was adorned with the decorations he had won. At the triumph of Papirius in 293 BC the infantry and cavalry marched or rode past wearing their decorations: 'Many civic, rampart and mural crowns were to be seen'.[123] Valerius Maximus tells us that on the nine occasions when Siccius Dentatus followed the triumphal carriage of his generals the eyes of the city were drawn to him by the number of his decorations. These decorations 'went before him'; who carried them we are not told, his slaves perhaps?[124]

It is unlikely that decorations were ever worn on the battlefield. A number of literary passages have been used to indicate that they were, but each is capable of more than one interpretation. The first passage comes from Caesar's Gallic wars. The Roman army, caught unawares by the enemy, had no time to prepare properly for battle neither to remove the covers from their shields, to put on their helmets nor to put on their *insignia* – *ad insignia accommodanda*.[125] The word *insignia* has here been construed as meaning military decorations. The term certainly *can* be used in this sense – Livy, for example, refers to the *corona obsidionalis* worn by Publius Decius as one of his *insignia* – but equally it has a much wider application, meaning any sort of distinguishing mark or trait.[126] For example, in AD 69 when the armoury was opened up for Otho's soldiers to collect arms and equipment, they are described by Tacitus as having seized them in a disorderly fashion with no attempt to distinguish praetorian or legionary by their proper *insignia*. Elsewhere Varro, discussing the *paludamentum*, a cloak, describes it as the *insignia*, the distinguishing mark, of soldiers specifically of a general: *Paluda a paludamentis. Haec insignia atque ornamenta militaria*. In a non-military context Livy notes that fine clothing and an elegant appearance are the *insignia* of women.[127] So wide therefore are the applications of the word that the context alone can determine in what sense it is being used. In the Caesarian context there is nothing to indicate that decorations rather than other distinctive pieces of military equipment are meant. Tacitus uses the word in an equally ambiguous fashion when describing the mutinous Rhine army in AD 14. Drusus was sent to put down the revolt and was met by the legions in grim mood *neque insignibus fulgentes* ('nor resplendent with their *insignia*'). This passage recalls the description, also by Tacitus, of the march of Vitellius' troops into Rome *armis donisque fulgentes*.[128] In this latter passage when *dona* are meant they are clearly specified. *Insignia* is an imprecise term; it is doubtful if it would be used, without further clarification, in so precise a sense.

Another ambiguous passage belongs to the period of the civil war of AD 69: the seventh legion mutinied outside Verona where they had been set to build an outer rampart to the city. Antonius Primus attempts to restore order, appealing personally to those soldiers whom he knew and to others distinguished by military honours (*et aliquo militari decore insignem*).[129] This phrase could be taken to mean that the men were actually wearing military decorations but on the other hand it could equally well indicate simply that these men were distinguished by having, in the past, received military honours. Given the context of the passage, a mutiny occurring during a building job, commonsense indicates the latter alternative. To wear decorations in battle was to risk loss or damage to what were intrinsically, as well no doubt as sentimentally, valuable items. It is a moot point as to whether they would have been safer firmly attached to their owner or left behind in camp or baggage train.

There were certain non-military occasions on which *dona* could be brought out. Polybius tells us that those who received decorations were made famous on their return to their homes, for they took part in religious processions when only those on whom awards had been bestowed by the consul were allowed to wear decorations.[130] At the games, too, crowns could be worn. According to Livy soldiers (presumably those who had just been involved in the war against the Samnites) first wore *dona* at the games in 292 BC. We learn from Pliny too that the *corona civica* was worn at the games, in fact, by implication, at all public spectacles, since the recipient of the civic crown was entitled to wear it for the rest of his life.[131] Finally we see them on show in a court room when a witness quotes his distinguished military record as evidence of good character. It is not clear from the text whether the man was actually wearing the decorations or whether they were simply displayed before him. The word used, *gerens*, could equally well mean either.[132]

When not being worn by or processed before their owners the *dona* would presumably be deposited somewhere safe. This might be at the family home or, in the case of the soldiers of the Principate, in the strongroom of the fort or fortress where the unit's valuables were kept. Alternatively they might be put on display. This certainly was the case with the spoils of the enemy which, according to both Polybius and Livy, were kept in a most conspicuous place, fastened to the walls of the house that they might serve as a visible reminder of the bravery of the men who had been awarded them.[133] Sulla, having been presented by his army with a siege crown after the siege of Nola during the Social War is said to have had the scene of the award painted on the walls of his villa:[134] the siege crown itself, being made of grass, would not have been a suitable subject for permanent display. This reference to *militaria* painted on the walls of a villa recalls the decoration in the atrium of the villa at Oplontis in Campania. Architectural motifs are painted on the walls and a row of oval shields adorns the spaces between the pseudo-columns, perhaps in com-memoration of some military episode in the life of a sometime owner of the villa.[135] Pliny expresses some doubt as to the veracity of the tale about Sulla, but what is important in the present context is that the story is consistent with the whole idea of using decorations, spoils and the like as outward signs of the inward quality of courage: it is precisely that same desire for recognition which led Sertorius to regard with pride the loss of an eye, a loss which he prized above decorations, because unlike the *dona* which could be displayed only on particular occasions it was with him always, a permanent and visible testament to his bravery.[136]

CHAPTER VII

IMPERIAL SCALES OF AWARD · THE SENATORS

Senators are, in relation to their overall numbers, exceptionally well represented in the statistics of decorated soldiers. This point is clearly illustrated in Table A. Not only were they, as officers, in the sorts of position that naturally drew attention to them but their exploits were of interest to the historians: they were the aristocracy, members often of famous families whose deeds were of more than local significance. Moreover, they belonged to the inscription-minded levels of society and were commemorated not only by their tombstones but often by texts set up in their honour, as for example by cities of which they were patron.

There were several stages in their careers at which senators could find themselves in a position to win military glory. While a well-connected patrician senator could rise through the senatorial magistracies without undertaking any military command, a plebeian senator who wished to pursue a successful career would have to employ his talents in the service of the Emperor, holding commands in the legions, governing the provinces where the empire's military might was concentrated, provinces where there were wars to be fought, Britain, Germany, Pannonia, Moesia, Dacia, Syria. As Alföldy has pointed out, by the middle years of the second century AD the only senators who had any hope of the consulate were those who were active in the imperial administration or who performed some other form of service to the emperor, that is the patricians who served as *quaestor Augusti* and acted as *comes*, or companion, to the emperor when he was on campaign, and those plebeian senators who commanded the legions and governed the imperial praetorian provinces.[1] The emperor's concern was to provide himself with senators competent to govern on his behalf in areas where the army played a vital offensive and defensive role: hence the emperor's men needed to combine civil with military experience. The emperor would ensure that his nominees were elected to the necessary qualifying magistracies, to the quaestorship, praetorship and consulate, so that the imperial provinces were provided with governors of the right calibre and experience. These are the men who figure large in the statistics of decorated soldiers. Fig. 3 summarizes the typical career ladder of such a man, indicating the steps by which he would progress to high command, though omitting the range of civil administrative posts which he might also hold from time to time on his way to the top. A year or two spent in Rome as curator of one of the Italian roads or in charge of the water supply was of value not so much for the experience of the job itself but because it gave the senator an opportunity to spend some time close to the seat of power, in close touch with the emperor for whom he was deputizing in the provinces. In addition to serving the emperor in the capacities indicated, a senator – particularly a patrician senator – might also accompany the *princeps* on campaign in the capacity of *comes* or companion. These companions were, like the tribunes and legates, eligible to win military decorations. With but one exception the senators decorated as *comites* were ex-consuls; the one exception is Publius Aelius Hadrianus, the future emperor, who when not yet quaestor accompanied Trajan to the first Dacian war.

The determining factor as far as the size of the award was concerned was the position held within the hierarchy of senatorial magistracies, whether the decorations were won before entering the senate as quaestor, that is merely with tribunician status, as ex-quaestor, as ex-praetor or ex-consul. Hence if a man held a legionary tribunate and followed this by an extraordinary command, as for example over a vexillation sent on campaign, the same scale of award would apply to both posts unless a magistracy intervened. Similarly the same basic scale applied to the legionary legate and the legate of a one legion province who combined the role of legionary commander with that of provincial governor: both were *praetorius*, ex-praetors. For the same reason the governor of a three-legion province was decorated on the same scale as the governor of a two legion province: both were ex-consuls.

Clear scales of award for these different categories of senator had emerged by the mid-Flavian period, and once established they did not undergo any apparent alterations or additions; they had no need to. The structure of the senatorial career itself changed not at all between the Flavian period and the date at which decorations generally ceased to be awarded: all that altered from time to time was the rating of the individual provinces as boundaries were changed or legions moved. The basic scales of award were as follows:

Tribunicius	2 coronae (muralis, vallaris)	2 hastae	2 vexilla
Quaestorius	—	—	—
Praetorius	3 coronae (muralis, vallaris, aurea)	3 hastae	3 vexilla
Consular	4 coronae muralis, vallaris, aurea, classica)		4 vexilla

As no military posts were normally held between the quaestorship and the praetorship no allowance was made for decoration at this rank in the set scales.

In practice of course a man might be appointed to an extraordinary command at this stage in his career or he might, exceptionally, serve as imperial *comes*. In such a case the award made could in theory be down-graded to that of the ex-tribune or upgraded to that of the ex-praetor, the determining factor presumably being the nature and degree of responsibility of the job in hand and the dignity of the recipient when he actually received his reward. There is no clear uncomplicated example to illustrate the point, not surprisingly for the very fact of a senator being appointed to a military post in the interval between his quaestorship and praetorship implies that something untoward was occurring. One such case is that of Cn. Domitius Tullus who was ex-quaestor when appointed to the command of a group of auxiliary units (*praefectus auxiliorum omnium adversus Germanos*). It was only while holding this command that he was designated praetor. Tullus held this command either in succession to or at the same time as his brother, Cn. Domitius Lucanus, who had already been praetor prior to going to Germany. Lucanus and Tullus both received military decorations: Lucanus naturally received them on the praetorian scale and so too, not surprisingly, did Tullus who was apparently fulfilling precisely the same duties as had his brother and who was moreover praetor by the time he actually received his decorations. However, such examples as there are of senators below the rank of praetor holding such commands all belong to the pre- or early Flavian period before all such irregularities in the senatorial career had finally been ironed out.

Table B shows the decorations known to have been awarded to senators in the period from Domitian to Commodus. The Hadrianic period stands out as being distinctly anomalous. There are only two clear cases dating to this time but both are odd. Lollius Urbicus was an ex-praetor who had already held a legionary command when he was appointed to serve as a legate with Hadrian in the Jewish war. The decorations he received, a single gold crown and a *hasta*, are considerably less than a tribune, let alone a legionary legate, might normally expect to receive and comparable to the award made at the same period to senior centurions (for example Arrius Clemens, table I and p. 194). It is less than was awarded during the same campaign to the unknown senator who probably succeeded Urbicus as legate of *X Fretensis* in Judaea and who received two crowns (*muralis* and *vallaris*) in addition to a single *hasta*. The records of decorations given to two other Hadrianic senators, Fuficius Cornutus and C. Iulius Thraso Alexander are defective, so little useful information can be drawn from them: the one thing that is clear is that in neither case has the maximum award for a senatorial tribune been given, both having received only a single *vexillum*. The conclusion which emerges from this rather sparse evidence is consistent with the picture painted by the equestrian *dona* of the same period (below, p. 176): Hadrian was distinctly sparing in his awards to his more senior officers. He in no way followed the trend which had been firmly established in the Flavian and Trajanic periods

TABLE B SENATORIAL DONA · DOMITIAN TO COMMODUS

DATE	NAME	RANK	DECORATIONS		
			coronae	*hastae*	*vexilla*
Domitianic	T. Iulius Maximus				
	Manlianus	trib leg	2	[2]	1
	L. Roscius Celer	trib vex	2	2	2
	[–.S]atrius Sep [. . . . . .]	trib leg	2	2	2
	P. Baebius Italicus	leg leg	3	3	[3?]
	L. Caesennius Sospes	leg leg	3	3	3
	M. Cornelius Nigrinus	leg prov (cos)⎫	8⁴	8⁴	8⁴
	M. Cornelius Nigrinus	leg prov (cos)⎭	4	4	4
	L. Funisulanus Vettonianus	leg prov (cos)	4	4	4
Trajanic	L. Minicius Natalis	leg leg	3	3	[3?]
	IGLS I 123	[leg leg]	[3?]	3	2
	L. Catilius Severus	leg prov (cos)	3?	[4?]	4
	Q. Glitius Atilius Agricola	leg prov (cos)	4	4	4
	Q. Sosius Senecio	comes (cos)⎫	8⁴	8⁴	8⁴
	Q. Sosius Senecio	comes (cos)⎭	4	4	4
	CIL XII 3169	? (cos)	[4?]	4	[4?]
Hadrianic	Q. Fuficius Cornutus	[trib leg]	1+	?	1
	C. Iulius Thraso Alexander	[trib leg]	[2?]	2	1
	Q. Lollius Urbicus	leg imp (praet)	1	1	0
	CIL XI 6339	leg leg	2	1	0
Antonine	[– Iunius Maximus]	trib leg	2	[2?]	1
	IRT 552	trib leg	2	?	1+
	Q. Antistius Adventus	leg leg	3	3	2
	M. Claudius Fronto	leg leg/leg aux	4	4	4
	C. Vettius Sabinianus	leg prov (praet)	3	2	2
	M. Pontius Laelianus	comes (cos)	4	[4?]	[4?]

and which was resumed by the later Antonine emperors. He was a law unto himself. This fits well with the character of Hadrian as it emerges from the literary sources. He was much concerned with the restoration of firm discipline to the army, stamping out laxness and irregular practices. He shared camp fare and expected nothing of his men which he himself was not ready to endure, presumably expecting his officers to do likewise rather than indulging themselves in the assumed privileges of rank. Tightening up on decorations fits into this general pattern: it is significant that Hadrian's parsimony where his officers were concerned did not extend to the centurionate and below.

Leaving aside therefore the Hadrianic period, the pattern of senatorial *dona* is singularly consistent. The full two-fold, three-fold and four-fold scales are maxima: the award often falls below this but never much so and with but one exception it is always the number of *hastae* and *vexilla* which is reduced, never the number of crowns. However many *hastae* and *vexilla* were combined with them it is clear that the two, three and four crowns were almost invariably given and always in the same combinations, the *muralis* and *vallaris* to the tribune, the *muralis*, *vallaris* and *aurea* to the ex-praetor, the *muralis*, *vallaris*, *aurea* and *classica* (or *navalis*) to the ex-consul. During the Principate no-one but a consular is known ever to have received a naval crown: while gold, mural and rampart crowns were also distributed in various combinations among centurions, equestrians and other senators, not even the most eminent of these qualified for the naval crown. The decorations of the praetorian prefect were closely comparable to those of the consular: they differed in just the one respect, that they lacked the naval crown (below, p. 206). The *corona navalis* therefore emerges as the signature of the ex-consul. The reason for its pre-eminence probably lies in its rarity value; it is the crown which, during the republican period, was used least, there being just one or possibly two attested examples of its award (above, p. 74). The one apparent exception to this rule relating to the naval crown, the case of M. Claudius Fronto, is in fact the exception which proves the rule. Claudius Fronto won his military decorations on the occasion of the Parthian war of Marcus and Verus in which he served in two praetorian posts, first as legate of legion *I Minervia* which he took east for the war from its base in Dacia, and then as commander of an army of legionaries and auxiliaries campaigning in the east, in Armenia, Osrhoene and Anthemusia. Before the war had ended he left the battle front, becoming involved in AD 165 in recruiting for Marcus' two new legions, *II* and *III Italica*. He won military decorations on the full consular scale, four *coronae*, four *hastae* and four *vexilla* although he had campaigned as ex-praetor and not as ex-consul. However, if his award was deferred to the occasion of the Parthian triumph in AD 166, as it very probably was, he may well have held the rank of consular at the time he actually received the decoration. The precise date of his consulate cannot be proved but he is known to have been a *comes* of Verus during the German war which began in AD 166, and all the known *comites* of this period were of consular rank, while prior to his death in AD 170 he had been governor first of Moesia Superior and then of Moesia plus Dacia during the reorganisation of the administration of these provinces. There can be little doubt that he was appointed consul in 165 or 166 and hence received the *dona* fitting to his present rather than to his past status.

The one apparent departure from standard practice is the case of Catilius Severus: he was decorated as governor of Cappadocia and Armenia Major and Minor, a post which must date to the time of Trajan's Parthian war, to that short period between the conquest of greater Armenia and its abandonment by Hadrian. The command was a consular one of some significance and yet a crown, the *corona aurea*, has been omitted from the standard consular combination. Trajan was consistently generous in his awards to senators, rarely dropping below the maximum, so the case of Severus is a strange anomaly both within its period and within senatorial *dona* as a whole. It would be convenient to explain it away as a stone-cutter's error, and indeed this may well be the correct explanation, but without corroborative evidence this convenient hypothesis can be neither proved nor disproved.

Hadrian apart, the emperors from the Flavian period onwards awarded decorations to senators on a consistent basis, unvarying in the numbers of crowns, but flexible as regards the *hastae* and *vexilla*: in this way it was possible, within the parameters laid down, to recognize individual merit. Even these variations seem to fall into a pattern; frequently one *vexillum* less than the norm was awarded, occasionally one *vexillum* and one *hasta* less, giving the following:

Tribunicius	max	2 coronae	2 hastae	2 vexilla	
		2	2	1	?
	min	2	1	1	?
Praetorius	max	3	3	3	
		3	3	2	
	min	3	2	2	
Consular	max	4	4	4	
		[4	4	3	]
	min	[4	3	3	]

In practice not all of these gradations are attested. Catilius Severus apart, there is no evidence for the consular ever receiving other than the maximum and it may well be that the other hypothetical combinations were never used. All three possibilities for the ex-praetor are attested. There are several examples of the top scale for the tribune and probably one each for the middle and lower scales, though some little doubt surrounds both of these cases. The senator whose name has been restored as that of Iunius Maximus won two crowns, one *vexillum* and multiple *hastae* – cor. mur. et vall. hastis puris vexillo – although the number of *hastae* is not specified the fact that they never exceed the number of crowns (excluding again the odd case of Catilius Severus) leaves little doubt that two *hastae* were intended. The lowest of the three scales for the tribune may be represented by the case of T. Iulius Maximus Manlianus, though this is by no means certain. The inscription which records his career is defective: he certainly won two crowns and one *vexillum* but the number of *hastae* is indeterminate – coronis murali et vallari h [. . . . .] *vexillo* – considerations of spacing make the reading *hasta pura* rather more likely than *hastis puris*.

Excluding yet again the anomalous Catilius Severus there is no attested fluctuation in the consular scale. The only deviation from the four-fold

pattern is when a consular records eight-fold decorations, as for example
Sosius Senecio who won a double consular award on the occasion of Trajan's
Dacian wars, or the Flavian senator M. Cornelius Nigrinus Curiatius
Maternus decorated in Domitian's campaigns on the Danube. These totals
could represent a single massive award or, perhaps more likely, two
decorations on the four-fold scale. This clearly is what occurred in the case of
the two Antonine senators who have been credited with eight-fold *dona*, C.
Aufidius Victorinus *bis donis donatus* (though the scale of his award has been
totally restored) and T. Pomponius Proculus Vitrasius Pollio *bis donis
m[ilitaribus donato cor]onis muralibu[s II vallar. II aur. II c]las[sicis II hastis puris
VIII vexillis VIII]*. This reconstruction of the *dona* differs from that offered by
Henzen in CIL. After the reference to the mural, rampart and gold crowns he
preferred to read . . . *has[tis puris IIII vexillis IIII]*. This restoration is unlikely
on two counts. A double consular award is indicated both by the explicit
statement *bis donis donatus* and by the existence of more than one mural crown:
hence the number of *hastae* and *vexilla* must also be doubled from four to
eight. Secondly a consular decoration without a naval crown is an oddity, but
it is an oddity that is more apparent than real, based on a faulty reading of the
broken stone. The fragment of a letter which Henzen believed to be the right-
hand upright of an H is better restored as the vertical stroke of an L (no cross-
bar is apparent), so allowing the restoration *[c]las[sicis]*, instead of *has[tis]*. Thus
Pollio's *dona* are restored to normality, to the unwavering consular scale of
award.

The Hadrianic period apart, there is no discernible variation in the patterns
of senatorial awards from Domitian to Commodus, and no evidence for the
period after Commodus. The system which survived these years unaltered is
first apparent in the early years of the Flavian emperors and it is probable that
it was Vespasian who brought order to what had earlier been an unregimented
and still somewhat *ad hoc* system of reward. This is consistent with the fact that
it is in the Flavian period that certain irregularities in the senatorial career
ladder itself were brought to an end.[2] Of particular relevance is the
regularising of the legionary command as a praetorian post which would no
longer, or only in very exceptional circumstances, be held by those below the
status of *praetor*. Hence the *dona* of the *legatus legionis* emerge as those of a
praetorius, the same as those of a praetorian provincial governor. Hitherto it
was not unknown for legionary commands to be bestowed on senators of
more junior rank: a nice example is provided by Tacitus.[3] In AD 60 when the
election for praetors was held there were found to be three more candidates
than posts to be filled; the emperor consoled the three disappointed candidates
by appointing them instead to commands of legions. Thus, if a *legatus legionis*
could be an ex-praetor, an ex-quaestor or even (exceptionally) less, there can
be no easy equation between reward and senatorial rank as later occurred. The
problem of tracing and dating the development of senatorial *dona* is further

exacerbated by the shortage of evidence for the early imperial period and by the complications of civil unrest. Of the eleven relevant Vespasianic and Julio-Claudian inscriptions known to date, five appertain in some way to the year 69, and one is a reward connected with the suppression of the Pisonian conspiracy of 65, irregular contexts not conducive to regular rewards even if such existed at the dates in question.

The basic evidence for this early period is set out in table C and includes nothing earlier than Claudian. Material of the crucial Augustan period is entirely lacking. Neither of the two Julio-Claudian instances for which evidence of scale of award survives bear any relation to the standard schemes characteristic of later periods. Coiedius Candidus was decorated with three crowns and a *hasta* when serving as tribune of legion *VIII* in the Mithridatic war and Nonius Asprenas was rewarded, it would appear, for some part played in putting down the conspiracy of Piso, receiving five crowns, eight *hastae* and four *vexilla*. One other Claudian example, the unknown senator of CIL v 7165, is too fragmentary to be very informative. The inscription appears to record an imperial *comes* decorated by Claudius (on the occasion of the British war?) with at least three crowns. The *comes* was most probably of consular standing and it is therefore of note that the *corona classica* is included among the decorations, though it does not feature in the liberal allocation of crowns to the non-consular Nonius Asprenas. The *corona classica* had perhaps already by this early date emerged as the mark of the ex-consul.

TABLE C SENATORIAL DONA · CLAUDIUS TO VESPASIAN

DATE	NAME	RANK	DECORATIONS		
			coronae	*hastae*	*vexilla*
Claudian	L. Coiedius Candidus	trib leg	3	I	0
	CIL V 7165	comes (cos)	3+	?	?
Neronian	L. Nonius Asprenas	? (tribunicius)	5	8	4
Vespasianic	L. Antistius Rusticus	trib leg	3	3	3
	Cn. Domitius Tullus	praef aux omn (quaest)	3	3	3
	A. Larcius Lepidus	leg leg (quaest)	3	2	2
	. . . . Firmus	trib leg vice leg	3	3	?
	Cn. Domitius Lucanus	praef aux omn (praet)	3	3/2	3/2
	M. Hirrius Fronto	? (praet?)	2+	[3?]	[3?]
	Valerius Festus	leg leg	4	4	4
	P. Glitius Gallus	?	0	I	0

The first examples of a recognizably organized system, bearing any relation to what became normal practice, appear early in the reign of Vespasian. With just a couple of exceptions the awards of that emperor conform from the outset to a pattern of standard combinations. The major difference between this and later periods is the absence, for reasons already indicated, of an easy correlation between size of reward and status.

The two odd awards are those of Glitius Gallus and Firmus. Gallus was awarded a single *hasta* during the censorship of Vespasian and Titus in 73–74. The career of this patrician senator includes no military posts whatever, so it is certain that the decoration was a reward for loyalty in 69 and has no connection with bravery in the field. Firmus' rewards too may well have some connection with the events of the civil war, though in a very different way from that of Gallus. While his political allegiance was right and assured him of reward, his *dona* do appear to relate to action in the field. The inscription which records the career is fragmentary, but the post held by Firmus has been restored very plausibly by Domaszewski to read *tr(ib.) mil. leg. IIII [Scyth(icae) vi]c(e) leg(ati)* military tribune of *IIII Scythica*, acting legate. There were two fourth legions in existence at this time, *IIII Scythica* and *IIII Macedonica*, but since the latter fought on behalf of Vitellius it is singularly unlikely to be the legion of a man highly honoured by Vespasian. *IIII Scythica* was stationed at this period in Syria, a province which from the outset supported the Flavian cause. Its governor, Mucianus, marched west in 69 canvassing support for Vespasian, and it is possible that the legate of *IIII Scythica* and perhaps part of the legion accompanied him, leaving the senatorial tribune, Firmus, as acting commander. All this is, however, pure speculation for we have no concrete evidence for the activities of *IIII Scythica* at this time. Its participation in the Jewish war of Vespasian and Titus is not directly attested – a fact which may be of some significance since we do have a good account of the war. An alternative context, suggested by Birley, is the annexation of Commagene in AD 72, though the participation of *IIII Scythica* in this campaign too is a matter of conjecture and not firm evidence.[4] The absence of the legate on this occasion can be simply explained by death or incapacitation. Firmus was very inexperienced to take over the command of a legion in time of war, but the very fact that it was war-time provides a ready reason for such a sudden promotion. For his exploits in the field, and no doubt also because of his allegiance to the Flavian cause, Firmus received *dona militaria* and *ornamenta praetoricia*, this latter presumably meaning the dignity of the praetorship, the honour without the reality of the magistracy for which he was, in all probability, too young to qualify (later on in his career he held a normal praetorship). When Firmus held the post in which he earned his decorations he was merely *tribunicius*: in the interval between the deed and the award he advanced to *quaestor* and on the occasion of the award was made, theoretically at least, *praetorius* – assuming that this is what is meant by *ornamenta praetoricia*.

The *dona* which he received approximate to those which later became characteristic of the ex-praetor – including, of course, the legionary legate – consisting of three crowns, an *aurea* and (hypothetically) a *muralis* and *vallaris* (there is no justification for, and every reason against, the *corona classica* restored by Dessau) and three *hastae*. The record of the decorations is defective, but there is certainly no room on the stone to restore *vexilla*: in this respect alone the scale of award differs from the later standard praetorian award.

For the rest, the Vespasianic awards are the familiar standard combinations, though in a number of cases the relation between rank, status and reward is complicated by promotion intervening between deed and reward, just as happened to Firmus. Antistius Rusticus, for example, won his decorations as a tribune and received them as a praetor, while Valerius Festus appears to have been decorated as a consular for deeds performed as *praetorius*. Both these irregularities arise directly or indirectly from the peculiar circumstances of civil war.

Antistius Rusticus, consul in AD 90 and legate of legion *VIII Augusta* under Vespasian, Titus and Domitian (that is at least from 79 to 81), served his first military command as tribune of *II Augusta* in Britain at a date which should fall around about 70. The career is detailed in reverse chronological order and the record of *dona* appears between the tribunate and the legionary command. It is this fact which led Groag to attribute the decorations, decorations normal for an ex-praetor, to the post in *VIII Augusta*.[5] This is unlikely. On chronological grounds it would be difficult to find a context for such an award. *VIII Augusta* was stationed at this period in Upper Germany at Strasbourg: it will have participated in AD 74 in the trans-Rhine expedition for which Cornelius Clemens won triumphal ornaments, and just possibly in Rutilius Gallicus's campaign against the Bructeri in 77–78, though it was rather a long way south for this war which involved mainly the lower German army.[6] In 83 it will have been involved in Domitian's war against the Chatti. Participation in any one of these campaigns would have involved Rusticus in an inordinately long period of legionary command. Leaving aside therefore the presupposition that the *dona* must be those of an ex-praetor, hence of a legionary legate, the phrasing of the text is perfectly consistent with the decorations being linked to the post of tribune – *leg. divi Vesp. et divi Titi et imp. Caesaris Domitiani Aug. Germanici leg. VIII Aug., curatori viarum Aureliae et Corneliae, adlecto inter praetorios a divo Vespasiano et divo Tito, donis militaribus donato ab iisdem corona murali cor. vallari corona aurea vexillis III hastis puris III, trib. mil. leg. II [A]ug.*

It is of note that here, as in the case of Firmus, the *dona* are associated with elevation to the rank of praetor. Did Rusticus too perform some service for the Flavian cause? The army of Britain was equivocal in its allegiances during the Year of the Four Emperors; it swayed with the wind of change. *II Augusta,* however, had good reason to be attached to the Flavian house for it had played a distinguished role in the Claudian invasion of Britain while commanded by Vespasian himself: it is known to have been the first legion in Britain to declare for Vespasian in AD 69.[7] Was Rusticus its tribune at this crucial time? Several of the rewards which Vespasian distributed to his supporters were delayed for some years – many of them, for example that of Glitius Gallus, were given during the censorship of 73–74 which was also the occasion for the elevation to patrician status of several Flavian supporters, including the later governor of Britain, Cn. Iulius Agricola – and this could have been the occasion for the award made to Antistius Rusticus who was, at the same time, elevated to a praetorship and hence given the *dona* fitting to his new status. Such an interpretation of the evidence explains why the text makes no mention of the campaign to which the decorations belong: there was no campaign as such.

Precisely the same is true in the case of Valerius Festus. C. Calpetanus Rantius Quirinalis Valerius Festus received decorations on a consular scale from an unnamed emperor on an unspecified occasion. The inscription which records the career of Festus is in strict chronological order: even the consulate and a priesthood appear in their correct position and not, as is so often the case, at the beginning or end of the text, moved out of sequence to give them greater emphasis. The *dona* are recorded after the consulate which was held in AD 71 and before the post of *curator alvei Tiberis et riparum* which Festus held in 73.[8] The *dona* cannot therefore be associated with subsequent consular governorships in Spain and Pannonia – in any case there is no evidence for campaigning in these areas at the correct period to provide the necessary context – and must be referred back to incidents which occurred earlier in the career. In AD 69–70 Festus held the post of legate of *III Augusta*, and during his sojourn in Africa he is known to have been instrumental in suppressing trouble with the Garamantes who had intervened in and exacerbated a quarrel between the cities of Oea and Lepcis Magna.[9] However, this minor encounter is unlikely to account for a major collection of decorations. Tacitus provides another and more likely context, the dubious role played by Festus in the murder of Lucius Piso in 70.[10] Piso was proconsul of the province of Africa where the army was not favourably disposed towards Vespasian. Supporters of Vitellius, fleeing from Rome, urged Piso to rebel against Vespasian, hinting that the Gallic provinces too were hesitating in their allegiance, that Germany was ready to rise up and that, since it was already rumoured abroad in Rome that Piso was plotting against the government, he might as well actually do so since his position and his life were already endangered. Tacitus hints that Festus, an ambitious and extravagant young man, may have been implicated in inciting Piso to rebel: certainly, however, it was he who instigated his death, sending Carthaginian and Moorish auxiliaries to kill him. Thus an incipient rebellion was nipped in the bud: Festus had proved his loyalty to the

Flavian house. His reward came soon; a consulate in 71 and, immediately following, military decorations on a scale commensurate with his present dignity.

A further case of rewards being delayed to the year in which Vespasian and Titus held the censorship is that of the Domitii brothers who served as commanders of an army of auxiliaries against the Germans (*praefecti auxiliorum omnium adversus Germanos*). The careers of these two virtually inseparable brothers are not easy to follow: the context for the command in Germany has been variously interpreted, but the most satisfactory solution to the problem is that advanced by Alföldy.[11] He suggests that the most likely context for the extraordinary command in Germany is the campaign led by Cerealis against the Batavians who lived near the mouth of the Rhine, when a large number of auxiliaries were concentrated in that area. Domitius Lucanus held the prefecture subsequent to serving as praetor, Tullus prior to the praetorship. Immediately after the German command the brothers were sent to Africa, Tullus being praetor designate at the time he was appointed to the (normally praetorian) post of *legatus propraetore ad exercitum qui est in Africa*. While absent he was promoted *inter praetorios*. The secondment of these two apparently staunch Flavian supporters to Africa in the early 70s, probably 71–72, makes good sense given the unrest of that province under Piso and Festus in 70. Both Lucanus and Tullus were awarded military decorations which are recorded together with adlection *inter patricios*, the date with little doubt, the censorship of 73–74, the reason their activities against the Batavians in 70 and their political allegiance. The confusing order of the inscriptions falls into place as the result of Vespasian's tardiness in rewarding his supporters, a tardiness for which, as we have seen, there are good parallels. Lucanus and Tullus both received the three-fold *dona* of the ex-praetor, Lucanus *praetorius* when he won the decorations and still of the same rank when he was awarded them, Tullus ex-quaestor when he won the decorations, *praetorius* by the time he received them.

Another cause for confusion in the early Flavian *dona* is, as has already been indicated, the absence of a rigid career pattern. While the sequence of magistracies was firmly set, the position to be occupied by such relatively new posts as that of *legatus legionis* was not. The appointment could be held at various different stages in the career. Larcius Lepidus, for example, served as legate of *X Fretensis* during the later stages of the Jewish war, having been appointed to this command direct from *quaestor*, subsequently holding the tribunate of the plebs which in later times would regularly precede legionary command.[12] This legionary appointment appears to have been Lepidus' first military post, there being no evidence that he ever served as laticlave tribune. The text of the inscription recording his career is slightly defective but the restoration in CIL of a tribunate in one of the *Adiutrix* legions is not possible for neither of them existed at the time at which Lepidus is supposed to have been serving in them. While holding this legionary appointment Lepidus was decorated by Vespasian and Titus: his award comprised three *coronae*, two *hastae* and two *vexilla*, that is it was on the same sort of level as was regularly given to holders of praetorian posts (including, of course, *legati legionum*). It was under Vespasian that the legionary command became firmly fixed at the level of ex-praetor: this was no more than regularising what was already becoming common practice. The political upheavals of the civil war no doubt exerted stresses and strains on the regular career ladder. Lepidus may well have owed his promotion to *legatus legionis* in large part to the fact that he had previously been serving as *quaestor* of Crete and Cyrene, a province which, as Tacitus points out, had quickly come over to allegiance to the Flavians.[13]

Despite all these complications, by the early 70s Vespasian was clearly awarding decorations in combinations familiar from later periods. There can be little doubt that it was he who introduced these regular scales of award. The initial use of these combinations was unconventional by comparison with later usage, but this is to view the situation with hindsight. In the early 70s there were no conventions. The practices which he developed under somewhat abnormal conditions were subsequently applied with ease and clarity.

CHAPTER VIII

IMPERIAL SCALES OF
AWARD ·
EQUESTRIANS

The *dona* of the equestrians, like those of the senators, appear to have emerged into a clear and recognizable form during the early Flavian period. The development of the *dona* fits neatly into the picture of the developing equestrian career structure which changed from an *ad hoc* system of appointments in the early first century to a clear promotion ladder set up by the time of Vespasian and augmented by the addition of an extra rung when Hadrian established the *militia quarta*.[1] Initial service as prefect of a 500-strong infantry regiment was followed by an angusticlave tribunate in a legion or, from the Flavian period onwards, the command of a 1000-strong infantry unit, thence to the prefecture of a 500-strong cavalry unit and for the very best there was, from the time of Hadrian onwards, the prefecture of a 1000-strong cavalry unit. From there the equestrian officer moved on to a career in the procuratorships and great prefectures where he would have to compete for promotion with men who had risen via the centurionates in Rome and the provinces. Fig. 14 summarizes the known promotion patterns, juxtaposing the equestrian career and the centurion career. It shows the situation as it existed about the middle of the second century AD after Hadrian had created the fourth equestrian military grade. Milliary *alae* existed prior to this date; they first appear in the Flavian period but from then until the 120s their command was regarded simply as an alternative to the command of a quingenary *ala*, both on the third rung of the career ladder.

In the later Republic and early years of the Principate no proper career structure existed either for the equestrian or the centurion, nor was there a clear separation between those who commanded auxiliary units and those who served as centurions in the legions. Appointments to auxiliary commands were made on an *ad hoc* basis: sometimes a native chief might be used to lead the men of his own tribe; sometimes a legionary centurion or *primus pilus* might be given the post, or it might even fall to a senator.[2] Nor was there any established order in which posts would be held; the prefecture of an *ala* might precede or it might follow command of an auxiliary cohort or a legionary

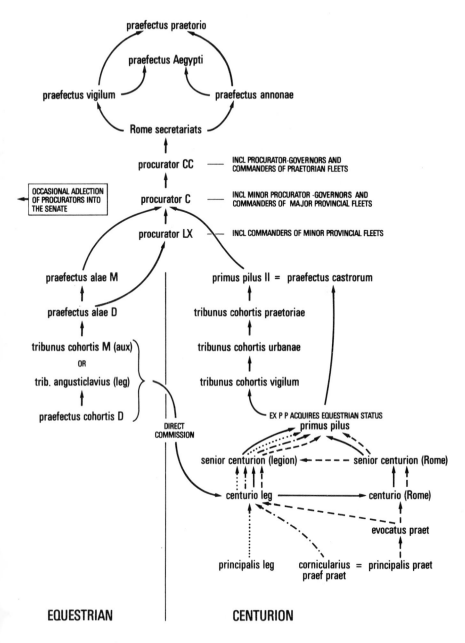

14   Equestrian and centurion career structure

tribunate; commands of auxiliary infantry or cavalry could come before, between or after legionary centurionates and the primipilate. The unstructured nature of auxiliary command at this date reflects the rather disorganized and spontaneous way in which the units had been raised as required to make good the deficiencies of the legionary army, by providing the necessary cavalry and light-armed troops to complement the heavy infantry of the legions. As the *auxilia* were fully integrated into the Roman army, becoming an increasingly large and significant part of the military machine, so they developed their own career structure. The importance of the auxiliary cavalry (for each legion had only 120 mounted men attached to it) naturally tended to make the cavalry prefectures the senior commands. Despite an attempt by Claudius to reverse the sequence and assert the seniority of the legionary tribunate, a seniority based only on its antiquity, the natural order prevailed: *praefectus cohortis quingenariae* to *tribunus legionis angusticlavius* to *praefectus alae quingenariae*.[3] With the development of milliary units in the Flavian period the post of *tribunus cohortis milliariae* became an alternative to the legionary post, and finally under Hadrian the command of a milliary *ala* was established as a separate promotion. As the equestrian career developed so were centurions excluded from auxiliary commands, except on a temporary basis when an unexpected vacancy occurred, arising, for example, from the sudden death of an equestrian officer. But the centurion no longer had need of these auxiliary commands; he now had his own career structure (Fig. 14).[4]

Pre-Flavian period

The status of auxiliary command during this disorganised formative period is clearly reflected in the decorations awarded to the officers. Where there was no promotion ladder as such there could be no ascending scale of decoration. Throughout the Julio-Claudian period officers of all types of auxiliary unit received precisely the same award, the same moreover as was received by angusticlave tribunes of legions, *primi pili* and *praefecti castrorum*. Table D lists the evidence. Prior to the Flavian period none of these officers received awards comprising other than one crown and one *hasta*. Commonly that crown was a *corona aurea* but occasionally it might be a *muralis*, as in the case of M. Stlaccius Coranus and Anicius Maximus, or a *vallaris*. Three possible exceptions to this rule merit further discussion. The decorations awarded to Ti. Claudius Balbillus have conventionally been restored as comprising one crown, one *hasta* and one *vexillum*. It was while serving as tribune of legion *XX* during Claudius's British war that Balbillus received *dona* of which we now have an incomplete record: [. . . . .]*m*[. . . . .] *Claudio*[. . . . *hasta*] *pura* [. . . . .]. Only the reference to the *hasta* and the name of the awarding emperor are extant. Keil restored the stone to read: [*d.d. in triu*]*m*[*pho a divo*] *Claudio* [*corona* . . . . . *et hasta*] *pura* [*et vexillo*], his spacing implying more than one crown. Pflaum varied this slightly despite accepting the same basic framework [*d.d. in triu*]*m*[*pho a divo*] *Claudio* [*corona murali et vexillo et hasta*] *pura.*[5] In view of the complete absence of *vexilla* from the known *dona* of pre-Flavian equestrians these restorations must be viewed with deep suspicion. Moreover, the drastic abbreviation *d.d.* (for *donis donatus*) is out of place in a text of so early a date which is in all other respects written out much more fully. Any restoration is hypothetical but something like [*donato ab i*]*m*[*p. divo*] *Claudio* [*ob bellum Britannicum hasta*] *pura* [*corona aurea?* . . . . .] would neatly fit the space available and eliminate the more obvious anomalies.

TABLE D   EQUESTRIAN DONA · PRE-FLAVIAN

NAME	RANK	CORONAE			HASTAE	VEXILLA
		m.	v.	a.		
Sex. Caesius Propertianus	trib leg		I		I	o
Ti. Claudius Balbillus	trib leg et praef fabr	[I?		]	I	[o?]
–. Cornelius N[–	trib leg		I		I	o
C. Fabricius Tuscus	praef alae D		I		I	o
C. Iulius Camillus	trib leg		I		I	o
L. Laetilius Rufus	trib leg	I			I	o
C. Purtisius Atinas	praef alae D		1?		1?	o
C. Stertinius Xenophon	trib leg et praef fabr		I		I	o
M. Stlaccius Coranus	pf coh D/trib leg/pf alae D	I			I	o
M. Vergilius Gallus Lusius	praef coh D		1?		1?	o
compare						
P. Anicius Maximus	praef castrorum	I			I	

The inscription relating to M. Vergilius Gallus Lusius raises a different sort of problem; it records the award of two *hastae* and more than one gold crown by Augustus and Tiberius in the middle of a career of typical early first century type: *prim. pil. leg. XI, praef. cohort. Ubiorum peditum et equitum, donato hastis puris duabus et coronis aureis ab divo Aug. et Ti. Caesare Aug.* The number of crowns is not specified, but generally where this occurs it is safe to assume the same number as that of the previous type of award mentioned, hence in this case two. The fact that this collection of *dona* is precisely double the standard for the period arouses suspicion. Nowhere else are Augustus and Tiberius recorded as giving decorations together; Tiberius awarded decorations on his own even within the lifetime of Augustus. It is thus in both respects more satisfactory to suggest that two separate awards are in question here, perhaps both won as prefect of the cohort of Ubii, perhaps one as prefect and one in the earlier post of *primus pilus* of legion *XI*. Legion *XI* moved from Moesia to Dalmatia at about this period and is known to have participated in the *bellum Illyricum* of AD 6–9. The *cohors Ubiorum* was in Germany in the early first century. It had moved to Moesia Inferior by AD 99 but is almost certainly to be equated with one of the cohorts of Ubii referred to by Tacitus as operating in the district of Marcodurum (Duren) in 69.[6] The unit was probably moved away from the Rhineland by Vespasian in his tidying-up operations after the civil war when, as a result of the lesson learnt in the revolt of Civilis who played on the local loyalties of the troops stationed in lower Germany, he moved auxiliary units away from the areas where they had been raised. Both Germany and Illyricum at this period offered opportunity for active campaigning and winning decorations.

The tombstone of C. Purtisius Atinas presents a problem similar to that of Gallus Lusius. No decorations are mentioned in the text, but depicted on the two sides of the stone are three legionary standards, one *torques*, two *armillae*, two *hastae* and two *coronae aureae* (pl. 7b). The extant portion of the stone, for half of it is missing, lists posts as *primus pilus* and *praefectus equitum*, and while the *torques*, *armillae* (and missing *phalerae*?) belong to a hypothetical early part of the career, it is likely that the two *coronae* and two *hastae* belong to two separate awards as senior centurion or *primus pilus* and/or *praefectus equitum*.

The Flavian period

By the early years of the second century there had developed a graduated scale of awards with *vexilla* in addition to *hastae* and *coronae* being available to the equestrian. The evidence for when this change occurred is inconclusive. The earliest unequivocal example of the appearance of a *vexillum* among the *dona* of an equestrian officer belongs to the end of the first century, to Q. Attius Priscus, who enjoys the distinction of being the one and only soldier known to have been decorated by Nerva. He held the post of tribune of legion *I Adiutrix* when decorated in a *bellum Suebicum*, receiving *corona aurea*, *hasta pura* and *vexillum*. Nerva was no military innovator – indeed his brief reign gave him no time for innovation – so the developments must come either in the Flavian period or at the very end of the Julio-Claudian era. It can be argued that it was Domitian who awarded military decorations to M. Arruntius Claudianus;[7] if this is indeed so, Claudianus supplants Priscus as the earliest clear example of an equestrian receiving a *vexillum*, for Claudianus' *dona* comprised one *hasta* plus more than one crown and *vexillum*. However the dating of the relevant part of the military career to the period of Domitian is by no means certain. Subsequent to completing the *militia equestris* Claudianus held two procuratorships and was then adlected into the senate where he held, *inter alia* the post of legate of *II Traiana*. His tenure of this post is the only datable feature of the career. A *terminus post quem* is provided by the date of the creation of the unit by Trajan prior to the start of first Dacian war in 102. In about 120 *II Traiana* moved to Egypt, and thereafter it was commanded by an equestrian prefect and not a senatorial legate on account of the emperor's ban on senators entering Egypt. Hence Claudianus' command of the legion must belong to the first two decades of the second century. If it falls in the later part of this time span the decorations would fall neatly into the period of Trajan's Dacian wars. If, on the other hand, Claudianus commanded the legion very soon after its creation, the decorations would be pushed back to the Dacian wars of Domitian. Nothing permits closer dating between these two extremes. The absence of the name of the awarding emperor (which does often indicate that the emperor in question is Domitian) is not of any great significance in a text which treats the military part of the career so peremptorily, not even indicating the names of the units commanded, while the suggestion that the command of the Moesian fleet must pre-date the division of Moesia by Domitian in AD 86 – which would push the cavalry command to the early 80s – is without foundation. Since the dating of this career is doubtful the reign of Nerva and not that of Domitian must remain our *terminus ante quem* for the changes in the pattern of equestrian *dona*.

Nor is it possible to establish a firm *terminus post quem*. Certainly the three examples of decorations by Claudius give no hint of change. The *vexillum* attributed to Balbillus, being a restoration and a dubious one at that, proves nothing. The other two Claudian examples, those of C. Iulius Camillus and C. Stertinius Xenophon, are however conclusive. Both were legionary tribunes when decorated and both received the single crown and *hasta*. No examples of the *dona* of *praefecti equitum* survive for this period, but in view of the fact that Claudius regarded the legionary tribunate as the higher ranking command, had a graduated scale existed at this time, it would have been the tribune and not the cavalry prefect who enjoyed the higher reward. What of Nero and Vitellius? The two relevant texts are unhelpful. M. Stlaccius Coranus was decorated by either Claudius or Nero; the omission of the name of the emperor concerned with the award is perhaps indicative of Nero, but by no means conclusively so, though the fact that the cavalry command followed the legionary tribunate instead of preceding it as Claudius would have it, is consistent with a Neronian date. Coranus' *dona* are recorded at the end of his military career, hence following the cavalry prefecture but not necessarily to be associated with it. The first post in the career was held in Germany, the next two in Britain. The continuation of the wars of conquest in Britain would offer a context for the winning of military decorations, but there was also sporadic campaigning in Germany at this period, against the Frisii and the Chauchi in 47, the Chatti in 50 and 51, and in 58 trouble with several tribes across the Rhine involving the intervention of the governor and the army of lower Germany. Hence it is not possible to attribute the *dona* with any confidence to one post rather than another, though the more major wars of conquest in Britain may be preferred.

The same problem arises with Sex. Caesius Propertianus, for both the units in which he served, *cohors III Hispanorum* and legion *IIII Macedonica*, were stationed in upper Germany. No campaign and no emperor is mentioned, but the disbanding of *IIII Macedonica* in AD 70 provides a *terminus ante quem* for the tribunate. Subsequently Propertianus became *procurator imp.* (again unnamed) *a patrimonio et hereditatibus et a libellis*, an appointment which Pflaum would date to the reign of Vitellius.[8] Hence the *dona* were awarded either by Nero or Vitellius; if by Vitellius the context must be the civil war, the post must be the legionary tribunate. Domaszewski preferred to see the decorations as those of a *praefectus cohortis* though he offered no possible context: his contention sprang from the belief that it was Claudius who reformed the equestrian *dona* and hence that had Propertianus been decorated as a tribune he would have received more than the single crown and *hasta* with which he is credited.[9] The argument is circular for there is no independent evidence of a Claudian reform on the lines proposed by Domaszewski.

TABLE E   EQUESTRIAN DONA · VESPASIAN TO NERVA

DATE	NAME	RANK	DECORATIONS		
			coronae	*hastae*	*vexilla*
			m. v. a.		
Vesp	C. Minicius Italus	praef coh D	I	I	I
	Ti. Claudius Heras	praef coh D/trib leg	I	I	o
	–. Pompeius Faventinus	pf coh D/trib leg/pf alae	I	I	[I?]
Dom	Ti. Claudius Alpinus	pf coh D/trib leg/pf alae			
	C. Iulius Karus	praef coh D	I I I	I	o
	Cn. Octavius Titinius Capito	praef coh/trib leg	I	I	o
Nerva	Q. Attius Priscus	trib leg	I	I	I
Dom/Traj	M. Arruntius Claudianus	praef alae et vexill praet	[I?]	I	I	2?

The crucial inscriptions are therefore those relating to the wars of Vespasian, Titus and Domitian. Excluding the uncertain case of Arruntius Claudianus there are six of those in total (Table E), but that of Ti. Claudius Alpinus is useless for the present purpose as it gives no indication of the scale of *dona* won. Certainly one and probably both of the two Domitianic examples record the *dona* of a *praefectus cohortis*, so the absence of a *vexillum* is of no significance; they could not be expected to show a graduated system even if one existed. C. Iulius Karus indeed received *dona* on an unprecedented scale of three *coronae*, one *hasta* but no *vexillum*: this is different from anything seen before but also unparalleled by anything that came after. There is no doubt that Karus was only in the *militia prima* when he acquired this collection. When the inscription which records his career was erected he had held only two military posts, that of prefect of the *cohors II Asturum* and military tribune in legion *III Cyrenaica*. *III Cyrenaica* was stationed in Egypt from about AD 11 until some time in the first decade of Hadrian's reign when it moved to Bostra in Arabia. At no time did it go west or send any vexillations west, specifically to Britain, and it was in a British war that Karus won his decorations. A *cohors II Asturum*, on the other hand, is attested in Germania Inferior in 80, was still there in 89 when it acquired the titles *pia fidelis Domitiana* for its loyalty during the revolt of Saturninus, but had moved to Britain some time before 105.[10] Though the text is not specifically dated, a Domitianic context is probable. There is a *terminus post quem* of 89 and a *terminus ante quem* of 128. The inscription was set up jointly by detachments of *III Cyrenaica* and *XXII Deiotariana*: these two legions shared a single camp in Alexandria some time between 119 and 128 or possibly 123 when *III* moved to Arabia and *XXII* disappeared from the Roman army lists.[11] The joint dedication must, logically, belong to the period when the two units were garrisoned together – hence before 128. There was a war in progress in Britain at the time of Hadrian's accession in 117, but the generosity of the decoration is hardly in keeping with the parsimony with which Hadrian normally rewarded his officers. Mann and Jarrett have made out a good case for dating the war to the late Domitianic period.[12] Their case rests on the equation of the *dilectus* mentioned on the inscription – the legionary detachments who set the stone up at Cyrene had been sent into the province to carry out a recruiting drive – with the appearance of recruits engaged in a road-building programme outside Cyrene in AD 100. If Karus was involved with recruiting in the closing years of the first century his post as *praefectus cohortis* falls into the last years of the reign of Domitian (who died in 96) or into the brief reign of Nerva. The case of Karus with its unparalleled *dona* attests at least a move away from the standard of the early first century.

Cn. Octavius Titinius Capito received the familiar combination of one crown, one *hasta*, but there is no evidence on which to decide what post he held at the time. He served in only the first two *militiae* before embarking on a procuratorial career, but the names of the units are not specified nor the location of the war in which he fought. Two of the three Vespasianic awards, both recording one crown and one *hasta*, pose a similar problem. C. Minicius Italus almost certainly was only in the first *militia* when decorated, while Ti. Claudius Heras might well have been, though here again it is not made clear with which post the *dona* should be associated.[13] Heras served first as prefect of a *cohors Ituraeorum* and then as tribune in two eastern legions, *XII Fulminata* and *III Cyrenaica*. *Cohortes Ituraeorum* are attested in Germany, Pannonia, Syria and Egypt and at a later date in Dacia: since the unit titles are not given in full any one of these could in theory be the unit in question. In practice the eastern bias of the career makes the Syrian or Egyptian unit the more likely. Both the legions in question are known to have taken part in Vespasian's Jewish war and an eastern *cohors Ituraeorum* was in a position to have done so. Hence decoration could have been in either the *prima* or *secunda militia*.

The crucial text must therefore be that recording the career of Pompeius Faventinus, a text which is now lost and survives only in corrupt form in a sixteenth-century manuscript.[14] The *dona* comprise a *corona aurea* and a *hasta pura*: the lacuna between the *hasta* and the name of the awarding emperor could be filled in one of two ways: there could be either a reference to the campaign in which the decorations were won or there could be another decoration; if the latter the obvious candidate is a *vexillum*, and this is the alternative which has generally been adopted, for example by Steiner, by Domaszewski and more recently by Alföldy.[15] If the name of a campaign is to be restored the possibilities are a German or a Jewish war, these being the only two areas of campaigning for which Vespasian is known to have awarded decorations. The Jewish war, *bellum Iudaicum*, keeps closest to the text we have, but this interpretation raises a major problem; none of the units concerned is known to have served in the east. All have Spanish or German connections which means that the war in question ought to be a German one. The *cohors VI Asturum* probably formed part of the garrison of lower Germany. There is no indisputable evidence for its whereabouts at this time – indeed the present inscription is the only proof of its existence – but it has been restored by Nesselhauf on a lower German diploma of AD 80, last of a series of units listed in ascending numerical order, following a *cohors VI Thracum*. There is no other known *cohors VI* (or higher) which would fit better.[16] If in Germany in 80 it had probably been there throughout the 70s, moved in perhaps (direct from Spain?) in the military reorganisation which followed the civil war. Legion *VI Victrix* in which Faventinus spent his tribunate left Spain as a result of the civil war and moved to lower Germany where it took part under Cerealis in the suppression of the Batavian revolt.[17] The name of the third unit in which Faventinus served is in doubt. Huebner restored it as the *ala II Flavia Hispanorum*, Stein as the *ala I Flavia Singularium c.R.* and Alföldy as the *ala Sulpicia c.R.*[18] Since the *ala II Hispanorum* is not known to have left Spain at this period, command of it would not have provided occasion for the winning of military decorations. The other two *alae* are both attested in lower Germany on a diploma of April 78 in which they are recorded as serving under Rutilius Gallicus who in 77–78 led a campaign against the Bructeri.[19] Hence Faventinus could have won his decorations in Germany in either 70, the suppression of Civilis, or 77–78, the war against the Bructeri, and could when decorated have been serving in either his first, his second or, unless the Huebner restoration is correct, his third *militia*. We can be sure therefore of neither the scale of award nor the post held when the decorations were won.

The material evidence relating to the *dona* of the Flavian period does not therefore provide incontrovertible proof that either Vespasian or indeed Domitian reformed the system, extending the scope and number of awards available. The case for change at this period rests largely on a theoretical basis. It was under Vespasian that centurions and primipilares finally ceased to hold equestrian military command: it was now that what had hitherto been a series of *ad hoc* appointments settled down into a regular career structure. The principle of reward according to rank was firmly entrenched by the period as is very clear from the study of all other categories of officer and men: it is inconceivable that the same should not also have been true of the equestrians. There is no good reason why Pompeius Faventinus should not have won a *vexillum* in addition to a *corona* and a *hasta*: there is every reason why he could have.

Trajanic period

It is not, however, until the Trajanic period that it is possible to see any pattern emerging: it is only then that there is sufficient evidence which is precisely enough dated. There are nine inscriptions which detail *dona* received in Trajanic wars: table F lists the cases in question.

TABLE F   EQUESTRIAN DONA · TRAJANIC

NAME	RANK	CORONAE			HASTAE	VEXILLA
		m.	*v.*	*a.*		
–. Aemilius Iuncus	praef coh D?		I		I	o
M. Vettius Latro	praef coh D	I			I	I
L. Aburnius Tuscianus	trib leg		I	I	I	I
T. Pontius Sabinus	trib leg	I			I	I
A. Pomponius Augurinus	praef coh M		I		I	I
M. Gavius Bassus	praef alae D	I			I	I
P. Prifernius Baetus	praef alae D?	I			I	I
P. Besius Betuinianus ⎫	praef coh D?		I		I	o
P. Besius Betuinianus ⎭	praef alae M	I			I	I

PRIMA MILITIA

M. Vettius Latro is straightforward: the decorations are linked to the post in which they were won and are clearly listed. The correlation is not quite so firm in the case of Aemilius Iuncus since the decorations are relegated to the end of the military part of the career. We know them to have been won in Trajan's Parthian war, that is some time between 114 and 117, but all the units in which Iuncus served either could have or are known to have participated. However the decoration most probably belongs to the prefecture of *cohors I Pannoniorum* for by the early 130s Iuncus was in post in his third civil appointment after completing the *militia equestris*.[20] Hence, if his career had progressed at a smooth and moderate pace, he should only just have embarked on his military career in the mid-110s. These two careers give the scale of award for a cohort prefect as either one *corona* plus one *hasta* or one *corona* plus one *hasta* plus one *vexillum*.

SECUNDA MILITIA

Two different scales of award are also attested for the second grade of the equestrian military hierarchy. Of the three officers decorated at this grade two received the lower award, one the higher, and of the two who received the lower award, one was a legionary tribune, the other commander of an auxiliary cohort. From this it would appear that there was no discrimination between auxiliary and legionary tribunes – their roles were different but their ranks the same – nor indeed is there any evidence for different treatment being meted out to commanders of peditate and equitate units. The prefect or tribune of a *cohors equitata* may have commanded more men than did his counterpart in an all-infantry unit but this gave him no technical seniority nor greater status. Pontius Sabinus was a legionary tribune serving with *VI Ferrata* in the Parthian war when he received his single *corona*, *hasta* and *vexillum*. Another tribune of this same legion, Aburnius Tuscianus, was decorated on the same occasion: it is particularly interesting therefore that he received what appears to be a higher award, two crowns instead of the one awarded to his fellow tribune. The attribution of the decoration is clear but its description is ambiguous. The Greek text records, in addition to one *hasta* and one *vexillum*, στεφάνῳ χρυσῷ τιχικῷ, *corona aurea vallaris*: this expression has been variously interpreted to mean that he won two crowns, a *corona aurea* and a *corona vallaris*, or that he won one crown only, a *corona vallaris* made of gold. An analogous case, that of the *corona aurea civica* of Didius Saturninus (above, p. 71), is of no use in elucidating the phrase since its interpretation too is a matter of dispute. The combination of a *vallaris* with an *aurea* rather than a *muralis* is an uncommon one though by no means unknown (cf. Rufellius Severus and possibly the unknown of CIL VIII 9372), while there is no known example (with the possible though doubtful exception of Saturninus) of the metal of which a crown was made being specified. The probability is that two crowns are intended.

The third equestrian to be decorated at this period while serving in the *secunda militia* is A. Pomponius Augurinus T. Prifernius Paetus. He held the post of ἔπαρχος σπείρης ά χειλιάνδρου , prefect of the first milliary cohort. The command is anomalous, a milliary cohort normally being commanded by a tribune and not a prefect. This led Pflaum to suggest that σπείρης *cohors*, had been wrongly inscribed in place of εἴλης ,*ala*, and in support of this contention he referred to the fact that a milliary *ala* is known to have been stationed in Dacia, the area to which the campaign in question belongs.[21] In theory this is quite possible. In the Trajanic period, prior to the introduction of the *quarta militia*, promotion from a command in the *secunda militia* to the prefecture of a milliary instead of a quingenary *ala* was normal, but in the present case it is most unlikely. Paetus was inexperienced. He had, if the evidence of the rest of the inscription is accurate, held only two equestrian military posts, the present one and an earlier legionary tribunate. He had gone direct to the legionary post without first serving as prefect of a quingenary cohort: he therefore had no experience of independent command. Such a man was not well suited for the command of a milliary *ala*, a post which normally was reserved for men of proven military talent. In fact such an hypothesis is unnecessary as an alternative explanation is ready to hand. Milliary cohorts were occasionally commanded by prefects instead of tribunes; for example cohorts *I* and *II Tungrorum* were clearly of milliary strength when commanded by the prefects who set up religious dedications at Housesteads and Birrens respectively.[22] An inscription from Teos in Asia records the existence of a *cohors I Thracum milliaria* with a prefect and not a tribune in charge. This unit was stationed in the Trajanic period in Judaea, which is the same province as that in which Paetus served his legionary tribunate (with *X Fretensis*).[23] It is fairly common practice for an equestrian officer to hold two commands within the same province. The name of the war in which the decorations were won is not specified but the omission of the names *Dacicus* and *Parthicus* from Trajan's titles (though *Germanicus* is included) suggests that the award ought to pre-date the assumption of *Dacicus* late in 102. Hence the decorations probably belong to the early stages of Trajan's first Dacian war. Now, although there is no specific evidence for any units from Judaea serving in Dacia, some eastern units certainly did: a diploma of AD 110 recording a grant to auxiliaries serving in lower Pannonia includes a detachment of cavalry from Syria (*vexillatio equitum ex Syria*).[24] There is nothing inherently improbable in a unit from Judaea having been transferred to the Danube area for the duration of the Dacian wars. If, however, the indication of Trajan's titles is misleading and they are not being used strictly correctly, the inscription need not pre-date the end of 102 and hence the war could be that against Parthia in 114–117 in which the Judaean army certainly took part. There is in any case little reason to doubt the accuracy of the text of the inscription and that the *dona* of Paetus, a gold crown, a *hasta* and a *vexillum* are those of a man in the *secunda militia*.

TERTIA MILITIA

We know of just four equestrian officers who, it can be argued, won military decorations when serving at this period as commanders of cavalry units. The least contentious of the four cases is that of M. Gavius Bassus who was decorated by Trajan in one of the Dacian wars, receiving one crown, one *hasta* and one *vexillum*. The inscription which records the career gives it in straightforward chronological order, and the reference to the *dona* follows immediately on the cavalry prefecture, though this of itself does not necessarily mean that the two are to be associated. However in this case the evidence suggests that they are. Bassus' second military command was as tribune of *I Adiutrix* in Pannonia; the unit appears without the titles *pia fidelis* which it acquired in AD 98, and if we assume that this omission is deliberate and not an error Bassus must have served in the legion before 98. Hence participation in and decorations for the Dacian war must have been as *praefectus alae*. The *ala* which Bassus commanded, the *ala Claudia nova*, was based at the time of the Dacian wars in Moesia Superior, a province which provided many units for the campaigns. The case for the attribution of the *dona* to the cavalry command stands or falls on the assumption that the legion's titles, or rather its lack of them, are significant. If this assumption is shown to be false the case collapses. Legion *I Adiutrix* also probably took part in the Dacian war, subsequently becoming part of the garrison of the newly created province of Dacia, and it could be conjectured that Bassus was decorated during his tribunate. We know that he was appointed to his first procuratorial post as *praefectus orae Ponticae maritimae* about 108, for he was in service at the time of Pliny's governorship of Pontus and Bithynia and is mentioned on a couple of occasions in the letters.[25] If Bassus was legionary tribune prior to 98 there must have been a hiatus somewhere in his career: if the date of 98 disappears so does the hiatus. However a gap in an equestrian military career is by no means impossible. The *militae* were a series of individual appointments with no guarantee of immediate promotion from one step to the next. When the tenure of one post came to an end the equestrian might or might not be given another command at once: ability of the candidate and availability of a suitable post would both play their part, for the higher up the ladder the fewer the posts (on the question of promotion see below, p. 240). Even an able man might have to enjoy an enforced return to civilian life from time to time – as happened, for example, to M. Valerius Maximianus.[26] A second factor which might be thought to mitigate against the *dona* being those of a *praefectus alae* is their scale, precisely the same as the higher of the two awards known to have been made to a *praefectus cohortis* and the lower of awards won by men in the *seconda militia*. There is however a parallel.

P. Prifernius Paetus Memmius Apollinaris, like Gavius Bassus, received one crown, one *hasta* and one *vexillum* from Trajan in a Dacian expedition. Even the crown is the same in both cases, a *corona muralis*. Again reference to the *dona* is made at the end of the military part of the career, immediately following the cavalry prefecture. There is in this case no explicit evidence for the dates at which any of the commands were held, so it is necessary to examine the known locations and movements of the units concerned in order to determine which might have taken part in a *bellum Dacicum*. The place of garrison of *cohors III Breucorum* at this time is uncertain though there is some evidence that it might have been in Britain.[27] Legion *X Gemina* was stationed in Germania Inferior from after the civil war of 69 until the early second century: it moved to Pannonia some time after the first Dacian war, its last firmly dated appearance on the Rhine being about 101–103/4 during the governorship of Q. Acutius Nerva.[28] It could have taken part in the second war.[29] The *ala I Asturum* is attested in Moesia Inferior as late as 99, but it subsequently moved to Dacia where the only specifically dated reference to it belongs to the year 200.[30] The most likely context for the move is of course the Dacian wars of Trajan. Hence if Apollinaris won his *dona* in the first war it must have been as *praefectus alae*; if in the second war it could have been either as *praefectus* or as *tribunus legionis*. Consideration of Apollinaris' later career provides some clue towards the elucidation of this problem. His fourth procuratorship was held in Thrace, a post which he must have filled when it was a ducenarian procurator governorship rather than a centenarian financial procuratorship, hence before the reorganisation of the government of that province in about 110. It would not have been possible for Apollinaris to have held four procuratorships between decoration in the second Dacian war in 105–6 and this terminal date of 110. Hence the award must belong to the first war and specifically to the prefecture of the *ala*. Even if the *cohors III Breucorum* had been in a position to take part in the Dacian campaign, decoration in this post would make the timing of the career unmanageable – advancement is swift even if Apollinaris was ready to embark on the procuratorships as early as 103. Thus the only interpretation which satisfactorily fits the known facts of the career is to suggest that the decorations were received in the first Dacian war and that they are those of a *praefectus alae*, paralleling exactly the *dona* of Gavius Bassus.

The third example is unhelpful. The inscription which records the decorations won by P. Cassius Secundus is not a tombstone or statue base but a religious dedication by Secundus to the goddess Aecorna: it thus records not a complete career but simply the present status and honours of the dedicator: *Aecornae Aug., P. Cassius Secundus praef. alae Brit. milliariae c.R. bis torquatae, donis donatus bis bello Dacico ab imp. Caesare Nerva Traiano Aug. Ger. Dacico coronis vexillis hastis*.[31] Clearly both decorations were won during the course of Trajan's Dacian wars: but what post or posts did Secundus hold on the two occasions when he distinguished himself? Was he decorated twice as *praefectus alae milliariae*, the post he held when he set up the dedication; was he decorated once in this post and once in a previous post or twice in previous posts? All these combinations are possible, none can be proven, though the likelihood is that one at least of the awards belongs to the cavalry prefecture. The *ala* itself is attested as *bis torquata*. The present inscription is the earliest piece of dateable evidence to describe it thus and there is no reliable *terminus post quem* for the award of the title, but the balance of probability is that the unit was honoured once if not twice in the course of the Dacian campaigns of Trajan. An alternative hypothesis would attribute the first award to the unit to the Dacian and Sarmatian campaigns of the emperor Domitian though its participation in this war is by no means certain.[32] Šašel suggests that this first award may belong to Domitian's Chattan war, given that we have no positive evidence for the whereabouts of the unit at this period.[33] Certainly the unit distinguished itself under Domitian; on two inscriptions it is credited with the titles *Domitiana* and *civium Romanorum* but on neither of these texts is it also called *torquata*.[34] Hence the decoration may well belong to a subsequent occasion.

It is commonly accepted that while the *ala Britannica* did take part in the second of Trajan's Dacian wars it was absent from the first.[35] This assumption springs from the fact that the *ala* is attested on a diploma of November 102 which records the grant of privileges to men serving in units in Pannonia.[36] The inclusion of the *ala Britannica* in this list does not mean, however, that it was physically in Pannonia when the grants were made: this is simply the province to which the unit belonged whether or not it was temporarily absent on campaign. Witness for example the diploma of September of 114 which also relates to units of the Pannonian army, including the *ala Britannica*:[37] the phrasing here is different – the grant is made to units which are in the province and also to one which is on an expedition: . . . *sunt in Pannonia inferiore. . item ala I Flavia Aug. Britannic. m. c.R. missa in expeditionem* – the absence on campaign is made explicit but the implication is the same, that a unit temporarily absent is still considered to belong to the province from which it set out and to which any men due for discharge would presumably have to return with their unit to collect their diplomas. Soldiers are being discharged from the unit while it is away on campaign. There is no evidence therefore to deny the participation of the *ala Britannica* in the first as well as the second of Trajan's Dacian wars. In theory there is no reason why Cassius Secundus could not, in the duration of a three or four year equestrian military appointment, have commanded the unit and won distinction with it in both the wars, though the phrasing of the inscription does not require it, it is a natural inference that at least one of the decorations belongs to the cavalry prefecture.

The dedication was set up at the very most eight years after the conclusion of the second Dacian war (Trajan is *Dacicus* but not yet *Optimus*, a title he assumed in 114), and conceivably very soon after the end of the campaigning, an *ex voto* by an officer who had not only survived the fighting but who had made a name for himself as well, for himself and for his unit. But this is conjecture.

The decorations won by Secundus comprise *coronae*, *hastae* and *vexilla*, more than one of each type of award. No officer of this period below the *tertia militia* is known to have received, on any one occasion, more than one *hasta* and one *vexillum* (in addition to a crown or crowns); hence the second award should comprise a minimum of one crown, one *hasta* and one *vexillum*, given that the number of *hastae* and *vexilla* does not normally exceed the number of crowns. The Secundus inscription does no more than conform with what one might expect: the standard of award does not fall below the already established minimum but because of the imprecision of its phrasing it cannot be shown to rise above this minimum. This lack of precision is all the more frustrating given that Cassius Secundus held a command somewhat different from that of Gavius Bassus and Prifernius Paetus: they were prefects of quingenary *alae*, he the prefect of a milliary *ala*. It was not until the reign of Hadrian that the prefecture of an *ala milliaria* became a separate and higher step on the equestrian career ladder, the *militia quarta*. At the time when Secundus held the post it was simply an alternative appointment on the *militia tertia*, technically therefore of the same grade as the prefecture of the *ala quingenaria*. They ranked the same and were presumably paid the same: the one may in practice have attracted greater prestige than the other – the subsequent elevation of the milliary command to higher status suggests that it did – but in theory their scales of award should have been parallel.

There is possibly another example of the decoration of a *praefectus alae* on the same scale as that attributed to Gavius Bassus and Prifernius Paetus: this is the contentious case of P. Besius Betuinianus. The career of Betuinianus is recorded in straightforward chronological sequence on an inscription from Tingis in Mauretania Tingitana. The problem with this career is that as so often the *dona* are recorded out of order right at the end of the inscription. It is worth listing, in order, the points made on the stone:

praefectus cohortis I Raetorum
tribunus legionis X Geminae piae fidelis
praefectus alae Dardanorum
procurator imperatoris Caesaris Nervae Traiani Augusti Germanici
    Dacici monetae
procurator provinciae Baeticae
procurator XX hereditatium
procurator pro legato provinciae Mauretaniae Tingitanae

donis donato ab imperatore Traiano Augusto bello Dacico corona
murali vallari hastis puris vexillo argenteo

Two crowns, (probably) two *hastae* and one *vexillum* were won in Dacia, by
far the most generous award yet encountered for an equestrian with the
exception of Arruntius Claudianus (above, p. 162) to whom we shall return.
The fact that the *dona* are referred to immediately after the procurator
governorship of Mauretania led Carcopino to suggest that the two belong
together.[38] This is singularly unlikely. As we have seen there is nothing
unusual in references to *dona* being moved out of chronological sequence in
order to put them in a position of prominence at the end of a text, while it
would be strange if a ducenarian procurator in charge of a provincial auxiliary
army were to receive a lesser award than a laticlave tribune who was junior to
him. Most significant of all is the point made by Pflaum that a procurator
governor could not normally campaign outside his province while retaining
authority over his troops: he concludes that unless Betuinianus received the
title of *dux* or *praepositus* – and there is no reason to believe that he did – he
cannot have gone to Dacia in command of his army.[39] Hence the *dona* must
belong to the period of the *militia equestris*.

Each of the units in which Betuinianus served was in a position to have
taken part in one or both of the Dacian wars. A *cohors I Raetorum* is attested in
Raetia in 107 while the *ala Dardanorum* was stationed in Moesia Inferior where
it is well attested by diplomas dating between 99 and 134.[40] Legion *X Gemina*
was still in lower Germany at the time of the first war but had probably
moved to Pannonia in time to take part in the second (above, p. 171). The
generous scale of the decorations recorded have given rise on the one hand to
the belief that they constitute a single award to a senior officer, that is to the
praefectus alae, and on the other to the suggestion that the decorations listed are
a combined total of two awards, one of one crown plus one *hasta*, the other of
one crown, one *hasta* and one *vexillum*.[41] Domaszewski believed that the first
award was won as *praefectus cohortis*, the second as *tribunus legionis*, Ritterling
and Pflaum that the first was as *praefectus cohortis*, the second as *praefectus alae*;
all attributed one award to each of the two Dacian campaigns. Of the
Domaszewski and the Pflaum/Ritterling interpretations the latter is the more
plausible. Betuinianus was holding his fourth procuratorial appointment
before 114 – the inscription was erected before Trajan had assumed the title
Parthicus – and these appointments would fit in much more comfortably if
Betuinianus had reached the third rung of the equestrian career ladder by the
time he was decorated. If he was only *tribunus legionis* in 105–6 it would leave
five posts, one military command and four procuratorships to be fitted in in
eight years, not impossible but unlikely. The issue was simplified for Nagy by
the assumption that neither *I Raetorum* nor *X Gemina* participated in either
campaign and that the *ala Dardanorum* took part only in the first. The belief

that the *ala Dardanorum* played no part in the second was based on the fact that it is mentioned on a diploma of AD 105 which records grants made to units in Moesia Inferior.[42] This fact in no way implies that the unit had to be in Moesia at the time the grant was made. Diplomas were, we know, awarded to men in units on campaign; there was no reason for delaying the formal procedure of the grant of privileges to men in a unit simply because it was temporarily away from its home province.[43] Indeed men were even discharged when on campaign though in the present case involving the *ala Dardanorum* the grants recorded in the diploma are being made to serving soldiers.[44] Nor does there appear to be any firm foundation for belief in the non-participation of *X Gemina* and *I Raetorum*. *X Gemina* certainly was not in a position to take part in the first war but its move Danube-wards suggests very strongly that it did take part in the second. As far as we know *I Raetorum* could have fought in both: there is no positive evidence that it did but neither can it be proved that it did not. The possibility cannot be dismissed.

For Nagy the award of two *coronae*, two *hastae* and one *vexillum* to a *praefectus alae* was consistent with the scheme of equestrian *dona* as he saw it. He put forward a case for an upper and a lower scale of award for each rank as follows:

prima militia:	1 corona + 1 hasta
	1 corona + 1 hasta + 1 vexillum
secunda militia:	1 corona + 1 hasta + 1 vexillum
	2 coronae + 1 hasta + 1 vexillum
tertia militia:	2 coronae + 1 hasta + 1 vexillum
	2 coronae + 2 hastae + 1 vexillum

The dual scales of the *prima* and *secunda militiae* are clearly attested: the extension of the scheme to the *tertia militia* is more a matter of logical deduction than of concrete evidence. The decorations of neither of the *praefecti alae* so far examined conform to this scheme, by the terms of which both should have been decorated as tribune.[45] There is no clear example of a cavalry prefect commanding a quingenary *ala* receiving a reward on either of the scales proposed by Nagy but there is nothing inherently improbable in the suggestion that he should have done: it is worth noting in this context that the prefect of a milliary *ala* in the Antonine period received two crowns, two *hastae* and two *vexilla* which is the logical extension of the scheme to the *quarta militia* (below, p. 179). The major problem of such a scheme is simple: it is deceptively neat, it cannot be applied rigidly and therefore does not work as a clear guide to the rank of equestrians when decorated. The one *praefectus alae* whose *dona* approximate to the scale suggested by Nagy are those of Arruntius Claudianus, (attested by an inscription discovered since he wrote), an equestrian whose early career belongs according to one argument to the period of Domitian but who could equally well, on present evidence, be

Trajanic. The problem regarding the dating of the career has already been considered (above p. 162). Claudianus received *dona* comprising two crowns, one *hasta* and more than one *vexillum*.

It would be unwise to use any hypothetical scale of awards to help elucidate the problem of Besius Betuinianus. The fact that a *praefectus alae* clearly could get as small an award as single *corona*, *hasta* and *vexillum* means that the Domaszewski/Pflaum/Ritterling hypothesis cannot be ruled out of court. On the other hand an award as large as that proposed by Nagy is, on the evidence of the case of Claudianus, perfectly feasible.

In summary therefore the evidence for equestrian *dona* in the Trajanic period gives the following picture:

prima militia: 1 corona + 1 hasta
                  1 corona + 1 hasta + 1 vexillum
secunda militia: 1 corona + 1 hasta + 1 vexillum
                  2 coronae + 1 hasta + 1 vexillum
tertia militia: 1 corona + 1 hasta + 1 vexillum
                  2 coronae + 2 hastae + 1 vexillum ?
                  2 coronae + 1 hasta + 2 vexilla ?

While there is some suggestion here of a graduated scale of award it is not so rigid a one as was applied to senatorial *dona*. Another feature of equestrian *dona* of which little account has so far been taken is the nature of the crowns awarded: in fact no significant pattern emerges:

prima militia: vallaris + 1 hasta
                  muralis + 1 hasta + 1 vexillum
secunda militia: vallaris + 1 hasta + 1 vexillum
                  muralis + 1 hasta + 1 vexillum
                  vallaris + aurea + 1 hasta + 1 vexillum
tertia militia: muralis + 1 hasta + 1 vexillum
                  muralis + 1 hasta + 1 vexillum
                  muralis + vallaris + 2 hastae + 1 vexillum ?
                  aurea + ? + 1 hasta + 2 vexilla ?

The inescapable conclusion here as in the case of the crowns awarded to centurions (below, p. 185) is that either the crowns were awarded completely at random, which is singularly unlikely, or that each signified something particular in the conduct of the man who won them.

Hadrianic period

TABLE G   EQUESTRIAN DONA · HADRIANIC

NAME	RANK	CORONAE	HASTAE	VEXILLA
M. Statius Priscus	trib. leg.	0	0	1
Sex. Cornelius Dexter	praef. alae D.	0	1	1

Hadrianic equestrian decorations are few in number and small in size just as were the senatorial *dona* of this same period. The two examples present no complications. Statius Priscus and Cornelius Dexter were both decorated in the Jewish war, the one in the *secunda*, the other in the *tertia militia*. It is idle to speculate what the *dona* of the *prima militia* might have been! It is doubtful if Hadrian was operating a system of award strictly according to rank for it is notable that these two awards are comparable to or smaller than those made at the same period to senior centurions. Arrius Clemens and Albius Felix for example each received a gold crown and a *hasta* from Hadrian (below, p. 194). Senators did little better. There is here more than a hint of the republican practice of decoration more by merit than status.

Antonine period

No example of equestrian *dona* awarded by Antoninus Pius is known: the evidence resumes with the Parthian wars of Marcus and Verus and the German wars of Marcus, Verus and Commodus in the 160s and 170s.

TABLE H   EQUESTRIAN DONA · ANTONINE

NAME	RANK	CORONAE			HASTAE	VEXILLA
		m.	*v.*	*a.*		
M. Cl. Faustus						
Secundus	praef. coh./trib.coh?	[	I	]	I	I
P. Cominius Clemens	trib. leg.	I			I?	o
C. Iulius Corinthianus	trib. vex. Dacorum	I			I	I
M. Macrinius Avitus						
Catonius Vindex	praef. alae. M.	I	I		2	2
CIL VIII 9372	praef. alae. M.?	[		]	2	[ ]
L. Aurelius Nicomedes	proc. + cura copiarum	I			I	I

PRIMA MILITIA

There is no clear example of the decorations of an equestrian in the *prima militia* though M. Clodius Faustus Secundus may belong to this category. The interpretation of this career is highly speculative and is discussed in some detail below (p. 181). If Secundus was *praefectus cohortis* when decorated this gives a scale of one crown, one *hasta* and one *vexillum*. The record of the *dona* is fragmentary, the extant portion mentioning only the *hasta* and the *vexillum*: since these two awards were very rarely awarded without a *corona* (the one example is Hadrianic) a single crown has been restored.

SECUNDA MILITIA

The two equestrians decorated in the *secunda militia* each received a different award, that of Clemens being, the Hadrianic example apart, the lowest attested decoration of a legionary tribune. The inscription relating to Cominius Clemens is fragmentary but the relevant portions can be restored with some confidence. Clemens was serving as tribune in *II Adiutrix* when decorated by Marcus and Verus in the Parthian campaign.[46] This much is clear. Verus was not concerned with *dona* for the German war for he died very soon after it began, while *II Adiutrix*, stationed at this period in Pannonia Inferior, is known to have moved east for the Parthian war under the command of Q. Antistius Adventus: *leg. secunda Adiutricis translato in eam expeditione Parthica*.[47] That part of the inscription which records the *dona* of Clemens is mutilated but considerations of spacing leave no doubt that only a single crown, a *corona muralis*, and one *hasta* were won, there being no room to restore a *vexillum*. This award is lower by the one *vexillum* than that made to Corinthianus when serving as tribune in charge of a detachment of Dacians sent to a Parthian war. The career is not specifically dated, no emperor is mentioned by name, but the Parthian war must be either that of Marcus and Verus or that of Severus and Caracalla: it cannot be the Trajanic war as two emperors were involved in the award. Mommsen believed the later of the two occasions to be the more likely but for no stated reason.[48] One clue to the date lies in the phraseology, *sacratissimi imperatores* ('most sacred emperors'). The epithet *sacratissimi* as applied to members of the imperial household is well attested in the mid-to-late Antonine period – to quote but one example it appears in the inscription relating to M. Valerius Maximianus (see below) – but is rare in the Severan. Corinthianus' subsequent career is also instructive. He went on to command two *alae*, both of them stationed in Dacia. The *ala Campagonum* formed part of the garrison of the province of Dacia Apulensis while the unnamed milliary *ala* is to be associated with the *ala I Batavorum*, since the findspot of the inscription was in Apulum where this unit is attested.[49] Now after the Parthian wars of Marcus and Verus the focus of military activity shifted to the Danube area and remained there for some time. Again M. Valerius Maximianus provides a useful parallel, for he followed service in the Parthian war with a multiplicity of commands in the Danubian area. The close similarity between the careers of Corinthianus and Maximianus is good reason for accepting an Antonine date for the former.

TERTIA MILITIA

No evidence is available for the *dona* of the *tertia militia*. M. Valerius Maximianus won decorations at this period as prefect of an *ala quingenaria*, the *ala I Aravacorum*, but his is a special case. Having killed an enemy king he received *spolia opima* (above, p. 59), not conventional *dona*: he was also promoted to the prefecture of a milliary *ala*.

QUARTA MILITIA

The Antonine period provides our first and only examples of the *dona* of an officer on the fourth grade of the *militia*. Valerius Maximianus won decorations at this rank (in addition to those won in his previous post) but does not specify the composition of the award. M. Macrinius Avitus Catonius Vindex does. He was prefect of the *ala contariorum* when decorated with two *coronae*, two *hastae* and two *vexilla* for services in the first German war. The record of the *dona* is dissociated from the post to which they belong, a fact which led Steiner to believe that the *dona* were won during service as a laticlave tribune, for Vindex had been adlected into the senate shortly after embarking on a procuratorial career.[50] The *dona* are precisely those of a senatorial tribune but we know Vindex to have been adlected *inter praetorios* where a three-fold and not a two-fold scale of decoration would have been appropriate. The timing of the career leaves no doubt as to the post held when the decorations were won. They were awarded by Marcus alone and could therefore belong to any stage within the first German war: the context for the award does not necessarily, as has been suggested, have to post-date the death of Verus in 169 particularly in view of the fact that the award of a decoration, if left until the end of the war, can be many years later than the deed which it commemorates; and Verus died well before the end of the German war.[51]

Vindex was clearly involved in the German war in its early stages. In the winter of 166/7 he was prefect of a cavalry unit sent against an invading force of Obii and Langobardi who had crossed over the Ister.[52] This literary reference does not make clear which of his two cavalry prefectures he held at this time but if it was the exploit for which he was decorated, and the association is an attractive and perfectly feasible one, he is likely to have been in the *quarta militia* at the time, given the scale of the award which is higher than any hitherto attested for an equestrian officer. The decoration is the same as that of a senatorial tribune and given the rank at which Vindex was adlected into the senate a correlation of level between the post of *praefectus alae milliariae* and that of *tribunus laticlavius* is perfectly acceptable. An angusticlave tribunate in a legion constituted a post in the *secunda militia*: senior to the tribunes was the *praefectus castrorum* (roughly parallel to the *tertia militia*) and then the senatorial tribune of comparable seniority therefore to the *quarta militia*, the *praefectus alae milliariae*. These comparisons are not, of course, exact. As Dobson has pointed out, the pay of the *praefectus castrorum* should be comparable to that of the *praefectus alae milliariae* rather than to that of the *praefectus alae quingenariae*, thus boosting the *tribunus laticlavius*, in terms of pay at least, above the *praefectus alae milliariae*.[53] But pay and relative seniority do not always go exactly hand in hand. For example on the Dobson figures the *primus pilus* earns two and half times as much as a *tribunus angusticlavius*, his superior. However, despite these problems, it is clear that there is no need to believe with Nagy that the *dona* are too high for an equestrian officer and must be attributed to the provincial governorship of Dacia Malvensis.[54]

Another example of decoration in the *militia quarta* may be postulated. The unknown officer commemorated by CIL VIII 9372 won in a German war a decoration which comprised two *hastae*, at least one *corona* and a totally unknown number of *vexilla*. Given that the number of *hastae* normally parallels or falls below the number of crowns two *coronae* may be restored plus hypothetically one or two *vexilla*. The text is very defective and nothing conclusive remains of any of the equestrian military posts: it can be restored at will to demonstrate either three or four *militiae*. The equestrian *militiae* were immediately followed by procuratorial posts, the first of which was in Moesia superior, a centenarian appointment.[55] Promotion to a centenarian post without prior service in a sexagenarian one strongly supports the contention that the unknown served in a milliary *ala*: the equestrian who had completed the *quarta militia* was invariably promoted direct to a centenarian post while those who completed only three grades often went first to a sexagenarian procuratorship. What little remains of the *dona* is consistent with their being those of a *praefectus alae milliariae*. Such an interpretation does not however rest on the firmest of foundations and collapses entirely if it could be shown that the German war in which the decorations were won is other than the German war of Marcus Aurelius, for the *quarta militia* did not exist at the time of earlier German wars.

The dating of the career to the Antonine period is based on the restoration of the TRA which is all that survives of the first extant line to read [*trib. leg. II*] *Tra*[*ianae*]. Legion *II Traiana* was not created until after the German wars of Domitian and Trajan: the next available context is the German war of Marcus. If the reference to *II Traiana* is discarded the *dona* could have been awarded by any of the emperors who adopted the cognomen *Germanicus*, that is Domitian, Trajan or Marcus. Vespasian can be counted out for the province of Moesia Superior in which the unknown served his first procuratorship was not created until AD 86 when Moesia was split. Domitian took the title *Germanicus* after the first of his German wars and carries it on some of the inscriptions which record *dona* for the war. Trajan also carries the title in an inscription recording *dona* for his German war.[56] Marcus took the title *Germanicus* in 172 during the course of the first German war, but subsequently dropped it (it disappears from his coinage late in 173) perhaps as a result of renewed revolt among the Quadi. He is not credited with the title on any of the texts recording *dona* for the war. Another factor which could point to a date earlier than the Antonine is the comparative lack of abbreviation of the text. Also the unknown is commemorated as procurator *Aug.* (of one

Augustus) and not *Augg.* (of more than one Augustus): Marcus and Commodus were joint *Augusti* at the conclusion of Marcus' German war, so if anything the inscription should be pushed a little later to the second German war begun by Marcus and Commodus and completed by Commodus alone on the death of Marcus (Commodus took the title *Germanicus* along with Marcus in 172). Much therefore depends on the restoration *II Traiana*, for the scale of the *dona* as conventionally restored is not sufficiently high to rule out decoration at any level other than that of the *quarta militia*. The case for decoration at that rank is an attractive one but it is by no means flawless.

TWO PROBLEM CASES

There are two cases of Antonine equestrian *dona* which do not, on first sight, fit into any of the categories discussed above. These are the cases of L. Aurelius Nicomedes and M. Clodius Faustus Secundus. These two men have one particular thing in common: both were given at some stage during their career a responsibility for army provisioning. Here the resemblance ends. L. Aurelius Nicomedes has already been discussed in some detail (above, p. 130). He is the freedman of Lucius Caesar who was elevated to the *ordo equester* by Marcus and undertook no equestrian military commands, proceeding direct to administrative posts, including that of *praefectus vehiculorum* together with the *cura copiarum*. As has been indicated his decorations – one crown, one *hasta* and one *vexillum* – are in absolute terms low, but his route to promotion was irregular and the job in hand though of obvious importance in wartime not strictly military. The *dona* are comparable to those regularly received by equestrians up to and including those in the *tertia militia*.

The same scale of award can be restored in the case of M. Clodius Faustus Secundus; what is not so clear is the post held by Secundus when he was decorated. The inscription recording the career survives in very fragmentary form. The relevant portion reads as follows: [. . . . .]*parationem frumenti i*[*n*] *provin*[. . . . .] *Maurorum in ex*[*p*]*editione Germ. p*[. . . . .] *vexillo et hasta p*[*u*]*ra donato et* [. . . . .]. The record of the *dona* is incomplete but a single crown can be restored on the assumption that never, except in the Hadrianic period, were a *hasta* and a *vexillum* given alone without a crown. Steiner in his article on *dona* included this inscription in a section on *dona* awarded in non-military posts, thus conveying implicitly (though he does not discuss the case explicitly) that he believed the decorations to be connected with the corn-gathering mission to which the early part of the text alludes: he accepted the Mommsen restoration [*misso ob com*]*parationem frumenti e*[*x*] *provi*[*ncia ad gentes*] *Maurorum in expeditione Germ. p*[. . . . .].[57] Although no military posts appear on the text thus reconstructed there is plenty of scope to restore them, for the entire right hand portion of the inscription is lost. Cagnat divorced the reference to the corn gathering from the German expedition and

inserted a military post as *praepositus*: [*misso ad com*]*parationem frumenti i*[*n*]
provin[*ciam* . . . . . *ob bellum*] *Maurorum in expeditione Germ. p*[*raeposito*
. . . . .].[58] Yet a further hypothesis has been put forward by Jarrett. On
analogy with the career of T. Flavius Macer he restores: [*curator ad com*]
parationem frumenti i[*n*] *provin*[*ciam* . . . . ., *praef. gentis*] *Maurorum, in expeditione Germ. p*[*raef. coh.* . . . . .].[59]

According to this interpretation the inscription records three separate posts:
responsibility for provisioning in an unknown province, a post as *praefectus
gentis* among the Moors and a command in the *militia prima* discharged during
the German war: the decorations attach to this last post. Clearly this is possible
but the phrasing, with the reference to the war preceding the post which is
coupled with it, is awkward. This problem can be circumvented if the
reference to the Moors is taken to be a reference to a unit of Moors serving in
the German expedition. Two *cohortes Maurorum* were stationed in Pannonia
Inferior in the second century, one of quingenary and one of milliary
strength.[60] The army of lower Pannonia certainly did take part in Marcus'
German war as is clear from the fact that the then governor of the province, C.
Vettius Sabinianus, himself received military decorations. The inscription
relating to Secundus could therefore be restored to read something as follows:
. . . [*curator ad com*]*parationem frumenti i*[*n*] *provinc*[*iam* . . . . ., *praef.* or
trib. coh.?] *Maurorum in expeditione Germ. p*[*rima? corona? et*] *vexillo et hasta
p*[*u*]*ra donato et* [. . . . .]. It still remains uncertain what rank Secundus held
when decorated, *prima* or *secunda militia*. One point in favour of the *prima
militia* is the difficulty otherwise in restoring a cohort prefecture: Secundus
could of course have omitted this post, passing straight to the *secunda militia*,
but this is less than probable. The scale of award at least equals the higher of the
two scales of award made to *praefecti cohortium* in the Trajanic period. It is
often assumed that Antonine equestrian *dona* were on a lower scale than
Trajanic ones. The only good evidence for this assumption is the single crown
and *hasta* awarded to Clemens as *tribunus legionis*. For the rest the comparatively few attested Antonine awards are directly comparable with Trajanic
examples, with the *dona* of the *quarta militia* neatly fitting into place as a fairly
generous extension of the practice as it existed in the earlier second century.

Conclusion

The *dona* of the *militia equestris* appear never to have developed into the fairly
rigid hierarchical form that the senatorial *dona* took on in the Flavian period
and retained thereafter. Neat schemes such as those put forward by Steiner, by
Domaszewski and more recently by Nagy can all be shown to be defective to
a greater or lesser degree. Bearing in mind the individuality of the emperors
each reign must be viewed separately, as a result of which it is only, the Julio-
Claudian period apart, under Trajan that there is evidence for all grades of the

militia equestris. It is significant therefore that the *dona* of the Trajanic period defy tight classification: the combination one *corona*, one *hasta* and one *vexillum* is attested for all grades of the *militia*, a fact which even Nagy's two-fold classification cannot encompass. One *corona* plus one *hasta* is, the Hadrianic period apart, the minimum award attested for any equestrian from Augustus to Commodus – and the evidence goes no later than this. From the Flavian period onwards when the *praefectura equitum* was securely established as the senior command, no cavalry prefect received less than one crown, *hasta* and *vexillum*. Lesser grades continued to receive a minimum of one crown plus one *hasta* though tribunes usually and prefects often received more than this minimum. The *dona* of the *praefectus alae milliariae* were suitably augmented as befitted the rarity, eminence and extreme importance of the post. Oddities such as Iulius Karus and Arruntius Claudianus clearly indicate that no rigid rules and regulations defined in exact terms what decorations should be awarded. There were probably guidelines and conventions: precedents were there to be followed at will. Despite a rough equation between scale of *dona* and position on the equestrian career ladder, the apparent vagaries of the system can be accounted for only if it is accepted that merit and individuality continued to play their part in determining the exact composition of award.

CHAPTER IX

IMPERIAL SCALES OF AWARD · CENTURIONS AND PRIMIPILARES

During the first half of the first century AD a proper career structure developed for the centurion separating his path to advancement off from that of the equestrian. Fig. 14 indicates the normal promotion pattern showing how the two careers, independent of one another at the lower levels, unite at the level of the procuratorships and thenceforth proceed as one. It will be convenient therefore to advance step by step through a typical centurion/*primipilaris* career, picking out the scale of *dona* appropriate to the different levels. Evidence is not available for every separate step of the way but it is possible tentatively to reconstruct hypothetical scales based on the general hierarchical principles involved.

During the Julio-Claudian period it was common as we have seen (above, p. 158) for a centurion or *primus pilus* to go on to command an auxiliary unit and receive the appropriate reward (the standard one *corona*, one *hasta*), so it is only after the creation of the separate equestrian career structure and the establishment of a regular promotion ladder for the centurion that we can expect to see a hierarchy of awards for the centurion and *primipilaris*.

One acute problem, in relation to the *dona* of the primipilaris, is the tendency to omit mention of the earlier posts held and to give the decorations as a total for the whole career. It is often difficult therefore to apportion the *dona* to the individual posts in which they were won. A case in point is that of Sextus Vibius Gallus who rose as high as *praefectus castrorum* but who details no earlier post than that of *trecenarius* (a senior centurionate).[1] His *dona* (*torques*, *armillae*, *phalerae*, three *coronae murales*, two *coronae vallares*, one *corona aurea*, five *hastae purae* and two *vexilla*) could belong to any stage in a career which may have begun with service in the ranks but more probably started with a direct commission to a centurionate. Problem careers such as that of Gallus can be elucidated only when, having established known or likely scales of award for the various posts involved, it may be possible to break the blocks of decorations down into their constituent parts. Discussion of such careers, even though they may involve decoration in the centurionate, is therefore left until the end of the chapter.

Centurions of the legions and Rome cohorts

The standard decoration of the centurion consisted of the *torques, armillae* and *phalerae* characteristic of soldiers in the ranks (below, p. 213) plus a single crown. This crown could be a *vallaris, muralis* or *aurea* but never a *classica* – a fact which underlines the exclusivity of the *corona classica* to the consular. Although this scale was the norm it was not invariable and could be added to or subtracted from as appropriate.

The first and most obvious variable factor in the *dona* of the centurion was the nature of the crown received. It is clear from Table I, which gives all available examples of the scales of *dona* of centurions, that the *corona vallaris* was by far the most common, followed by the *muralis* and the *aurea*. Of these three crowns the *aurea* was undoubtedly the least prestigious; this is the crown which was, invariably, awarded to the praetorian *evocatus* who occupied a position inferior to that of the centurion, and it is the crown which appears to have been most freely distributed during the years of the Republic in situations in which none of the other more specific types of crown were appropriate. The *corona muralis* on the other hand was not often awarded and so presumably acquired a rarity value. It is inconceivable that the award of these different crowns to centurions was made in a haphazard fashion, any more than it is likely in the case of the equestrians. The different types must have had some significance but it is not immediately clear just what this significance was. No apparent distinction was made between the awards given to centurions of the legions and those of the Rome cohorts. Technically the posts were of comparable ranking and the same scales of award applied to both. The case of Aemilius Paternus is particularly instructive; he was decorated three times, twice as legionary centurion and once as praetorian centurion and on all three occasions he received a *corona vallaris*. Likewise under Trajan, Marcius Celer was decorated as legionary centurion but he received a *corona muralis*. Of the four Vespasianic centurions, two certainly and two probably legionary, two received *vallares*, two *aureae*, one of each type going to the certain legionaries. Nor can it be shown that the directly commissioned man received a materially different award from the centurion who rose from the ranks. This is no more than one might expect but it does nevertheless leave unanswered the problem of the allocation of the different types of crown. Seniority cannot be shown to have any bearing on the issue. Returning to the case of Aemilius Paternus, a gap of at least nine and probably more like fourteen years separates his first and last awards and yet both were the same. The inevitable conclusion is that the distinction of the deed performed determined the award won. Such a conclusion is incapable of positive proof, arising as it does in such a negative fashion, from the impossibility of explaining the variations in any other way.

The centurion scale was further varied downwards by the complete omission of any type of crown, or upward by the addition of a further crown. Both these variants are rare but they do occur. Otherwise the one basic distinction which can be detected is that between the award of the ordinary and the senior centurions. In the legions a similar scale appears to have been awarded to all centurions in cohorts II–X; only the *primi ordines*, the centurions of the first cohort, received an appreciably different award. This is no more than one might expect for, as Wegeleben has shown, the centurions in cohorts II–X were equal in rank if not in seniority and it was only those who had been promoted into *cohors I* who held a higher rank.[2] Similarly among the centurions of the praetorian guard it is only those who ranked as senior, for example the *trecenarius* and the *princeps castrorum*, who received a larger decoration.

TABLE I   DONA OF CENTURIONS AND PRIMIPILARES

DATE	NAME	RANK	T A P	CORONAE			HAST	VEX
				a	v	m		
Julio–Claudian	L. Blattius Vetus	C leg or below	A P					
	M. Caelius	C leg or below	T A P	civica				
	C. Gavius Silvanus	C or evocatus	T A P	I				
	M. Petronius Classicus	C leg or below	T ? P					
	L. Refidius Bassus	C leg or below	? ? P	[		]		
	Q. Sertorius Festus	C leg or below	T P	I				
	CIL XIII 7556	C leg or below	T P	[		]		
	C. Purtisius Atinas	p p ?			I		I	
	M. Vergilius Gallus Lusius	p p ?			I		I	
	P. Anicius Maximus	praef castr					I	I
Neronian	M. Vettius Valens	p p	T A P					
	L. Antonius Naso	trib coh praet		I	I		2	2
Julio Cl/early Fl	C. Gavius Celer	C leg	T A	I				
Vespasianic	M. Blossius Pudens	C leg	T A P	I				
	L. Lepidius Proculus	C leg	T A P		I			
	C. Velius Rufus	C (leg ?)	T A P		I			
	CIL III 14387i	C (leg ?)	T A P	I				
Titus/Domitian	CIL XI 1602	senior C or p p		I			I	
Domitianic	L. Aconius Statura	C leg	T A P	I				
	Ti. Claudius Vitalis	C leg	T A P	I				
	Ti. Claudius Vitalis	C leg	T A P	I				
	T. Cominius Severus	C leg	T A P	I				
	L. Valerius Proclus	C leg	T A P					
	Q. Vilanius Nepos	C urb	T A					
	Cn. Pompeius Homullus	C ?	T A P					
	Cn. Pompeius Homullus	senior C		I			I	
	C. Velius Rufus	trib coh urb			I		2	2
	C. Velius Rufus	trib coh urb			I		2	2

TABLE I DONA OF CENTURIONS AND PRIMIPILARES

DATE	NAME	RANK	T A P	CORONAE a v m			HAST	VEX
Trajanic	L. Aconius Statura	C leg	T A P	I				
	L. Aemilius Paternus	C leg	T A P	I				
	L. Aemilius Paternus	C leg	T A P	I				
	L. Aemilius Paternus	C praet	T A P	I				
	Q. Geminius Sabinus	C leg	T A P	I				
	N. Marcius Celer	C leg	T A P		I			
	CIL v 546	C ?	T A P	[		]		
	Epigraphica XXII, 29	C leg	T A P	I				
Hadrianic	Q. Albius Felix	C leg (senior ?)		I			I	
	C. Arrius Clemens	trecenarius		I			I	
	–. Octavius Secundus	C leg	T A P	I				
	M. Sabidius Maximus	C leg	T A P		I			
	CIL XI 2112	p p ?	[			]	I	
Antoninus Pius	C. Cestius Sabinus	senior C/p p					I	
Marcus – Commodus	M. Petronius Fortunatus	C leg	T P	I	I			
	L. Petronius Sabinus	C leg (senior ?)		I	I		I	
	L. Petronius Sabinus	C leg (senior ?)		I	I		I	
	M. Bassaeus Rufus	praef praet		I	I	I	4	4
Severan	C. Didius Saturninus	C praet/p p		I + civ			I	
	M. Tillius Rufus	princ castr		I			I	
Undated	T. Cassius Secundus	C leg	T A P		I			
	M. Pompeius Asper	C ?	T A P					

PRE–FLAVIAN PERIOD

Clear evidence for the scale of a centurion's *dona* in the pre-Flavian period is lacking. On four of the relevant inscriptions the decorations are not mentioned at all, they are merely indicated by sculpture, while at the same time the career records are defective, being limited to the highest post held, in each case that of centurion. Marcus Caelius died as centurion of legion *XVIII* in the Varus disaster of AD 9; the very fine cenotaph set up in his honour at Xanten (Vetera) shows Caelius wearing *torques, armillae, phalerae* and a crown (pl. 2a). However the crown is a *corona civica* awarded for saving the life of a Roman citizen, which could have been won at any stage in the career, not necessarily as centurion. Had Caelius been decorated as a centurion on the same scale as is attested from the Flavian period, he would probably have won *torques, armillae, phalerae* and a crown (*aurea, vallaris* or *muralis*). Since the portrait sculpture could not show the man wearing two crowns, whoever commissioned the stone would presumably have required that the sculptor illustrate the more significant, that is the *corona civica*. There is no way, on the details available, to prove which is the correct alternative – decoration in the ranks without a centurion's crown but with the civic crown, or decoration as centurion with a centurion's crown (*muralis, vallaris* or *aurea*) plus the civic crown.

A similar problem arises with Q. Sertorius Festus, except that here the sculpture of the crown is badly abraded and not so well executed and has been variously interpreted as a *corona civica* or a *corona aurea* (pl. 2b). Festus is shown with the crown, *torques, phalerae* but no *armillae* and is described in the text as centurion of *legio XI Claudia pia fidelis*. The legionary titles are written out in full and for this reason, as well as on stylistic grounds, the erection of the tombstone is unlikely to post-date by many years the date of AD 42 when the legion, stationed in Dalmatia, won its honorary titles on the occasion of the revolt of Scribonianus. It may be that Festus won his decorations on the occasion of the rebellion – in which case he will probably have been a centurion at the time (unless of course he was promoted centurion because of his bravery): however it is equally likely that he won them on some earlier occasion during the pacification of the area when he could have been serving as centurion or in the ranks.

The tombstones of L. Blattius Vetus and M. Petronius Classicus likewise refer only to posts as centurion. The former won *dona* comprising two *armillae* and *phalerae* but apparently no *torques*, the latter *torques* and *phalerae* but no *armillae*, although the lower part of the stone is somewhat mutilated and they could have appeared there: in both these cases the *dona* are depicted but not mentioned in the text (pl. 10b, 13c). Steiner believed Vetus to have been a centurion when decorated but apparently for no other reason than that a centurionate is the only post mentioned on the stone. Such precise allocation of the *dona* is not possible. The military service pre-dates the disbanding of *IV Macedonica* in AD 69. The legion served in Spain until its move to Mainz in upper Germany in AD 43, too late to participate in the Augustan and Tiberian campaigns on the Danube. It is probable therefore that the decorations belong to the period of the Augustan campaigns in Spain in which the unit no doubt took part. The fact that the stone was erected at Ateste in Italy, Vetus' birthplace and the place to which he retired, rather than at the location where he served, makes it impossible to tie down its date any more precisely: he could have returned to Italy from either Spain or from Germany and there is no way of knowing which. Hence the progress of the career cannot be timed and the *dona* ascribed to their correct place in it. If the practice of giving a crown to a centurion could be shown to date back to the early years of the Principate decoration in the ranks would be the more likely alternative. So also with Petronius Classicus who died as centurion of *VIII Augusta*. The stone was erected at Poetovio in upper Pannonia, presumably the place where Classicus served, so his career must pre-date the move of *VIII Augusta* to Moesia about AD 45. The context for the decorations is assumed to be the Illyrican wars, but it is impossible to determine the capacity in which Classicus was serving at the time, as centurion or in the ranks.

Two inscriptions which suggest that the later standard centurion award did emerge during the pre-Flavian period are those relating to Gavius Silvanus and Gavius Celer. Silvanus won *torques*, *armillae*, *phalerae* and a *corona aurea* from Claudius in the British war. The text which records his *dona* gives no details below the post of *primus pilus* but we know from a chance reference in Tacitus that in AD 65 Silvanus held the post of *tribunus cohortis praetoriae*.[3] It is clear as Dobson has shown that in 43 he cannot have held a command any higher than that of centurion, while he might even have been *evocatus*.[4] The career is extremely close in timing to that of M. Vettius Valens whom we know to have been *evocatus* in 43 when decorated by Claudius *bello Britannico*, with the same award as that given to Silvanus. Since the *corona aurea* does later appear to be characteristic of the *evocatus* (below, p. 210) and is only comparatively rarely awarded to a centurion, there is a good case to be made for Silvanus being praetorian *evocatus* when decorated by Claudius. This being so, our one piece of direct evidence for the scale of a centurion's *dona* at this period disappears; however we are left with a strong piece of circumstantial evidence. If, by the time of Claudius, the *evocatus* regularly received an award comprising a crown in addition to the *torques*, *armillae* and *phalerae* the centurion cannot have received less. Hence the 'normal' scale must have been in existence by the 40s, earlier than any of the other officers' scales of award can be shown to have developed.

The inscription relating to Gavius Celer is consistent with this evidence. This stone depicts a crown, a *corona aurea*, two *torques* and two *armillae*. The text tells us that Celer was a centurion in legion *III Augusta*; he died in service aged forty-three having served just twenty-three years (pl. 6b).[5] The stone is not precisely dated but its findspot at the legionary fortress of Ammaedara in Africa Proconsularis indicates a date which falls about the middle of the first century AD before the move of *III Augusta* to Theveste in the early Flavian period. A pre-Flavian date is vey probable, the wars of the Tiberian age against Tacfarinas providing a likely context.

FLAVIAN PERIOD

A consistent picture regarding the *dona* of the centurion emerges under Vespasian. Four centurions decorated at this period provide evidence of the scale of award: all received *torques*, *armillae*, *phalerae* in combination with a crown. Two received *coronae aureae*, Blossius Pudens as centurion of legion *V Macedonica* and the *ignotus* of CIL III 14387[i] while holding what was probably a legionary centurionate; two received *coronae vallares*, Lepidius Proculus as centurion of either *V Macedonica* or *XV Apollinaris* (probably the former), and Velius Rufus probably in a legionary post. Proculus' *dona* are recorded at the end of the career, immediately following reference to the primipilate.

However, they are clearly out of order for the legion in which Proculus served as *primus pilus*, *XIII Gemina*, did not serve in the Jewish war for which the *dona* were given, while two of the legions in which he held centurionates, *V Macedonica* and *XV Apollinaris*, both did. The former is the more likely. The inscription set up in Proculus' honour at Ariminum (Rimini) was erected by the *salinatores civitatis Menapiorum*, salt workers of the city of the Menapii, that is roughly the area of Flanders. There are two occasions in his career when Proculus could have come into contact with the Menapii, as *primus pilus* of *XIII Gemina* when it was briefly in that area to put down the revolt of Civilis or as centurion of *VI Victrix* which, from AD 70 until the early 120s was stationed in lower Germany. If he was there with *XIII Gemina* he must have won his *dona* as centurion of *XV Apollinaris*, the legion in which he was serving immediately prior to his primipilate; if he was there as centurion of legion *VI Victrix*, the *dona* must belong to a preceding centurionate, that is in *V Macedonica* (he was centurion first of *V Macedonica*, then *VI Victrix*, then *XV Apollinaris*). To have been with *XIII Gemina* in lower Germany in AD 69 means leaving the east before the completion of the Jewish war: this is less likely than the contention that he transferred to *VI Victrix* on the completion of the war.

The text relating to Velius Rufus gives no post lower than that of *primus pilus*, but it is possible on the known dating of the career to assign the *dona* with confidence to an unmentioned centurionate. Rufus served in 83 in Domitian's German war as *primus pilus* in command of vexillations from nine legions; the *dona* were won some thirteen years previously in the Jewish war of Vespasian and Titus. Rufus must therefore have been a centurion when decorated. The legion or legions in which he served as centurion are not stated but the inscription was set up by a veteran of *XV Apollinaris*, a legion which is known to have taken part in the Jewish war and which is not mentioned in any other context on the stone. Conjecturally, Rufus may have been decorated as centurion of *XV Apollinaris*.

Only a single post is mentioned in the case of Blossius Pudens, the unfortunate centurion who died after being nominated to but before he could take up a primipilate. There is no reason to doubt the association of decoration in the Jewish war with the specified centurionate in *V Macedonica*.

The unwavering standard attested under Vespasian and Titus is not sustained through the reign of their successor. Aconius Statura and Cominius Severus, both received *torques*, *armillae*, *phalerae* and a *corona vallaris*, the former in Domitian's *bellum Germanicum et Sarmaticum*, the latter in his Dacian war. In neither case is there any reason to doubt the attribution of the *dona* to posts in the centurionate for neither held any higher rank and both are likely candidates for having obtained their centurionates by direct commission.

Vilanius Nepos did not fare so well. Although a centurion when decorated he won only *torques* and *armillae*. There is no doubt as to his rank despite the fact that his tombstone does not give details of his earlier career. Nepos was decorated by Domitian on three occasions, in his two Dacian wars and in the intervening campaign in Germany. The unit in which he served as centurion, *cohors XIII Urbana* which was normally stationed in Carthage, is known from independent evidence – the career of one of its tribunes, Velius Rufus – to have crossed over to Europe to take part in Domitian's Rhine and Danube wars. So small an award to a centurion is not without parallel at this period. Pompeius Homullus, for example, appears to have received an award comprising only *torques, armillae* and *phalerae*, though the case is complicated by the fact that the *dona* for the career as a whole are recorded in a block at the end of the military part of his life. In a military career which began with a direct commission and ended with a second primipilate Homullus won *torques, armillae, phalerae, corona aurea* and *hasta pura* from an emperor left unnamed, doubtless Domitian. There is no reason to associate the *dona* with the post which they immediately follow, that of tribune of the fifth praetorian cohort. This particular combination of awards is unparalleled as a single decoration but splits easily into two, one comprising the minor awards, one of *corona* plus *hasta*. Since Homullus appears never to have served in the ranks, the first award, that of *torques, armillae* and *phalerae*, must have been won as centurion see also below, p. 193).

A crown was also omitted from the *dona* of L. Valerius Proclus who was decorated as centurion of *V Macedonica* in a Dacian war. Domaszewski's attribution of the *dona* to the post of *optio ad spem* (second in command of a century, awaiting a centurionate) has nothing to commend it.[6] The career is recorded in strict chronological order and the decorations are in place in mid-sequence. Domaszewski gives no reason for his suggestion which presumably springs from the belief that the *dona* are too low to be those of a centurion. The career of Proclus has been dated to the Trajanic period by Birley, but a good case can be made out for its being Domitianic and hence roughly contemporary with those of Nepos and Homullus.[7] The case for a Trajanic date rests on the close parallel between the career of Proclus and that of Ti. Claudius Vitalis. Both careers included centuionates in the Danube area with decorations in a Dacian war, followed by service in legions *XX Valeria victrix* and *IX Hispana* in Britain. Birley argued that the transfer from the Danube to Britain can best be explained in terms of reinforcements of the army of Britain during a period of active campaigning, and he went on to suggest a likely context at the time of Hadrian's accession when, according to the Augustan History life of Hadrian, the Britons could not be held under Roman rule.[8] War in the northern part of the province was followed by the construction of Hadrian's Wall. According to Birley's hypothesis the Dacian wars must fall into the reign of Trajan, 101–2 and 105–6.

This hypothetical timetable for the careers of Vitalis and Proclus raises a severe chronological problem in the case of Vitalis. If Vitalis was transferred to

Britain *c.* 117 he must have served a minimum of eleven years as centurion of *I Minervia*, the legion in which he won his second set of decoration in the Dacian wars, since no other post interposes between that in *I Minervia* and the move to *XX Valeria victrix* in Britain. He also appears to have served eleven years in his last military post as *princeps posterior* in the second cohort of *VII Claudia*, though the wording of the inscription is ambiguous on this point. These two posts alone would therefore account for twenty-two years' service out of a life of only forty-one years. Vitalis received his centurion's commission *ex equite Romano*, so saw no service in the ranks, but even if he was commissioned as young as eighteen years of age the rest of the career simply will not fit in. The gap between the second Dacian war and the move to Britain cannot have been so long as is required by a Trajanic dating of the decorations. An alternative context for the move to Britain is to be found in the postulated trouble in Britain in the mid-Trajanic period (below, p. 226). However another emperor fought two Dacian wars in quick succession and that was Domitian (86–92). Trouble in the Danube area at this period was also quickly followed by unrest in Britain.[9] Hence Vitalis and Proclus could have remained on the Danube into the early 90s and then transferred to Britain in a general reinforcement of the army of that province. Vitalis' subsequent move back to the Danube region, to *VII Claudia* in Pannonia Inferior, could then have been occasioned by the Suebic war begun by Nerva in AD 96. The one soldier known to have been decorated in this campaign, Attius Priscus, was a tribune of *I Adiutrix* which was also a Pannonian legion. Dating the decorations of Proclus and Vitalis to the Domitianic period has the further merit of providing a ready explanation of the omission of the name of the awarding emperor, an omission which is rare under Trajan but normal in the case of those Domitianic inscriptions which were erected after the death and *damnatio memoriae* of that emperor. This same timing of the military career of Vitalis (and hence also of Proclus) holds good if the eleven-year period is taken to apply to the whole period of service rather than simply to the last post; the phrasing – *milit(avit) (centurio) in (cohorte) II pr(inceps) annis XI* – allows of either interpretation.

Returning therefore to the scale of decoration, the omission of the crown from the award made to Proclus provides a contemporary parallel to the cases of Nepos and Homullus. So small an award would stand alone in the Trajanic period when no centurion is known to have received other than the standard *torques, armillae, phalerae* and a crown.

It may also be conjectured that the *dona* of Pompeius Asper belong to the Domitianic period. The career of Asper makes no reference to the decorations which are illustrated on the very fine sculptured slab (Pl. 12a). *Torques, armillae* and *phalerae* are shown but no crown. Asper probably obtained the centurionate by direct commission: no posts below that of centurion are shown and the sequence of commands held is that characteristic of a *centurio ex equite Romano.* The stone has been dated to the early second century by Lesquier and to the Vespasianic period by Hofmann.[10] A Domitianic date would be consistent with this range.

While the Domitianic period provides the first clear evidence for downward variation in the *dona* of the centurion, it also provides the first case of a higher award. If it is accepted that the collection of *dona* won by Pompeius Homullus should be split into two separate awards, the later of the two, that of the single crown and *hasta*, has still to be accounted for. After service as centurion Homullus became *primus pilus* and then rose via the Rome tribunates to be *primus pilus iterum*. The second decoration he received is considerably less than was awarded at this same period to the tribunes of urban and praetorian cohorts (below, p. 205), so it ought to belong to an earlier stage in his career. It is unfortunate that the units in which Homullus served as centurion are not named for it makes the allocation of the *dona* little more than educated guesswork. Domitian is known to have awarded decorations for his campaigns on the Rhine in 83 and 89 and his Danubian wars between 86 and 92. He also conducted a war through his governor Cn. Iulius Agricola in Britain in the first half of the 80s; no certain cases of decoration in this British war are at present known, but since the general in charge was awarded triumphal ornaments it is very likely that certain of the officers and men also received rewards.[11] Homullus served his first primipilate in legion *II Augusta* at a date which cannot be far removed from AD 86/87: the possibility of decoration as *primus pilus* in the British war which culminated in the victory of Mons Graupius in 84 cannot, therefore, be entirely excluded, but it is probably slightly too early. An award as senior centurion either in Britain or in the Danubian campaigns would accord better with the known dating of the career. Hence both sets of *dona* are likely to belong to the unspecified centurionates, the second of the two awards to a senior post, an hypothesis which fits well with later evidence (below, p. 194) which strongly suggests that the crown and *hasta* were commonly awarded to members of the *primi ordines*, the centurions in the first cohorts of the legion, and those holding more senior praetorian posts such as *trecenarius* and *princeps castrorum*.

TRAJANIC PERIOD

If Valerius Proclus is excluded as Domitianic, and the evidence is very strong in this direction, all Trajanic centurions without exception received the same basic award. Six officers account between them for eight separate awards, six including a *corona vallaris*, one a *corona muralis* and one unknown. Six of the recipients won their *dona* as legionary centurions, just one, Aemilius Paternus, as *centurio cohortis praetoriae*. (These figures refer only to cases where the *dona* are given in detail.) Paternus was decorated on three separate occasions, receiving the same on each occasion, and on the third of these, in the

Parthian war, he must have been serving in the praetorian guard for none of the legions in which he held the posts as *centurio*, *trecenarius* or *primus pilus* is known to have taken part in the Parthian war or to have been in a position to do so. His last centurionate was served in the fourth praetorian cohort and he might well, in this capacity, have accompanied Trajan to the East.

The one Trajanic centurion who won a *corona muralis* was N. Marcius Platorius Celer, a centurion in *XVI Flavia* during the Parthian war. His rank, his seniority, his legion, the context of the award – none of these can adequately account for his receiving a crown which, as far as is known, is different from those received by all his contemporaries. The reason must lie in what it rewards.

The decorations won by Geminius Sabinus do not appear, on first sight, to be those of a centurion. The scale is right but the *dona* are listed between the post of *primus pilus et princeps peregrinorum* and that of *praefectus legionis X Fretensis*. The inference that they must belong to one of these posts is wrong. The primipilate will, in this instance, have been served in Rome and not with a legion in the provinces and hence cannot be connected with the German campaign in which the distinction was won. Nor can the unit in question be *X Fretensis*, stationed at this period in Judaea. Despite the order of the text the *dona* must be associated with a centurionate. Sabinus served in *I Adiutrix* and *XIV Gemina* both of which were stationed in Pannonia, geographically in a position to have taken part in the war. *I Adiutrix* certainly did participate for another of its officers, the equestrian tribune, Attius Priscus, was decorated by Nerva at an earlier stage in the same war.

HADRIANIC PERIOD

It is of particular note that the awards which Hadrian made to his centurions are no more and no less generous than those of his predecessors. The undoubted paucity of Hadrianic awards to senators and equestrians is in no way reflected in the decorations received by his more junior officers. Two out of the four centurions in question received *torques*, *armillae*, *phalerae* and a crown, Octavius Secundus a *corona aurea*, Sabidius Maximus a *corona muralis*, both on the occasion of the Jewish war. The other two cases are on a scale larger than that hitherto encountered for anyone below the primipilate (with the one exception of the Domitianic centurion Pompeius Homullus). Arrius Clemens was serving as *trecenarius* in the seventh praetorian cohort when he received *hasta pura corona aurea*. The post of *trecenarius* in the praetorian guard is the equivalent of that of the *primi ordines*, the senior centurions, in the legions, so remembering that the *primi ordines* ranked higher than the *secundi* to the *decimi ordines*, the high award need occasion no surprise. Clemens' award is paralleled by that made to Albius Felix, also a centurion and in the circumstances probably a senior one though this cannot be proved. The inscription recording the career of Felix notes only two posts, that of *cornicularius praefecti praetorio* (adjutant to the praetorian prefect) and centurion of legion *XX Valeria victrix*. Praetorians who rose to the centurionate via the post of *cornicularius praefecti praetorio* rather than through *evocatio* invariably went direct to a legionary post and remained in the legions without service in a Rome cohort before advancement to the primipilate.[12] Hence Felix could have remained a long time in the one legion and risen within it to the *primi ordines* without any specific indication being given of the fact on his tombstone. He was decorated on two occasions, once in the Parthian war of Trajan (114–117) and once in an unspecified Hadrianic campaign. The first decorations were almost certainly won before he obtained his commission as they do not include a crown: as we have seen Trajan consistently gave his centurions a crown of some description. It is unfortunate that the Hadrianic campaign is not named for this makes it impossible to estimate with any confidence the number of years that elapsed between the two sets of decorations, and hence the degree of seniority of Felix at the time of his second award. He would need, on average, about ten years' service as centurion to have attained the ranks of the *primi ordines*.

There are two areas where he is most likely to have been decorated, Britain and Judaea. Legion *XX* was stationed at this period in Britain so the answer would appear on the surface to be obvious. However there is reason to believe that some troops from Britain may have gone east in the early 130s, accompanying the governor of the province, Sex. Iulius Severus, who, as the best general of his day, was summoned to Judaea to put down the Bar Kochba revolt.[13] One pointer to such a transfer of troops is the inscription honouring C. Ligustinus Disertus, a legionary centurion who served first in legion *XX*, then in *IIII Scythica* and then moved back to *XX*.[14] The text is not specifically dated, but stylistically belongs to the later first or early second centuries AD. Legion *IIII Scythica* was stationed at this period in Syria. It was unusual for an individual soldier to be transferred for no good reason all the way across the Empire when he moved from one centurionate to another, and these moves are, as Eric Birley first pointed out, best understood in terms of a period when both units were operating in the same area.[15] Another text which points in the same direction is that on an altar set up at Maryport in the northern part of the province of Britain by M. Censorius Cornelianus, a native of Nîmes in Gallia Narbonensis, perfect (or, less probably, *praepositus*) of *cohors I Hispanorum* and centurion of legion *X Fretensis*.[16] *Cohors I Hispanorum* was the garrison of Maryport: *X Fretensis* was stationed in Judaea. A link could have been established between the two units if the cohort had sent men to fight in the Jewish war. However in neither this case nor that of Disertus is any reference made either to Hadrian or his Jewish campaign and in neither case is the text closely and specifically dated to the Hadrianic period: the association is, however, an attractive one. Thus it may be that despite the failure to make explicit reference to a sojourn in the East, Albius Felix did in fact accompany Severus to the Jewish war and there win his military decorations. If this is so he will have been a centurion of some fifteen or sixteen years standing, in all probability a member of the *primi ordines*.

On the other hand a case can clearly be made out for Felix having been decorated in Britain for there is known to have been fighting there in the early years of Hadrian's reign.[17] If this is the context for the award Felix will have been a relatively new centurion at the time. Further trouble in Britain has been postulated for Hadrian's reign but the evidence is equivocal.[18] Pontius Sabinus and Maenius Agrippa are both known from epigraphic evidence to have taken part in a Hadrianic *expeditio Britannica*: the dating of this *expeditio* is crucial. Pontius Sabinus came to Britain in charge of a vexillation of 3,000 men, and the date of his command depends on the estimate of the amount of time which must have elapsed since the one firmly dateable event in his career, decoration as an equestrian military tribune in Trajan's Parthian war, 114–117. After this tribunate Sabinus obtained a direct commission into the centurionate and held commands in *XXII Primigenia* and *XIII Gemina* before becoming *primus pilus* in *III Augusta*. Immediately after the primipilate he brought the vexillations to Britain. The post of *primus pilus* is normally of just one year's duration,[19] but centurionates can be held for as long or as short a period as is required; hence any estimate of the date at which Sabinus came to Britain can be little more than an informed guess. However, it would be rather pushing things to bring him over as early as the time of troubles at the very beginning of Hadrian's reign. Against this Dobson has argued that this stage of Sabinus' career would have to be swift if, having transferred from the equestrian to the centurion career ladder, he was to keep pace with his contemporaries in terms of promotion.[20] This is true but it takes no stock of Sabinus' possible reasons for choosing to relinquish an equestrian in favour of a centurion career. He was doing well in the *ordo equester*: there is no reason to doubt that he would have gone smoothly on to the third and possibly even the fourth *militia*, thence to the procuratorships. If swift promotion was his concern he could have stayed where he was. As Dobson himself has pointed out elsewhere, one of the reasons for opting for a centurion instead of an equestrian career was the quality of the life itself, continuous service among men of like interests and a longer period spent actually soldiering.[21] If these were the reasons it would be invidious to rush Sabinus too quickly through this part of his career in order to keep him at level pegging with his counterparts in the equestrian *militiae*. Sabinus' move to Britain could in theory belong to the early 120s but would fit equally happily into the middle of the decade. What of Maenius Agrippa? Agrippa served as prefect of a quingenary cohort and then, instead of proceeding to the *secunda militia* was sent by Hadrian on an expedition to Britain (*electo a divo Hadriano et misso in expedition—Brittanicam*).[22] His next command kept him in Britain as tribune of *cohors I Hispanorum equitata* which was stationed at Maryport in Cumbria. It is this tribunate which provides our only dating evidence for the *expeditio*.

Of the inscriptions relating to the *cohors I Hispanorum* at Maryport some attest it as being of quingenary strength, that is with a prefect in charge, some as milliary with a tribune in command. Birley argued that the unit was initially quingenary and was subsequently enlarged, hence that Maenius Agrippa, as tribune, cannot have been in command until the end of the 120s at earliest, there being four prefects to fit in between the foundation of the fort in *c.*122 and his command. Jarrett suggests that the sequence be reversed on the grounds that the fort which is an estimated size of 1.9ha. internally (2.64ha. over the ramparts) is too large to have been built for a quingenary cohort. Hence the unit must initially have been milliary and later been either reduced in size or, more likely, had a substantial detachment sent away on a long term basis leaving the parent formation *de facto* a quingenary cohort with a prefect in charge. This being the case, Agrippa could have commanded the unit at any time between the early 120s and the change of establishment strength which, in order to accommodate four prefects before the abandonment of the site in about 140, must have taken place by *c.* 130. If he was tribune, at latest, in 128–130 the *expeditio Brittannica* in which he participated can have been no later than 127. This certainly eliminates the possibility of the *expeditio* belonging to the early 130s but it does not preclude the suggestion of activity later than that which opened Hadrian's reign in 117. There must, for example, have been some very good reason behind the decision radically to alter the design of the still unfinished Hadrian's Wall, a decision which was put into operation *c.* 124.

Thus the British expedition should belong to some time in the first five or six years of Hadrian's reign. There can be no certainty that by this time Felix would have joined the *primi ordines* but for a soldier of obvious merit such as he, it is by no means impossible. For present purposes, however, a career which allows of such widely varying interpretations cannot be used as evidence. It is not inconsistent with the picture presented by the cases of Octavius Secundus and Arrius Clemens, but neither does it provide good independent supporting evidence for it.

ANTONINE AND SEVERAN PERIODS

Cestius Sabinus is unique in being the only soldier known to have been decorated by Antoninus Pius. The award which he received, a single *hasta*, is also unique for a centurion. Sabinus' recorded military career began with a centurionate in legion *VII Claudia* and ended as tribune of the thirteenth urban cohort in Carthage. He probably obtained his centurionate by a direct commission – in which case we have a complete record of his career. The decoration is recorded out of sequence at the end of the inscription which is given in reverse chronological order. No indication is given of the context for the decoration. According to the Augustan History Pius fought wars through his legates against the Britons, Moors, Germans, Dacians, Jews, in Achaia and in Egypt.[23] None of the units in which Sabinus served was in a position to have fought in Britain, Judaea, Achaia or Egypt and he will not have gone to any of these places with the praetorian guard, for the emperor did not personally conduct any of the campaigns of his reign. Four of the legions could have or did take part in campaigning in Dacia or Germany so in theory the decoration could have been received as centurion, senior centurion or *primus pilus*. *VII Claudia* (in which he held an ordinary centurionate, his first post), stationed at this period at Viminacium in upper Moesia, could have fought against the Dacians across the Danube. *II Adiutrix* in which he held an ordinary centurionate, *VIII Augusta* in which he held a senior centurionate and *I Adiutrix* of which he was *primus pilus* (stationed in lower Pannonia, upper Germany and upper Pannonia respectively) could have fought in the German war. Moreover, a military diploma records the presence of auxiliary units from the two Pannonias on an expedition to Mauretania Caesariensis in August 150:[24] it is not inconceivable that the auxiliaries were accompanied by a legionary detachment. Hence there are four different posts at three different levels which Sabinus could have held when decorated. The opposite approach must be taken, using the scale of award to suggest the rank involved. The use of a *hasta* might, on analogy with earlier and later practice, imply a senior post, the primipilate in *I Adiutrix* or the senior centurionate in *VIII Augusta*, but in the absence of contemporary parallels it is impossible to be certain.

The one clear example of a centurion's decoration awarded by the later Antonine emperors suggests a trend towards a more generous scale. Petronius Sabinus was decorated twice by Marcus during the German war of 169–175, receiving on each occasion a *hasta pura* and two *coronae*, a *vallaris* and a *muralis*. Sabinus was certainly a senior centurion at the time of the awards for by the death of Marcus in 180 he had attained a second primipilate and embarked on a procuratorial career. Nevertheless the decoration is one crown in excess of that hitherto normally awarded to a senior centurion.

Similar generosity appears in the case of the *dona* of Petronius Fortunatus – a fact which leads one to believe that the Parthian war in which Fortunatus was decorated was that of Marcus and Verus rather than that of Severus and Caracalla. Fortunatus was awarded *torques, phalerae* and two crowns, a *muralis* and a *vallaris, ob virtutem in expeditione Parthica*. He enjoyed a military career which spanned a period of fifty years and involved service in thirteen different legions. The very earliest date for the beginning of the career is *c.* 150, since the penultimate legion in which he served, *II Parthica*, was not created until 197 on the occasion of Severus' second Parthian war. The *dona* are recorded out of order at the end of the career and several of the legions mentioned are known to have participated in the eastern wars of the Antonine and/or Severan periods. *VI Ferrata* and *III Gallica* in Syria and *XV Apollinaris* in Cappadocia were stationed conveniently in the East and thus close at hand for any war against the Parthians. *I Minervia* from lower Germany is known to have taken part in the Parthian war of Marcus and Verus under its legate M. Claudius Fronto who received military decorations, while vexillations from all four German legions, hence including *I Minervia* and *XXX Ulpia* in which Fortunatus served, took part in the second Severan campaign under the command of Claudius Gallus (*praepositus vexillationum IIII Germanicarum expeditione secunda Parthica*).[25] If Fortunatus was decorated in the Antonine war (162–166) it will have been within at most twelve to sixteen years of the beginning of his military service, that is within about eight to twelve years of becoming centurion, hence most probably as centurion of either *VI Ferrata*, his second command, or *I Minervia*, his third command or just conceivably *III Gallica*, his sixth command. If the decoration was won in the Severan period it could belong to any of the units indicated above known to have served in the east at this time. If the decorations belong to a comparatively early stage in the career (as must be the case if they are Antonine, and could be if they are Severan) they are of a magnitude comparable only to Marcus' award to Petronius Severus. If they belong to a later stage, to a senior centurionate, they are completely unparalleled. Hence an Antonine context would best fit the available evidence.

From the little evidence available it would appear that Severus reverted to earlier scales of award. Tillius Rufus was serving as *princeps castrorum*, a senior praetorian centurion, when decorated by Severus and Caracalla with a *corona aurea* and a *hasta pura* together with the further honour of equestrian status. The only other centurion decorated in the Severan period, Didius Saturninus, received the same award, less the elevation to the *ordo equester*. It remains uncertain whether he had risen to the primipilate. The career inscription records a total of three separate occasions on which Saturninus was decorated: on the first two occasions he received the *dona* of a man in the ranks, on the third *coron(a) aurea civica et (h)asta pura argent(ea)*. The reference to the crown has been taken as implying one single crown, a *corona civica* made of gold. For reasons already discussed (above, p. 71) it is here interpreted as referring to two separate crowns, a *corona civica* and a *corona aurea*: the omission of the *et* between the two crown is readily paralleled (witness for example the *coronam muralem vallarem* of Petronius Fortunatus), while if the gold is describing the civic crown the *aurea* would surely come after the *civica* to balance the *argentea* which comes after the *hasta*. Saturninus' decorations are (the *corona civica* apart) the normal one crown one spear of the senior centurion. Saturninus must have been in the ranks of the praetorian guard when he was first decorated by Marcus and Verus in the Parthian and German wars of AD 162–166, 166–175 (he cannot have been a legionary for he later saw service as a centurion in the guard). He will have been recruited in 150 at the earliest, in the mid-160s at latest, and received his *evocatio* some time between the mid-160s and the late

170s or very early 180s. Unless he remained a long time as *evocatus* he will have attained his centurion's *vitis* some time between *c.* 165 and *c.* 180. Saturninus' tombstone gives us no detail of his career below the rank of *primus pilus*, but we known from praetorian discharge lists of AD 204 that he was serving as a centurion in the praetorian guard in that year.[26] Severus and Caracalla who jointly awarded him his third set of decorations, were jointly responsible for awards connected with the second Parthian war and will presumably have together made the presentations for the British war of 207–211 (though none are specifically attested). Either of these provides a possible context for the decorations of Fortunatus. On the earlier of these two occasions he will have been a centurion of at very least seventeen years standing, on the later occasion of at least twenty-seven years standing, in both cases almost certainly as a senior centurion if not as *primus pilus*.

CONCLUSION

Throughout the period of the Principate the *dona* of the centurion remain remarkably consistent for both ordinary and senior centurion. The pattern appears to have been established by the time of Claudius and to have persisted, little changed, to the end. It is surprisingly Domitian and not Hadrian who shows a tendency towards smaller awards, while what little evidence there is hints at an otherwise unsuspected Antonine generosity. The legionary and the praetorian were treated on precisely equal terms and it is only when the senior posts in both arms of the service were reached that scales of award change upwards. It is of note here that the most senior of the senior centurions, the *primus pilus*, apparently received no more. He was after all still a centurion, albeit one of a singular eminence.

Auxiliary centurions and decurions

By far the greater majority of the centurions and decurions of the *auxilia* were recruited from the ranks: such recruits would be non-citizens and therefore, from the Flavian period onwards, apparently not eligible to win decorations (above, p. 121). Occasionally a soldier might be promoted from the ranks of a legion to an auxiliary centurionate or decurionate and these men would of course be in a position to receive decorations. One example of this occurring is Tiberius Claudius Maximus, promoted from legionary *vexillarius equitum* to *duplicarius* of an *ala*. He was decorated on a total of three occasions, once while serving with legion *VII Claudia*, once as *explorator alae* and finally as *duplicarius alae*, the *ala* in question being *II Pannoniorum*. The text of the inscription gives no indication of the scale of award while reliefs on the stone depict just two *torques* and two *armillae* (pl. 8a). These can be no more than symbolic, giving little indication of what Maximus actually received.

There are three other possible examples of auxiliary decurions receiving *dona* – Rufinus and T. Flavius Capito, both dating to the Flavian period, and the problematic L. Cas(sius) Caen(icus?). The text relating to Rufinus is fragmentary but we know that he was decurion of an *ala Moesica* and that his tombstone was set up by his friend and heir who was a legionary centurion. The *dona*, again sculpted but not mentioned in the text, are only partly extant: the remaining fragment of the stone shows part of a set of *phalerae* and a *torques* (fig. 13). The *dona* of Capito are neither listed nor depicted: their existence is merely referred to in the words *donis donat(us)*. The case for these two decurions both being Roman citizens is argued elsewhere (above, p. 122). Finally, the text commemorating Cas(sius) Caen(icus?), decurion of the *ala I Gig(?)* has been read as recording *torques* and *phalerae*. This reading is, however, by no means certain. Nor is it possible, in any of these cases to prove that the *dona* belong to the decurionate rather than to earlier service in the ranks.

The only possible example of the *dona* of an auxiliary centurion is that of the non-citizen Caeno (above, p. 123). Caeno was centurion in a *cohors Hispanorum*: he died at the age of forty-four after nineteen years' service, clearly no Roman citizen. The text of the stone is brief, naming the one post, mentioning no campaign and alluding to no decorations. The case for decoration rests on the object depicted between the upper and lower parts of the text (pl. 9b). This has been variously interpreted as a *corona* or a *torques* though it lacks the usual characteristics of a crown.[27] The simplest types are generally shown with the ribbon fastening suspended from them (e.g. pl. 6a, b, c): this is a simple pennanular object, plain terminals abutting one another, with no attempt at the leaf decoration characteristic of the *corona aurea* (and this is the only type of crown it could be) and only a pecking of the surface most closely paralleled on the *torques* of Marcus Caelius (pl. 2a). But what, in this context, is the significance of a single *torques*? Is it Roman or native? Is it the personal ornament of a Celt or a military decoration? Auxiliary soldiers certainly did continue to be allowed to wear certain of their native ornaments – for example, Flavinus the standard-bearer of the *ala Petriana* from near Corbridge in Northumberland is depicted on his tombstone with a *torques* about his neck – so the latter of these two alternatives is by no means impossible.[28] A third possibility is also worth considering. Certain auxiliary units are known to have earned the battle honour *torquata* (below, p. 220) and it is not inconceivable that members of units so honoured might have had a *torques* depicted on their tombstone in the same way as did soldiers who had won individual decorations. The problem with this hypothesis is that the unit in which Caeno served is not known to have been so honoured, and is not so designated on the inscription in question. The text mentions only that Caeno served in a *cohors Hispanorum* without specifying which of the Spanish cohorts was the one in question. The answer is supplied by the findspot, Vindonissa, for tile-stamps from this site attest the *cohors III Hispanorum*. Tile-stamps do not, it is true, always refer to the unit in garrison but the coincidence of name suggests that on this occasion they do. The Caeno text poses a problem to which there is at present no wholly satisfactory answer.

There is insufficient evidence to make any useful comparisons between the *dona* of the auxiliary and the legionary for in all cases concerning auxiliary decurions and centurions the record of the *dona* is defective; the one feature which may be of significance is the apparent absence of any indications of a crown among the *dona* of the auxiliary. In view of the discrepancy in pay and status between the two the scale of award may well have differed also.

Primus pilus

The *primus pilus*, officer in command of the first century of the first cohort of a legion, was the most senior of the *primi ordines* (fig. 14). It might be anticipated that on a hierarchical scale of military decorations the *primus pilus* would receive an award equal to or slightly in excess of that of the other senior centurions. It is therefore disconcerting to find that the one clear and unequivocal example of the *dona* of a *primus pilus* evidences a scale comparable to that of a man in the ranks or an ordinary centurion receiving less than the average. The case in question is that of M. Vettius Valens who as *primus pilus* of *VI Victrix* was decorated by Nero with *torques*, *armillae* and *phalerae* in connection with activities against the Astures of north-west Spain. This award is less than Valens himself received at a considerably earlier stage of his career when, as praetorian *evocatus* he participated in the Claudian invasion of Britain. In order to get around the anomaly Domaszewski suggested that the stone mason had, in error, omitted reference to a crown:[29] even if this were so – and there is no way of proving it one way or the other – the award would still be comparatively low, making no acknowledgement of the pre-eminence of the *primus pilus* among the centurions. It may well be that the encounter in which Valens participated was of so minor a nature as to merit no more than a minor decoration. Whatever guidelines might have existed as to normal scales of award it becomes clear again and again that there were no hard and fast rules: there could not be. Whatever care might be taken to accommodate rewards to the particular needs of a highly stratified society it was always necessary to be able to make allowances for individual circumstances: the size of a reward remained ultimately at the emperor's discretion.

A case can be made for two earlier and rather more generous examples of the decoration of *primi pili*. In the Julio-Claudian period as we have seen the commands of auxiliary units were of comparable ranking to and were often held by *primipilares*. The equestrian awards of this time were remarkably consistent and one might therefore expect the *primipilaris* commander of an auxiliary *ala* or cohort to receive decorations at least comparable to those of an equestrian commander. Two cases where this probably did occur have already been alluded to (above, p. 161). M. Vergilius Gallus Lusius and C. Purtisius Atinas each received total decorations comprising two *coronae* and two *hastae*, most plausibly understood, in view of the apparent rigidity of equestrian *dona* of the period, as two separate awards of one *corona* and one *hasta*. Both these men held primipilates and it is as likely as not that one of the awards in each case was won as *primus pilus* if not as senior centurion.

The scale of one crown and one *hasta* is the same as that which is later attested for the senior centurion (above, p. 194) and which becomes arguably the standard also for the *primus pilus*. For example an unknown soldier buried at Florence in the late first century received from a son of Vespasian, that is either Titus or Domitian, military decorations comprising a *corona aurea* and a *hasta pura*. The inscription is too fragmentary to restore with any certainty: a centurionate in *XX Valeria victrix* (in Britain) was preceded (according to the Domaszewski restoration) by the post of *trecenarius* and followed by that of *primus pilus*.[30] All three of these posts were in the *primi ordines*, so any one of them could merit the award of a *corona* and *hasta*. The fact that the reference to the decorations follows the (hypothetical) primipilate may or may not be significant. A similar uncertainty surrounds the interpretation of the career of another unknown centurion who is commemorated on a fragmentary inscription from Clusium in north-central Italy. This man followed service in the praetorian guard with *evocatio*, Rome centurionates, a post as *trecenarius*, a legionary centurionate and the primipilate of *VI Ferrata*.[31] He was decorated, probably as *evocatus*, by Trajan in the Dacian wars and again by Hadrian in an unspecified campaign, receiving on this latter occasion a *hasta* and further decorations (a *corona aurea*?) now missing. The *dona* are recorded out of order at the end of the inscription. If the Hadrianic decoration belongs to the Jewish war a period of at least twenty-six years separates it from the Trajanic decoration and the post of *evocatus* (from 106 at latest to 132 at earliest): hence the primipilate in *VI Ferrata* would, both chronologically and geographically, provide a likely context. However it is by no means certain that the *dona* do belong to the *bellum Iudaicum* so that this solution, neat as it is, cannot be regarded as definitive. A third tentative case for decoration in the primipilate can be argued for Didius Saturninus. His *dona* (a crown and a *hasta*) could belong to his year as *primus pilus* but an equally good case can be made in support of one of the other senior centurionates (above, p. 199).

Thus we have five tentative examples of the *dona* of a *primus pilus* being, like that of the other senior centurions, a crown (commonly a *corona aurea*) plus a *hasta pura*. The evidence of the block records of *dona* tends towards the same conclusion. Some of the crowns and *hastae* won by Sextus Vibius Gallus and T. Statius Marrax must belong to the primipilate (below, p. 207).

Praefectus castrorum

The only straightforward example of the *dona* of a *praefectus castrorum* dates to the Claudian period before the development of the separate centurion and equestrian career structure. It is no surprise therefore to find that on the occasion of Claudius' British war P. Anicius Maximus received the norm for the equestrian of the period, one *corona* (in this case a *muralis*) and one *hasta*. With the development of the *primipilaris* career this scale would appear not to have gone unchanged. This much is clear from the fact that Sextus Vibius Gallus, who never rose beyond the rank of *praefectus castrorum*, received a formidable total of *dona* comprising six crowns (three *murales*, two *vallares*, one *aurea*), five *hastae*, two *vexilla*, *torques*, *armillae* and *phalerae*. The allocation of these decorations to individual posts is complicated by the fact that only the highlights of the career are mentioned on both the inscriptions which record it. Gallus probably began his military service with a direct commission; the fact that he later held the post of *trecenarius* indicates either a direct commission or service with the praetorian guard[32] and in view of his assumed eastern origin service in the guard is unlikely at this date. Assuming therefore that the *torques*, *armillae*, *phalerae* and one of the crowns belong to an ordinary centurionate, five crowns, five *hastae* and two *vexilla* remain to be allocated to senior centurionates, the primipilate or the post of *praefectus castrorum*. We know Gallus to have been an ex *primus pilus* in AD 115, so his career encompasses the periods of active campaigning under Domitian and Trajan.[33] Legion *XIII Gemina*, the only unit mentioned by name and the unit in which Gallus served as camp prefect, was stationed in Pannonia until the conquest of Dacia when it moved to Apulum, forming part of the garrison of the newly conquered province. It certainly took part in the Dacian wars of Trajan. There is no shortage of campaigns to which to attribute the *dona*. The evidence regarding the scale of award normally made to the *primus pilus* gives no hint of the *vexillum* ever having been included: hence the two *vexilla* won by Gallus must belong to the camp prefecture. Did the *praefectus castrorum* receive one *corona*, one *hasta* and one *vexillum*, the same award as that commonly made to the equestrian tribune and *praefectus alae* but appreciably less than that of the laticlave tribune to whom he was subordinate? Working on this hypothesis two decorations as *praefectus castrorum* would leave three *coronae* and three *hastae* unallocated, simply accounted for as three separate awards as senior centurion and *primus pilus*. An alternative interpretation of the few facts available is put forward by Dobson who suggests that the camp prefect received two *coronae*, two *hastae* and one *vexillum*, that is a combination comparable to that won by the laticlave tribunes and prefects of milliary *alae*.[34] In this case two awards as *praefectus castrorum* following on one in an ordinary and one in a senior centurionate would satisfactorily account for the recorded collection. Until further positive evidence is forthcoming either solution must be considered possible. It is in either case highly probable that it was Vespasian who augmented the *dona* of the prefect, reorganizing the *primipilaris* decorations at the same time as he brought into line those of the equestrians.

Tribunus cohortis vigilum

The tribune of the *vigiles*, like the men under his command, had no opportunity for winning military decorations.

Tribunus cohortis urbanae

The tribunes of the urban cohorts, all of them stationed in cities (Rome, Carthage and Lyon), normally had little or no opportunity to distinguish themselves in battle for their role was basically that of an urban police-force. However we know that in the 80s part or all of *cohors XIII urbana* from Carthage was transferred to Europe to take part initially in Domitian's Dacian war. While there one of its centurions was decorated (Vilanius Nepos above, p. 191) and also its tribune, C. Velius Rufus who received two sets of *dona*, one probably in the Dacian war and one in the ensuing campaign against the Marcomanni, Quadi and Sarmatae. On each occasion Rufus received one *corona muralis*, two *hastae* and two *vexilla*.

Tribunus cohortis praetoriae

The one example of the *dona* of a praetorian tribune belongs to the reign of Nero when Lucius Antonius Naso was decorated for an unspecified reason, probably in connection with the suppression of the revolt of Vindex. The name of the awarding emperor has been mutilated on the inscription which gives Naso's career, but it is known from the Histories of Tacitus that Naso was dismissed by Galba in AD 69 from a post as *tribunus cohortis*.[35] The inscription is broken and the record of the *dona* incomplete though it can reasonably be restored to indicate two crowns, two *vexilla* and two *hastae*: [. . . *corona valla*]*ri corona au*[*rea*] *vexillis* [*duob*]*us ha*[*stis puris*] *duabus*. Suitably this is one crown in excess of the award received (some years later) by the urban tribune.

Primus pilus bis

There is no attested example of the decorations of the *primus pilus II*, a particularly unfortunate lack in view of the interesting position which he occupied. Dobson argues very convincingly that the *primus pilus II* performed the same job as did the *praefectus castrorum*, he simply arrived at it by a different route (fig. 14), proceeding from *primus pilus* to the Rome tribunates and thence to *primus pilus II*, instead of from *primus pilus* direct to *praefectus castrorum*.[36] As far as *dona* are concerned there is an inbuilt contradiction in his position. On the one hand it could be assumed that he would be decorated as *praefectus castrorum* which to all intents and purposes he was. On the other hand his enhanced seniority, the fact that he had served in the Rome tribunates should bring him *dona* on a par with or even in excess of those of the praetorian tribune: in this case he would be receiving rewards on at least the same scale as the senatorial tribune of the legion, the second-in-command to whom he, as third-in-command, was subordinate. There is an intriguing disharmony between job, rank and status – a situation not without parallel in the modern British army. How the Roman high command coped with the problem is, in the absence of any evidence, a matter of speculation.

Praefectus praetorio

The two examples of the *dona* of a praetorian prefect both date to the mid-Antonine period: one is a man who rose to the prefecture via the primipilate, the other via the *militia equestris*. M. Bassaeus Rufus the *primipilaris* received from Marcus and Commodus an award comprising three *coronae*, four *hastae* and four *vexilla*. T. Furius Victorinus the equestrian was decorated by Marcus and Verus, receiving three *coronae* and an indeterminate number of *hastae* and *vexilla*. There is no reason to suppose that the differing avenues of advancement would have made any difference to the scales of award so the *dona* of Victorinus can reasonably be assumed to be comparable to those of Rufus. Thus the scale for the praetorian prefect comes very close to that of the consular governor – a reflection of the great importance of the prefect, the highest ranking of the non-senatorial officials who, being based in Rome in close proximity to the emperor, was a man of singular influence. The one difference between the *dona* of the praetorian prefect and the consular commander is that the former lacks the *corona classica*, the hallmark of the ex-consul.

Summary

The scales of decoration of the centurion and *primipilaris*, like those of the equestrians and the senators settled down into a clear pattern in the Flavian period. The basic scales were emerging prior to this but it was not until a proper career structure was available that it is possible to think in terms of any sort of graduated system.

TABLE J   SCALES OF AWARD · CENTURIONS AND PRIMIPILARES

	CORONA	HASTA	VEXILLUM	TAP
Praetorian centurion	I			I set
Legionary centurion coh. II–X	I			I set
Auxiliary centurion	?			I set
Senior praetorian centurion	I	I		
Legionary centurion coh. I				
(incl. primus pilus)	I	I		
Praefectus castrorum	I?	I?	I?	
	or 2?	2?	I?	
Tribunus cohortis vigilum	—	—	—	
Tribunus cohortis urbanae	I	2	2	
Tribunus cohortis praetoriae	2	2	2	
Primus pilus bis	?	?	?	
Praefectus praetorio	3	4	4	

The centurions and *primipilares*, particularly those who rose from the ranks, enjoyed a military career longer than that of any of the other categories of soldier, and those whose term of service coincided with a particularly active period in terms of warfare were in a position to amass large collections of *dona*: the German and Illyrican wars of Augustus and Tiberius, the activities on the Rhine, in Britain, across the Danube and in the East under Domitian and Trajan, the Parthian and German wars of Marcus, Verus and Commodus all these provide concentrated periods of active campaigning. It was quite common practice for soldiers who won large collections of *dona* at such periods to record these decorations en bloc instead of individually campaign by campaign. Examples of this practice are listed in table K.

TABLE K   COLLECTIONS OF DONA · CENTURIONS AND PRIMIPILARES

		HIGHEST		DONA		
DATE	NAME	POST HELD	COR.	HAST.	VEX.	T.A.P.
Republic	C. Vibius Macer	?	I	2	—	2 sets
Aug. – Tib.	C. Allius Oriens	centurion	3	—	—	I set
Aug. – Claud.	L. Rufellius Severus	trib. praet.	4	I	—	—
Aug. – Tib.	T. Statius Marrax	prim. pil.	5	I	—	I set
Domitianic	Cn. Pompeius Homullus	p.p.II	I	I	—	I set
Dom. – Traj.	Sex. Vibius Gallus	praef. castr.	6	5	2	I set
Late 1st-2nd cent.	Ti. Claudius Iunianus	praef. castr. ?	2+	[?	?]	I set?
2nd cent.	(EE VIII 478)	trib. praet.	3	[?	?]	?

An attempt has already been made to break down the collections of Pompeius Homullus and Vibius Gallus. The unknown soldier commemorated on a fragmentary inscription from Capua (EE VIII 478) was believed by Domaszewski, largely on account of his having three crowns, to be a praetorian prefect.[37] This identification has been challenged by Dobson who makes the point that the promotion from praetorian tribune direct to praetorian prefect which is necessitated by Domaszewski's hypothesis, is completely unparalleled except in the upheavals of the civil war of 69.[38] Three crowns as a single award are admissible only for a praetorian prefect, a legionary legate or an imperial praetorian governor, none of which is feasible in the present context. Hence the *dona* must represent a total amassed over an entire career. The unknown rose as high as *tribunus praetoriae* during a military career which could belong to the Trajanic-Hadrianic period or to the wars of the Antonine emperors. The reference to a subsequent post in 'both Syrias' (*Syria utraque*) dates that part of the career to after 135 when Hadrian created Syria Palaestina and before the readjustment of the boundaries of the Syrian provinces by Severus in 194. Too little survives of the *dona* or the career to do more than indicate the existence of a collection of *dona* rather than a single award.

Another fragmentary inscription which appears to record a collection of *dona* is that relating to Ti. Claudius Iunianus (fig. 7). The middle and left half of the stone survive in two fragments which depict two mural crowns, one at centre bottom and one at the bottom left hand corner. Jantsch suggested that a third mural crown be restored at the bottom right corner, a restoration which can be justified only on the grounds of symmetry.[39] If the reliefs are an accurate reflection of what was won there is no logical reason for them to be symmetrical. The text is very defective. One or more mural crowns are mentioned as are *torques*, in the plural. The record of the career survives only as [. . . . .] *leg. XXII Primig[e]n[iae* . . . . .] *p.p., princeps* [. . . . .]. giving a probable sequence of *princeps castrorum, primus pilus* and a post in legion *XXII Primigenia*, presumably *praefectus castrorum*. Two or more crowns and *torques* could easily have been won in the career as it is known or can reasonably be inferred, but there is insufficient evidence on which to allocate the *dona* in detail to the posts to which they belong.

The same is true in the case of Vibius Macer. The decorations are shown in relief on the stone commemorating him, but the text mentions none of the posts held, nor indeed the fact that he was a soldier (fig. 5). The career probably belongs to the late Republic rather than to the imperial period which means that there can be no easy correlation between decorations won and posts held. The man was probably a legionary who rose to the centurionate and held one or more of the commands then available to a legionary centurion.

The remaining three collections of *dona* have two features in common, their approximate date and the fact that each records a large number of *coronae* in proportion to other types of award. The text which records the career of

Rufellius Severus states that the *dona* belong to just two separate awards: in no way can these be made to fit into the schemes outlined above. Likewise the three crowns of the centurion Allius Oriens and the five of the *primus pilus* Statius Marrax are inconsistent with the later imperial 'standard' centurion's awards. This is perhaps symptomatic of the period to which they belong, at the end of the republican tradition and forerunners of the imperial system with crowns apparently still being awardçd individually and alone, though whether they still retained their traditional significance at so late a date is doubtful.

CHAPTER X

IMPERIAL SCALES OF AWARD · BELOW THE CENTURIONATE

Evocati

From the third quarter of the first century AD the term *evocatus* as a military rank became restricted almost exclusively to those praetorian soldiers who, having completed their sixteen-year term in the ranks, were being retained for service in the centurionate. They were officially designated *evocatus* until such time as a centurionate became available. Normally a soldier would not spend long as *evocatus* since he was, by definition, marked out for promotion; however, the not insignificant number of soldiers who died as *evocati* does suggest that not all those retained with a view to promotion did in fact make the grade. Also occasionally the rank would be retained while a particular job was being carried out; for example Vedennius Moderatus spent twenty-three years as *evocatus et architectus armamentarii*, having been not so much retained as recalled from retirement, no doubt because of his special skills in the field of artillery. Similarly Pellartius Celer spent twenty-seven years as *evocatus et armidoctor*, in charge of arms training. During the Republic and early Empire the term *evocatus* was applied more widely, denoting any soldier, praetorian or legionary or auxiliary, who had been retained for some reason. Both these categories are represented in the corpus of decorated soldiers and it is of interest that, as far as the evidence goes, the scale of award to both categories was the same and can be followed back to the later years of the Republic.

Cassius Dio described *evocati* in the following terms: 'These last-named (i.e. *evocati*) Augustus began to make a practice of employing from the time when he called again into service against Antony the troops who had served with his father, and he maintained them afterwards; they constitute even now a special corps and carry rods like centurions.'[1] Thus the *evocati* occupied a position transitional between those of the *principalis* and the centurion, a position which is reflected in their *dona* which is in excess of the award made to the *miles*, *immunis* or *principalis* but at the lower end of the centurion's scale. In all cases where the *dona* of the *evocatus* are recorded clearly and in full the reward comprises *torques*, *armillae*, *phalerae* and a *corona aurea*. The three most straightforward examples are those of Tatinius Cnosus, Statius Celsus and the

210

TABLE L   THE DONA OF EVOCATI

DATE	NAME	RANK	DECORATIONS
Caesar	C. Canuleius	evoc. leg.	t.a.p., cor.
Augustus	C. Iulius Macer	evoc. aux.	clipeus, coronae, aenuli aurei
Augustus–Tiberius	Antiochus	evoc. aux.	—
Claudius	C. Gavius Silvanus	evoc. praet./ centurio	t.a.p., cor. aur.
Claudius	M. Vettius Valens	bf. + evoc. praet.	t.a.p., cor. aur.
Titus	L. Pellartius Celer	evoc. praet.	d.d. et cor. aur.
Domitian	C. Vedennius Moderatus	evoc. praet.	—
Domitian	L. Tatinius Cnosus	evoc. praet.	t.a.p., cor. aur.
Trajan	CIL XI 2112	evoc. praet.	t.a.p., cor. aur.
Trajan	C. Statius Celsus	evoc, praet.	t.a.p., cor. aur.
Trajan	C. Nummius Constans	evoc. praet./ centurio leg.	t.a.p., cor. aur.

unknown of CIL XI 2112: in none of these cases is the rank of the recipient nor the composition of the award in any doubt. Cnosus was decorated by Domitian during his wars on the Rhine or Danube in the 80s and then moved on to centurionates in the Rome cohorts. Celsus served as *evocatus* long enough to be decorated as such in both of Trajan's Dacian wars, after which he received a commission in legion *VII Gemina* in Spain, while the unknown was decorated by Trajan in one of the Dacian wars, subsequently rising at least as high as the primipilate.

A slight variant on the pattern is presented by the case of Vettius Valens. Valens was serving in the praetorian guard during the Claudian invasion of Britain; his award is referred to in the following terms: *benef(iciario) praef(ecti) pr(aetorio) donis donato bello Britan(nico) torquibus armillis phaleris, evoc(ato) Aug(usti) corona aurea donat(o)*. He received *torques, armillae* and *phalerae* as a praetorian *principalis* and then, having been designated *evocatus*, a gold crown was added to the reward. Such a procedure is in some ways analogous to what went on in the early Flavian period when an award was earned at one rank, promotion intervened between the winning and the receiving, and the scale of the decoration was augmented to the higher rank (above, p. 156). It is possible that Valens was designated for decoration while serving as *beneficiarius* but that his sixteen-year term expired while he was still actively engaged in Britain; he was retained as *evocatus* and, perhaps on the occasion of the British triumph in AD 44, was given the appropriate awards. A similar sequence of events would explain the odd wording of the text relating to L. Pellartius Celer Iulius Montanus – *bello Iudaico donis donatum et corona aurea ab divo Tito*: he was given decorations and a gold crown, the decorations referred to presumably being *torques, armillae* and *phalerae*. Celer was discharged by Domitian (hence before AD 96) after forty-three years service, presumably twenty-seven as *evocatus et armidoctor*: he thus obtained his *evocatio* some time between 54 and 69 so it is certain that he was *evocatus* when decorated by Titus.

The wording of the texts relating to Valens and Celer led Mommsen to believe that the gold crown was the characteristic award of the *evocatus* and that in no case did an *evocatus* also receive *torques, armillae* and *phalerae*, the award of the simple *miles*.[2] Where a crown was linked with these minor decorations Mommsen believed that two discrete awards were involved. There is little justification for this belief. Steiner on the other hand interpreted these two inscriptions as meaning that *torques, armillae, phalerae* and a *corona aurea* was the characteristic award of the *evocatus* but that a gold crown alone would be given where the minor awards were already held.[3] This is an interesting idea which could certainly be sustained by reference to Valens and Celer alone. However it is out of step with everything else we know of Roman practice regarding *dona*. Decorations major and minor were repeated, several times if necessary: there is no good example among the *evocati*, but to use the nearest available analogy several centurions are known to have received the full *torques, armillae, phalerae* plus *corona* on two or even three occasions (table I): the case of Valens is different because only one campaign, in the middle of which he received his promotion, is involved. Steiner went on to suggest that, as the gold crown was the sign of the *evocatus*, each of those cases of decoration where a *corona aurea* was combined with a *hasta pura* constitutes not one but two separate awards – an initial award, as *evocatus*, of *torques, armillae, phalerae* and a *corona aurea*; and a later award of a *hasta* which resulted in the suppression, in the texts concerned, of the minor decorations. This is to misrepresent the evidence. As we have already seen (above, p. 185) not only *evocati* but centurions received the gold crown, while the combination in a single award of a gold crown and a *hasta* fits neatly into an ascending scale of decoration as the award appropriate to the senior centurion as well as to the more junior equestrian officers.

The fact that a centurion was eligible to win the same combination of awards as was the *evocatus* gives rise to problems of interpretation in certain careers. Nummius Constans, for example, received this particular combination from Hadrian in the Jewish war having earlier in his career received from Trajan the *dona* of a *miles* on the occasion of the Parthian war. An interval of a minimum of fifteen and a maximum of twenty-one years' service separates the two awards, so if Constans had enlisted only shortly before transfer to the East under Trajan he could have been *evocatus* at the time of Hadrian's Jewish campaign. Alternatively if he had already seen fourteen or fifteen years service by 114 he would almost certainly have been a centurion by 132: he held commands in *III Cyrenaica* and *VII Claudia* and the former unit certainly took part in the Jewish war. The two interpretations are equally viable. The same problem arises over Gavius Silvanus. Only the highest posts he held, and this includes nothing lower than *primus pilus* of *VIII Augusta*, are recorded on his tombstone. The text ends with a reference to decoration by Claudius in the British war, *torques, armillae, phalerae* and *corona aurea*. A reference to Silvanus in the Annals of Tacitus informs us that in AD 65 he held the post of praetorian tribune;[4] hence in 43 he should have been no more than a centurion and very possibly *evocatus*. The timing of the career is very similar to that of Vettius Valens whom we know to have become *evocatus* during Claudius' British war and who by AD 66 was holding his first procuratorial post, just two steps further up the career ladder than Silvanus had reached by the previous year.

The only other praetorian *evocatus* known to have been decorated is Vedennius Moderatus. The scale of award is not stated but the case is worth noting as it is the only example of decorations being awarded to a soldier concerned with artillery: Moderatus was *evocatus, architectus armamentarii*.

Of the three non-praetorian *evocati* who were decorated only one, Caius Canuleius, is known to have received decorations comparable to those of the praetorian *evocati*: the fact that he did so is of particular interest because of his early date. He belongs not to the Principate but to the late years of the Republic, decorated, in all probability, during Caesar's Gallic wars. The legion in which he served, legion *VII*, is known to have taken part and his brother Quintus, also serving in *legio VII*, was killed in Gaul.[5] The type of crown which Caius Canuleius received is not specified, but it may well have been a *corona aurea*.

No detail is given of the composition of the award made to Antiochus, while the wealth of gifts bestowed on Iulius Macer is the one and only apparent exception to the very constant standard of award of the *evocati*. The exceptionality goes deeper than just the composition of the reward which consisted of a shield, crowns and gold rings. The award is a rare example of an unofficial decoration given not by the emperor but by the man's comrades. Herein no doubt lies the reason for the abnormality of the gift: it is *sui generis* and not an exception to any general rule.

Milites, immunes and principales

The wide range of decorations, which in the later republican period the ordinary soldier might aspire to winning, was severely restricted during the Principate; to all intents and purposes he could hope for no more than the minor awards, *torques, armillae* and *phalerae*. All the crowns, with the single exception of the *corona civica*, were now reserved for officers, as were *hastae purae* and *vexilla*. Though in theory the *corona civica* was within the reach of the man in the ranks, in practice the latest example for which there is evidence of its being awarded to a soldier below the rank of centurion belongs to the period of Tiberius and the war against Tacfarinas in Africa.[6] This same episode is also the latest attested case of a simple *miles* receiving a *hasta*.

This tendency towards rewarding the rank and file with lesser decorations is already clearly discernible in the literature of the Republic. A simple *miles* could in theory, and occasionally did in practice, win a crown, but he was far more likely to receive a *torques* while the officer in command would receive something more substantial. As early as the beginning of the first century BC the combination of awards which was to become characteristic of the man in the ranks first appears. It was in 89 BC that the cavalrymen in the *turma Salluitana* won *torques, armillae* and *phalerae* in addition to *cornucula, patellae* and double grain rations. *Torques, armillae* and *phalerae* subsequently recur regularly in combination as the decoration of the *miles, immunis* and *principalis*. There is no discernible difference between the *dona* of the ordinary ranker and those of the *immunes* and *principales*, nor does the legionary appear to have been treated differently from the praetorian soldier despite the gulf in pay and status which divided them. For example Arrius Clemens as *eques cohortis praetoriae* received from Trajan precisely the same award as did Albius Felix as *cornicularius praefecti praetorio*, adjutant to the praetorian prefect, a post from which promotion was direct to the centurionate before the completion of sixteen years service and *evocatio*. Both these men received *torques, armillae* and *phalerae* and so too did many legionaries who never rose higher than *miles* or *eques* (table M).

While all three awards were very commonly received together one or more might be omitted. Indeed it is possible that sometime after the reign of Trajan *phalerae* disappeared altogether from the *dona* of the ordinary soldier (though they were certainly retained for centurions). Certainly they are not attested any later than Trajan, though as there are only three relevant examples for the whole period from Hadrian to Severus this may be due to no more than lack of evidence. No legionary with *phalerae* is attested after the Domitianic period, but then no decorated Trajanic legionaries are known. Steiner sought to explain the absence of *phalerae* by appealing to the passage in Polybius which states that the *phalera* was the award of the *eques* while the *patella* was awarded to infantrymen. This explanation clearly will not do. The Polybius passage refers to practices in the middle of the second century BC, to an army very different from that of the Principate: already by 89 BC we have cavalrymen being awarded *patellae* and by the Augustan period *milites* with *phalerae*.

The various possible combinations of award are indicated in table M. One point which emerges very forcibly from this table is the lack of precision with regard both to the rank of the recipient and to the scale of the award. There is a frustrating lack of detail on the tombstones of many of these soldiers. If the man had retired he may be designated *veteranus* or *emeritus* instead of specifying in which particular posts he had served. Alternatively only the highest post reached may be named, particularly if a centurion's commission had been obtained. The problems to which this gives rise have already been considered in discussion of the centurionate (above, p. 184). As we have seen omission of a crown constitutes by no means conclusive proof that the man in question was of lower rank than centurion. Frequently in the case of the soldiers of the Julio-Claudian period the texts of their tombstones give no indication of *dona*, which are attested only by the sculpture which decorated the stones. The unreliability of such evidence needs no re-emphasis here. In the absence of text there is no way of knowing whether the reliefs are intended to be accurate or merely symbolic. However there is one thing which the sculpture does indicate which the texts do not and that is the numbers of individual pieces awarded. Though crowns, *hastae* and *vexilla* are commonly quantified in the inscriptions, *torques*, *armillae* and *phalerae* never are – a fact which suggests that the numbers were standard. Such an assumption does not altogether square with the pictorial evidence. *Torques* and *armillae* were, it does appear, conventionally awarded in pairs. There are exceptions but these are in the minority. *Phalerae* on the other hand appear in sets of nine, seven or five, nine being the commonest number. Whether these differences reflect actual variations or whether they are the product of artistic licence is difficult to say. The sculptor who executed the Caelius stone (pl. 2a) depicted five large *phalerae* in very fine detail: unless he made the individual discs smaller he could not fit any more than five into the space available (Caelius's hand covers the position of another possible disc) but if he made them smaller he could not include such intricate designs. Was the number of *phalerae* merely a matter of convenience for the sculptor? The one authentic set of *phalerae* which survives, the Lauersfort *phalerae* (above, p. 94), consists of nine circular pieces (the number most commonly illustrated by sculpture) plus one kidney-shaped piece. The significance, if any, of the different designs to which the *torques*, the *armillae* and the *phalerae* were made is again obscure. There is for example no direct correlation between rank and fineness. Caius Marius was no more than an *eques legionis* when he received a set of *phalerae* finely decorated with rosettes and mythological figures, while the *aquilifer* Cn. Musius is credited with a set of plain discs.

A second fact which emerges very clearly from table M is the disproportionate number of cases from the pre-Claudian period. Of the forty-one examples of individual award which are either precisely or approximately dated, seventeen certainly belong to the wars of Augustus and Tiberius and a further eight (listed as Claudian or pre-Claudian) may do. A mere fifteen awards are attested for the next century and a half and of these only six are legionary. Not a single legionary ranker is known to have received military decorations during the whole of the Trajanic wars in Dacia and Parthia. This is hardly an accurate reflection of the continuing importance of the legions in the major wars of the Empire. Auxiliary units were certainly taking over much of the work of control on the frontiers but the legions were still of prime importance on the battlefield. There is no shortage of officers from the legions on the rolls of honour for the Dacian and Parthian wars or for the campaigns of Hadrian and the Antonines in which the legionaries are again notable by the paucity of their numbers. The group of four praetorians decorated by Trajan stands out in marked contrast; superficially it looks as though the soldiers of the Emperor's bodyguard were receiving preferential treatment. The true explanation is probably rather more fundamental. A study of the inscriptions which provide our basic facts about the *dona* of the Principate in general and this period in particular at once reveals another contrast between the praetorian and the legionary. The praetorian stones are, in general, considerably more detailed: a wordy inscription is an expensive inscription, and the praetorian earned more than did his legionary counterpart. This same financial factor has already been invoked to explain the glut of fine legionary tombstones of the Augustan period. Augustus' generosity to his armies will

TABLE M   THE DONA OF MILITES, IMMUNES AND PRINCIPALES

DATE	NAME	RANK	TEXT *t a p*	RELIEF *t a p*
Republic	Q. Annaeus Balbus	miles leg		
	Q. Annaeus Balbus	miles leg		
	Turma Salluitana	eques alae	T A P	+ cornuculum, patella, frumentum duplex
Aug – Tiberius	M. Aemilius Soterias	eques leg	T A P	
	L. Antonius Quadratus	miles / signifer leg	T A	2 2 ?
	L. Blattius Vetus	miles / C leg		2 9
	M. Caelius	miles / C leg		2 2 5 + cor civ
	L. Coelius	signifer leg	T A P	
	M. Fraxsanias	eques / miles leg	T A P	
	L. Gellius Varus	miles leg	T A P	2 2 ?
	M. Helvius Rufus	miles leg	T + hasta + cor civ	
	C. Iulius [. . . .]ius	miles (leg)	T A	
	L. Leuconius Cilo	miles leg		2 + cor aur
	M. Petronius Classicus	miles / C leg		2 5 +
	Q. Sertorius Festus	miles / C leg		2 9 + cor aur
	C. Vettius	eques leg		2 2 9
	M. Vireius Celer	? leg	T A P	
	CIL III 8438	miles leg		2 2 ?
	CIL XIII 7556	miles / C leg		2 9
Claudian or pre-Claudian	A. Baebius	? leg	? A ?	
	P. Baebius	eques leg	? A ?	
	Q. Cornelius	miles leg		2 1 9
	–. Lucius	?		2 ? 7+
	C. Marius	eques leg		2 2 9
	Cn. Musius	aquilifer leg		2 1 9
	L. Refidius Bassus	miles / C leg		? ? 7+
	A. Volsonius Paulus	miles leg		2
Claudius	M. Vettius Valens	beneficiarius praef pract	T A P	
Vespasian-Titus	C. Vedennius Moderatus	miles praet		

TABLE M   THE DONA OF MILITES, IMMUNES AND PRINCIPALES

DATE	NAME	RANK	TEXT			RELIEF		
			t	a	p	t	a	p
Domitian	Ti. Claudius Maximus	vexillarius eq leg ⎫						
	Ti. Claudius Maximus	explorator alae ⎭				2	2	
	P. Tedius Valens	signifer leg	T	A	P			
	CIL VI 37298	? praet						
Trajan	Q. Albius Felix	cornicularius praef praet	T	A	P			
	C. Arrius Clemens	eques praet	T	A	P			
	C. Caesius Silvester	miles praet	T	A	P			
	C. Nummius Constans	miles praet	T	A	P			
Hadrian	T. Camulius Lavenus	miles leg	T	A				
Marcus –	C. Didius Saturninus	miles praet	T	A				
Commodus	C. Didius Saturninus	miles praet	T	A				
	L. Murrius Fronto	miles leg						
Marcus or Severus	C. Titurnius Quartio	eques leg	T	A		1	2	
Undated	L. Avaenius Paser	miles praet					2	
	T. Nasidius Messor	eques speculator						
	M. Praeconius Iucundus	tubicen leg						
	A. Saufeius Emax	optio praet	T	?	?			
	T. Valerius Germanus	imaginifer leg						
	T. Valerius Germanus	imaginifer leg						
	AE 1915, 112	signifer praet				2	9	+cor aur

have left sufficient money in the hands of the soldiers' families to pay for the fine memorials which appear in disproportionate quantities in the early years of the first century AD. It can be no coincidence that the majority of praetorians whom we know to have been decorated in the ranks subsequently rose to higher and more lucrative posts, one to senior centurion and five to *primus pilus* and beyond. Also in four cases the stones were not tombstones set up at the expense of the families of the deceased but honorific inscriptions erected by the cities of which these men were patrons. Further, it is possible that the legionary who rose through the ranks to later eminence would not wish his earlier career to be recorded: the omission of all posts below (commonly) the centurionate might be extended to include any honours won during that period. Hence the apparent scarcity of legionary rankers decorated during the second century may be no more than a result of the bias in the evidence.

One positive factor which points towards this same conclusion is the number of soldiers listed on military *laterculi* of the mid to late second century who are designated *d.d.*, interpreted as *donis donatus*: the figures are one in fifteen on a legionary list concerning legion *VII Claudia* and roughly double this on a praetorian list of slightly earlier date (above, p. 136). These figures suggest a considerably greater use of *dona* to reward the men in the ranks than would appear from individual career records.

CHAPTER XI

BATTLE HONOURS OF
THE ROMAN ARMY

While it was very rare for a member of an auxiliary unit, other than its commanding officer, to win military decorations in an individual capacity, it was fairly common for the unit itself to be honoured in some way. The legions, the praetorian guard and the fleets too could be collectively honoured, with the award being permanently commemorated by the incorporation of appropriate honorary titles in the unit's official name. For example a unit might be designated 'victorious' or 'unconquered', it might be allowed to incorporate the emperor's name into its title thus indicating imperial favour (a practice comparable to that by which certain regiments in the British army became known as the King's or Queen's Own), it might receive a block grant of Roman citizenship or be collectively decorated.

The evidence for these various grants comes in the surviving titulature of the units concerned. Once granted an honorary title a unit would presumably have had the right to use that title for the rest of its existence unless it subsequently disgraced itself and was stripped of its honours. In theory therefore it should not be difficult to establish approximately when such an award was made and even to tie it down to a particular campaign. In practice this is frequently not possible simply because our surviving documents, official as well as unofficial, are surprisingly erratic in their use of these honorary titles. There is no apparent logic behind the pattern of use and even such formal documents as military diplomas frequently do not attribute to a unit titles which it is known to have borne. For example the *cohors I Breucorum* is referred to on a career inscription erected in AD 105 as the *cohors I Breucorum c. R. (civium Romanorum*, of Roman citizens): a diploma of AD 107 calls it simply *I Breucorum*, while another of 121/5 adds in the *c.R.* The title is retained on an inscription of the reign of Pius dropped on a diploma of AD 153/7 and never again resumed.[1] Hence it will be apparent that the earliest surviving dated reference to a title can in no way be guaranteed to be at all close to the date when that title was bestowed, and that conversely the omission of such a title does not mean that none had been bestowed. One might expect that, particularly in the case of career inscriptions, the closer the record to the date of the award the higher the probability that the title will be used: but again this cannot be relied upon in practice. For example, there is every reason to believe that the *cohors I Brittonum* earned the titles *Ulpia torquata pia fidelis civium Romanorum* during Trajan's second Dacian war. The 'Ulpia' in the title points to Trajan as the originator of the award, while a diploma of AD 110 records a special grant of citizenship made in 106 to this very unit in acknowledgement of its conduct during the Dacian expedition (*pie et fideliter expeditione Dacica functis*).[2] Yet in another diploma issued the same year the *p.f.* does not appear and in the career inscription of M. Aemilius Bassus who commanded the unit in 110 it is called simply *coh. pr. Brittonum*.[3] Subsequent references to the unit omit all titles but the *Ulpia*.

Apart from these battle honours being recorded verbally in a unit's official titles it is highly probable that they were also recorded visually in the unit's standards. The official *signa* of all types of unit – auxiliary, legionary and praetorian – were decorated with a wide range of devices some inspired by military symbolism, some recalling the origins of the unit, others connected with its subsequent history: eagles, thunderbolts, half-moons, and ships' prows commonly appear, and also *phalerae*, *coronae* and *vexilla*. The shafts of legionary *signa* tend to be dominated by plain *phalerae* but often have a crown at the top (fig. 15). One of the standards depicted on the relief from S. Marcello in Rome includes both a simple *corona aurea* and a *corona muralis*, both of which presumably have some significance in the battle history of the unit concerned (pl. 4a). Praetorian standards tend to be rather more ornate. Two very fine ones are illustrated on the tombstone of Pompeius Asper from Rome (pl. 12a). Working from the bottom upwards they comprise a crown, an *imago*, another crown, a plaque giving the name of the unit (*coh. III pr.*), a scorpion, another *imago*, a *corona muralis*, a winged victory, a crown, an eagle framed within what appears to be a *torques*, a cross-bar and another crown encircling the point. These two identical *signa* are the only standards believed to show a *torques*. In his commentary on this relief Durry expressed a doubt that a *torques* was really intended, suggesting that what we see is in fact a crown viewed from on top.[4] Certainly the eagle is usually encircled by a crown, and this is the device which is employed on the other of the three standards on the Asper relief. However, the sculptor who executed this relief was clearly very competent: had his intention been to show crowns and not *torques* there is no reason to believe that he could not have done so accurately. Other praetorian standards, notably some particularly fine examples illustrated on Trajan's Column, include *coronae navales* and *vallares* (pl. 4b).[5] Auxiliary *signa*, too, incorporate military decorations, most commonly *phalerae* and *coronae aureae*. All these decorations on standards may echo a practice, specifically recorded only in the case of the auxiliary cavalry and infantry, of awarding military decorations to entire units.

L . G E L L I V S

O V F. V A R V S

V E T E R. L E G X I I I

G E M I N A E

15   Tombstone of L. Gellius Varus (after Ianus Gruterus: stone now lost)

Torquata and armillata

Among the honorary titles awarded to military units these two alone imply the presentation of military decorations to the unit as a whole, rather than to the individuals therein. Only the *torques* (*torquata*) and the *armilla* (*armillata*) are attested in this way, though the appearance of various types of crown and also of *phalerae* on military standards could be taken to suggest that units might also be *coronata* and *phalerata*, though there is no epigraphic evidence to bear this out. The title *armillata* is attested in the case of one unit only, the *ala Siliana*, and this is on record once as *armillata* and once as *bis armillata* having apparently received the honour on two completely separate occasions.[6] The title *torquata*, or *bis torquata*, is known to have been awarded to a total of eleven or possibly twelve units, five or six cohorts and six *alae*, and to have been used for a fairly restricted period. With just one possible exception all the block grants of both *torques* and *armilla* belong to the Flavian, Trajanic and Hadrianic periods (cf. Table N). The one possible exception, the grant to the *cohors I Lepidiana*, may, in view of the problems of close dating outlined above, be more apparent than real. The decorations of the *cohors Lepidiana* are recorded just once, on a dedication by the unit to Septimius Severus: the stone is fragmentary but neither the date nor the decorations (*bis torquata*) are in doubt.

TABLE N   DECORATED UNITS

ALA

I Fl. Aug. Brittannica	torquata	Trajan	Dacia
	bis torquata	Trajan	Dacia
Gall. et Thrac. Classiana	torquata	Flav/Traj	Britain
	bis torquata	Traj/Hadr	Britain
Moesica	torquata	Vespasian	Rhineland
Gallorum Petriana	torquata	Flav/Traj	Rhine/Britain
	bis torquata	Traj/Hadr	Britain
Gallorum Tauriana	torquata	Vespasian	Rhineland
Siliana	torquata	Domitian	Danube
	torquata et armillata	Trajan	Dacia
	bis torquata et bis armillata	Traj/Hadr	Parthia/Danube

COHORS

I Breucorum	torquata	pre-Antonine	?
	bis torquata	pre-Antonine	?
I Brittonum M.	torquata	Trajan	Dacia
I Hispanorum (?)	torquata	Trajan ?	Dacia ?
Lepidiana	torquata	Dom/Traj ?	Danube ?
	bis torquata	Trajan ?	Dacia ?
VIII Raetorum	torquata	Trajan	Dacia
III Thracum	torquata	pre-Antonine	?
	bis torquata	pre-Antonine	?

The stone comes from the Euphrates area.[7] *Cohors I Lepidiana* is known to have moved east from the Danube area, where it is attested in Pannonia and thereafter Moesia Inferior, to take part in Trajan's Parthian war. Prior to its move it is attested on three diplomas, on none of which is it called either *torquata* or *bis torquata*.[8] On the first of these diplomas, dating to AD 80, it bears no title, on the second, of 90, it is designated *c.R.* and on the latest which belongs to the early second century even this title is dropped. Hence it is possible that the *torquata* was acquired at the time of the Dacian wars of Trajan in which it may well have participated, being based at the time in lower Moesia, a province which certainly provided units for the Dacian campaigns. One subsequent reference to the unit which, from its findspot in Asia Minor, post-dates the move east, describes it simply as *c.R.*[9] All we can therefore be sure of is that the unit had twice been decorated by the time of Septimius Severus: the context for both awards might well be the Parthian wars of the 190s, but in the light of all other evidence for the dating of this type of award it is perhaps more likely that they belong to the Domitianic or Trajanic encounters on the Danube, or the Trajanic war against the Parthian empire.

Activities on the Rhine in the early Flavian period account for the two earliest examples of a unit being decorated. The *ala Tauriana* is described as *c.R. torquata victrix* on two military diplomas, one dating to the years 114/7 the other to 122.[10] At this time the unit was based in Mauretania Tingitana to which it had moved, via Spain, in the mid-Flavian period, by AD 88 at the latest. It is attested in Gaul in AD 69 and was in all probability still in the Rhineland at the time when it was commanded by Sextus Attius Suburanus, *praefectus alae Taurianae torquatae* some time during the 70s.[11] It was certainly *torquata* by the time it moved to Spain. A likely context for the award is provided by Vespasian's activities on the Rhine, probably Cerealis' campaign against the Batavi in 69–70 or the war of 77–78 against the Bructeri (unless it had already been transferred to Spain by this date) in which C. Minicius Italus distinguished himself as commander of the *cohors II Varcianorum equitata*, another of the units of the Lower German army.[12] It is during one of these two same campaigns, probably the later, that the *ala Moesica* played a distinguished part. This unit is described as the *ala Moesica felix torquata* on an inscription from Rome in honour of Titus Staberius Secundus who is known from the evidence of a diploma to have commanded the *ala* in AD 78. The governor of Germany named in this diploma is Rutilius Gallicus whom we know to have led the campaigns against the Bructeri in 77–78.[13] The only other inscription to describe the *ala Moesica* as *torquata* is a fragmentary text from Augst which is too defective to help with dating: however it is of note that a veteran of the unit, one Rufinus, is known to have received individual military decorations in Germany some time in the second half of the first century (fig. 13). The *ala Moesica* very probably became *felix* at the same time as it was *torquata*. Given the problems of the evidence there is nothing positively to exclude the possibility that these awards go back considerably further than the record of them. However in the case of these German units it would be necessary to push the context well back into the early years of the first century to find a period of active campaigning. The early 70s, on the other hand, emerge as the period in which the making of block awards to whole units established itself as a regular practice, for it is to these same years that the earliest examples of block grants of citizenship can also be attributed (below, p. 227).

Thereafter it was Trajan who made most use of this device for rewarding units, employing it particularly frequently during the Dacian and Parthian wars. The bulk of the units decorated twice belong to this period. The *cohors I Brittonum milliaria Ulpia torquata p.f., c.R.* was certainly decorated at this time as were the *ala I Flavia Augusta Brittanica milliaria c.R. bis torquata*, probably twice in Dacia, and the *cohors VIII Raetorum c.R. equitata torquata* which moved from Moesia to Dacia after the second Dacian war, in all probability winning its *torques* during the war of conquest, though it is not specifically attested until AD 129.[14]

It is to the Trajanic period also that the first example of the award of the title *armillata* belongs. The *ala Siliana c.R. bis torquata bis armillata* was decorated on three separate occasions in the late first and early second centuries. Its titles are recorded variously as *torquata*, *torquata et armillata* and *bis torquata bis armillata*.[15] In all three cases the titles appear on the career records of prefects who commanded the unit, Claudius Paternus Clementianus, M. Vettius Latro and L. Valerius Firmus. Only the second of these is closely dated, for Latro himself received military decorations at an earlier stage in his career when in charge of the *cohors I Alpinorum* during Trajan's first Dacian war.[16] His command of the *ala Siliana*, his next but one post, should therefore fall about the years 105/108, during and perhaps slightly after the second Dacian war. Taking the evidence of the unit's titles at its face value, Clementianus command should come slightly before this, that of Firmus slightly after. Exactly the opposite order was proposed by H.G. Pflaum who believed Firmus's command to predate that of Latro;[17] however this hypothesis is based on the assumption that the differing forms of the unit's titles have no chronological significance, an assumption which is not based on any independent dating evidence. The *ala Siliana* is known to have been stationed in AD 78 in Germania Inferior. By 84 it had moved to Pannonia where it remained until some time after 110 when it transferred to Dacia. It is attested in Dacia Porolissensis from 133 to 164.[18] The award of the first *torques* may well belong to the same occasion as that on which the unit acquired the title *c.R.*, a title first attested in AD 98.[19] The occasion in question is perhaps one of Domitian's Danubian campaigns. The second award thus falls into place in one of Trajan's Dacian wars. The third is impossible to date with any certainty, but Hadrian's Suebo-Sarmatian war of 118 would fit both chronologically and geographically, or perhaps Trajan's Parthian war in which units from Dacia are known to have participated.

If the *cohors I Hispanorum* is correctly credited with a *torques* the Trajanic campaigns in Dacia provide the most likely context for its award. The case is, however, an insecure one, based on the interpretation of some tile-stamps from the fort at Românasi (Largiana) in Dacia (fig. 16).[20] *Torquata* is restored from

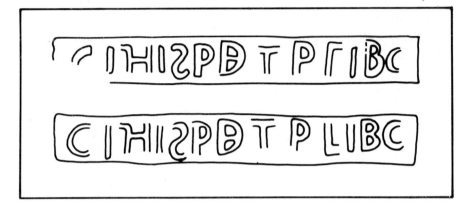

16 Tile-stamps from Românasi (Largiana)

the single letter T, an abbreviation unparalleled in any other text, though, it should be added, the decoration of no other unit is attested on a tile-stamp (which is, of course, too small to accommodate a long text), but rather on tombstones, building inscriptions and diplomas. If the findspot of the tiles is anything to go by the *cohors I Hispanorum* in question was stationed on the western frontier of Dacia Porolissensis and Margaret Roxan has made out a good case for identifying this unit with the *cohors I Flavia Ulpia Hispanorum equitata civium Romanorum* which moved from Moesia to Dacia to take part in Trajan's Dacian wars and is attested as part of the garrison of Dacia by February 110 and specifically in Dacia Porolissensis by July 133 until at least 164.[21] This unit clearly distinguished itself in the Trajanic period – witness the title *Ulpia* – so it is not inconceivable that it was decorated, though conclusive proof that it was is lacking. Even if the putative decorated unit is not to be identified with the *I Flavia Ulpia Hispanorum* the point remains that as part of the second century garrison of the frontier province of Dacia it had plenty of opportunity to distinguish itself in battle.

Two units probably earned the distinction in Britain in the Flavian, Trajanic and Hadrianic periods. These are the *ala Petriana* and the *ala Classiana*. The *ala Petriana* is recorded on an undated inscription from Carlisle as the *ala Petriana milliaria torquata c.R.* (fig. 17) and on a career inscription of one of its

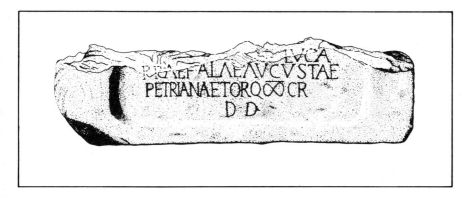

17   Inscription of the ala Petriana from Carlisle

commanding officers, C. Camurius Clemens, as *milliaria c.R. bis torquata*.[22] The career of Clemens is reasonably closely dated: prior to commanding the *ala Petriana* he was tribune of *cohors II Ulpia Petraeorum milliaria equitata*, a post he cannot have held until the unit was raised following the annexation of Arabia by Trajan in AD 106. His command of the *ala Petriana* was a third and not a fourth military post and must therefore predate the creation by Hadrian of the *militia quarta*. Hence the *ala Petriana* was *bis torquata* by the very early years of Hadrian's reign. The date of the text which calls it simply *torquata* cannot be pinned down quite so precisely, though it clearly postdates the upgrading of the unit from quingenary to milliary establishment which occured some time after AD 98 and before 122 or the prefecture of Camurius Clemens, whichever is the earlier.[23] The elevation of the unit from *torquata* to *bis torquata* must therefore belong to the Trajanic or early Hadrianic period, but the only firm date we have for the initial award of the title *torquata* is the *terminus ante quem* provided by the elevation to *bis torquata*. The omission of the title from the diploma of AD 98 need not be at all significant. However, it remains to consider what likely contexts there were for the award of decorations. The *ala Petriana* moved to Britain from the Rhineland some time in the Flavian period. It was at Mainz in AD 56 when it is attested on a dedication in honour of Nero. It was still in the Rhineland during the civil war but may well have been transferred to Britain by Vespasian during the reorganization of army dispositions which followed on his coming to power. An inscription of the unit, still quingenary, from Hexham in Northumberland suggests that it at one time formed the garrison of the nearby fort of Corbridge and it could best be accommodated in the fort as it was in its primary phase *c.* 90- *c.* 105.[24] If the unit was still in Upper Germany in 73–4 it might have taken part in Cornelius Clemens' activities beyond the Rhine (Clemens won triumphal ornaments *ob res in Germania prospere gestas*);[25] if it had moved to Britain by that time it would have had plentiful opportunity to distinguish itself during Agricola's campaigns in Scotland in the 80s, during the troubles of the late Domitianic or early Trajanic period in which C. Iulius Karus won individual military decorations or the encounters of the early second century, some time between 103 and 117, in which *cohors I Cugernorum* earned the titles *Ulpia Traiana c.R.* and the *cohors I Vardullorum* became *cohors I Fida Vardullorum c.R.*[26] There was trouble again in Britain during the early years of Hadrian's reign as is attested by his biographer and by the careers of Pontius Sabinus and Maenius Agrippa, both of whom took part in a Hadrianic *expeditio Britannica* (above, p. 196).

The *ala Gallorum et Thracum Classiana* is credited with the titles *invicta bis torquata* on just one of the texts which record it, the career inscription of one of its prefects, C. Caesidius Dexter.[27] Dexter's career cannot be dated with precision, but must belong to the latter part of the first or first half of the second century AD. In the year 105 the unit formed part of the army of Britain where it remained until at least 122.[28] At some stage in its history it was stationed in lower Germany, probably after rather than before its sojourn in Britain, though there has been some difference of opinion on this point.[29] A tombstone of a veteran of the unit, an ex-decurion, from Cologne suggests that at some time the *ala* was operating in the eastern part of the Empire, for the man comes from Galatia, the area which is now central Turkey. A hypothetical sequence of events might be that the unit came to Britain at some time in the first century, perhaps at the time of the Claudian invasion, perhaps later, transferred out east some time after 122 and possibly in 132 with Iulius Severus who was posted from his governorship in Britain to take command in Hadrian's Jewish war, and subsequently returned west, to Germania Inferior.[30] If this sequence is correct, one and probably both of the decorations should belong to British wars, perhaps to the Agricolan campaigns in Scotland, or to the troubles in the province during the reigns of Trajan and Hadrian. Already by 105 the unit bore the title *c.R.* and it may be that the grant of one of the *torques* accompanied the citizenship grant. The acquisition of the title *invicta* ('invincible') perhaps belongs to the same occasion.

Two further units, the *cohors I Breucorum* and the *cohors III Thracum* are attested as *bis torquata*, both on early Antonine inscriptions from the province of Raetia, but in neither case is there sufficient positive evidence about the movements of the unit to attribute the decorations to specific campaigns.[31] However in neither case need the awards be post-Hadrianic. The *cohors Lepidiana* apart, there are no possible later examples of the use of the titles *torquata* or *armillata*: it was a short-lived and comparatively rare phenomenon, introduced in the Flavian period, attested not at all for the period of active warfare in the 160s to the 180s and apparently falling out of favour very soon after its heyday in the wars of the late first and early second century.

C(ivium) R(omanorum)

From the time of Claudius onwards the auxiliary soldier received the Roman citizenship as of right on the completion of twenty-five (or in the early period sometimes rather more than twenty-five) years of service. From the early second century onwards the grant invariably coincided with discharge, for by then the period of service had stabilized at twenty-five years, but during the first century the grant could be made (and under Claudius and Nero always was made) to serving soldiers.[32] To earn this privilege and also that of *conubium*, the right to contract a legal marriage with a non-Roman woman, the soldier had only to complete, without any serious blemish on his record, the statutory quarter-century term of service. This standard grant was unconnected with war or distinguished service.

These grants to auxiliary soldiers (and also to soldiers of the praetorian guard and the fleets) were recorded on bronze tablets set up in Rome, until AD 90 at various places on the Capitol, thereafter on a wall behind the temple of the deified Augustus, the templum divi Augusti ad Minervam. A copy of the text (in modern parlance a military diploma), naming the individual recipient, his rank on retirement and his unit, was given to each soldier receiving the grant so that, if called upon to do so, he could prove his new enhanced status. Falsely to claim Roman citizenship was a crime punishable by death.

The grant of citizenship to auxiliaries could also be used in another way, not as acknowledgement of twenty-five years service but as a reward for meritorious behaviour in the field. The entire membership of a unit could be given citizenship before the twenty-five year term was completed. We have already seen this occuring in the republican period in the case of the grant by Cn. Pompeius Strabo to the cavalrymen of the *turma Salluitana* in 89 BC *virtutis caussa* (above, p. 127). It became a relatively common practice during the Principate, for in all a total of about fifteen per-cent of the known auxiliary units came to bear the honorary title *c.R.*, *civium Romanorum*, of Roman citizens. In the years of military crisis of the mid-Augustan period a number of auxiliary units were raised from among Roman citizens: these units, *cohortes voluntariorum* and *ingenuorum* also bear the title *c.R.* but in this case it is indicative of status on recruitment, not status won. When a block grant of citizenship was made to a unit only those members serving at the time of the grant were enfranchised, and possibly not even all of these, but only those actually present at the encounter where the honour was won. It does not imply that all subsequent recruits to the unit automatically received citizenship; they would have to earn it in the normal way, so that within twenty-five years of the title being won an *ala* or *cohors c.R.* could well be composed, in common with all auxiliary units, entirely of *peregrini* (non-Romans).

An example of such a premature grant of citizenship as a reward for distinguished service occurs in the context of Trajan's second Dacian war. A special diploma issued in 110, records a grant of citizenship to soldiers still serving in *cohors I Brittonum milliaria* in acknowledgement of their faithful service on the Dacian expedition (*pie et fideliter expeditione Dacica functis*):[33] the unit acquired thereby the titles *p(ia) f(idelis), c(ivium) R(omanorum)*, in addition to becoming *Ulpia torquata*. This special grant was actually made in August 106, the year of the conclusion of the second Dacian campaign, at Darnithitis, a site in Dacia, presumably at a ceremony similar to those in which individual soldiers received their rewards. Indeed it may well be that at the same ceremony the then commanding officer of the unit, whose name we do not know, did receive military decorations. The reason for the four-year delay between the grant of the citizenship and the issue of the certificate proving it can only be conjectured: the problem is tied up with the larger question of what purpose this special diploma was designed to fulfil. The function of the normal diploma was presumably to serve as proof of status should that status ever be challenged. As serving soldiers the recipients of the special grant would have had less need to prove their citizenship: this need would not really arise until they were discharged, hence a four year gap before the issue of the proving certificate would not be of consequence so long as the soldiers in question remained in service for those four years. A comparable time-lag is, however, known to have occurred in a case where the soldiers in question *had* been discharged. A group of auxiliaries from Pannonia Inferior and Dacia Porolissensis discharged by Marcius Turbo (hence no later than 119 when he was appointed praetorian prefect), did not receive their diplomas until August 123.[34] In addition to their special diploma, the soldiers of *I Brittonum* appear also to have received normal diplomas on discharge. In AD 110 a total of fourteen units stationed in Dacia were discharging men who had completed their twenty-five year term:[35] included in this total, and receiving all the normal privileges, is the *cohors I Brittonum c.R.* Clearly many of the men discharged at this time from this unit did not need the grant of Roman citizenship for themselves, they already had it – in which connection it is interesting to note that the man to whom the surviving diploma was awarded, a footsoldier of the *cohors I Brittonum*, already bears the names of a Roman citizen, M. Ulpius Longinus – but they did still need the grants of *conubium* and of Roman citizenship for their children.

This ordinary diploma would have served as proof of Roman citizenship from time of discharge; the purpose of the special diploma must therefore be something rather different. Perhaps it was a prestige document, the auxiliary's equivalent of the legionary's decorations, or perhaps it was issued in case it ever became necessary to prove status prior to discharge. It appears to have been prepared at much the same time as the normal 110 diploma – the names of the witnesses are precisely the same on both documents – which reinforces the impression that it was a document needed after but not necessarily before discharge. As it stands this special diploma is unique, but it is probable that it was originally one of many and that similar documents were issued to all those soldiers who received citizenship *virtutis causa*.

A similar case may be attested by a fragmentary diploma from Dacia. This diploma, which was awarded to a [Marcus?] Ulpius, son of a non-Roman, Landio, is dated by Roxan on the basis of the names of the witnesses, to the early years of Hadrian's reign.[36] A man discharged by Hadrian but who had acquired his citizenship under Trajan had in all probability been honoured as a result of participation in campaigning: the findspot of the diploma, Românași (Largiana) in northern Dacia, suggests Trajan's Dacian wars. The name of the unit in question has not survived, but Russu suggests that a *cohors I Hispanorum* be restored, this being, on the evidence of tile stamps, the unit in garrison at Românași.[37] The problem of the garrison of Românasi has already been touched upon (above, p. 224), but if Roxan's hypothesis is accepted the unit in question is part of the *cohors I Flavia Ulpia Hispanorum c.R.*, a unit which clearly earned one honorific title, Ulpia, under Trajan, and may well have won another, *c(ivium) R(omanorum)*. It is not credited with the title *c.R.* on any of the diplomas recording its sojourn in Moesia Superior where it was stationed prior to its move to Dacia, but nor does it bear it on the Dacian diplomas other than those of AD 110.[38] Hence [Marcus?] Ulpius son of Landio could have acquired his citizenship when the men of *cohors I Hispanorum* received the block grant, presumably on account of the Dacian wars.[39]

Men serving in the Roman fleets also acquired citizenship on discharge in the same way as did auxiliaries, and they too could win it for wartime services. There survives a diploma dating to the year 71 which records the citizenship grant, as per normal, to men just discharged from one of the fleets but combined with the same grant made before discharge (*ante emerita stipendia*) to those who had served courageously and industriously in an unnamed campaign (*quod se in expeditione belli fortiter industrieque gesserant*).[40] In view of the date of the document the campaign in question is probably the Jewish war, the fleet the *classis Syriaca*: alternatively, the occasion may be the Civil War. This special award, unlike that made to the Trajanic auxiliaries in Dacia, included *conubium* and citizenship for the children of those rewarded.

One group of soldiers who did not normally profit from grants of citizenship on discharge were the men who served in the national *numeri*, the irregular units. However, they too could and did receive extraordinary grants in recognition of meritorious service, a fact which is attested by a small group of diplomas relating to two different units, a *numerus Palmyrenorum sagittariorum* and a unit of Moorish cavalry.[41] Four of the texts record a grant made to the Palmyrene archers who were serving in Dacia Superior, whence they had been sent from Syria, during the governorship of Sex. Iulius Severus. Two of the texts date to the year 120, two to 126.[42] The privilege granted was that of Roman citizenship for the soldiers themselves: the grant did not extend to the children, born or unborn, nor was the right of *conubium* given. No mention is made in any of the documents of length of service nor of the reason for the grant, though this latter may be conjectured from the dates of the documents. In the early years of Hadrian's reign there was trouble with the tribes beyond the lower and middle Danube, the Sarmatian Iazyges who lived to the west of the province of Dacia in the plain between the rivers Theiss and Danube and the Roxolani who dwelt by the Danube mouth. The consular governor of Dacia, C. Iulius Quadratus Bassus, fell at the end of AD 117 in battle against the Sarmatians: he was replaced by the *primipilaris*, Q. Marcius Turbo, to whom Hadrian granted an exceptional united command over the provinces of Dacia and Pannonia Inferior. The Augustan History records that the Roxolani soon came to terms.[43] The Iazyges continued to resist and Hadrian invested Turbo with powers comparable to those of the prefect of Egypt in order to give him the necessary authority to deal with the problem.[44] The Palmyrene archers, stationed in the northern part of Dacia, may well have been involved in this episode. The block grant of citizenship attested by these documents is reflected in the name of the unit which came to bear the title *c.R.*, and by the number of soldiers serving in it who bear the nomen Aelius, indicating citizenship acquired under Hadrian.[45]

Another fragmentary document, this one of the reign of Antoninus Pius, records the grant of some privilege (most probably citizenship) to a unit of *Mauri equites* (or *equites* and *pedites*) serving in Upper Moesia. The reason for the grant is unclear, but troops in Moesia may well have been involved in the fighting against the Dacians to which Pius' biographer alludes.[46]

In neither of these two examples is the reason for the award recorded on the extant portion of the diploma, but in both cases it is a reasonable assumption that distinction in battle lies behind it. The soldiers of the *numeri*, in common with those of the *auxilia*, were apparently ineligible for military decorations: the grant of citizenship was the one way in which they could be recompensed for their services in wartime, a grant made all the more significant by the fact that the privileges of citizenship did not come their way as a matter of course on expiry of their period of service.

Legionaries of course did not normally stand to profit by these special citizenship grants since they were, by definition, citizen soldiers. Any non-Roman admitted to a legion would normally be given the citizenship on enlistment. However the civil wars of AD 69 produced an anomaly. The pressure on normal recruiting channels was such that in order to fulfil the requirement for extra legionaries unusual sources were tapped. Legion *II Adiutrix* was raised from the men of the Ravenna fleet, just as a few years earlier Nero had used marines as the basis of legion *I Adiutrix*. These men were non-Romans and so it was necessary to grant them citizenship: hence the series of so-called 'legionary diplomas'. Three record ordinary grants of citizenship on discharge. One gives citizenship to men being discharged *ante emerita stipendia* as war casualties – though they are receiving a full honourable discharge (*honesta missio*) and not the more normal discharge of the wounded (*missio causaria*) – and one, dating to AD 70, is a grant to veterans who have served twenty years or more instead of the normal twenty-five (or twenty-six in the case of the fleets), presumably an early discharge in recognition of their particular service.[47]

Leaving aside the *ad hoc* grants of the Republic and one possible Claudian case, the earliest examples of the block award of citizenship to non-citizen units belong to the Flavian period. It appears to have been introduced first as one of the devices by which Vespasian rewarded those who fought for the Flavian cause, ironing out certain anomalies which had crept into the army as a result of irregular recruiting, and then been extended as a more regular means of rewarding non-citizen soldiers. The earliest diploma to record a unit as *c.R.* belongs to the year 88 and relates to the army of Syria.[48] If the units designated *c.R.* (the *ala I Flavia* and the *cohortes II Italica* and *II Thracum*) were in Syria at the time of their award the most likely context is the Jewish wars of Vespasian and Titus. Individual career records take the date back to the 70s. C. Minicius Italus commanded the *cohors I Breucorum eq. c.R.* in the very early 70s, while Pompeius Faventinus was decorated by Vespasian some time during a military career which culminated in the prefecture of an *ala* whose exact name is disputed but which was certainly *c.R.*[49]

The one possible pre-Flavian example is that of the *ala Vettonum*. The unit is described as *c.R.* on a tombstone of one of its troopers, Lucius Vitellius Tancinus, from Bath.[50] Tancinus' father, Mantaius, bears only the single name of the non-citizen so it follows that Tancinus should have acquired citizenship in his own right, no doubt by military service and in all probability on the occasion of the block award to the unit in which he was enrolled. The names Lucius Vitellius provide the date. As Mann has pointed out, in AD 47–48 Lucius Vitellius shared the censorship with the emperor Claudius: such an occasion would provide a most suitable opportunity for bestowing rewards, as for example on a unit which had taken part in the invasion and conquest of Britain.[51] An alternative view has, however, recently been advanced by Paul Holder who argues for a Flavian date for the inscription. Holder believes that Tancinus' father Mantaius was a Roman citizen, a Lucius Vitellius Mantaius. He points to the propensity among Spaniards to use the father's *cognomen* instead of the *praenomen* for filiation.[52] Hence Tancinus did not acquire the citizenship in his own right but received it via a citizen father: in this case it would be the father's acquisition of the citizenship which dated to the Claudian period, and not the son's. The son's tombstone, attesting a unit designated *c.R.*, need not then be pre-Flavian: the *ala Vettonum* thus falls into line as one of the Vespasianic unit grants. Holder's hypothesis requires that a Roman citizen would have opted to join a non-citizen unit rather than a legion, unusual for the date in question, though not impossible. While there is no doubt that the use of block citizenship grants was put on a regular basis by Vespasian, there is no reason why the practice should not have occurred sporadically prior to this: indeed, as we have seen, it has republican precedents. Given Claudius' known idiosyncrasies regarding Roman citizenship it is quite in character for him to have made a grant of this sort and also to have required that the new citizens take not his names, as would have been normal, but the names of his co-censor. Further, the use of the censorship as an occasion for giving out rewards would provide a nice parallel for the actions of Vespasian and Titus in 73–74.

C.L.

There is just one example of a unit bearing the title *C.L.* This is the *cohors II Tungrorum* which was stationed in the mid-second century at Birrens in south-west Scotland and in the third century at Castlesteads on Hadrian's Wall. Three inscriptions from Birrens attribute this title to it: two are undated altars, the third a building inscription of the year Dec. 157–Dec. 158. Of the three Castlesteads inscriptions which give it the title two are only roughly dated to the third century, the third is of 241.[53] The abbreviation *C.L.* is conventionally expanded to read *c(ivium) L(atinorum)*: this interpretation has until very recently been followed unquestioningly by the various commentators on the Birrens and Castlesteads stones. The basic problem arises from the fact that, unlike *c.R.*, *p.f.*, and all the other standard abbreviations, nowhere is the meaning of *C.L.* written out in full. It is a basic rule on inscriptions that an abbreviation is used only if its significance will be clear to its readers. It is unfortunate that the complete lack of comparative material for this particular abbreviation means that any modern interpretation can be no more than an educated guess at the various possibilities. Latin citizenship was a status intermediate between that of *peregrinus* (non-Roman), and full *civis Romanus*. During the period in question the *ius Latii* could be granted to individual cities with the effect that its magistrates would become Roman citizens. There is no evidence to show that the individual citizens of these cities became Latins and it has further been suggested that the only Latin citizens who existed during the Principate were the *Latini Iuniani*, freedmen who had been informally manumitted in accordance with the provisions of the *Lex Iunia Norbana*.[54] Hence the idea of a grant of Latin citizenship to a body of soldiers in the provinces in the second century AD is anachronistic: it would be meaningless. An attractive alternative interpretation of *C.L.* has recently been put forward by Wolff who suggests the phrase *c(oram) l(audata)*.[55] The basis for this suggestion is the inscription in honour of the equestrian officer, M. Valerius Maximianus. The text records that Maximianus, having slain an enemy leader, was publicly praised, *coram laudato*, and presented with the spoils.[56] A variant on this theme of praise, as for example *cum laude* or the like, is also possible but until corroborative material is forthcoming, purely hypothetical.

Descriptive titles

Both legionary and auxiliary regiments received, *honoris causa*, names descriptive of the qualities which they were deemed to have displayed in battle. One well known case is that of the legions of Britain which distinguished themselves in the suppression of the rebellion of Boudica in AD 60/61: legion *XIV* became *XIV Martia* (after Mars, the god of war) *victrix* (victorious), legion *XX Valeria* became *XX Valeria victrix*. Despite the fact that the role of the legions was thus publicly acknowledged there is no evidence that any individual members of the army in Britain received military decorations on this occasion. The title *victrix* was also bestowed by Trajan on legion *XXX* which he himself raised in the very early second century in order to strengthen his army for the war against Dacia and the subsequent annexation of the province. This same legion later earned the additional *cognomina, pia fidelis* ('loyal and faithful'), in recognition of its support of the Severan cause in the civil war of the late second century. These particular titles were most suitable for awarding to units which remained true to the imperial house in times of civil stress and they were frequently used in such contexts. For example on the occasion of the revolt of Camillus Scribonianus in Illyricum in AD 42 Claudius designated legions *VII* and *XI* which remained faithful as *Claudia pia fidelis*, while Domitian awarded the titles *pia fidelis Domitiana* to the units of the lower German army after their suppression of the revolt of Saturninus in AD 89: the *Domitiana* was dropped after the death and *damnatio memoriae* of the emperor but the *pia fidelis* was retained. Other titles bestowed on legions include *felix* happy (by Vespasian on *IIII Flavia* and by Elagabalus on *II Parthica*), *fortis* strong (by Trajan on *II Parthica*), *vindex* protector (by the African emperor Septimius Severus on the single legion of Africa, *III Augusta*) and *firma* firm (by Vespasian or Domitian on *XVI Flavia*).

A similar range of epithets was used of the auxiliary units. As with the legions *pia fidelis* was by far the most common. The *ala Gallorum et Thracum Classiana* in addition to being *c.R.* and *bis torquata* was described as *invicta*, unconquered, a title which it carried in the early second century and probably won in the troubles in Britain under the Flavian emperors or Trajan while the *cohors I Augusta Nerviana* stationed in Mauretania Caesariensis in AD 107 enjoys the apparently unique distinction of being called *velox*, swift.[57]

Imperial titles

Imperial titles are frequently incorporated into a unit's name, often though by no means invariably signifying a battle honour. The meaning of the imperial title varies according to the position it takes. If inserted in a primary position, as for example in *cohors I Aelia Dacorum* or *ala Ulpia contariorum*, the title commonly indicates not battle honours but simply the emperor responsible either for initially raising the unit or for altering in some way its composition, for example upgrading from quingenary to milliary establishment. There are, however, exceptions to this generalization. Units called *Augusta* do not all by any means belong to the period of Augustus. This is clear in the case of *cohors II Augusta Dacorum* which cannot have been raised until after the completion of the conquest of Dacia in AD 106 or the *ala I Flavia Augusta Britannica* which must postdate the conquest of Britain by Claudius in the 40s, and presumably belongs to the Flavian period. In cases such as these *Augusta* is being used as a particular mark of honour: this fact is made particularly clear in the case of the unit known as the *ala Augusta ob virtutem appellata*, an *ala* called *Augusta* because of its bravery. In this instance the unit has dropped its conventional title in favour of the honorific one instead of, as is more common, combining the two. This dual practice in relation to auxiliary titles reflects the dichotomy which also existed among the legions: *XXX Ulpia* was so called because it was raised by Trajan, *VII* and *XI Claudia* were so called because they were honoured by Claudius.

From the early third century onwards it became common practice for all types of unit to add at the end of their title an epithet derived from the name of the reigning emperor – *Antoniniana, Severiana, Gordiana* and the like. These names were dropped and a new one taken up as soon as there was a change of emperor and there is little connection with merit. The granting of the title might be delayed because of the dubious loyalty of the troops concerned – it has for example been suggested that the reason why the units of the army in Britain did not adopt the title *Antoniniana* until after AD 213 was because their loyalty to Caracalla was suspect[59] – but it does not appear to have required any positive action to win it. An early example of this usage occurs in the context of the Saturninus revolt when Domitian granted the titles *p.f. Domitiana* to the units of the Lower German army, in this case a grant connected with a more specific event than was later the norm.

Finally, imperial titles can appear after a unit's normal ethnic or descriptive name, often linked with other honorary titles and hence indicating the emperor responsible for these awards. An example of this is the *cohors I Brittonum milliaria Ulpia torquata p.f. c.R.*, the unit honoured by Trajan on the occasion of the second Dacian war (above, p. 228).[60]

Conclusion

Only one of these titles, that indicating Roman citizenship, can be shown to have had any substance as far as the individual members in the honoured unit were concerned. It is possible, though by no means certain, that the soldiers

serving in the units designated *torquata* or *armillata* did receive individ'
torques and *armillae*. For the rest the titles are purely honorary, reflecting
on the units that bore them but bringing no demonstrable practical b'
the men who won them. Increased rations or other such perks ma'
been given as rewards to these soldiers, as is frequently seen to '
literature of the republican period, but in the absence of an'
point this is pure conjecture. The promise of citizenship   .ory
completion of service remains the one reward which r'   .ne way
of the auxiliary soldier.

CHAPTER XII

DECORATION, PROMOTION AND PRESTIGE

At the outbreak of civil war in 49 BC the army of Pompey was swelled by recruits who joined up in the hope of prizes and promotion (*spe praemiorum et ordinum*).[1] The prizes of war included plunder, donatives and decorations, while promotion to a higher rank with its enhanced pay and prestige was certainly easier to come by in war than in peace for it would be accelerated for those who survived by the deaths of those men into whose shoes they would step. Moreover, a soldier who had distinguished himself in battle, even if he did not receive immediate promotion, had marked himself out as a warrior of quality: he had brought attention on himself in a way which would stand him in good stead in the future. Promotion might thus be given as a reward in itself, instead of *dona militaria*; it might accompany *dona* or it might come at a later stage as an incidental spin-off of decorations received on an earlier occasion.

There are a number of examples in the accounts of Caesar's Gallic and Civil wars of promotion being used as a prize for valour. Indeed, if the literary evidence reflects the situation accurately, Caesar used promotion quite frequently as a method of rewarding his troops: there are on the other hand singularly few examples of *dona* in the whole of the Caesarian corpus. During engagements between the armies of Caesar and Pompey at Dyrrhachium in the summer of 48 BC one of Caesar's camps suffered a severe attack: none of the men inside the camp had escaped unwounded. The situation was saved largely through the splendid resistance of the centurion Scaeva whose shield, when brought up for inspection at the end of the battle, was found to be pierced with 120 holes. Caesar rewarded him for his bravery with a gift of two hundred thousand *sesterces* and promoted him from his post in the eighth cohort to that of *primus pilus*, senior centurion in the first cohort.[2] The soldiers in the cohort that had been with him all received double pay, clothing, food supplies and *dona militaria*. The double pay could have been either a once-off gratuity or a permanent doubling of their stipendia.

The linking of promotion with a money payment recurs some two and a half centuries later when Caracalla rewarded T. Aurelius Flavinus – who probably held the rank of centurion at the time – with 75,000 *sesterces*.[3] Details of the promotion are not given but Flavinus retired as *primipilaris*, so he may well have been advanced to the centurionate of the first cohort or, if he already held a post in the *primi ordines*, he may have moved up to *primus pilus*. This inscription postdates the last secure reference to soldiers receiving military decorations proper and so provides a clue as to the practice which came to act as a substitute (below, p. 248). Caesar and Caracalla were not alone in using promotion in this way. At the very end of the third century BC Spurius Ligustinus had been promoted for his bravery in the war against Philip of Macedon. Just over a century later, in 102 BC during Marius' campaign against the Cimbri and Teutones who had invaded Gaul, Sertorius received two distinctions. Firstly he was decorated for his courage in mingling with the soldiers in the enemy camp in order to find out what they were planning; subsequently he performed so many brave and cunning deeds that Marius 'promoted him to positions of honour and trust'.[4] Over a century and a half later during Vespasian's Jewish War we find the troops who are besieging Antonia, one of the strongpoints within the city of Jerusalem, vying with one another to be seen by their emperor performing deeds of outstanding bravery, 'every man convinced that his promotion would date from that day if he distinguished himself in the fight'. Their hopes had been inspired by the words of their general, for on the eve of the assault Titus had harangued the troops, promising that those who led the onslaught would be rewarded, that those who survived would command those who had been their equals.[5]

The combination of *dona* with promotion is explicitly recorded on two inscriptions. The earlier example is that of Tiberius Claudius Maximus, the legionary soldier who transferred into an auxiliary cavalry unit, with the rank of *duplicarius*. He received military decorations a total of three times during his career, in the Dacian wars of Domitian and Trajan and during the Parthian war, and on the second of these occasions he was promoted to the rank of decurion in recognition of the fact that he had killed the Dacian king, Decebalus: *factus decurio in ala eade(m) quod cepisset Decebalu(m) et caput eius pertulisset ei Ranisstore.*[6] The promotion did not involve a transfer but was within his own unit to a post which must have fallen vacant through the death or promotion of its previous holder. Some years later an equestrian officer, Marcus Valerius Maximianus, was honoured by the emperor Marcus Aurelius for a rather similar deed.[7] During the German war of AD 166–175 he killed with his own hand Valao, the king of the Naristae. His reward was promotion from the third to the fourth *militia*, to the command of an *ala milliaria*, one of only ten such posts which existed throughout the whole of the Roman empire.

The association of *dona* with promotion is attested also in the literary evidence. The testimony of Josephus is clear: after the fall of Jerusalem Titus called an assembly for the purpose of presenting rewards to those of his soldiers who had fought with outstanding courage. He gave them *coronae, torques, hastae* and *vexilla* and promoted every man to a higher rank.[8] This same link between *dona* and promotion is hinted at also by Vegetius, but the precise significance of what he has to say is far from clear. In his treatise *de Re Militari* Vegetius lists among the *principales* of the *antiqua legio* soldiers whom he calls *torquati simplares, torquati sesquiplicares* and *torquati duplares*. He explains that these men are so called because they have won a gold *torques* as a reward for bravery and that they receive respectively basic corn rations, rations and a half, and double rations.[9] It is by no means certain to what date the *antiqua legio* belongs, though the consensus of modern opinion would assign it to the third century. Vegetius himself was writing towards the end of the fourth century AD but he was drawing on a chronologically very wide variety of sources: if he considered the legion of which he was writing to be *antiqua* it clearly must have differed from that with which he himself was familiar, while it certainly is not the army of the first two centuries of the Principate. Parker and Sander have ascribed it to some time in the period from Gallienus to Diocletian, while Birley would put it rather earlier, under Severus.[10] Problems arising from an assumed late third century date for the *antiqua legio* are discussed further in relation to the end of military decorations (below, p. 249); what is significant here is the inclusion of these *torquati* among the *principales* (junior officers) of the legion. There is clearly implied some connection between bravery, decoration and promotion.

The allusion to double rations recalls the description of the *duplicarius* by Varro, who was writing in the mid–first century BC; a *duplicarius*, he says, is a soldier who has earned double rations (*duplicia cibaria*), on account of his valour.[11] This reward was given, according to Livy, to the soldiers of Publius Decius who helped rescue the army of the consul Cornelius which had been ambushed in a deep defile as it marched away from Saticula (east of Capua) during the campaign against the Samnites in 343 BC.[12] The double rations were awarded to them in perpetuity. During the Principate the term *duplicarius* came to designate a rank or, more precisely, a pay-grade, to signify those soldiers who received double pay by virtue of holding a particular post. Similarly a *sesquiplicarius* was a soldier receiving pay and a half. Standard-bearers, for example, were *duplicarii*, the *armorum custodes* (men in charge of arms) were *sesquiplicarii*. Prior to the professionalization of the army and the need to create a career structure for the men in the ranks, pay-grades of this type were not needed: a man could be given a bonus of double pay or double rations for his greater experience or, in the present context, his fighting qualities. Hence he could be *duplicarius* while holding any post. With the crystallization of the structure of the army in the later Republic and early Empire the term was transferred to describe a *principalis* who received double pay by virtue of the job he did. This went so far in the auxiliary cavalry that the term *duplicarius* became synonymous with one particular post, that of second-in-command of the troop or *turma*: presumably he was the only man in the unit who received double pay. At this stage in the development of the term it would not be accurate automatically to describe as *duplicarius* a man who received double pay or double rations as a reward for valour. An analogous case of the name of a rank or post changing its significance appears to have occurred with the *cornicularius*. The name was probably originally applied to a soldier who won a *corniculum* but in the Empire the *cornicularius* was an adjutant, who could be either *sesquiplicarius* or *duplicarius*, taking his rank from the seniority of the officer he served.

The equation of the term *duplicarius* with a soldier who has been decorated recurs in the early third century. Aurelius Iovinus is described on his tombstone as *miles torquatus et duplarius*.[13] The stone is not specifically dated, mentioning neither the campaign nor the emperor concerned in his award, but it ought to post-date the proliferation of M. Aurelii which resulted from the mass grant of citizenship by the Constitutio Antoniniana of M. Aurelius Antoninus, Caracalla, for Iovinus lacks a *praenomen*. This appears to be a reversion to something akin to republican practice, for Vegetius's *torquati* are included among the *principales* of the *antiqua legio* not because they held a particular post but because they had been decorated in battle. As a corollary they were granted certain privileges and enhanced status which accounts for their inclusion among the junior officers. However it should be noted that Vegetius uses the term *principalis* very loosely, including in this category posts which in the first and second centuries would have been classed as *immunis*, that is carrying with them immunity from fatigues but not extra pay. This being so the problem of Vegetius' *torquati* disappears; they emerge as a privileged group of soldiers some of whom received additional rations though not additional pay, who had been 'promoted' in terms of their status and perhaps granted immunity from fatigues but who had not been promoted in terms of the actual post they held.

Promotion and enhancement of status have thus been used as a reward in themselves and as a corollary to military decorations. But further than this it is notable that a large proportion of those men who received decorations had particularly successful careers. This is unlikely to be fortuitous. Immediate promotion as a direct reward for bravery depended on the availability of a suitable vacant post for the candidate to go to: this would not always be forthcoming, though war casualties would create more openings than would normally become available at any one time. However even if immediate promotion were not forthcoming, once a soldier had indicated his suitability for advancement by the qualities he demonstrated in battle and had been appropriately recompensed there and then with *dona militaria* he was a marked man, marked out for promotion when the time was right. That this was so is indicated by Caesar's choice of centurions for his newly raised fourteenth legion: he promoted men, *virtutis causa*, from the lower ranks of other legions to the higher ranks of this.[14] One such man was Quintus Fulginius who died during the civil wars while holding the rank of centurion in the first maniple of *hastati* of legion *XIV*, having risen to this rank, Caesar tells us, through his extraordinary bravery.[15]

The greater precision of the epigraphic material relating to the soldiers of the Principate makes it possible to examine in some detail this assumed link between decoration and advancement. The relation between military prowess and promotion varied of course from one category of soldier to another. The influence of decorations is likely to be least in the case of the senator whose career prospects were intimately tied up with imperial politics. The favour or disfavour of individual emperors could materially affect his chances, and events outside the field of battle could prove the decisive factors in furthering or ruining his promotion prospects. Military activity was, after all, only one aspect of the role of the senator. The career of Caesennius Sospes, for example, appears to have suffered a temporary set-back on the death of Domitian, probably as a result of his connection with the abolished Flavian dynasty. He had served with distinction on the Danube in AD 92, winning the military decorations appropriate to his rank as legionary legate, and yet he did not become consul until twenty-two years later; in the normal way of things he might have anticipated the consulate in 97 or 98. Domitian was assassinated in 96.[16] Leaving out of account those patricians who did not require military commands in order to attain the consulate and those plebeians who followed a 'senatorial' rather than an 'imperial' career and thus eschewed practically all military activity, the army could bulk quite large in the life of a senator. A career in the service of the emperor started with a legionary tribunate, led on to the command of a legion and then to governorships of provinces which held one, two or more legions in addition often to substantial numbers of auxiliary units. Appointment to the necessary qualifying magistracies would be assured for those whom the emperor favoured and whose careers he needed to advance in order to provide himself with men of the right calibre to govern his provinces. Bravery and the skills of military command exhibited during the tenure of a post as legionary tribune or legate, confirmed by the successful application of these qualities in times of war and acknowledged by the award of military decorations will certainly be factors of significance when weighing up suitability for higher command; but equally the senator must have the abilities of a magistrate. The higher posts in the emperor's service were governorships involving civil administration as well as military command. *Dona* might serve to confirm an opinion of ability in a senator, it is doubtful if they ever had much if any influence on his promotion.

The position was very different for the equestrian officer whose military career consisted of a succession of commands of auxiliary units (though at the second level he could go for a legionary tribunate instead). Competition for posts was keen and at the higher levels the number of qualified candidates was far in excess of the number of jobs available. Military ability must have played a major part in determining promotion prospects and although patronage alone might obtain an initial appointment to the prefecture of a quingenary cohort it could not be relied upon to ensure a steady rise. An efficiency bar clearly operated, for the number of posts decreased with each step on the latter. It lay therefore with the officer himself to prove his competence and hence his suitability for advancement. It has been estimated that in the mid-second century AD the number of posts in each grade of the *militia equestris* was as follows:[17]

Prima militia   270 posts as *praefectus cohortis auxiliaris*
Secunda militia   181–191 posts: 40–50 as *tribunus cohortis auxiliaris*
                                                141 as *tribunus angusticlavius legionis*
Tertia militia   90 posts as *praefectus alae quingenariae*
Quarta militia   10 posts (at maximum) as *praefectus alae milliariae*

Less than 4 per cent of those embarking on an equestrian military career could hope to command an *ala milliaria* and just nine times as many, a third of the total entrants, to command an *ala quingenaria*. It is a striking fact that of the eight detailed careers analysed by Birley of men who attained the *quarta militia* four record decorations at some stage during their military service. Further, the vast majority of all the decorated equestrians completed at least the *tres militiae*, a notable achievement when only one third of the total of those who embarked on the *militiae* can have done so. Of the forty-one decorated equestrians about whose careers there is reasonably good information, only four failed to reach the third grade. Of the remaining thirty-seven, eleven retired or died after the *tres militiae* and all but five of the rest went straight on to procuratorial careers, two (and possibly three) being adlected into the senate. Ti. Claudius Alpinus and Statius Priscus are the certain senators: P. Cassius Secundus is a matter of some speculation. The one inscription recording Secundus as an equestrian officer attests him in his third *militia* as *praefectus alae milliariae* (under Trajan). However, as J. and A. Sašel have pointed, out there exists a homonym, P. Cassius Secundus, suffect consul in AD 138, and imperial legate in Africa immediately prior to this (say 135–138) but whose earlier career is not known. It is tempting to identify these two Cassii with one another, all the more in view of the hypothesis put forward by Groag that the senator, P. Cassius P.f. Dexter was the son of P. Cassius Secundus, senator: the voting tribe in which Cassius Dexter was enrolled was *Claudia*, the same tribe as that to which belonged the city of Emona in Dalmatia, which is where P. Cassius Secundus, equestrian, set up his dedication to the local deity Aecorna.[19] The five exceptions who did not go direct from *tertia militia* to procurator rose to be prefects of milliary *alae*: of these five, four subsequently had distinguished procuratorial careers, one rose to be praetorian prefect and three were adlected into the senate. Equestrians with military experience were particularly suited to certain procuratorial posts such as the fleet commands and the governorships of procuratorial provinces, and it has been noted that, in the Flavian and Trajanic periods in particular, decorated equestrians feature very largely among certain categories of procurator.[20]

All of this is more than pure coincidence. Even granted that three or four of the equestrians were decorated in the last post they held and cannot therefore have been promoted on account of the *dona*, the remaining figures are quite striking. At the very least it would appear that, all other things being equal, the decorated man would be given preference. A conscious selection process had to take place every time an equestrian military appointment became vacant. At the end of his (probably three-year) tenure of a post the record of each officer who wished to be considered for reappointment would have to be scrutinised to assess his suitability for further employment. If he was considered unsuitable or if, in the face of the competition, there was no post available for him, he would simply return to civilian life. If he exhibited the right qualities he would be given another command either on the next rung of the ladder or, occasionally, at the same level as that of the command he had just relinquished. His credentials, which presumably included a report from the governor of the province in which he had just served, would certainly mention any particular distinctions, including military decorations.[21] Though the receipt of military decorations would not in itself be sufficient to ensure promotion or even continued service, the courage and spirit that it represented clearly were. The man who sought advancement did well to draw himself to the attention of the emperor and the provincial governors who had the equestrian military commands in their gift.

The same is true of all other officers and men in the ranks. Of the decorated 'other ranks' just under a third overall rose to the centurionate. Out of the twelve praetorian soldiers who were decorated below the rank of *evocatus* only two certainly failed to obtain a centurionate, and one of these died before he had completed the sixteen years qualifying service. One became *evocatus* and was then retained for twenty-three years as *architectus armamentarii*, in charge of artillery, while two of the stones are too mutilated to show what became of the soldiers commemorated. Of the seven who did attain centurionates one rose to be a senior centurion in a legion, four retired or died as *primus pilus*, one as *praefectus castrorum* and one rose to be procurator of Lusitania. Only eight praetorian *principales* are known to have risen to the primipilate during the second century, and four of these are decorated soldiers. Of the praetorians decorated as *evocati*, those already picked out for advancement, two attained but did not move beyond the centurionate, two reached the rank of *primus pilus* and one went on to be tribune of a praetorian cohort. Just one continued in office as *evocatus*, but this was clearly a special case for the man in question remained in service for a good quarter century as *evocatus et armidoctor*, the man in charge of arms training, retained in this grade presumably for his specialist knowledge.

The legionaries decorated in the ranks do not have quite such a distinguished record, partly perhaps because the competition here was rather fiercer. Praetorians had to vie with directly commissioned men for access to the centurionates of the Rome cohorts (praetorian guard, urban cohorts and *vigiles*) but they could also obtain commissions in the legions, and in the second century more praetorians entered legionary than entered Rome centurionates. The legionary on the other hand had to compete with both praetorians and directly commissioned men and was moreover ineligible for any of the Rome centurionates. Something between 13 and 25 per cent of decorated legionaries, that is between one in seven and one in four, obtained a commission as centurion. The large discrepancy in this figure is due to a combination of the small size of the sample and problems created by the nature of the evidence. The bulk of the legionaries in question date to the early first century when the tendency was to give not a full career record but merely to name the highest post held. Hence it is not always possible to correlate the decorations with the post in which they were won. Marcus Caelius, for example, records only a post as centurion but it is very possible that he was decorated while still in the ranks. Only the scale of the award, particularly the omission of a crown, will indicate the rank of the recipient, but even this is not conclusive for there are a number of clear examples of centurions, and even one *primus pilus*, receiving awards on the scale more commonly associated with the 'other ranks'. It is very likely that a number of soldiers decorated in the ranks and subsequently promoted centurion have been recorded as having been decorated as centurions. Including four cases where there is good reason to believe that this occurred, eight out of thirty-three decorated legionaries became centurion: excluding these dubious cases the figure is four out of twenty-nine.

But how good were the chances of the average legionary of obtaining a centurionate? Ignoring for the moment the directly commissioned men and praetorians, some 5,000 men in any one legion would be seeking fifty-nine posts as centurion. Analysis of a random selection of tombstones which indicate length of service as centurion suggests an average sixteen year tenure: this would mean that about four posts became available each year to be competed for by about 200 in any one year group. This number of men would not in practice be competing for the post since there would already have been considerable weeding out of potential candidates: however the point at issue here is the overall probability of a member of a particular year-group obtaining a centurionate. Using the the Model Life Tables published by the United Nations it can be estimated that 70–75 per cent of each year's intake would survive to the age of thirty to thirty-five, the optimum years for recruitment to the centurionate. This would produce something between a maximum of thirty-eight and a minimum of thirty-five possible contenders for each post. These are of course very crude figures, leaving out of account a number of important factors. The non-legionary element has been completely ignored because it is so difficult to quantify and no cognizance has been taken of the fact that of the fifty-nine centurionates in each legion, five are senior posts including that of *primus pilus* which are held for one year only. Both these factors would tend to reduce the promotion prospects below the figure quoted. The samples are too small and the variables too great to do anything more than provide a rough basis for comparison, but even so the contrast is a striking one: at best the average legionary had a one in thirty-five chance of becoming a centurion, at worst the decorated legionary had a one in seven chance. That is, on the given figures a legionary who distinguished himself in battle was at least five times as likely to receive promotion as were his peers.

Of the centurions who received decorations over half rose to the primipilate and beyond. True these men did not become *primus pilus* on average any younger than did their undecorated colleagues: the age range from about fifty to seventy-two with a preponderance in the early to mid-fifties is much the same as that for the primipilate as a whole. But if the career was not made any swifter it appears to have been made surer – a 50 per cent advancement to the primipilate is high compared with the estimated average of about 30 per cent.[24] The soldier who had been decorated is likely to succeed because he is the sort of man whose qualities are at a premium in an army: he is the sort of man who would probably succeed in any case, but when a post fell vacant the inclusion of *dona* in his references would doubtless stand him in good stead.

Decorations certainly brought with them prestige. The recipients of these gifts, according to Polybius became famous not only in the army but also in their homes.[25] Even entry into the Roman senate might be effected by the man who had brought honour on himself on the battlefield. For example, when in 216 BC there was a review of the composition of the senate in order to fill the places of those who had died since the last census, those considered for entry included firstly men who had already held lesser offices and then those who had the spoils of the enemy fixed to their houses or had received the *corona civica*.[26] Indeed the prestige attached to the holder of the civic crown was such that, according to Pliny, when he attended the games not only did he sit next to the senate, but the senators should rise at his entry.[27] The equestrian officer, M. Valerius Maximianus, was elected into the senate, and the reason for this was clearly his abilities as a soldier. During his equestrian military career he had moved from one battle front to another, distinguishing himself in action and receiving decorations on three separate occasions. He was just gaining access to the upper cadres of procuratorial administration which would have taken him away from active military involvement, when he was adlected into the senate as praetor and given an unparalleled six legionary commands.[28] Maximianus rose in status as a direct result of his military qualities: he became a senator not out of any sense of altriusm on the part of the emperor but because in a period of active warfare he was needed in the army and this was the one way in which his undoubted talents in this direction could be kept at work. Similar reasons account for the elevation to the senate of M. Macrinius Avitus Catonius Vindex who had received military decorations when serving as prefect of a milliary *ala* during Marcus' first German war.[29] His adlection to the senate, like that of Maximianus, dates to the 170s. Finally there is the case of Furius Victorinus, an equestrian who rose eventually to the praetorian prefecture. He did not actually embark on an active senatorial career as did Maximianus and Victorinus but was awarded consular ornaments and continued to serve as praetorian prefect. This ennoblement was dated by Stein to the reign of Antoninus Pius but is more likely to belong to the period of Marcus and Verus and to represent an honour bestowed on him as a consequence of his conduct in the Parthian war in which he participated as praetorian prefect and in which he won military decorations.[30]

There are, to date, just three known examples of centurions being elevated to equestrian status and in each case this elevation is coupled with military decorations. Enrolment in the *ordo equester* brought with it both a rise in status and presumably a considerable money payment in order to provide the necessary equestrian census. It did not of itself necessarily effect any change in the career pattern of the recipient – though it did in theory open up another avenue of advancement through the equestrian *militiae*. Since this avenue had, for the committed soldier, no apparent advantages over the centurion career, such movement as there was between the two career structures being in the opposite direction, it is not surprising that none of the three recipients in question took it.[31] L. Aconius Statura was decorated, for the second time in his life, by Trajan on the occasion of the Dacian wars. He was a legionary centurion when decorated and granted equestrian status, but he continued in the rank of centurion for the rest of his military career. Gavius Fronto and Tillius Rufus were also centurions when similarly honoured but both of them rose eventually to the primipilate.[32] The decorations awarded to Tillius Rufus comprised a *corona aurea* and a *hasta pura* and it was partly the link between these *dona* and the grant of the *equus publicus* which led Domaszewski to suggest that the *hasta pura* was an award characteristic of the equestrian.[33] There is a total of six examples of the *hasta* being awarded to soldiers of the rank of centurion or below but in only one of these cases, that of Tillius Rufus, is equestrian status referred to. Had the award of the *hasta* carried with it automatic equestrian status there would have been no need to make the explicit statement that Rufus had been *equo publico exornatus.* The implication is clearly that none of the other five did receive equestrian status – there is no reason whatever from their subsequent careers to believe that they had – and that Rufus did but only by a completely separate grant.

The significance of the possession of military decorations in both military and civil contexts is demonstrated in a number of different ways. They are frequently quoted by officers and men wishing, for one reason or another, to establish their credentials. C. Marius, for example, addressed the assembled people of Rome after he had been appointed consul and assigned the province of Numidia. His province carried with it command in the war against Jugurtha, and in order to encourage the young men present to enlist in his army he harangued them according to Sallust, with these words: 'I cannot to inspire confidence show the portraits triumphs and consulates of my ancestors but if necessary my *hastae, vexillum* and *phalerae* and other military decorations, not to mention my wounds, all received on the front of my body. These are my portraits, these my nobility, titles which have not been inherited but which I have won at the expense of fatigue against numerous dangers.'[34] Here Marius is using his decorations as evidence of his own quality as a soldier: they are similarly used in Livy's account of the ex-centurion Spurius Ligustinus. In 171 BC a levy was raised for the war against Perseus, king of Macedon, who had broken a treaty with Rome and invaded her allies: in view of the emergency permission was granted to the consul to enrol ex-centurions and soldiers up to fifty years of age. A number of these veterans appealed to the tribunes against this decision, being unwilling to undertake further military service particularly when there was no guarantee that they would be appointed to posts equal to or higher than those which they had held at the time they retired. Spurius Ligustinus however came forward as a willing volunteer, willing, we are told, to serve at whatever rank he is appointed. He boasted of his previous military service and of the thirty-four occasions on which he had received military decorations: as a result he was appointed to the post of *primus pilus*.[35]

Not only could decorations be used to obtain preferment, they might also help to retain it. After the mutiny of the Rhine army in AD 14 there was a revision of the list of centurions of the legions involved. The legions were purged of undesirable elements and only if the tribunes approved the energy and integrity of a centurion was he allowed to retain his commission. The evidence on which the tribunes based their decision included the number of campaigns in which a centurion had participated, what distinctions he had earned and what decorations he had won.[36]

In a civil context too *dona* could be used as evidence of good character. For example, a witness at the trial of Spurius Oppius in 449 BC, in order to prove his *bona fides*, is said to have quoted his military record which included twenty-seven campaigns and eight decorations which he proudly displayed for all to see, while Marcus Manlius himself on trial in 384 BC for plotting against the state, sought to rehabilitate his character by detailing his military career with its many distinctions and its forty decorations, among them two mural and eight civic crowns. His protestations were, however, in vain: he was condemned and flung as a traitor from the Tarpeian Rock.[37]

In view of the fact that decorations were widely used in this way as proof of good character and a qualification for advancement it is not surprising to find that certain qualities were looked for in those to whom they were to be presented and that the standards of those who had won them might be expected to be higher than the average. Marcellus, for example, was forbidden to award *dona* to those who had fled the field of battle at Cannae (above, p. 128), while the actions of Sulla the dictator were deemed by Pliny to be all the more despicable if it was true, as was claimed, that Sulla had once won the *corona obsidionalis*.[38] Distinction and prestige bring with them increased responsibility: when in 471 BC the consul Appius Claudius had suffered a defeat at the hands of the Volsci, largely through the stubborn disobedience of his army, he punished them by decimation. Every tenth man was put to death but also those whose fault had been particularly great, soldiers who had lost their weapons, standard-bearers who had lost their standards, centurions and *duplicarii*.[39] *Duplicarii* in this context must be understood in the sense in which Varro defined it, soldiers who received double rations *ob virtutem*, men who because of their bravery had been set up above their colleagues. By their ignoble behaviour they betrayed the whole basis of their enhanced status and for this they paid dearly. The corollary to Roman military decorations was improved promotion prospects, honour and prestige and the inescapable responsibilities which rank and status carry with them. It is hardly surprising therefore to find that false boasting of valour to win distinction was regarded as an offence. Our evidence on the point is Polybius who includes such boasting in a category of offence which he contrasts with what he calls crimes. However it is clear from what follows that such ignoble behaviour was regarded very seriously and that the penalty was death.[40]

CHAPTER XIII

THE END OF DONA

The wars of Severus and Caracalla in the last years of the second century and the early third are the last in which *dona* in the imperial tradition are known to have been awarded in any numbers. Claudius Gallus was decorated by Severus and Caracalla jointly when he commanded detachments from the four German legions sent to fight in the second Parthian war in 197, and although we are not explicitly told so this same war must be the occasion on which Tillius Rufus received both military decorations and equestrian status. The context for the last decoration of Didius Saturninus could be even later, conceivably the British campaigns of 208–211. Here the evidence for military rewards changes sharply in its character and falls off dramatically in quantity. In place of the symbolic *dona* a more practical form of reward is attested, a reward consisting of a money payment, increased rations or promotion. The sole example of a reward made by Caracalla alone is of a money payment: T. Aurelius Flavinus, a centurion, having shown valour in the face of the enemy, the Carpi, received a gratuity of 75,000 sesterces and was promoted. He eventually rose to the primipilate, retired and went on to enjoy civic distinction, bolstered no doubt by the money he had won in service.

Of roughly the same period is the tombstone of Aurelius Iovinus, a veteran of legion *XIII Gemina*, who is described as *miles torquatus et duplarius*, a soldier decorated with a *torques* and given double rations. There is no mention of the other *dona* traditionally associated with the ordinary soldier, the *armillae* and the *phalerae*. This is true also in the case of the award made to C. Antonius Flavinus, a centurion of legion *II Augusta*, whose tombstone records a gold *torques* and double corn rations (*torq. aur. et an. dupl.*) rather than the traditional decorations of the *ordinatus*. The stone is not dated but a third century context would not be out of place. There was campaigning against the tribes of northern Britain at both the beginning and the end of the century and sporadic trouble from seaborne raiders from both mainland Europe and Ireland. Successful encounters with these enemies are attested by the assumption of the title *Britannicus Maximus* by Carinus and Numerian

(283–284) and by Diocletian and Maximian in 285.

The award received by the two Flavini and by Iovinus is echoed by Vegetius when he speaks of a grade of soldier called *torquati*, enhanced in rank and prestige and in some cases enjoying double rations.[1] Vegetius' *torquati* are *principales* of his *antiqua legio* which would appear to date to the third century and probably to the latter part of it, prior to the military reforms of Diocletian. This being so it suggests that the practice of awarding the *torques* to valorous soldiers may have continued for some decades beyond the period for which we have epigraphic evidence of it. It is unfortunate that our source here, Vegetius, is not an author in whom one can place much confidence. Neatly described by one modern commentator as a 'congeries of inconsistencies' the work (which was written in the late fourth century) is carelessly cobbled together, with little understanding, from material of widely different dates.[2]

The evidence of these three texts points towards a change of direction over the question of military rewards: practical gifts in the form of money and increased rations appear to be replacing symbolic decorations. This is a shift of emphasis rather than a completely new idea, a harking back to a practice which was commonplace during the days of the Republic but which, during the Empire, had been largely though not totally replaced by the use of *dona*. The use of promotion as a reward, with its corollary of extra pay, has already been noted: this features sporadically through Republic and Principate. The increase of rations is more characteristic of the Republic and so too is the making of money payments. The case of the centurion Scaeva and his heroic defence of one of Caesar's camps at Dyrrhachium in 48 BC links together the various types of reward. Scaeva himself received 200,000 sesterces (the equivalent of well over a hundred times his annual pay) and promotion: his men, double pay, bounties, grain and clothing, in addition to military decorations. Another example of the making of money payments by Caesar occurred after an engagement in Spain in 45 BC when Pompey's forces had been successfully repulsed. Of the troops involved in the action two groups were singled out for their valour, the *turma Cassiana* who received 3,000 denarii (12,000 sesterces) and the light-armed troops whose reward was slightly less, 2,000 denarii.[3]

Hereafter individual money payments *ob virtutem* became rare. There is one example in the 160s arising from the Parthian war of Marcus and Verus. Iunius Maximus, the man who brought back to Rome the glad news of the Parthian victory, took part in the war as the senior tribune in legion *III Gallica*: he was duly awarded military decorations on a scale consistent with his rank, but received in addition a *donativum extraordinarium* – an extraordinary donative.[4] The subject of ordinary donatives has already been touched on (above, p. 59). In their distribution individuals were not singled out. They were awarded to entire armies, to each man according to his rank and the type of unit to which he belonged, not according to what he himself might have accomplished. They commemorate high days and holidays. The case of Iunius Maximus is something rather different. Here there is a clear association with the man's individual exploits: the donative is linked with the *dona*. It is but a short step from here to the dropping of the *dona* and the grant of a donative, a money payment, alone as happened at the time of Caracalla in the case of Aurelius Flavinus.

For about a century and a half after the reign of Caracalla none of our sources, literary (apart from the Vegetius passage already noted), epigraphic or numismatic, have anything of value to say about decorations: this gap in the evidence does not however coincide with a period for which evidence in general is in short supply. The third century is generally well represented epigraphically. For example of the 236 *primipilaris* careers studied by Dobson seventy-one (30 per cent) belong to the third century; this compares with sixty-two (26 per cent) in the preceding century. Devijver's equestrian prosopography comprises a total of over 1900 careers of which about 18 per cent are third century (post–Severan), 32 per cent second century. Hence there is no shortage of career inscriptions, many of them mentioning *bella* and *expeditiones*; the lack of any epigraphic evidence for military decorations becomes, therefore, all the more significant. Four litarary references for the later third century can be virtually ignored. All come from the pen of the author of the Lives of the emperors Aurelian (270–275) and Probus (276–282) in the Augustan History. These particular biographies contain little that is of value. The collections of *dona* attributed to Aurelian and Probus are unprecedented and unparalleled. In return for freeing Rome from the threat of the Goths Aurelian, we are told, was given by the Republic thirteen crowns (four mural, five rampart, two naval, two civic), ten *hastae purae*, four *vexilla bicolora*, four red general's tunics, two proconsul's cloaks, a bordered toga, a palm embroidered tunic, a gold decorated toga, a long under-tunic, and an ivory chair.[5] The *dona* of the soldier appear here side by side with certain of the *ornamenta triumphalia*, the insignia of the triumphing general: the *vexilla bicolora* are unparalleled but recall the *vexillum caeruleum* won by Agrippa. It is a list such as might be composed from a reading of honorific inscriptions and the writings of earlier historians, particularly those who detail the fabulous collections of awards won by the heroes of the early Republic, men such as Siccius Dentatus and Spurius Ligustinus. The same is true of the assemblage with which Probus is credited.[6] Probus is reported to have taken part in the Sarmatian war fought during the reign of the emperor Valerian. The *dona* which he is supposed to have won comprise four *hastae purae*, two rampart crowns and one civic crown, four *vexilla*, one gold *torques*, two gold *armillae* and a sacrificial patera weighing five pounds. A further civic crown was awarded to him for saving the life of a kinsman of Valerian, one Valerius Flaccus. The minor awards of the ordinary soldier and the major prizes of the officer are here combined in a way which has not been seen since the hey-day of the Republic. The utter unreliability of the source for these awards, the author's known propensity for fabrication and the bizarre nature of the collections themselves combine to throw deep suspicion on the validity of these references.

A further century passed before the next reference to *dona*, the context here being the wars of the emperor Julian, the source the historian Ammianus Marcellinus, an altogether more reliable writer. Marcellinus was writing in the last quarter of the fourth century, not many years after the events of the year AD 363 to which the military decorations belong. Military crowns – *coronae navales, obsidionales, civicae* and *castrenses* – were awarded for heroic deeds performed with unshaken courage. Those who fought particularly valiantly were presented, we are told, with siege crowns, a type of decoration not attested since the last days of the Republic. As far as one can tell from what is a very generalized account, the awards were being made without regard to rank as would be appropriate in the imperial system, and with little regard to the nature of the deed performed as formed the basis for the republican system. However, it is probably no coincidence that soldiers participating in a siege, that of Maizomalcha, were rewarded with *coronae obsidionales* (siege crowns). Originally the siege crown had been presented to the man who was responsible for relieving a siege so the use of the crown by Julian is not strictly according to ancient custom, but there may well have been an attempt here to revive what was believed to be the true republican practice.[7] The whole episode smacks of that conscious antiquarianism on the part of Julian which is made explicit in Ammianus' remark that the public commendation of the award winners was done according to 'ancient custom' (*veterum more*). If Julian was reviving an ancient but largely disused practice it would not be surprising if he did things somewhat differently from the way in which they had been done in the republican and imperial periods.

The fact that what appears to be a revival of the practice of awarding distinguished service with military crowns takes place under the emperor Julian may be of some significance. Julian was a non-Christian emperor, commonly known as Julian the Apostate because he tried to revive pagan religion and to restore the traditional gods of Rome to their former eminence. The crowning of soldiers and triumphing generals was a part of Rome's pagan heritage which, if the arguments advanced by Tertullian in his *de Corona Militis* accurately reflect contemporary Christian attitudes, had no part to play in a Christian society. According to Tertullian the soldier who had accepted Christ as his crown could not accept any earthly crown: the whole practice of wearing crowns is condemned for a variety of reasons, notable amongst which is the fact that, as pagan literature shows, it inevitably involves idolatry. Hence it must be forbidden.[8] Tertullian cites the case of a soldier who, having been awarded a crown, refuses to put it on because he is a

Christian; as a result of this action he was imprisoned and awaited martyrdom. It is unclear whether this incident is actual or, as has been argued elsewhere, hypothetical.[9] It is thus of uncertain value as evidence for the award of decorations at the period in question (early third century) but of considerable interest for the light it sheds on the attitude to military awards which could have been adopted by contemporary Christians.

Sporadic references to *dona* continue into the fifth century and beyond, but they are exceedingly rare. Flavius Aetius, appointed *magister militum* of the armies in the west in 433, was awarded *dona* (*donis militaribus ornatus*) and had a statue set up in his honour by the Senate and People of Rome for the part he played in securing Italy at a time when the Goths and Burgundians had been active in Gaul, taking advantage of native revolt to attack the cities near them (435–6). It is unfortunate that the inscription which records the honours afforded Aetius does not specify what these *dona militaria* were, *dona* of the traditional type or gifts of a more general nature, even perhaps a money payment.

The latest recorded example of the granting of *dona* of a recognizably Roman pattern takes us into the sixth century, well beyond the fall of the Roman Empire in the West, in fact to the attempt by Justinian to reconquer Italy from the Ostrogoths.[10] The Byzantine army was led by Belisarius, a general noted for his humane treatment of his soldiers. According to the historian Procopius, Belisarius rewarded those who had distinguished themselves with *armillae* and *torques*. Procopius had accompanied Belisarius on this Italian campaign (535–540), and earlier on his Persian and African wars, and was Belisarius' confidante: he had direct first-hand acquaintance with military affairs and there is therefore no reason to doubt his testimony. The tenor of the passage in question which is devoted to the praise of Belisarius, his meekness, his humility and his extraordinary kindness to his soldiers does suggest that such rewards as Belisarius gave were unusual. However, the fact remains that a practice which we first see emerging in the sixth century BC can still be detected in the sixth century AD: the rewards which Belisarius gave to his soldiers are in direct line of descent from the *dona* of the Republic and Principate. Belisarius, however, was apparently giving the rewards of his own grace and favour. It is not suggested that he is presenting the *dona* on behalf of the state: the award is quoted as one piece of evidence of Belisarius' generosity, the *torques* and *armillae* take on the complexion of personal gifts as much as formal military decorations.

The literary and epigraphic evidence thus point to a phasing out of military decorations until they become an unusual rather than the standard method of acknowledging outstanding valour. The pictorial evidence points to a new development in the use of military decorations, specifically of the *torques*. Reliefs in stone and metal dating from the fourth century AD onwards regularly show members of the imperial guard wearing a *torques*, and wearing it not in earlier Roman military fashion but in the more normal and logical position for it, around the neck. Probably the best-known example of soldiers thus adorned is the mosaic of Justinian from the church of S. Vitale in Ravenna. This mosaic, which is one of a pair (the other depicts the empress Theodora), shows the emperor with bishop Maximian. To the emperor's right stand six soldiers, members of the emperor's bodyguard: the three clearly visible at the front carry spears and oval shields and around their necks are gold bands with a diadem (jewel or enamel) at the front.[11] The mosaic dates to the year 547. Soldiers similarly clad are illustrated on the base of the obelisk of Theodosius I, erected in the Hippodrome at Istanbul in 390. The four sides of the base are decorated with reliefs depicting ceremonial groups attending the Hippodrome. On two sides the emperor and his entourage, presumably in the royal box, are flanked by soldiers all of whom wear *torques*, in this case a neck-ring with a leaf-shaped pendant at the front.[12] Members of Theodosius's guard are also depicted on a *missorium*, a large flat silver dish, made to celebrate the emperor's *decennalia* in 388.[13] Theodosius appears enthroned at the centre, flanked by his son Arcadius and co-emperor Valentinian II: on either side of this group stand two soldiers each with oval spear and shield and each with a *torques* about his neck. For the emperor's bodyguard at least the *torques* had clearly become a standard piece of dress uniform and it has taken on this aspect by the later part of the fourth century. It is no longer a *donum militare*, a military decoration in the earlier sense of that term.

The beginning of the end as far as proper military decorations are concerned would appear therefore to be the Severan period. They are attested in traditional fashion up to and including the reign of Septimius Severus. The accession of Caracalla introduces a new element. The date is significant. The principate of Caracalla is precisely the time when the promulgation of the *Constitutio Antoniniana* led to the spread of Roman citizenship to all free-born men. Throughout the first two centuries of imperial rule a clear distinction had been maintained between the legions and the *auxilia*, the citizen and the non-citizen units or, to be more precise, between citizen and non-citizen soldiers. The one was eligible for *dona*, the other, broadly speaking, was not. The edict of 212 completely subverted this distinction. If the reason for the failure of the auxiliaries to receive *dona* has been correctly interpreted as being their peregrine status, there would not in theory be any reason why, after 212, all soldiers should not be eligible to receive *dona*: all, that is, or none. The change in status would presumably have required some adjustment of the basis on which decoration were apportioned and this could have gone one of two ways; either all soldiers could have become eligible for award or the whole practice could have been discontinued. The auxiliaries played a vital role in the defence of the Empire; to extend *dona* to all categories of soldier would be roughly to double the number of those eligible. In the event things would appear to have gone the other way. The practice virtually died out and was replaced by a more practical form of benefit, promotion, a money payment or increased rations, this last a particularly significant form of reward in periods of severe inflation. Traditionally the military decorations had been made of gold and silver; such profligate use of the noble metals would have been unthinkable in a third century context when the coinage itself was seriously debased. In view of all these circumstances a reward in money or in kind represented a more practical way of honouring the brave, and one with sound republican precedents. The wheel had gone full circle.

APPENDIX I

CHRONOLOGICAL TABLE

This table includes two broad categories of material: dates of general historical significance and dates relating to events referred to in the text.

BC 753	Foundation of Rome (traditional date)
753–510	Seven kings of Rome (traditional date)
509	Fall of monarchy: foundation of the Republic with two annual magistrates.
496	Battle of Lake Regillus: Rome against the Latin League
483–474	War with Veii
428–425	Rome at war with Fidena, ally of Veii
	428 A. Cornelius Cossus dedicates the breastplate of Lars Tolumnius as *spolia opima* in the temple of Jupiter Feretrius
396	Veii falls to Rome after long siege
390	Roman defeat at the battle of the Allia: Gauls sack Rome (387 according to Polybius)
360s	Sporadic Gallic raids into Italy
354	Rome-Samnite alliance against the Gauls
343–341	First Samnite war
340–338	Latin war
	338 Latin league dissolves
326–304	Second Samnite war
	321 Roman defeat at Caudine Forks
298–290	Third Samnite war
	295 Samnites, Gauls and Umbrians defeated at Sentinum
	293 Samnites defeated at Aquilonia
282–272	War with Tarentum and King Pyrrhus of Epirus
	279 Victory of Pyrrhus at Asculum
	275 Romans defeat Pyrrhus near Malventum
	272 Surrender of Tarentum

BC 264–241   First Punic war

260 Naval victory off Mylae

247 Hamilcar Barca launches Carthaginian offensive in Sicily

241 Naval victory off Egadi Islands: Romans occupy Sicily

227   Foundation of New Carthage following Carthaginian conquests in Spain

226   Ebro treaty

225   Invading Gauls defeated at Telamon

222   Roman victory over Gauls at Clastidium: M. Claudius Marcellus slays Insubrian chieftan Viridomarus and dedicates his armour as *spolia opima*; surrender of the Gallic Insubres

218–201   Second Punic war: Hannibal attacks across the Alps

218 Defeat of P. Cornelius Scipio at the Ticinus

218 Battle of the Trebia: defeat of Scipio and Ti. Sempronius Longus

217 Roman naval victory off the Ebro

217 Defeat of C. Flaminius at Lake Trasimene

217 Q. Fabius Maximus (Cunctator) appointed dictator

216 Battle of Cannae: defeat of Roman army under L. Aemilius Paullus and C. Terentius Varro

215 Hasdrubal defeated at Dertosa

213–211 Roman siege, conquest and sack of Syracuse

212 Roman alliance with Syphax of western Numidia against Carthage

212 Hannibal victorious at Capua

211 Roman siege and conquest of Capua

209 P. Cornelius Scipio conquers New Carthage

208 Battle of Baecula: Hasdrubal breaks into Italy

207 Battle of the Metaurus river: Hasdrubal defeated

206 Battle of Ilipa: end of Carthaginian rule in Spain

204 Scipio crosses to Africa

202 Battle of Zama: Carthaginian army destroyed: Scipio receives honorary title *Africanus* and celebrates a triumph

214–205   First Macedonian war: alliance of Hannibal with Philip V of Macedonia

200–190   War with Gauls: suppression of the Boii and Insubres

200–196   Second Macedonian war

197 Victory of Romans under T. Quinctius Flamininus at Cynoscephalae

197   Insurrection in Spain

195   M. Porcius Cato sent to Spain with a consular army

192–188   War with Antiochus III of Syria

191 Antiochus defeated at Thermopylae

190 Battle of Magnesia: Antiochus defeated by Romans under L.

BC	
	Cornelius Scipio and Scipio Africanus
	188 Peace of Apamaea
183	Death of Hannibal
181–179	First Celtiberian war
172–167	Third Macedonian war
	168 Battle of Pydna: Roman victory under L. Aemilius Paullus
153–151	Second Celtiberian war
151	Carthage declares war on Masinissa
149–146	Third Punic war
	146 Carthage taken by P. Cornelius Scipio Aemilianus: the city rased to the ground and its inhabitants sold into slavery. Scipio Aemilianus celebrates a triumph, receives honorary title *Africanus Minor*
143–133	Third Celtiberian (or Numantine) war
	133 Fall of Numantia
135–132	Slave war in Sicily
113–101	War with the Cimbri and Teutones
	105 Cimbri and Teutones destroy Roman army at Arausio
	104–100 Marius consul
	102 Victory of Marius over the Teutones at Aquae Sextae
	101 Victory of Marius over the Cimbri at Vercellae
112–106	Jugurthine War
91–88	Social war
	89 Cn. Pompeius Strabo besieges Asculum: victories of Strabo and L. Cornelius Sulla
88–84	First Mithridatic war
	88 Mithridates overruns Asia Minor
	86 Sulla defeats Mithridates
	85 Treaty of Dardanus
83–81	Second Mithridatic war
82–79	Dictatorship of Sulla
74–63	Third Mithridatic war
	74 Mithridates invades Bithynia: L. Licinius Lucullus given command against him
	71 Lucullus defeats Mithridates
	63 Death of Mithridates
73–71	Verres' governorship of Sicily
73–71	Slave war of Spartacus
	71 Crassus defeats Spartacus
67	Gnaeus Pompey given extraordinary powers to deal with the problem of piracy in the Mediterranean
63–62	Catiline conspiracy: exposed and suppressed by Cicero
60	Foundation of first triumvirate: Caesar, Pompey and Crassus
59–51	Caesar's conquest of Gaul

BC	56	Conference of Luca: triumvirate renewed
	55–54	Invasions of Britain
	49–46	Civil war
		49 Caesar crosses Rubicon
		48–47 Alexandrian war
		47 Caesar's victory at Zela over Pharnaces of Pontus
		46 Caesar's victory at Thapsus
		Caesar celebrates triumph in Rome
	44	Murder of Caesar
	43	Foundation of second triumvirate: Antony, Lepidus and Octavian
	42	Battle of Philippi: defeat of Brutus and Cassius
	38	Triumvirate renewed
	36	M. Vipsanius Agrippa defeats Sextus Pompey at Mylae and Naulochus
	31	Battle of Actium: Agrippa defeats Antony and the Egyptian fleet
	30	Capture of Alexandria: suicides of Antony and Cleopatra
	29	Octavian celebrates triumph
	29–28	M. Licinius Crassus campaigns in Balkans: slays Deldo, king of the Bastarnae: claims and is refused the right to consecrate *spolia opima*: Bastarnae pushed back beyond the Danube
	27	Octavian designated AUGUSTUS
	27–AD 14	AUGUSTUS
	27	Augustus campaigns in Gaul
	26–25	Campaigns in Spain against the Cantabri and Astures
	16–13	Augustus campaigns in Gaul
	15	Drusus and Tiberius defeat Raeti and Vindelici: advance to area of upper Danube
	13–9	Campaign of Agrippa and Tiberius in Illyricum
	12–9	Drusus campaigns in Germany: Elbe reached
		9 Drusus dies
	8–6	Tiberius campaigns in Germany
		7 Tiberius celebrates a triumph
AD	4–6	Tiberius campaigns in Germany
	6	Revolt in Pannonia and Illyricum
	6–9	Tiberius campaigns in Illyricum
	9	The Cherusci, led by Arminius, destroy three legions under the command of C. Quinctilius Varus: area between Rhine and Elbe abandoned
	10–11	Tiberius in Germany
	12	Tiberius celebrates triumph
	14–37	TIBERIUS
	14	Mutiny among the armies in Pannonia and Germany
	14–16	German campaigns led by Germanicus
	17	Germanicus celebrates triumph

AD 17–24   Rebellion of Tacfarinas in Africa

19   Arminius killed

21   Revolt of Florus and Sacrovir in Gaul

28   Revolt of Frisii

34–36   War with Parthia

37–41   GAIUS (CALIGULA)

39   Campaign in Rhineland

40   Manoeuvres on the Gallic coast (planned 'invasion' of Britain)

40   Ptolemy of Mauretania murdered: Mauretania revolts

41–54   CLAUDIUS

41   Campaign against the Chauchi

41–2   Campaign in Mauretania

42   Revolt of L. Arruntius Scribonianus in Dalmatia

43   Invasion of Britain

44   Claudius's British triumph

45   Claudius restores Mithridates to throne of Armenia

46   Thrace made a province

48   Rebellion of the Iceni in Britain

50   Chatti invade Germany

53   Parthians occupy Armenia

54–68   NERO
        Campaign against the Astures of Spain

58–63   Corbulo campaigns in Armenia

60–61   Rebellion of Boudica in Britain suppressed by Suetonius Paulinus

65   Conspiracy of Piso fails: Seneca obliged to commit suicide

66–70   Jewish war
        67 Josephus surrenders to Vespasian
        68 Attack on Jerusalem begins
        70 Capture of Jerusalem: Vespasian and Titus celebrate triumph

68   Revolt of C. Iulius Vindex in Gaul joined by S. Sulpicius Galba and M. Salvius Otho in Spain

69   YEAR OF THE FOUR EMPERORS: Galba, Otho, Vitellius, Vespasian

69   Suppression of trouble in north Africa between Oea and Lepcis Magna

69–79   VESPASIAN

69–70   Suppression of the revolt of Civilis and the Batavians by Q. Petilius Cerealis

71   TITUS given proconsular *imperium* and tribunician power

71–84   Conquest of Britain continued under the command of:
        71–74 Q. Petilius Cerealis
        74–78 Sex. Iulius Frontinus
        78–85 Cn. Iulius Agricola

Appendix I

<table>
<tr><td>AD</td><td>72</td><td>War in Commagene: the ruler deposed and Commagene added to Syria</td></tr>
<tr><td></td><td>73–74</td><td>Censorship of Vespasian and Titus</td></tr>
<tr><td></td><td>73–74</td><td>Campaign in Germany under Cn. Pinarius Cornelius Clemens</td></tr>
<tr><td></td><td>77–78</td><td>Rutilius Gallicus's campaign against the Bructeri</td></tr>
<tr><td></td><td>79–81</td><td>TITUS</td></tr>
<tr><td></td><td>79</td><td>Eruption of Vesuvius</td></tr>
<tr><td></td><td>81–96</td><td>DOMITIAN</td></tr>
<tr><td></td><td>83</td><td>Campaign against the Chatti: triumph celebrated</td></tr>
<tr><td></td><td>85</td><td>Decebalus, the Dacian king, defeats the legate of Moesia</td></tr>
<tr><td></td><td>86–89</td><td>Dacian war</td></tr>
<tr><td></td><td></td><td>88 Dacians defeated at Tapae</td></tr>
<tr><td></td><td></td><td>89 Domitian celebrates triumph</td></tr>
<tr><td></td><td>89</td><td>Revolt of Saturninus, governor of Upper Germany: suppression of Saturninus and the Chatti with whom he had allied himself by Appius Maximus, governor of Lower Germany</td></tr>
<tr><td></td><td>92</td><td>Campaign against the Suebi, Sarmatae and Marcomanni</td></tr>
<tr><td></td><td>96–98</td><td>NERVA</td></tr>
<tr><td></td><td>97–98</td><td>War in Germany against the Suebi: campaigning begins under Nerva, completed by Trajan</td></tr>
<tr><td></td><td>98–117</td><td>TRAJAN</td></tr>
<tr><td></td><td>101–102</td><td>First Dacian war</td></tr>
<tr><td></td><td>105–106</td><td>Second Dacian war</td></tr>
<tr><td></td><td></td><td>106 Death of Decebalus: Dacia made a province</td></tr>
<tr><td></td><td>112</td><td>Dedication of Trajan's forum and column</td></tr>
<tr><td></td><td>114–117</td><td>Parthian war</td></tr>
<tr><td></td><td></td><td>114 Armenia annexed</td></tr>
<tr><td></td><td></td><td>115 Mesopotamia annexed</td></tr>
<tr><td></td><td>115</td><td>Jewish revolt</td></tr>
<tr><td></td><td>117–138</td><td>HADRIAN</td></tr>
<tr><td></td><td>117–122</td><td>War in Britain</td></tr>
<tr><td></td><td>122</td><td>Construction of Hadrian's Wall begins</td></tr>
<tr><td></td><td>122</td><td>Moorish revolt</td></tr>
<tr><td></td><td>132–135</td><td>Jewish war following the revolt of Bar Kochba</td></tr>
<tr><td></td><td>134</td><td>Alans invade Parthia</td></tr>
<tr><td></td><td>138–161</td><td>ANTONINUS PIUS</td></tr>
<tr><td></td><td>139–142</td><td>Campaign in Britain followed by construction of the Antonine Wall</td></tr>
<tr><td></td><td>152</td><td>Expedition against the Moors</td></tr>
<tr><td></td><td>157–158</td><td>Campaign against Dacian tribes</td></tr>
<tr><td></td><td>161–180</td><td>MARCUS AURELIUS</td></tr>
<tr><td></td><td></td><td>161–169 LUCIUS VERUS as co-ruler</td></tr>
<tr><td></td><td></td><td>175–180 COMMODUS as co-ruler</td></tr>
<tr><td></td><td>162–166</td><td>Parthian war conducted by Lucius Verus</td></tr>
</table>

AD	
	166 Marcus and Verus celebrate triumph
166–175	First German war against the Marcomanni, Quadi and Sarmatae
	170 Invasion of Italy by Marcomanni and Quadi
175	Revolt of Avidius Cassius in Syria
176	Erection of Marcus Column, triumphal column with scenes from the first German war
178–180	Second German war: offensive ends on the death of Marcus
180–192	COMMODUS
180–184	War in Britain: a Wall crossed and a Roman general killed
193–197	Civil war: Septimius Severus, Clodius Albinus and Pescennius Niger fight for the imperial throne
	194 Death of Pescennius Niger
	197 Albinus defeated near Lugdunum
193–211	SEPTIMIUS SEVERUS
	198–211 CARACALLA as co-ruler
	209–211 GETA as co-ruler
197–199	War in Parthia
208–211	Severan campaigns in Britain: Severus accompanied by his sons, Caracalla and Geta
211	Severus dies at York: Caracalla concludes British campaign
211–212	CARACALLA and GETA co-rulers
212–217	CARACALLA sole rule
212	Constitutio Antoniniana
213	Campaign on the Rhine against the Alamanni

Dona Militaria were awarded very rarely hereafter: contexts in which they are known to have been given are:

355–363	JULIAN (Caesar from 355, Augustus from 360)
363–364	Persian war (brought to an end by JOVIAN 363–364)
425–455	VALENTINIAN III
430s	Campaign against invading Goths and Burgundians
527–565	JUSTINIAN (Emperor in the East)
535–553	War against the Goths in Italy conducted first by the general Belisarius and subsequently by Narses

APPENDIX II

RECIPIENTS OF MILITARY DECORATIONS

This list includes all persons known, by name, to have received military decorations. It does not include records of awards to unnamed soldiers unless the soldiers in question can be identified by individual career records. For abbreviations see note at beginning of References and Notes, p. 273.

A THE REPUBLIC

M. Aemilius Lepidus: Valerius Maximus 3.1.1
M. Aemilius Scaurus: Aurelius Victor *de Viris Illustribus* 72.3
Albius Tibullus: *vita Tibulli*
Q. Annaeus Balbus: CIL VIII 14697=10605=ILS 2249
Basillus: Appian *Mithridatica* 7. 50–51
M. Calpurnius Flamma: Pliny *Nat. Hist.* 22. 5
L. Calpurnius Piso Frugi: Valerius Maximus 4.3.10; Pliny *Nat. Hist.* 33.38
C. Canuleius: ILLRP 497=CIL I 624=CIL x 3886=ILS 2225
Q. Canuleius: ILLRP 497=CIL I 624=CIL x 3886=ILS 2225
M. Castricius: Cicero *in Verrem* 3. 185
Cleomenes of Syracuse: Cicero *in Verrem* 5. 110
P. Cornelius Scipio Aemilianus: Pliny *Nat. Hist.* 22.6; Velleius Paterculus 1.12.4
S. Cornelius Merenda: Pliny *Nat. Hist.* 33.38
L. Cornelius Sulla Felix: Pliny *Nat. Hist.* 22.7
M. Cossutius: Cicero *in Verrem* 3. 185
P. Decius Mus: Festus 208L; Livy 7.37.1; Pliny *Nat. Hist.* 16.8, 22.5
Sex. Digitus: Livy 26.48.5
Q. Fabius Maximus: Aulus Gellius 5.6; Pliny *Nat. Hist.* 22.5
Hostius Hostilius: Pliny *Nat. Hist.* 16.11
C. Iulius Caesar: Suetonius *Iul. Caes.* 2
G. Laelius: Livy 26.48.5; Silius Italicus *Punica* 15.254–262
–. Laelius: Lucan *Bell. Civ.* 1.357
L. Licinius Murena: Cicero *pro Murena* 11
Sp. Ligustinus: Livy 42.34.11
M. Manlius Capitolinus: Livy 6.22.7; Pliny *Nat. Hist.* 7.103, 16.12

262

T. Manlius Torquatus: Livy 7.10.14

Gn. Marcius Coriolanus: Plutarch *Coriolanus* 3. 2–3

C. Marius: Sallust *Bell. Iug.* 85.29

Milo of Lanuvium: Silius Italicus *Punica* 13. 364–5

Sp. Nautius: Livy 10.44.3–4

C. Octavius: Suetonius *Augustus* 8.1

Sp. Oppius: Livy 3.58.8

L. Orbilius Pupillus: Suetonius *de Grammaticis* 9

Sp. Papirius: Livy 10.44.3–4

Cn. Petreius Atinas: Pliny *Nat. Hist.* 22.5

Q. Rubrius: Cicero *in Verrem* 3. 185

L. Siccius (Sicinius) Dentatus: Aulus Gellius 2.11.2; Ammianus 25.3.13; Dion. Hal. 10.37; Festus 208L; Pliny *Nat. Hist.* 7.101–2, 16.12, 22.5; Valerius Maximus 3.2.24

M. Terentius Varro: Pliny *Nat. Hist.* 7.115, 16.6–7

Q. Trebellius: Livy 26.48.5

Trebonius: Plutarch *C. Marius* 14, 3–5

M. Tullius Cicero: Aulus Gellius 5.6

M. Valerius: Livy 7.26.10

M. Vipsanius Agrippa: Livy *Perioch.* 129; Seneca *de Benef.* 3.32.4; Dio 49.14, 51.21; Pliny *Nat. Hist.* 16.6–7; Velleius Paterculus 2.81.3; Suetonius *Augustus* 25.

Cavalrymen serving in the *turma Salluitana*: ILLRP 515=CIL vi 37045=ILS 8888=AE 1909, 30

Sanibelser Adingibas f.
Illurtibas Bilustibas f.
Estopeles Ordennas f.
Torsinno Austinco f.

Bagarensis:
Cacususin Chadar f.

– – –*cilicenses*:
– – – – – – Sosimilus f.
– – – – – – irsecel. f.
– – – – – –elgaun f.
– – – – – – iespaiser f.

Ilerdenses:
Otacilius Suisetarten f.
Cn. Cornelius Nesille f.
P. [F]abius Enasagin f.

Begensis:
Turtumelis Atanscer f.

Segienses:
Sosinadem Sosinasae f.
Sosimilius Sosinasae f.

Urgidar Luspanar f.
Gurtano Biurno f.
Elandus Enneges f.
Agirnes Bennabels f.
Nalbeaden Agerdo f.
Arranes Arbiscar f.
Umargibas Luspangib. f.

Ennegenses:
Beles Umarbeles
Turinnus Adimel. s.f.
Ordumeles Burdo f.

Libenses:
Bastugitas Adimeis f.
Umarillun Tarbantu f.

Sucosenses:
Belennes Albennes f.
Atullo Tautindals f.

Illuersensis:
Balciadin Balcibil f.

Appendix II

B THE EMPIRE

I   SENATORS

For fuller references to the careers of the senators cf PIR and PIR2.

P. Aelius Hadrianus: CIL III 550=ILS 308; HA *v. Hadriani* 3.6–7

Q. Antistius Adventus: ILS 8977=AE 1893, 88; ILAlg II 613=AE 1914, 281; ILS 1091; ILAlg II.2, 4681

L. Antistius Rusticus: AE 1925, 126

C. Aufidius Victorinus: AE 1957, 121+AE 1958, 26.

P. Baebius Italicus: IGRR III 551=ILS 8818=AE 1897, 115

C. Bruttius Praesens Lucius Fulvius Rusticus: AE 1950, 66

L. Caesennius Sospes: CIL III 291+6818=ILS 1017

C. Caesonius Macer Rufinianus: CIL XIV 3900=ILS 1182

C. Calpetanus Rantius Quirinalis Valerius Festus: CIL V 531=ILS 989; CIL VI 1237; CIL III 11194–6; CIL II 2477; CIL II 4802–3; CIL II 4837; AE 1974, 401

L. Catilius Severus: CIL X 8291=ILS 1014

M. Celer Velleianus: Velleius Paterculus 2.115.1

C. Cilnius Proculus: AE 1926, 123; CIL XI 1833; CIL XVI 46=ILS 9054.

M. Claudius Fronto: CIL III 1457=ILS 1097; CIL VI 1377+31640=ILS 1098.

–. *Claudius Gallus*: AE 1957, 123; CIL VI 2741 cf 18126=AE 1913, 11; CIL III 1564

–. *Claudius Maximus*: CIL III 10336=ILS 1062; CIL XVI 99; CIL XVI 104.

L. Coiedius Candidus: CIL XI 6163=ILS 967.

M. Cornelius Nigrinus Curiatius Maternus: CIL II 3788+*Saitabi* 19 (1969) 23; CIL II 6013; CIL II 3783; CIL XIV 4725

Cn. Domitius Lucanus: CIL XI 5210=ILS 990; IRT 527

Cn. Domitius Tullus: CIL XI 5211=ILS 991; IRT 528

Flavius Aetius: AE 1950, 30

Q. Fuficius Cornutus: ILS 8975=AE 1897, 19; CIL XVI 91+suppl.; IGRR I 609; AE 1937, 180; AE 1957, 266

L. Funisulanus Vettonianus: CIL III 4013=ILS 1005; CIL XVI 30; CIL XVI 31

Q. Glitius Atilius Agricola: CIL V 6977=ILS 1021a; CIL XVI 47; CIL XVI 48; CIL V 6976, 6978, 6980 (text similar to 6977); CIL V 6974, 6975, 6979, 6981, 6982, 6983 (dona not mentioned).

P. Glitius Gallus: CIL XI 7492=3098=ILS 999.

M. Hirrius Fronto Neratius Pansa: AE 1968, 145=J. Roman Stud. 1968, 170f.; IGRR III 125; IGRR III 223.

T. Iulius Maximus Manlianus: CIL XII 3167=ILS 1016; CIL XVI 164.

C. Iulius Thraso Alexander: AE 1952, 220; AE 1924, 75.

[Iunius Maximus]: AE 1972, 576+ZPE 35 (1979), 195–212.

A. Larcius Lepidus: CIL X 6659=ILS 987; *Inscr. Creticae* 4, 292

Q. Lollius Urbicus: CIL VIII 6706=ILS 1065=ILAlg II 3605; ILAlg II 3446.

Magius Celer Velleianus: Velleius Paterculus 2.115.1

L. Minicius Natalis: CIL II 4509+6145=ILS 1029; CIL VI 31739; CIL VIII

22785=AE 1894, 72; CIL VIII 2478; CIL XVI 64

L. Nonius Asprenas: AE 1952, 232=IRT 346

M. Ostorius Scapula: Tacitus *Annals* 12.3; 16.15

Q. Pompeius Falco: CIL X 6321=ILS 1035; CIL III 12117=ILS 1036; CIL XVI 69; CIL III 7537.

Q. Pompeius Sosius Priscus: CIL VI 31753; CIL XIV 3609=ILS 1104; CIL VI 1490=ILS 1106

T. Pomponius Proculus Vitrasius Pollio: CIL VI 1540=31675=ILS 1112

M. Pontius Laelianus Larcius Sabinus: CIL VI 1497+1549=ILS 1094+1100.

C. Popilius Carus Pedo: CIL XIV 3610=ILS 1071

L. Ragonius Urinatius Larcius Quintianus: CIL VI 1502=ILS 1124; CIL VI 1503; CIL VI 2112

L. Roscius Aelianus Maecius Celer: CIL XIV 3612=ILS 1025

–. Satrius Sep[– – – – – –]: CIL X 135=ILS 2719

Q. Sosius Senecio: CIL VI 1444=ILS 1022.

M. Valerius Maximianus: AE 1956, 24

C. Velleius Paterculus: Velleius Paterculus 2.121.4

C. Vettius Sabinianus Iulius Hospes: AE 1920, 45=ILA 281

Q. Voconius Saxa Fidus: TAM 1201+1201A

[–. ––––––] Firmus: CIL XI 1834=ILS 1000

Unknown: CIL III 14387d=IGLS 2775

        CIL V 36

        CIL V 7165

        CIL VIII 12536=ILS 988

        CIL VIII 25422

        CIL IX 2849

        CIL IX 3380=ILS 974

        CIL XI 6399

        CIL XII 3169

        AE 1922, 38

        AE 1930, 79

        AE 1964, 192

        AE 1972, 394

        IGLS I 234

        ILG 419

        ILTG 85

        IRT 552

        Atti Lincei 1969, 10=CIL IX 431+437

II EQUESTRIANS

For fuller references to the careers of equestrians cf Devijver *Pros. Mil. Eq.*

L. Aburnius Tuscianus: ILS 9471=AE 1911, 161

–. Aemilius Iuncus: AE 1935, 167; IGRR IV 351; AE 1903, 116; AE 1974, 596

C. Annius Flavianus: CIL VIII 17900=ILS 1436

M. Arruntius Claudianus: AE 1969–70, 595a=AE 1972, 572

A. Atinius Paternus: CIL VI 1838=ILS 2727

Q. Attius Priscus: CIL V 7425=ILS 2720

L. Aurelius Nicomedes: CIL VI 1598=ILS 1740

P. Besius Betuinianus C. Marius Memmius Sabinus: CIL VIII 9990=ILS 1352

C. Caelius Martialis: AE 1934, 2

Sex. Caesius Propertianus: CIL XI 5028=ILS 1447

L. Calidius Camidienus: CIL XI 7978; CIL XVI 42

P. Cassius Secundus: Archeološki Vestnik 28 (1977), 334

P. Cassius [– – – – – –]: AE 1912, 20

Ti. Claudius Alpinus: CIL V 3356=ILS 2710; CIL V 3337–8; CIL III 13250=ILS 5968; EE IX 676

Ti. Claudius Balbillus: AE 1924, 78

Ti. Claudius Heras: IGRR III 230=AE 1897, 123

M. Clodius Faustus Secundus: CIL VIII 12066=EE V 1210.

P. Cominius Clemens: AE 1890, 151; CIL V 8659=ILS 1412; *Not. Scav.* 1923, 230

Sex. Cornelius Dexter: CIL VIII 8934=ILS 1400; CIL III 553; CIL VIII 8925

–. Cornelius N[– – – – –]: CIL III 2018

Q. Cornelius Valerianus: CIL II 2079=ILS 2713; CIL II 3272

Sex. Decius: CIL XII 2430

C. Fabricius Tuscus: ZPE 13 (1974), 161f.=J.M. Cook *The Troad* (Oxford 1973), inscr. no 50

T. Furius Victorinus: ILS 9002=AE 1907, 152=CIL V 648*; AE 1916, 47=CIL VI 39449; IGRR III 1103=ILS 8846

M. Gavius Bassus: AE 1969–70, 595b=AE 1972, 573

C. Iulius Camillus: CIL XIII 5093=ILS 2697 add.

C. Iulius Corinthianus: CIL III 1193=ILS 2746

C. Iulius Karus: AE 1951, 88

L. Iulius Vehilius Gratus Iulianus: CIL VI 31856=ILS 1327=AE 1888, 66; ILS 8869=IGRR III 1037=AE 1933, 208; CIL V 4343; CIL XIV 4378=AE 1928, 125

L. Laetilius Rufus: CIL IX 1614

M. Macrinius Avitus Catonius Vindex: CIL VI 1499=ILS 1107

L. Marcius Avitus: AE 1961, 358

C. Minicius Italus: CIL V 875=ILS 1374; CIL XIV 4456+*Epigraphische Studien* 9, 242 f.; CIL III 12053.

C. Nummius Verus: CIL XI 3100; CIL III 7739

Cn. Octavius Titinius Capito: CIL VI 798=ILS 1448; AE 1934, 154

L. Paconius Proculus: CIL VI 32933=ILS 2723

Ti. Plautius Felix Ferruntianus: CIL VIII 619+11780=ILS 2747

–. Pompeius Faventinus: CIL II 2637=AE 1966, 187=*Madrider Mitteil.* 6 (1965), 105f

A. Pomponius Augurinus T. Prifernius Paetus: ILS 8863=AE 1905, 6

T. Pontius Sabinus: CIL x 5829=ILS 2726

P. Prifernius Paetus Memmius Apollinaris: CIL IX 4753=ILS 1350; CIL III 5179

C. Purtisius Atinas: CIL XI 624

Ti. Robilius Flaccus: Epigraphica XXII, 27

M. Rossius Vitulus: ILA 455=AE 1914, 248=ILS 9015; CIL VIII 14454

M. Statius Priscus Licinius Italicus: CIL VI 1523=ILS 1092

C. Stertinius Xenophon: IGRR IV 1086; *Hist. Zeitschr.* 125 (1922); 236

M. Stlaccius Coranus: CIL VI 3539=ILS 2730

Q. Sulpicius Celsus: CIL VI 32934

M. Valerius Maximianus: AE 1952, 24

M. Vergilius Gallus Lusius: CIL x 4862=ILS 2690

M. Vettius Latro: ILT 720=AE 1939, 81; ILT 721; CIL VIII 8369=ILS 5961; AE 1951, 52

[– – – – – –] *Flavianus*: IGRR IV 964=ILS 8865

Unknown: CIL VIII 9372

        CIL VIII 26585

        CIL XI 5037

        CIL XII 5899

        CIL XIV 2110

        AE 1965, 348

        AE 1967, 287

        IGRR I 824

        IRT 98

        Inschr. von Olympia 357

III   MILITES, CENTURIONES, PRIMIPILARES

L. Aconius Statura: CIL XI 5992

P. Aelius Romanus: CIL VIII 2786=ILS 2659

L. Aemilius Paternus: CIL II 4461=ILS 2661

M. Aemilius Soterias: ILS 2321=EE VIII 530

Q. Albius Felix: CIL XI 3108

C. Allius Oriens: CIL XIII 5206

P. Anicius Maximus: CIL III 6809=ILS 2696

Antiochus: Mainzer Zeitschr. 69 (1974) 247=58 Ber RGK, 99

C. Antonius Flavinus: CIL II 115

L. Antonius Naso: CIL III 14387 ff+fff+k=ILS 9199=IGLS VI 2781; CIL III 6993=ILS 253

L. Antonius Quadratus: CIL v 4365=ILS 2272

Sex. Aquillius Severus: CIL III 1940

C. Arrius Clemens: CIL XI 5646=ILS 2081 add

T. Aurelius Flavinus: CIL III 14416=ILS 7178 cf AE 1961, 208; AE 1972, 548

Aurelius Iovinus: CIL III 3844+p. 1734=13398=ILS 2438=*Inscr. Iug.* 172

L. Avaenius Paser: AE 1927, 108

A. Baebius: CIL x 3883

P. Baebius: CIL v 1882

M. Bassaeus Rufus: CIL vi 1599+31828=ILS 1326; CIL XIV 4500; CIL iii 5171; CIL ix 2438

—. Blandius Latinus: CIL xii 2601

L. Blattius Vetus: AE 1893, 119

M. Blossius Pudens: CIL vi 3580=ILS 2641

M. Caelius: CIL xiii 8648=ILS 2244

Caeno: AE 1971, 276=AE 1972, 353

C. Caesius Silvester: CIL xi 5696; CIL xi 5674; CIL xi 5695, 5697–5700.1, 5694=ILS 2666a

T. Camulius Lavenus: CIL xii 2230

L. Cas(sius) Caen(icus)?: AE 1976, 296

T. Cassius Secundus: CIL iii 5334

C. Cestius Sabinus: CIL xi 6057

Ti. Claudius Iunianus: CIL iii 11667+ *Carinthia* I (1933), 175

Ti. Claudius Maximus: AE 1969/70, 583

Ti. Claudius Vitalis: CIL vi 3584=ILS 2656

L. Coelius: CIL v 7495=ILS 2337

T. Cominius Severus: CIL iii 10224=ILS 9193

Q. Cornelius: CIL xiii 6938

C. Didius Saturninus: CIL xi 7264=ILS 9194; CIL vi 32523 a+32624; CIL xi 6251

C. Flaminius Marcellus: *Arheološki Vestnik* 25 (1974), 247f

T. Flavius Capito: CIL iii 14453

T. Flavius Victorinus: CIL iii 1664

M. Fraxsanius: CIL iii 9885=ILS 2322

C. Gavius Celer: *Museo della Civiltà Romana: Catologo*, 167 no. 31

L. Gavius Fronto: *Revue des Études Grecques* 61 (1948), 201

C. Gavius Silvanus: CIL v 7003=ILS 2701

L. Gellius Varus: CIL v 5586

Q. Geminius Sabinus: ILT 779=AE 1923, 28

M. Helvius Rufus Civica: CIL xiv 3472=ILS 2637; Tacitus *Annals* 3.21

Icascaen?: see L. Cas(sius) Caen(icus)

C. Iulius Aetor: CIL iii 3158=ILS 3320

M. Iulius Avitus: CIL iii 7397

[C. Iulius?] Flavus: Tacitus *Annals* 2.9

C. Iulius Macer: CIL xiii 1041=ILS 2531

C. Iulius [– – – – –]lus: CIL viii 5209=ILAlg I 137

M. Iulius Maximus: AE 1962, 311

L. Lepidius Proculus: CIL xi 390; CIL xi 391

L. Leuconius Cilo: CIL v 4902

—. Lucius: CIL xiii 8061

N. Marcius Plaetorius Celer: CIL x 1202=ILS 2660

Q. Marcius Turbo: CIL xiv 4243; AE 1955, 255; CIL iii 14349²; CIL xvi 60; CIL
    iii 1462=ILS 1324; ILA 421

C. Marius: CIL xiii 8059

L. Murrius Fronto: CIL viii 27512=AE 1899, 39

Cn. Musius: CIL xiii 6901

T. Nasidius Messor: AE 1954, 162

A. Numisienus Gallus: CIL vi 3618

C. Nummius Constans: CIL x 3733=ILS 2083

–. Octavius Secundus: CIL iii 7334=ILS 2080

L. Pellartius Celer Iulius Montanus: AE 1952, 153

M. Petronius Classicus: CIL iii 4060

M. Petronius Fortunatus: CIL viii 217+p. 2353=ILS 2658 add

L. Petronius Sabinus: CIL xi 6055=ILS 2743; CIL xi 5898=ILS 1386

M. Pompeius Asper: CIL xiv 2523=ILS 2662=EE ix 726

Cn. Pompeius Homullus Aelius Gracilis Cassianus Longinus: CIL vi 1626=ILS 1385

M. Praeconius Iucundus: CIL iii 14358, 21a

C. Purtisius Atinas: CIL xi 624

C. Quintilius Priscus: CIL v 930

Q. Raecius Rufus: CIL iii 2917=ILS 2647

L. Refidius Bassus: CIL xiii 11837

L. Rufellius Severus: CIL xi 6224; CIL v 698=ILS 5889=*Inscr. Ital.* x.4,376

M. Sabidius Maximus: AE 1937, 101

A. Saufeius Emax: CIL iii 2887=ILS 9067

Q. Sertorius Festus: CIL v 3374

T. Servaeus Sabinus: CIL iii 14398=AE 1903, 77; AE 1930, 109

C. Statius Celsus: CIL iii 6259=ILS 2665

T. Statius Marrax: ILS 2638

L. Tatinius Cnosus: AE 1933, 87

P. Tedius Valens: *Inscr. Ital.* x.2, 253

L. Terentius Rufus: CIL ii 2424

M. Tillius Rufus: CIL x 5064=ILS 2667; CIL xiii 6762

C. Titurnius Quartio: ILS 9492=AE 1913, 48=ILA 434

L. Upturius Agrippa Aristianus: IGRR iii 398=CIG iii 4367k

T. Valerius Germanus: CIL iii 12498=AE 1891, 55

L. Valerius Proclus: CIL iii 12411=ILS 2666b=AE 1892, 106

C. Vedennius Moderatus: CIL vi 2725=ILS 2034

C. Velius Rufus: ILS 9200=AE 1903, 368=IGLS vi 2796

C. Vettius: CIL iii 4858=ILS 2466

M. Vettius Valens: CIL xi 395=ILS 2648

Sex Vibius Gallus: CIL iii 13648=6984=IGRR iii 1432=ILS 2663 add.; CIL iii
    14187 ⁴,⁵=IGRR iii 1433=ILS 4081; IGRR iii 1434

C. Vibius Macer: AE 1891, 15=EE viii 172

Q. *Vilanius Nepos*: CIL VIII 1026=ILS 2127

M. *Vireius Celer*: CIL III 2718

A. *Volsonius Paulus*: 27 Ber RGK, 144

[– – – – – –] *Numenius*: CIL VI 3617

[– – – – – –] *Rufinus*: CIL XIII 8503

Unknown: CIL III 2888+*Jahreshefte* VIII Beibl. 46

        CIL III 8438=ILS 2597

        CIL III 12913

        CIL III 14006

        CIL III 14387^i=ILS 9198=IGLS VI 2798

        CIL V 546

        CIL V 955

        CIL VI 37298=AE 1906, 166

        CIL X 3900

        CIL XI 1602

        CIL XI 2112

        CIL XIII 7556=ILS 2649 add

        AE 1915, 112

        AE 1942/3, 33

        EE VIII 478

        ILA 20

        Epigraphica XXII, 29

        Not. Scav. 1901, 327

Soldiers serving in *legio vii Claudia*: CIL III 14507

T. Aurelius Sinna	M. Aurelius Saturni
C. Valerius Valens	M. Valerius Marcellinus
M. Aurelius Dolens	C. Valerius Quintianus
L. Minicius Verissimus	–. Prupincus
–. Aurelius Mucco	C. Iulius Severus

Soldiers serving in *cohorts v, vi* and *vii Praet.*: CIL VI 2381=32522

Coh. v Praet	*Coh. vii Praet*
C. Hostilius Quintianus	L. C[– – – – – – – –]
M. Pacilius Fortunatus	L. Fusidius Cogitatus
L. Modus Felix	Q. Laetinius Firmus
Coh. vi Praet	C. Surinas Felix
L. Geminius Maximus	C. Ofilius Expectatus

IV   FREEDMAN

L. *Aurelius Nicomedes*: CIL VI 1598=ILS 1740

[– – – – – –] *Epaphroditus*: AE 1914, 279

[– – – – – –] *Numenius*: CIL VI 3617

Posides: Suetonius *Claudius* 28

V   UNCLASSIFIED

Unknown: CIL v 949
   CIL ix 1135
   CIL ix 3381
   CIL x 1713
   CIL x 3901
   CIL x 5712
   CIL xi 5036
   CIL xi 5049
   CIL xi 6227
   CIL xii 1575
   CIL xiv 4469 (indexed in CIL but does not appear in the text: cannot be traced at Ostia)
   CIL xiv 4475[a]
   AE 1924, 34
   Not. Scav. 1933, 496 no. 175
   Not. Scav. 1933, 497 no. 177
   Not. Scav. 1953, 276 no. 38
   Not. Scav. 1953, 296 no. 61?
   Atti Lincei 1969, 12

VI   FALSAE AND INSCRIPTIONS WITH DONA INCORRECTLY RESTORED

C. Bruttius Praesens: CIL x 408=ILS 1117
C. Caetronius Miccio: CIL ii 2423 as re-read by Alföldy, *Madrider Mitteil.* (1967), 185f
−. *Sextilius Marcianus*: CIL xiii 6728
T. Statilius Barbarus: CIL vi 1522=ILS 1144; IGRR 1 787
[− − −]*cilius Volus*[− − − − −]: CIL ii 19★
Unknown: CIL ii 1086=ILS 2712
   CIL v 3348

VII   UNITS ATTESTED AS TORQUATA OR ARMILLATA

ALAE
Ala 1 Flavia Augusta Britannica M., c.R., bis torquata: CIL iii 6748=EE v 41; AE 1908, 23; AE 1914, 241; *Arheološki Vestnik* 28 (1977), 334
Ala Gallorum et Thracum Classiana c.R., invicta, bis torquata: CIL xi 6033
Ala Moesica felix torquata: CIL vi 3538=ILS 2729 add.; *Festschrift Laur-Belart*, 129
Ala Gallorum Petriana M., c.R., bis torquata: RIB 957=CIL vii 929; CIL xi 5669=ILS 2728 add
Ala Siliana c.R., bis torquata, bis armillata: IBR 85=CIL iii 5775; IBR 86=CIL iii 5776=ILS 1369; AE 1939, 81=ILT 720; AE 1930, 92
Ala Gallorum Tauriana c.R., torquata, victrix: AE 1939, 60; CIL xvi 165; CIL xvi 169; CIL ii 2984

Appendix II

COHORTES

Cohors I *Breucorum c.R., val(ens ?), victrix, bis torquata*: CIL III
5918a=11931=IBR 276

Cohors I *Brittonum M., Ulpia torquata, p.f., c.R.*: CIL XVI 160; CIL XVI 163

Cohors I *Hispanorum D., T., p.f.* (?): CIL III 8074, 18a and b

Cohors I *Lepidiana bis torquata*: AE 1908, 22

Cohors VIII *Raetorum c.R., equitata, torquata*: AE 1960, 375

Cohors III *Thracum c.R., equitata, bis torquata*: 37 Ber RGK, 38 no. 81

REFERENCES AND NOTES

ABBREVIATIONS

AE	*L'Année Épigraphique* (Paris)
ANR W	ed. H. Temporini and W. Haase, *Aufstieg und Niedergang der römischen Welt: Geschichte und Kultur Roms im Spiegel der neuerer Forschung* (Berlin 1972 cont.)
Atti Lincei	*Atti della Accademia Nazionale dei Lincei*
Ber RGK	*Bericht der Römisch-Germanischen Kommission des deutschen archäologischen Instituts* (Frankfurt)
BMCRE	ed. H. Mattingly, *Coins of the Roman Empire in the British Museum* (London 1923–62)
BMCRR	ed. H.A. Grueber, *Coins of the Roman Republic in the British Museum* (London 1910)
Cichorius *Ala*	C. Cichorius, 'Ala', Pauly-Wissowa, *Real-Encyclopädie der classichen Altertumswissenschaft* 1, col 1224–1270
CIG	ed. A Boeckh et al., *Corpus Inscriptionum Graecarum* (Berlin 1828–1877)
CIL	ed. T. Mommsen et al., *Corpus Inscriptionum Latinarum* (Berlin 1866 cont.)
Devijver, Pros. Mil. Eq.	H. Devijver, *Prosopographia Militiarum Equestrium quae fuerunt ab Augusto ad Gallienum* (Louvain 1976, 1977)
Dobson, *Primipilares*	B. Dobson, *Die Primipilares. Entwicklung und Bedeutung Laufbahnen und Persönlichkeiten eines römischen Offiziersranges* (Cologne 1978)
Domaszewski, *Rangordnung*	A. von Domaszewski, *Die Rangordnung des römischen Heeres* (1908). 2nd. ed. B. Dobson (Cologne 1967)
EE	*Ephemeris Epigraphica. Corpus Inscriptionum Latinarum Supplementum* (Berlin 1872–1913)
IBR	ed. F. Vollmer, *Inscriptiones Baivariae Romanae sive Inscriptiones Provinciae Raetiae adiectis aliquot Noricis Italicisque* (Munich 1915)
IGLS	ed. L. Jalabert, R. Mouterde, J.P. Rey-Coquais, *Inscriptions Grecques et Latines de la Syrie* (Paris 1929–1970)

IGRR   ed. R. Cagnat et al., *Inscriptiones Graecae ad Res Romanas Pertinentes* (Paris 1911–1927)

ILA   ed. R. Cagnat, A. Merlin, L. Chatelain, *Inscriptions Latines d'Afrique: Tripolitaine, Tunisie, Maroc.* (Paris 1923)

ILAlg   ed. S. Gsell, H.-G. Pflaum, *Inscriptions Latines d'Algérie* (Paris 1922–1976).

ILG   ed. E. Espérandieu, *Inscriptions Latines de Gaule Narbonnaise* (Paris 1929)

ILLRP   ed. E. Degrassi, *Inscriptiones Latinae Liberae Rei Publicae* (2nd. ed. Florence 1965)

ILS   ed. H. Dessau, *Inscriptiones Latinae Selectae* (Berlin 1892–1916)

ILT   ed. A. Merlin, *Inscriptions Latines de la Tunisie* (Paris 1944)

ILTG   ed. P. Wuilleumier, *Inscriptions Latines des trois Gaules* (Paris 1963)

Inscr. Creticae   ed. M. Guarducci, *Inscriptiones Creticae* (Rome 1935–1950)

Inscr. Ital.   *Inscriptiones Italiae.* Academiae Italicae consociatae ediderunt (Rome 1931 cont.)

Inscr. Iug.   ed. V. Hoffiller, B. Saria, *Antike Inschriften aus Iugoslavien* (Zagreb 1938)

IRT   ed. J.M. Reynolds, J.B. Ward Perkins, *The Inscriptions of Roman Tripolitania* (Rome and London 1952)

Jahreshefte   *Jahreshefte des Österreichischen Archäologischen Instituts in Wien*

Not. Dig.   *Notitia Dignitatum*

Not. Scav.   *Notizie degli Scavi di antichità*

Pflaum, *Carrières*   H.-G. Pflaum, *Les Carrières Procuratoriennes Équestres sous le Haut-Empire Romain* (Paris 1960)

Pflaum, *Procurateurs*   H.-G. Pflaum, *Les Procurateurs Équestres sous le Haut-Empire Romain* (Paris 1950)

PIR   ed. E. Klebs, H. Dessau, P. de Rohden, *Prosopographia Imperii Romani, saec. I, II, III* (Berlin 1896–1898)

PIR2   ed. E. Groag, A. Stein, L. Petersen, *Prosopographia Imperii Romani, saec. I, II, III* (2nd. ed. Berlin 1933 cont.)

RIB   ed. R.G. Collingwood, R.P. Wright, *The Roman Inscriptions of Britain. Vol. I. Inscriptions on Stone* (Oxford 1965)

RIC   ed. H. Mattingly, E.A. Sydenham et al., *The Roman Imperial Coinage* (London 1923 cont.)

RMD   M.M. Roxan, *Roman Military Diplomas 1954–1977.* Institute of Archaeology Occasional Papers no. 2 (London 1978)

Steiner, *Dona Militaria*   P. Steiner, 'Die Dona Militaria', *Bonner Jahrbücher* 114/115 (1906), 1–98

TAM   ed. E. Kalinka, *Tituli Asiae Minoris* (Vienna 1901 cont.)

ZPE   *Zeitschrift für Papyrologie und Epigraphik*

NOTES

CHAPTER II   The nature of the evidence and its problems (pages 42–54)

1   Dion. Hal. 10.36.4–37.3

2   Varro in Fulgentius *Expositio Sermonum Antiquorum* 5; Verrius Flaccus in Festus 208 L; Valerius Maximus 3.2.24; Pliny *Nat. Hist.* 7.101–102; 16.10; 22.5; Aulus Gellius *Noctes Atticae* 2.11.2; Ammianus 25.3.13; Solinus *Collectanea Rerum Memorabilium* 1.102, 106

3   'Siccius Dentatus' Pauly-Wissowa, *Real-Encyclopädie der classichen Altertumswissenschaft*, 2nd. ser. 2, col. 2189–2190

4   Aulus Gellius *Noctes Atticae* 5.6

5   Pliny *Nat. Hist.* 16.6–14; 22.4–7

6   Polybius 6.39; Josephus *Bell. Iud.* 7.10–15

7   G.R. Watson, *The Roman Soldier* (London 1969), 89f.; B. Dobson, 'Legionary Centurion or Equestrian Officer? A Comparison of Pay and Prospects', *Ancient Society* 3 (1972), 196f

8   *Dona* are mentioned on AE 1890, 151 (Concordia); not mentioned on CIL v 1659=ILS 1412 (Concordia) or *Not. Scav.* 1923, 230 (Aquileia). The two inscriptions from Concordia come from the same area of the city: if they were erected adjacent to one another this might account for the suppression of detail on one of the texts. The same stone which omits the *dona* also summarizes instead of detailing the equestrian military commands.

9   *VIII Claudia*: CIL III 14507. *II Parthica*: AE 1964, 14+*Athenaeum* 1962, 85f. Praetorian guard: CIL VI 2381=32522

10 G. Alföldy, 'Zur Beurteilung der Militärdiplome der Auxiliarsoldaten', *Historia* 17 (1968), 215–227. J.C. Mann, 'The Development of Auxiliary and Fleet Diplomas', *Epigraphische Studien* 9 (1972), 233–241

11 H. Russell Robinson, *The Armour of Imperial Rome* (London 1975)

12 C. Cichorius, *Die Reliefs der Traianssäule* (Berlin 1896–1900), Plates I, Taf. XXXIV and Text 1,214–216

13 CIL III 13648=6984=ILS 2663 add=IGRR III 1432

14 AE 1969/70, 583. M. Speidel, 'The Captor of Decebalus: a New Inscription from Philippi', *J. Roman Stud.* 60 (1970), 142–153

15 CIL v 4365=ILS 2272

16 ILS 9492=AE 1913, 48=ILA 434

17 Tacitus *Hist.* 1.57.14

18 Pliny *Nat. Hist.* 33.44.153

19 F.G. Simpson and I.A. Richmond, 'The Roman Fort on Hadrian's Wall at Benwell', *Archaeologia Aeliana* 4th. ser. 19 (1941), 23–25

20 V.A. Maxfield, 'The Benwell Torc – Roman or Native?', *Archaeologia Aeliana* 5th. ser. 2 (1974), 41–47. RIB 1172, pl. XVII shows a Roman auxiliary soldier wearing a native *torques*.

CHAPTER III   The origin and development of Dona Militaria (pages 55–66)

1   Polybius 6.39; Onasander *The General* 34
2   Onasander *The General* 33. 1–3
3   Polybius 10. 13. 1–5
4   Valerius Maximus 8. 14.5
5   Livy 34. 57.7
6   Appian *Civil Wars* 1.6.51
7   Dionysius of Halicarnassus 9.16.8
8   Cicero *ad Atticum* 5.20.5
9   Plutarch *Lucullus* 24.4
10   Plutarch *Lucullus* 17.5–7; Appian *XII Mithridatica* 12.82
11   Plutarch *Marius* 21.2
12   cf Varro in Festus *opima spolia* 204L; Plutarch *Marcellus* 8
13   Servius *ad Aen.* 6.859
14   AE 1956, 124 and Pflaum, *Carrières* no. 181 bis
15   Polybius 6. 39
16   Livy 33.33.6
17   Josephus *Bell. Iud.* 6.317 and 7.15
18   Livy 39.7; 45.40.5; 45.43.7
19   Isidor *Orig.* 19.31.11 and 16
20   Plutarch *Themistocles* 17; Arrian *Anabasis* 7. 5.4–6; Demosthenes *de Corona*
21   Polybius 6.39
22   Caecilius fr. 250W=269R
23   Dio 51.21; Suetonius *Augustus* 25.3; Silius Italicus *Punica* 15.254–262; Sallust *Bell. Iug.* 85.29
24   Livy 26.48.13–14
25   Livy 10.44.3–5
26   Livy 24.16.9; 26.48.13–14; Silius Italicus *Punica* 15.254–262
27   ILLRP 515=CIL vi 37045=ILS 8888=AE 1909,30
28   ILLRP 497=CIL x 3886=ILS 2225
29   Suetonius *Augustus* 25.3
30   Tacitus *Annals* 3.21
31   Suetonius *Claudius* 17
32   J. Harmand, *L' Armée et le Soldat à Rome de 107 à 50 avant notre ère* (Paris 1967), 467
33   Plutarch *Sertorius* 4.2

CHAPTER IV   The decorations (pages 67–100)

1   Pliny *Nat. Hist.* 22.4
2   Livy 7.37.1–2
3   Some doubt has been thrown on the historicity of this event. cf E.T.

Salmon *Samnium and the Samnites* (London 1967), 195f. The narrative nevertheless remains of value for what it shows of an Augustan writer's view of fourth century tradition.

4   Pliny *Nat. Hist.* 22.6

5   Pliny *Nat. Hist.* 22.5

6   Ammianus Marcellinus 24.4.24

7   The publication of the stone fails to identify the type of crown intended. The illustrations on which fig. 5 is based appears in AE 1891. 15. A photograph of a squeeze of the stone appears in Steiner, *Dona Militaria*

8   Aulus Gellius *Noctes Atticae* 5.6.13–14. Pliny *Nat. Hist.* 16.12–13

9   Tacitus *Annals* 3.21

10   CIL XIV 3472

11   Livy 33.23.6

12   Aulus Gellius *Noctes Atticae* 5.6

13   Caecilius Statius fr. 250W=269R

14   Polybius 6.39.6–7

15   Cicero *pro Plancio* 30.72

16   Pliny *Nat. Hist.* 16.14. Pliny places the episode at the battle of the Trebia. Livy and Polybius assign it to the Ticinus.

17   Livy 21.46.7–10. Polybius 10.3. Laelius may not yet have known Scipio at the time of the encounter in question cf. F. Walbank, *A Historical Commentary on Polybius* (2 vols. Oxford 1957–67) II, 198–199. H. Scullard, *Scipio Africanus Soldier and Politician* (London 1970), 17, 29

18   Tacitus *Annals* 12.31; 16.15

19   Tacitus *Annals* 15.12

20   G.R. Watson, *The Roman Soldier* (London 1969), 116

21   Dio 53.16; *Res Gestae* 34

22   BMCRE Augustus 314 an *aureus* of 18–17 BC. Numerous others

23   H. Russell Robinson, *The Armour of Imperial Rome* (London 1975), 118–119

24   Arrian *Tactica* 34.2

25   H. Russell Robinson, *The Armour of Imperial Rome* (London 1975), pl. 318–323. *Vetusta Monumenta* (London 1747) Vol. IV, pl. I–III

26   Plutarch *Quaest. Rom.* 92

27   Pliny *Nat. Hist.* 22.4

28   Seneca *de Benef.* 3.32.4; Dio 49.14; Livy *Perioch.* 129.

29   Pliny *Nat. Hist.* 16.7; Steiner, *Dona Militaria*, 37.

30   Aulus Gellius *Noctes Atticae* 5.6.18; Festus *Navali corona* 157 L.

31   Pliny *Nat. Hist.* 16.7; 7.115; Livy *Perioch* 129; Seneca *de Benef.* 3.32.4; Velleius Paterculus 2.8.7

32   Suetonius *Claudius* 17

33   Dio 49.14; Aulus Gellius *Noctes Atticae* 5.6.19

34   BMCRE Tiberius 161. J.P.C. Kent, *Roman Coins* (London 1978), no. 174. I am grateful to Dr Kent for further information (*in lit.*) on the dating of this coin.

35 Suetonius *Caligula* 44.2, 46.1; Suetonius *Claudius* 17. 1–2; Dio 60.19–22.

36 Polybius 6.39.5; Aulus Gellius *Noctes Atticae* 5.6.16

37 Livy 26.48.5

38 Suetonius *Augustus* 25.3

39 H. Russell Robinson, *The Armour of Imperial Rome* (London 1975), 112–113

40 Aulus Gellius *Noctes Atticae* 5.6.17. Festus *Castrensi corona* 49 L.

41 Livy 10.46.3; 30.28.6

42 Valerius Maximus 1.8.6

43 Aulus Gellius *Noctes Atticae* 5.6.17; Festus *Castrensi corona* 49 L.

44 C. Cichorius, *Die Reliefs der Traianssäule* (Berlin 1896), Taf. xlii

45 Livy 7.10.14; 7.26.19; 10.44.3–5

46 Livy 26.48.5

47 Dion. Hal. 10.37

48 Sallust *Bell. Iug.* 85.29

49 Silius Italicus *Punica* 15.262

50 Dio 51.21; Suetonius *Augustus* 25

51 M. Rostovtzeff, 'Vexillum and Victory', *J. Roman Stud.* 32 (1942), 92–106

52 Josephus *Bell. Iud.* 7.15. CIL xiv 3612=ILS 1025 (Flavian); CIL viii 9990=ILS 1352 (Trajanic); CIL iii 1193=ILS 2746 (Antonine); CIL ix 2849 (undated)

53 CIL vi 1599+31828=ILS 1326; ILS 9002=AE 1907, 152=CIL v 648*

54 Polybius 6.39.3–4

55 Tacitus *Annals* 3.21

56 Sallust *Bell. Iug.* 85.29

57 *de Gente Populi Romani* in Servius *ad Aen.* 6.760

58 A. Alföldi, 'Hasta – Summa Imperii. The Spear as the Embodiment of sovereignty in Rome', *American Journal of Archaeology* 63, no. 1 (1959), 1

59 Josephus *Bell. Iud.* 7.15

60 cf. Homer *Iliad* 7.140

61 Festus 55L. A. Alföldi o.c. note 58

62 Josephus *Bell. Iud.* 7.15 CIL xi 7264=ILS 9194

63 T.G.E. Powell, *The Celts* (London 1958), 71–2. 'Torques o. Torquis', Pauly-Wissowa, *Real-Encyclopädie der classichen Altertumswissenschaft* 2nd. ser. 6 (1936), 1800–1805

64 Livy 7.10.4

65 ILLRP 515=ILS 8888=AE 1909, 30=CIL vi 37045

66 Caesar *Bell. Hisp.* 26

67 CIL iii 3158=ILS 3320

68 Pliny *Nat. Hist.* 33.37

69 Caesar *Bell. Hisp.* 26; Josephus *Bell. Iud.* 7.15

70 Suetonius *Caligula* 52

71 Isidor *Orig.* 19.31.16

72 Livy 1.11.8; Xenophon *Anabasis* 1.5.8

73 Polybius 2.29.8

74 Some examples of Celtic armillae appear in J. Déchelette, *Manuel d'Archéologie Préhistorique, Celtique et Gallo-Romaine* II.3 (Paris 1914), 1218f

75 Livy 10.44.3–5

76 Festus 41L

77 CIL XII 2230

78 A. Alföldi. 'Der frührömische Reiteradel und seine Ehrenabzeichen', *Deutsche Beiträge zur Altertumswissenschaft* 2 (1952), 17f

79 Suetonius *Claudius* 17

80 A collection of these is illustrated in H. Gabelmann 'Römische Grabmonumente mit Reiterkampfszenen im Rheingebiet', *Bonner Jb.* 173 (1973), 132–200. A good example from Britain is the tombstone of Longinus Sdapeze from Colchester RIB 201, pl. V.

81 Doorwerth: J.H. Holwerda, 'Een Vondst vit den Rijn bij Doorwerth', *Internationales Archiv Ethnographie* (suppl.) 32 (1933/4), pt.2. Newstead: J. Curle, *A Roman Frontier Post and its People: the Fort of Newstead in the Parish of Melrose* (Glasgow 1911), 298f. and pls. LXXII–LXXIV.

82 O. Jahn 'Die Lauersforter Phalerae', *Fest-Programm zu Winckelmanns Geburtstage am 9 December 1860. Herausgegeben vom Vorstande des Vereins von Altertumsfreunden in den Rheinlanden* (Bonn 1860); F. Matz, 'Die Lauersforter Phalerae', *Winckelmannsprogramm der archeologischen Gesselschaft zu Berlin* 92 (1932), 2–41.

83 J. Curle, o.c. note 81, 174f.; pl. XXXI.

84 Tacitus *Hist.* 1.57.14

85 The history of the site is conveniently summarized in J.E. Bogaers and C.B. Rüger, *Der Niedergermanische Limes* (Bonn 1974), 106–111

86 F. Matz o.c. note 82

87 Polybius 6.39.3

88 Nonnus *Dionysiaca* 9.125; 46.278; 47.9

89 Steiner, *Dona Militaria*, 11f

90 This point is reinforced by a passage in Aristotle's *Rhetoric* 1412b.35 where a shield and a *phiale* are compared. Aristotle quotes as the example of a good simile the statement that 'a shield (ἀσπίς) is the drinking-bowl (φιάλη) of Ares'. The ἀσπίς is circular. Elsewhere (Aristopho 14) the term ἀσπίς is used of a circular bowl.

91 Homer *Iliad* 23.270

92 CIL II 2079=ILS 2713; CIL II 3272

93 *Res Gestae* 34.2 ILS 82. CIL IX 5811

94 Livy 10.44–5

95 Suetonius *Gramm.* 9; anon. *de Vir. Ill.* 3.72.3

96 Fronto *ad Verum* p. 204 (Loeb edition). A letter of AD 165 to Lucius Verus

97 *Thesaurus Linguae Latinae* vol IV col. 958–959

98 G. Korre, *The Ram's Head as an Emblem of Valour* (Athens 1970).

99 One of the best known examples of a ram's head appearing in a Roman military context is on the fine silver helmet from Emesa in Syria, on which the animal's head stands proud on the middle of the brow. The

authenticity of this piece has however recently been challenged. C. Vermuele 'A Roman Silver Helmet in the Toledo (Ohio) Museum of Art', *J. Roman Stud.* 50 (1960), 8–11. H. Russell Robinson, *The Armour of Imperial Rome* (London 1975), 65

100 R. Amy, *L'Arc d'Orange,*xvth suppl. of *Gallia* (1962). O. Klindt-Jensen *Gundestrupkedeln* (1961), figs. 2.8

101 A. Ross, *Pagan Celtic Britain* (London 1967), 172f

102 A. Büttner, 'Untersuchungen über Ursprung und Entwicklung von Auszeichnung im römischen Heer', *Bonner Jb.* 57 (1957), 177–180

103 Pliny *Nat. Hist.* 10.40

104 Pliny *Nat. Hist.* 33.38

CHAPTER V   Triumphs and triumphal ornaments (pages 101–109)

1 The origins, development and whole significance of the triumph have been the subject of a detailed study by H.S. Versnel, *Triumphus* (Leiden 1970)

2 Suetonius *Augustus* 38

3 T. Mommsen, *Römisches Staatsrecht* (3rd ed. 1887), 132 followed by H.S. Versnel, o.c. note 1, 191f

4 Josephus *Bell. Iud.* 7.123–157. K. Lehmann-Hartleben, 'L'Arco di Tito', *Bullettino Comunale* 62 (1934), 89–122, Tav. II

5 Suetonius *divus Iulius* 37.2

6 Versnel o.c. note 1, 66–93; Dion. Hal. 3.61

7 Val. Max. 2.8.1; Livy 40.38; Cicero *in Pisonem* 26.62

8 Dio 43.42

9 Dio 49.42.3; 54.12.1–2; Suetonius *Augustus* 38

10 *Acta Triumphorum*; Pliny *Nat. Hist.* 5.5.36

11 Velleius Paterculus 2.115.3

12 Tacitus *Annals* 3.72; 3.74

13 Livy 4.19–20

14 Livy 4.32.4

15 Livy 4.20.5–11

16 See the discussion by H. Dessau, 'Livius und Augustus', *Hermes* 41 (1906), 142–151

17 Dio 51.25.2

18 R. Syme, *The Roman Revolution* (Oxford 1939), 302f

19 PIR2 L 186

20 Plutarch *Marcellus* 22; Aulus Gellius *Noctes Atticae* 5.6.20–22; Pliny *Nat. Hist.* 15.125; Festus *ovalis corona* 213 L

21 Suetonius *Claudius* 24; Dio 60.30.2 wrongly credits him with a triumph.

22 Dio 60.22.1; 23.1; Suetonius *Claudius* 17.2; Pliny *Nat. Hist.* 3.119

23 Livy 30.15

24 Suetonius *Augustus* 38.1; A.E. Gordon, 'Quintus Veranius, Consul AD 49' *University of California Publications in Classical Archaeology* Vol. 2, no. 5

(1952), appendix 2

25 Dio 54.24.8

26 Suetonius *Tiberius* 9.2

27 Pannonian campaign, Dio 54.31.4. L.R. Taylor 'M. Titius and the Syrian Command', *J. Roman Stud.* 26 (1936), 169–170 for the possibility of *ornamenta* for the Armenian campaign.

28 Dio 60.23.2

29 Dio 60.20.4

30 CIL IX 2847=ILS 971; E. Groag, 'Hosidius', Pauly-Wissowa, *Real-Encyclopädie der classichen Altertumswissenschaft* 8, col. 2490; PIR2 H 217

31 Suetonius *Vespasianus* 4.1

32 Suetonius *Claudius* 17.2

33 Dio exc. 61.31.7; Suetonius *Claudius* 24.3; Tacitus *Annals* 12.3.2; CIL XIV 2500=ILS 957; Gordon o.c. note 24, 318

34 Tacitus *Agricola* 40

35 Dio 55.10.3

36 Tacitus *Annals* 2.52; 3.21; 3.72; 4.23

37 Dio 58.4.8

38 Pliny *Epist.* 2.7

39 Tacitus *Hist.* 1.79.5

40 Gordon o.c. note 24, 311; Dio 55.10.3; Tacitus *Annals* 4.23. For discussion of the statues awarded to Volusius Saturninus cf. J. Reynolds, 'Roman Inscriptions 1966–1970', *J. Roman Stud.* 61 (1971), 142f. and W. Eck 'Die Familie der Volusii Saturnini in neuen Inschriften aus Lucus Feroniae', *Hermes* 100 (1972), 461–484 esp. 464f., 469–72

41 CIL XI 5212=ILS 1058

42 CIL VI 1540=31675=ILS 1112

43 CIL VI 1549=ILS 1100

44 CIL VI 1599+31828=ILS 1326

45 PIR P 558

46 CIL VI 1377+31640=ILS 1098

CHAPTER VI   The awarding of Dona (pages 110–144)

1 Aulus Gellius *Noctes Atticae* 5.6.21; Valerius Maximus 2.8.7

2 Plutarch *Cato Minor* 8.2

3 Tacitus *Annals* 15.72.1; for Nerva see also CIL XI 5743=ILS 273

4 H. Dessau, *Geschichte der römischen Kaiserzeit* Vol. 2.1 (Berlin 1926), 253

5 AE 1952, 232=IRT 346; Tacitus *Hist.* 2.9 (Nonius Asprenas). AE 1914, 279 (Epaphroditus)

6 CIL XI 1834=ILS 1000

7 AE 1925, 126

8 Tacitus *Hist.* 3.44

9 CIL XI 7492=ILS 999

10 Tacitus *Hist.* 4.4.2

11 CIL XI 5028=ILS 1447; Pflaum, *Carrières*, no. 37

12 Caesar *Bell. Civ.* 3.53.6 (Scaeva). Dio 49.14; Livy *Perioch* 129; Pliny *Nat. Hist.* 16.7; Suetonius *Augustus* 25.3; Dio 51.21.3 (Agrippa).

13 E. Ritterling 'Zu den Germanenkriegen Domitiens am Rhein und Donau', *Jahreshefte des österreichischen archäologischen Instituts* 7 (1904), beibl. 28f

14 Dio 68.3–4; CIL v 7425=ILS 2720

15 HA *v. Antonini Pii* 5.4; CIL XI 6057

16 CIL VIII 2786=ILS 2659

17 HA *v. Marci* 21.1

18 HA *v. Hadriani* 11.2; 12.1

19 AE 1951, 88

20 Suetonius *Domitianus* 6

21 CIL XI 395=ILS 2648 for an award in the campaign against the Astures.

22 IGRR IV 1086

23 B. Dobson, 'The Praefectus Fabrum in the Early Principate', in B. Dobson and M.G. Jarrett ed. *Britain and Rome* (Kendal 1966), 72–73

24 Aulus Gellius *Noctes Atticae* 5.6.24–26

25 Cicero *in Verrem* 3.185–7

26 Plutarch *C. Marius* 14.3–5

27 Polybius 6.37.9

28 Pliny *Nat. Hist.* 7.105–6

29 Pliny *Nat. Hist.* 16.14

30 Polybius 6.39. 1–2

31 Livy 26.48.13–14

32 Caesar *Bell. Afr.* 86

33 ILLRP 515=CIL VI 37045=ILS 8888

34 Suetonius *Augustus* 25; *Tiberius* 32.

35 CIL x 4862=ILS 2690; CIL v 4365=ILS 2272; CIL III 3158=ILS 3320; CIL III 2718 (Tiberius). AE 1972, 501 (Germanicus)

36 Tacitus *Annals* 3.21

37 HA *v. Marci* 21.1; 22.9.11; *v. Severi* 2.4

38 CIL VIII 2786=ILS 2659

39 CIL v 531=ILS 989. Tacitus *Hist.* 4. 49–50

40 Suetonius *Tiberius* 32

41 Polybius 6.15.7

42 Suetonius *Claudius* 17

43 Aulus Gellius *Noctes Atticae* 5.6.10

44 Dio 53.16

45 Dio 49.14

46 Suetonius *Divus Iulius* 2

47 Tacitus *Annals* 3.21 (Helvius Rufus); *Annals* 15.12 (Corbulo).

48 CIL XIII 1041=ILS 2531; Pliny *Nat. Hist.* 33.8

49   CIL II 2079=ILS 2713; CIL II 3272. Devijver *Pros. Mil Eq.* C 250

50   CIL VI 3617

51   CIL XII 2230

52   CIL VIII 1026=ILS 2127; ILS 9200=IGLS VI 2796=AE 1903, 368

53   *Mainzer Zeitschrift* 69 (1974), 247=58 Ber RGK, 99. This inscription is the
      first to record the rank (or pay-grade) *triplicarius*, though its existence has
      long been suspected cf. Domaszewski, *Rangordnung*, 71–72

54   P. Holder, *Studies in the Auxilia of the Roman Army from Augustus to Trajan*
      (British Archaeological Reports S 70, Oxford 1980), 28 and 287

55   The known fort at Mainz-Weisenau dates to the period Caligula –
      Claudius, but the existence of pottery and coins of Augustan – early
      Tiberian date indicates the existence of an earlier establishment. cf D.
      Baatz, *Mogontiacum. Neue Untersuchungen am römischen Legionslager in
      Mainz. Limesforschungen* 4 (Berlin 1962), 81–82

56   40 Ber RGK, 169. H.U. Instinsky, 'Grabstein eines berittenen
      Bogenschützen der Ala Parthorum et Araborum', *Germania* 36 (1958),
      72–95

57   CIL III 8746+G. Alföldy, 'Epigraphica', *Situla* 8 (1965), Sect. I no. 7

58   Tacitus *Annals* 6.37

59   AE 1969/70, 583

60   CIL XIII 8503

61   D.J. Breeze, 'The Organisation of the Career Structure of the Immunes
      and Principales of the Roman Army', *Bonner Jahrbücher* 174 (1974),
      263–278. P. Holder, o.c. note 54, 86–90

62   CIL III 14453

63   AE 1971, 276+1972, 353. H. Lieb, 'Zu den Hilfstruppen in Vindonissa',
      Gesselschaft pro Vindonissa. Jahresbericht 1971 (1972), 36–40. E. Meyer 'Ein
      spanischer Centurio in Vindonissa', *Madrider Mitteilungen* 13 (1972),
      190–195

64   AE 1914, 241

65   Published in A. Garcia Y Bellido, 'El "Exercitus Hispanicus" desde
      Augusto a Vespasiano', *Archivio Español de Arqueologia* 34 (1961), 114–160
      cf. AE 1963, 27. Re-read by P. Le Roux and A. Trancy, 'Problèmes
      Épigraphiques de la Province d'Orense', *Boletin Avriense* 5 (1975), 271–279
      to indicate a peregrine with *dona* and again in AE 1976, 296 to give a
      citizen soldier

66   Tacitus *Annals* 2.9

67   Tacitus *Annals* 11.16

68   E. Ritterling, *Fasti des römischen Deutschlands unter dem Prinzipat* (Vienna
      1932), 141. D. Timpe, *Arminius – Studien* (Heidelberg 1970), 41–44

69   P. Holder o.c. note 54, 28

70   J.C. Mann, 'The Role of the Frontier Zones in Army Recruitment',
      Quintus Congressus Internationalis Limitis Romani Studiosorum (Zagreb
      1963), 147f

71   P. Holder o.c. note 54, 29–30

72   Pliny *Nat. Hist.* 33.37

73   Dion. Hal. 10.37

74   Silius Italicus *Punica* 15.256. Caesar *Bell. Hisp.* 26

75   Livy 26.11.9

76   Plutarch *Marius* 28.2

77   ILLRP 515 = CIL VI 37045 = ILS 8888

78   Livy 25.7.4; Valerius Maximus 2.7.15

79   Livy 22.11.8; Livy *Perioch.* 74

80   Valerius Maximus 8.14.5

81   Suetonius *Claudius* 28.

82   AE 1914, 279. PIR2 E 69; W. Eck, 'Neros Freigelassener Epaphroditus und die Aufdeckung der Pisonischen Verschwörung', *Historia* 25 (1976), 381–384

83   CIL VI 3617

84   CIL VI 1598 = ILS 1740

85   H.-G. Pflaum, *Essai sur le Cursus Publicus sous le Haut-Empire romain* (Paris 1940), 261

86   Domaszewski, *Rangordnung*, 139

87   CIL III 1457 = ILS 1097

88   Pflaum, *Procurateurs*, 141–146

89   ILS 9200 = AE 1903, 368 = IGLS VI 2796 (Velius Rufus); CIL VIII 9990 = ILS 1352 (Besius Betuinianus).

90   Pflaum, *Carrières*, no. 163

91   AE 1934, 2

92   H.-G. Pflaum, 'Deux Carrières équestres de Lambèse et de Zama', *Libyca* (Arch.-Epig.) 3 (1955), 142–143

93   CIL X 6662 = ILS 1455

94   Plutarch *Pompey* 38.1

95   CIL XI 395 = ILS 2648; AE 1952, 153

96   CIL II 3788 + *Saitabi* 19 (1969), 23; CIL II 3783; CIL XIV 4725

97   AE 1956, 24

98   Polybius 6.39.1–2; Josephus *Bell. Iud.* 7.5–17

99   CIL III 1457 = ILS 1097

100   Caesar *Bell. Alex.* 77

101   Suetonius *Augustus* 8; *Claudius* 28

102   Velleius Paterculus 2.115.1

103   CIL XII 2230

104   M.J. Crook, *The Evolution of the Victoria Cross* (Tunbridge Wells 1975), Chapter 10

105   Josephus *Bell. Iud.* 6. 133–134

106   Caesar *Bell. Gall.* 1.52

107   Livy 26.48.5, 13–14

108   Valerius Maximus 1.8.6 (283 BC)

109   Valerius Maximus 8.14.5

110   Josephus *Bell. Iud.* 3.103–4; 7.13

111   Parthian war: CIL V 648* = ILS 9002. German war: CIL VI

1599+31828=ILS 1326. Parthian and German wars: CIL xi 7264=ILS 9194

112 CIL xi 6055=ILS 2743

113 P. Aelius Romanus: CIL viii 2786=ILS 2659. Detachment of iii Augusta on the Danube: CIL viii 619+11780=ILS 2747

114 *Athenaeum* 1962, 85–86; AE 1964, 14 omits the line which mentions the decorated soldier.

115 B.L. Montgomery, *Military Leadership* (London 1946), 13

116 Caesar *Bell. Gall.* 2.25

117 Polybius 6.24.9

118 Caesar *Bell. Gall.* 4.25

119 CIL xiii 8648=ILS 2244

120 ILLRP 497=CIL i 624=CIL x 3886=ILS 2225

121 Herodian 3.14.9

122 Tacitus *Hist.* 2.89

123 Livy 45.38.12; 10.46.3

124 Valerius Maximus 3.2.24

125 Caesar *Bell. Gall.* 2.21.5

126 Livy 7.37.1–2

127 Tacitus *Hist.* 1.38.1; Varro *de Lingua Latina* 7.37; Livy 24.7.9

128 Tacitus *Annals* 1.24; *Hist.* 2.89

129 Tacitus *Hist.* 3.10

130 Polybius 6.39.8–10

131 Livy 10.47; Pliny *Nat. Hist.* 16.13

132 Livy 3.58.8

133 Polybius 6.39.10; Livy 10.7.9

134 Pliny *Nat. Hist.* 22.6

135 A. de Franciscis, *The Pompeian Wall Paintings in the Roman Villa of Oplontis* (Recklinghausen 1975), pl. 12

136 Plutarch *Sertorius* 4.2

CHAPTER VII   Imperial scales of award: Senators (pages 145–157)

References to the source material for the individual decorated senators are given in Appendix II.

1 G. Alföldy, 'Consuls and Consulars under the Antonines: Prosopography and History', *Ancient Society* 7 (1976), 263 f.

2 W. Eck, 'Beföderungskritirien innerhalb der senatorischen Laufbahn, dargestellt an der Zeit von 69 bis 138 n. Chr.', ANRW ii.1 (1974), 172

3 Tacitus *Annals* 14.28

4 E. Birley, 'The Adherence of Britain to Vespasian', *Britannia* 9 (1978), 243–6. In this article Birley suggests that the man in question was perhaps a son of Cn. Avidius Celer Fiscillinus Firmus (cf W. Eck, *Senatoren von*

Augustus bis Vespasian (Munich 1970), 118)

5 PIR2 A 756

6 CIL XVI 23

7 Tacitus *Histories* 3.44

8 CIL VI 1237

9 Tacitus *Histories* 4.50

10 Tacitus *Histories* 4.38; 4.48–50

11 G. Alföldy, *Die Hilfstruppen in der römischen Provinz Germania Inferior. Epigraphische Studien* 6 (1968), 131–135; gives full references to earlier discussions of the careers

12 Josephus *Bell. Iud.* 6.43

13 Tacitus *Histories* 3.52

CHAPTER VIII   Imperial scales of award: Equestrians (pages 158–183)

References to the source material for individual decorated equestrians are given in Appendix II.

1 E. Birley, 'Alae and Cohortes Milliariae', *Corolla Memoriae Erich Swoboda Dedicata*. Römische Forschungen in Niederösterreich v (Graz 1966), 54–67

2 Caesar *Bell. Gall.* 3.59; 8.12; Tacitus *Annals* 2.10 (native chiefs). CIL IX 996, XI 711, XII 3177 (centurions or primipilares). Suetonius *Augustus* 38; ILS 911, 912 (senators)

3 Suetonius *Claudius* 25. H. Devijver, 'Suétone Claude 25 et les Milices Equestres', *Ancient Society* I (1970), 69–81

4 Dobson, *Primipilares*, 40f

5 H. Keil in *Forschungen in Ephesos* III (1923), 128. Pflaum, *Carrières* no. 15

6 CIL XVI 44 (Moesia Inferior). Tacitus *Hist.* 4.28 (Marcodurum)

7 Devijver, *Pros. Mil. Eq.* A 166

8 Pflaum, *Carrières* no. 37

9 Domaszewski, *Rangordnung* 137–9

10 CIL XIV 158 (Germania Inferior). CIL XVI 51 (Britain).

11 E. Birley, 'Britain after Agricola and the End of the Ninth Legion', in *Roman Britain and the Roman Army* (Kendal 1961), 23–24. H.G. Pflaum cited by F. Zevi, 'Miscellanea Ostiense', *Atti Lincei, Rendiconti Morali* ser. 8, 36 (1971), 457 n. 21.

12 M.G. Jarrett and J.C. Mann, 'Britain from Agricola to Gallienus', *Bonner Jahrbücher* 170 (1970), 181

13 V.A. Maxfield 'C. Minicius Italus', *Epigraphische Studien* 9 (1972), 242–245

14 *Codex Vaticanus* 5237 f.219

15 Steiner, *Dona Militaria*, 54. Domaszewski, *Rangordnung*, 200. G. Alföldy, 'Ein Hispanischer Offizier in Niedergermanien', *Madrider Mitteilungen* 6 (1965), 105–113

16 CIL XVI 158

17 Tacitus *Hist.* 4.68

18 CIL II 2637. E. Stein, *Die Kaiserlichen Beamten und Truppenkorper im*

römischen Deutschland unter dem Prinzipat (Vienna 1932), 132. G. Alföldy, o.c. note 15.

19 CIL XVI 23

20 Pflaum, *Carrières* no. 116

21 Pflaum, *Carrières* no. 72

22 RIB 1580=CIL VII 635; RIB 2104=CIL VII 1071

23 IGRR IV 1565; CIL XVI 33 (AD 86); CIL XVI 87 (AD 139)

24 CIL XVI 164

25 Pliny *Ep.* 10.21; 10.86A

26 G. Alföldy, 'P. Helvius Pertinax und M. Valerius Maximianus', *Situla* 14–15 (1974), 202

27 EE IX 1278

28 CIL XIII 7697, 7715, 7716

29 R. Syme, 'The First Garrison of Trajan's Dacia', *Laureae Aquincenses* I (1938), 267–286

30 CIL XVI 45 (AD 99); CIL III 1393 (AD 200)

31 J. and A. Sašel, 'Le Préfet de la Iᵉ Aile Britannique milliare sous Trajan à Emona', *Arheološki Vestnik* 28 (1977), 334–341

32 Cichorius, *Ala* 1235 followed by W. Wagner, *Die Dislokation der römischen Auxiliarformationen in den Provinzen Noricum, Pannonien, Moesien und Dakien von Augustus bis Gallienus* (Berlin 1938), 20

33 J. and A. Šašel o.c. note 31, 337

34 CIL III 15197=ILS 9140. L. Barkoczi, *Brigetio* (1951) 51 no. 1

35 For example by A. Radnóti and L. Barkoczi, 'The Distribution of Troops in Pannonia Inferior during the 2nd. Century', *Acta Archaeologica* I (1951), 195

36 CIL XVI 47

37 CIL XVI 61

38 J. Carcopino, *Le Maroc Antique* (Paris 2nd. ed. 1949), 179f

39 Pflaum, *Procurateurs*, 142f

40 CIL XVI 55 (AD 107); XVI 45, 78 (AD 99, 134)

41 T. Nagy, 'Die Ausziechnungen des P. Besius Betuinianus und das Problem der Dona Militaria zu Trajan's Zeitalter', *Acta Antiqua Academiae Scientiarum Hungaricae* 16 (1968), 289–295 (one award). Steiner, *Dona Militaria*, 84; E. Ritterling, 'Zu den Germanenkriegen Domitiens am Rhein und Donau', *Jahreshefte des österreichischen archaeologischen Instituts* 7 (1904), Beibl. 28f.; Pflaum, *Procurateurs*, 142–4 (two awards)

42 CIL XVI 50

43 CIL XVI 61

44 CIL XVI 99 is a diploma awarded in AD 150 to soldiers from units in Pannonia Inferior who were granted *honesta missio* when they were absent from their home province on an expedition to Mauretania: *dimissis honesta missione cum essent in expedition. Mauretan. Caesariens.* cf HA *v. Pii* 5

45 The case of Gavius Bassus, first published in 1972, was not available when Nagy wrote

46 Bertolini's restoration of I *Adiutrix* and the German war is most unlikely.

Two emperors were involved with the award of the *dona*, and these must
be Marcus and Verus; Verus is not known to have been associated with
the award giving for the German war for he died soon after it began. AE
1890, 151 follows the Bertolini restoration in *Not. Scav.* 1890, 173

47 ILS 8977

48 CIL III 1193

49 Cichorius *Ala* 1234

50 Steiner, *Dona Militaria* 84

51 J. Fitz, 'Auszeichnungen der Praefekten der Alae Milliariae', *Klio* 52 (1970),
    99f. argues for a date after the death of Verus

52 Petrus Patricius, *Excerpta de Legationibus Gentium* 6

53 B. Dobson, 'Legionary Centurion or Equestrian Officer? A Comparison of
    Pay and Prospects', *Ancient Society* 3 (1972), 193–207

54 T. Nagy, 'Les Dona Militaria de M. Macrinius Avitus Catonius Vindex',
    Hommages à Marcel Renard. Collection Latomus 102 (1969), 536–546

55 Pflaum, *Carrières*, no. 199

56 CIL VI 37298; IGRR III 551=ILS 8818 (Domitian). AE 1923, 28 (Trajan)

57 Steiner, *Dona Militaria*, 73

58 cf. CIL VIII 12066

59 M.G. Jarrett, 'An Album of the Equestrians from North Africa in the
    Emperor's Service', *Epigraphische Studien* 9 (1972), no. 46. T. Fl. Macer,
    CIL VIII 5351=ILS 1435

60 Coh. D: CIL III 3324, 3668; coh. M: CIL III 3542, 3545, 10673

CHAPTER IX   **Imperial scales of award: Centurions and primipilares**
(pages 184–209)

References to the source material for individual decorated officers are given in
Appendix II

1 On trecenarius cf. B. Dobson and D.J. Breeze, 'The Rome Cohorts
   and the Legionary Centurionate', *Epigraphische Studien* 8 (1969), 118–9

2 T. Wegeleben, *Die Rangordnung der römischen Centurionen* (Berlin 1913)

3 Tacitus *Annals* 15.50

4 Dobson, *Primipilares*, 200

5 The text of this inscription, which is now lost, exists only on the facsimile
   of the stone displayed in the Museo della Civiltà Romana, Rome.

6 Domaszewski, *Rangordnung*, 69

7 E. Birley, 'Promotions and Transfers in the Roman Army. II The
   Centurionate', *Carnuntum Jahrbuch* 1963/4 (1965), 22

8 HA *v. Hadriani* 5.2

9 M.G. Jarrett and J.C. Mann, 'Britain from Agricola to Gallienus', *Bonner
   Jahrbücher* 170 (1970), 181

10 J. Lesquier, *L'Armée Romaine d'Égypte d'Auguste à Diocletien* (Cairo 1918),
   543: H. Hofmann, *Römische Militärgrabsteine der Donauländer.*
   Sonderschriften des Osterreichischen Archaeologischen Instituts in Wien.

References and Notes

Bd. V (1905)

11 Tacitus *Agricola* 40

12 B. Dobson and D.J. Breeze, o.c. note 1, 101 career type B (2a)

13 Dio 69.13.2

14 CIL XI 5960

15 E. Birley, o.c. note 7, 29–30

16 RIB 814=CIL VII 371. For a recent discussion of the career cf R. Davies 'Cohors I Hispanorum and the Garrisons of Maryport', *Trans. Cumberland Westmorland Antiquarian Archaeol. Soc.* new series 77 (1977), 8–9

17 HA *v. Hadriani* 5.2

18 E. Birley, 'Britain after Agricola and the End of the Ninth Legion', in *Roman Britain and the Roman Army* (Kendal 1961), 26–29. For a contrary view Dobson, *Primipilares*, 236, M.G. Jarrett, 'An Unnecessary War', *Britannia* 7 (1976), 145–151 and M.G. Jarrett, *Maryport, Cumbria, a Roman Fort and its Garrison* (Kendal 1976), 17f

19 Dobson, *Primipilares*, 60

20 Dobson, *Primipilares*, 235–6

21 B. Dobson, 'Legionary Centurion or Equestrian Officer? A comparison of Pay and Prospects', *Ancient Society* 3 (1972), 193–207

22 CIL XI 5632=ILS 2735

23 HA *v. Pii* 5.4–5

24 CIL XVI 99

25 AE 1957, 123

26 CIL VI 32523a+37184; CIL VI 32624

27 H. Lieb, 'Zu den Hilfstruppen in Vindonissa', *Gesselschaft pro Vindonissa, Jahresbericht* 1971 (1972), 36–40. E. Meyer, 'Ein Spanischer Centurio in Vindonissa', *Madrider Mitteilungen* 13 (1972), 190–195

28 RIB 1172 and pl. XVII

29 Domaszewski, *Rangordnung*, 110

30 CIL XI 1602. The fragmentary text reads : [. . . .]c, 7 leg. xx[. . . . .]n. aur. hasta [pura . . . .] divi Vespasiani f.

31 CIL XI 2112

32 B. Dobson and D.J. Breeze, o.c. note 1, 118–119

33 IGRR III 1434 for Gallus as *primipilaris* in AD 115

34 Dobson, *Primipilares*, 223

35 Tacitus *Histories* 1.20

36 Dobson, *Primipilares*, 90f.

37 A. v. Domaszewski, 'Beiträge zur Kaisergeschichte', *Philologus 66* (1907), 171f. followed by Pflaum, *Carrières* no. 165

38 Dobson, *Primipilares*, 276 f

39 F. Jantsch, 'Ein Inschrift aus Allersdorf', Carinthia I heft. 2 (1933), 175–179

References and Notes

CHAPTER X   Imperial scales of award: Below the centurionate (pages 210–217)

References to the source material for individual decorated soldiers are given in Appendix II.

1   Dio 55.24.8. CIL VI 3416 shows an *evocatus* with a *vitis*
2   T. Mommsen, *Gesammelte Schriften*. VII *Epigraphische und Numismatische Schriften* (Berlin 1913), 451 and after him M. Durry, *Les Cohortes Prétoriennes* (Paris 1938), 121
3   Steiner, *Dona Militaria*, 77–78
4   Tacitus *Annals* 15.50
5   Caesar *Bell. Gall.* 8.8
6   Tacitus *Annals* 3.21

CHAPTER XI   Battle honours of the Roman army (pages 218–235)

1   CIL V 875=ILS 1374; CIL III 11930=IBR 278; probably to be restored on CIL III 11931=IBR 277; CIL XVI 55, 117, 183; AE 1961, 173=RMD no. 25
2   CIL XVI 160. See p. 228
3   CIL XVI 163; AE 1915, 58=ILS 9506
4   M. Durry, *Les Cohortes Prétoriennes* (Paris 1938), 198
5   C. Cichorius, *Die Reliefs der Traianssäule* (Berlin 1896) Taf. VIII, XXXIII A.v. Domaszewski, *Die Fahnen im römischen Heere*. Abhandlungen des archäologisch-epigraphischen Seminares der Universität Wien, Heft. 5 (Vienna 1885)
6   AE 1939, 81=ILT 720 (*armillata*); AE 1930, 92 (*bis armillata*)
7   AE 1908, 22
8   CIL XVI 26, 45, 58
9   AE 1890, 159
10 CIL XVI 165, 169
11 CIL XVI 159 in Mauretania Tingitana by 88; Tacitus *Hist.* 1.59.64 in Gaul; AE 1939, 60 in Rhineland; CIL II 2984 Spain
12 CIL V 875=ILS 1374
13 CIL VI 3538=ILS 2729 add; CIL XVI 23 (T. Staberius Secundus). Statius *Silvae* 1.4.89–93
14 Ala I Fl. Aug. Brit. CIL III 6748; AE 1908, 23; AE 1914, 241; *Arheološki Vestnik* 28 (1977), 334. Coh. VIII Raetorum AE 1960, 375
15 *Torquata*: CIL III 5775=IBR 85; CIL III 5776=IBR 86=ILS 1369. *Torquata et armillata*: AE 1939, 81=ILT 720. *Bis torquata et bis armillata* AE 1930, 92
16 AE 1939, 81=ILT 720; ILT 721
17 Pflaum, *Carrières*, no. 86
18 CIL XVI 23 (Germ. Inf.); CIL XVI 30, 164 (Pannonia). AE 1962, 255; CIL XVI 185; RMD 64 (Dacia Porolissensis).
19 CIL XVI 42
20 N. Gudea, 'Observatii cu Privire la Cohortele I Hispanorum din Dacia',

Studii si Cercetări de Istorie Veche si Arheologie 26 no. 3 (1975), 381–385, fig, 3; cf. CIL III 6283=8074, 18a and b

21 CIL XVI 57 (AD 110); RMD 35 (AD 133); CIL XVI 185 (AD 164). cf M. Roxan, 'Epigraphic Notes', *Epigraphische Studien* 9 (1972), 247–250 and *The Auxilia of the Roman Army raised in the Iberian Peninsula.* Unpublished London Ph.D. thesis (1973), 218–223. *Contra* N. Gudea, o.c. note 20

22 RIB 957=CIL VII 929. CIL XI 5669=ILS 2728

23 The date AD 98 depends on the restoration of the *ala Petriana* on CIL XVI 43. CIL XVI 69 for AD 122

24 CIL XIII 6820=ILS 2491 add (Mainz); Tacitus *Hist.* 1.70 (Rhineland); RIB 1172 (Hexham). J.P. Gillam, 'The Roman Forts at Corbridge', *Archaeologia Aeliana* 5th. ser. 5(1977), 53

25 CIL XI 5271

26 E. Birley 'Britain after Agricola and the End of the Ninth Legion', *Roman Britain and the Roman Army* (Kendal 1953), 24

27 CIL XI 6033

28 CIL XVI 51 (AD 105); CIL XVI 69 (AD 122)

29 CIL XIII 8306=ILS 2534 (Cologne) and CIL XIII 8668 (Kalkar) are tombstones of decurions of the unit. These have been variously dated to the first century by E. Stein, *Die kaiserlichen Beamten und Truppenkörper im römischen Deutschland unter dem Prinzipat* (Vienna 1932), 127 and by K. Kraft, *Zur Rekruitierung der Alen und Kohorten an Rhein und Donau* (Bern 1951), 148, to the second century or later by G. Alföldy, *Die Hilfstruppen in der römischen Provinz Germania Inferior* (Bonn 1968), 17–19

30 An alternative sequence starting in the East, thence to Lower Germany and finally to Britain, depends on the dating of the Cologne inscription (o.c. note 29) to the mid-first century and on the equation of this *ala Gallorum et Thracum* (*Classiana*) with the *ala Gallorum et Thracum* attested on a diploma of AD 54 (CIL XVI 3) which was stationed in the East. Margaret Roxan has however suggested that the unit on the diploma is the *ala Gallorum et Thracum constantium* which is attested as part of the garrison of Syria in AD 88 and 91 (RMD 3, 4), possibly still there in AD 139 (CIL XVI 87) and again in 186 (RMD 69), and which clearly did not move west. It was in the East under the command of the Dux Palestinae in the late fourth century (Not. Dig. Or. 34.33): cf M. Roxan, 'Pre-Severan Auxilia named in the Notitia Dignitatum' in ed. R. Goodburn and P. Bartholomew, *Aspects of the Notitia Dignitatum* (British Archaeological Reports S 15, Oxford 1976), 59–68 esp. Table IV and p. 62

31 CIL III 5918a, 11931; 37/38 Ber RGK, 81

32 G. Alföldy, 'Zur Beurteilung der Militärdiplome der Auxiliarsoldaten', *Historia* 17 (1968) 215–227. J.C. Mann 'The Development of Auxiliary and Fleet Diplomas', *Epigraphische Studien* 9 (1972), 233–241

33 CIL XVI 160

34 HA *v. Hadriani* 9.4 (prefecture of Marcius Turbo); RMD 21, 22

35 CIL XVI 163

36 RMD 20

37 I.I. Russu, *Dacia și Pannonia Inferior* (Bucharest 1973), 83

38 Moesia Superior: CIL XVI 39 (AD 94); RMD 6 (AD 96); CIL XVI 46 (AD 100). Dacia: CIL XVI 57 (AD 110); CIL XVI 163 (AD 110). Dacia Porolissensis: RMD 47 =CIL XVI 110 (AD 159); CIL XVI 185, RMD 63, 64, 66 (AD 164)

39 Paul Holder has interpreted this evidence rather differently, suggesting that [Marcus] Ulpius received an individual grant of citizenship: P. Holder, *Studies in the Auxilia of the Roman Army from Augustus to Trajan* (British Archaeological Reports S 70, Oxford 1980), 30. He follows Gudea's views on the question of which *cohors I Hispanorum* was at Românaṣi

40 CIL XVI 17

41 The question of grants to numeri was discussed by J.C. Mann, 'A Note on the Numeri', *Hermes* 82.4 (1954), 501–506, working with two very fragmentary diplomas, CIL XVI 68 and 114. Since he wrote three further documents have come to light which support the conclusions which he advanced: RMD 17, 27, 28

42 CIL XVI 68, RMD 17 (AD 120); RMD 27, 28 (AD 126)

43 HA *v. Hadriani* 6.1

44 HA *v. Hadriani* 7.3 Turbo's united command is reflected in the diploma RMD 21, dated to August 10, 123, which records grants of citizenship and *conubium* to men who served under Turbo in units stationed in the provinces of Pannonia Inferior and Dacia Porolissensis. Dacia Porolissensis, which did not exist by this name at the time of Turbo's command was created some time prior to 123, the date of this diploma, out of territory hitherto part of Dacia Superior. Dušanić and Vasić have argued that the joint award is connected with the campaign against the Iazyges and Roxolani: S. Dušanić and M.R. Vasić, 'Fragment of a Military Diploma from Moesia Inferior', *Germania* 52 (1974), 408–425 and RMD 22 note 3

45 AE 1944, 56 (Use of title *c.R.*). CIL III 1471, 7693, 7999, 14216 (Aelii)

46 CIL XVI 114. HA *v. Antonini Pii* 5.5

47 CIL XVI 7–11; no. 10 records the grant *ante emerita stipendia*, no. 11 records the grant to those who have served twenty or more years

48 CIL XVI 35

49 C. Minicius Italus CIL V 875=ILS 1374 cf. V.A. Maxfield 'C. Minicius Italus', *Epigraphische Studien* 9 (1972), 242–245. He held his next post in 73–4. Pompeius Faventinus CIL II 2637=AE 1966, 187

50 RIB 159=CIL VII 52

51 B. Dobson and J.C. Mann, 'The Roman Army in Britain and Britons in the Roman army', *Britannia* 4 (1973), 198 fn. 34. E. Birley, 'Roman Garrisons in Wales', *Archaeologia Cambrensis* 102 (1953), 9–19

52 P. Holder o.c. note 39, 30–31, 52

53 RIB 2092, 2104, 2110 (Birrens). RIB 1981, 1982, 1983 (Castlesteads)

54 J.C. Mann Review of G. Rupprecht, *Untersuchungen zum Dekurionenstand in den nordwestlichen Provinzen des römischen Reiches, Germania* 54 (1976), 513. F. Millar, *The Roman Emperor and his World* (London 1976), 630f

55 H. Wolff, 'Die Cohors II Tungrorum milliaria equitata c(oram)? l(audata)? und die Rechtsform des ius Latii', *Chiron* 6 (1976), 267–288

56 AE 1956, 24

57 CIL XI 6033 (ala Gallorum et Thracum Classiana); CIL XVI 56 (cohors I Augusta Nerviana).

58 P.S. Austen and D.J. Breeze, 'A New Inscription from Chesters on Hadrian's Wall', *Archaeologia Aeliana* 5th ser. 7 (1979), 116f. RIB 893, 894, 897, 946

59 E. Birley, 'A New Inscription from Chesterholm', *Archaeologia Aeliana* 4th. ser. 40 (1934), 129f

60 The question of unit titles in the first and early second centuries is discussed more fully in P. Holder o.c. note 39, Chap. 2,3

CHAPTER XII   Decoration, promotion and prestige (pages 236–247)

1 Caesar *Bell. Civ.* 1.3

2 Caesar *Bell. Civ.* 3.53

3 CIL III 14416=ILS 7178

4 Livy 42.34.5 (Spurius Ligustinus); Plutarch *Sertorius* 3.3

5 Josephus *Bell. Iud.* 6.135; 6.53

6 AE 1969/70, 583

7 AE 1956, 24

8 Josephus *Bell. Iud.* 7.15

9 Vegetius 2.7

10 G.R. Watson, *The Roman Soldier* (London 1969), 25–27; E. Birley, 'The Epigraphy of the Roman Army', *Actes du deuxieme congrès internationale d'Épigraphie grecque et latine*. Paris 1952 (1953), 234

11 Varro *de Lingua Latina* 5.90

12 Livy 7.37.1

13 CIL III 3844+13398=ILS 2438

14 Caesar *Bell. Gall.* 6.40

15 Caesar *Bell. Civ.* 1.46.4

16 CIL III 6818=ILS 1017. The career is discussed in detail by R. Syme, 'The Enigmatic Sospes', *J. Roman Stud.* 67 (1977), 38–49

17 E. Birley, 'Alae and Cohortes Milliariae', *Corolla Memoriae Erich Swoboda Dedicata*, Römische Forschungen in Niederösterreich v (Graz 1966), 54f

18 E. Birley o.c. note 17, 58

19 PIR2 C 521 (P. Cassius Secundus); PIR2 C 490 (P. Cassius Dexter); J. and A. Šašel 'Le Préfet de la Iᵉ Aile Britannique milliare sous Trajan à Emona', *Arheološki Vestnik* 28 (1977), 338–9

20 Pflaum, *Procurateurs*, 218

21 For credentials cf. Pliny *Ep.* 10.87

22 *Age and Sex Pattern of Mortality. Model Life-Tables for Under-developed Countries.* United Nations Department of Social Affairs, Population Branch, New York (1955). For their application to the study of the Roman population cf. K. Hopkins 'On the probable age structure of the Roman population', *Population Studies* 20 (1966–67), 245–264 and of the Roman army in particular J. Rainbird, *The Vigiles of Rome.* Unpublished Durham University PhD thesis (1976), Section 5.2.10 and Appendix III

23 Dobson, *Primipilares*, 60–63

24 Dobson, *Primipilares*, 63, 150

25 Polybius 6.39

26 Livy 23.23.6

27 Pliny *Nat. Hist.* 16.13

28 AE 1956, 24

29 CIL vi 1499=ILS 1107

30 ILS 9002=AE 1907, 152=CIL v 648★. PIR2 F 584

31 B. Dobson, 'Legionary Centurion or Equestrian Officer ? A Comparison of Pay and Prospects', *Ancient Society* 3 (1972), 193–207

32 *Revue des Études Grecques* 61 (1948), 201 (Gavius Fronto); CIL x 5064=ILS 2667, CIL xiii 6762 (Tillius Rufus)

33 Domaszewski, *Rangordnung*, 117 and 137

34 Sallust *Bell. Iug.* 85.29

35 Livy 42.34.11

36 Tacitus *Annals* 1.44

37 Livy 3.58.8 (Sp. Oppius); 6.20.7 (M. Manlius)

38 Pliny *Nat. Hist.* 22.6

39 Livy 2.59.11

40 Polybius 6.37

CHAPTER XIII   The end of Dona (pages 248–254)

1 Vegetius *de Re Militari* 2.7. See also p. 238f

2 G.R. Watson, *The Roman Soldier* (London 1969), 26

3 Caesar *Bell. Hisp.* 26

4 Fronto *ad Amicos* 1.6. G. Alföldy and H. Halfmann, 'Iunius Maximus und die Victoria Parthica', *Zeitschrift für Papyrologie und Epigraphik* 35 (1979), 195–212

5 HA *Aurelian* 13. 2–4

6 HA *Probus* 5. 1–3

7 Ammianus 24. 4. 24

8 Tertullian *de Corona* 7.1; 9.1

9 A. v. Domaszewski, *Die Religion des römischen Heeres* (Berlin 1895), 95

10 Procopius *History of the Wars* 7. 1–8

11 G. Bovini, *I Monumenti Antichi di Ravenna* (Milan 1954), pl. 43

12 G. Bruns, *Der Obelisk und seine Basis auf dem Hippodrom zu Konstantinopel* (Istanbul 1935). D. Strong, *Roman Art* (Pelican History of Art. London 1976), 169–170, pl. 254, 255

13 D. Strong, o.c. note 12, 167 and pl. 250

SELECT BIBLIOGRAPHY

Alföldi, A.	'Hasta – Summa Imperii. The spear as Embodiment of Sovereignty in Rome', *American Journal of Archaeology* 63 no. 1 (1959), 1–27
Alföldy, G.	'Ein Hispanischer Offizier in Niedergermanien', *Madrider Mitteilungen* 6 (1975), 105–113
Alföldy, G.	*Die Legionslegaten der römischen Rheinarmeen.* Epigraphische Studien 3 (Cologne 1967)
Alföldy, G.	*Die Hilfstruppen in der römischen Provinz Germania Inferior* Epigraphische Studien 6 (Dusseldorf 1968)
Alföldy, G.	'Zur Beurteilung der Militärdiplome der Auxiliarsoldaten', *Historia* 17 (1968), 215–217
Alföldy, G.	*Fasti Hispanienses. Senatorische Reichsbeamte und Offiziere in den spanischen Provinzen des römischen Reiches von Augustus bis Diokletian* (Wiesbaden 1969)
Alföldy, G.	'Consuls and Consulars under the Antonines: Prosopography and History', *Ancient Society* 7 (1976), 263–299
Alföldy, G. and Halfmann, H.	'Iunius Maximus und die Victoria Parthica', *Zeitschrift für Papyrologie und Epigraphik* 35 (1979), 195–212
Birley, E.	'Alae and Cohortes Milliariae', *Corolla Memoriae Erich Swoboda dedicata. Römische Forschungen in Niederösterreich* (Cologne 1966), 54–67
Breeze, D.J.	'The Organisation of the Career Structure of the Immunes and Principales of the Roman Army', *Bonner Jahrbücher* 174 (1974), 245–292
Büttner, A.	'Untersuchungen über Ursprung und Entwicklung von Auszeichnungen im römischen Heer', *Bonner Jahrbücher* 157 (1957), 127–180
Cichorius, C.	'Ala', Pauly-Wissowa *Real-Encyclopädie der classichen Altertumswissenchaft* I, col. 1224–1270
Cichorius, C.	'Cohors', Pauly-Wissowa, *Real-Encyclopädie der classichen Altertumswissenschaft* IV, col. 231–356
Cichorius, C.	*Die Reliefs der Traianssäule* (Berlin 1896–1900)

Devijver, H.	'Suétone, Claude 25 at les Milices Équestres', *Ancient Society* 1 (1970), 69–81
Devijver, H.	*Prosopographia Militiarum Equestrium quae fuerunt ab Augusto ad Gallienum* (Louvain 1976–1977)
Dobson, B.	'Legionary Centurion or Equestrian Officer? A Comparison of Pay and Prospects', *Ancient Society* 3 (1972), 193–207
Dobson, B.	*Die Primipilares. Entwicklung und Bedeutung, Laufbahnen und Persönlichkeiten eines römischen Offiziersranges* (Cologne 1978)
Dobson, B. and Breeze, D.J.	'The Rome Cohorts and the Legionary Centurionate', *Epigraphische Studien* 8 (1970), 100–124
Domaszewski, A. von	*Die Fahnen im römischen Heere*. Abhandlungen des archäologisch-epigraphischen Seminares der Universität Wien (Vienna 1885)
Domaszewski, A. von	*Die Rangordnung der römischen Heeres* (1908) 2nd. ed. B. Dobson (Cologne 1967)
Durry, M.	*Les Cohortes Prétoriennes*. Bibliothèques des Écoles Françaises d'Athènes et de Rome, fasc. 146 (Paris 1938)
Eck, W.	*Senatoren von Vespasian bis Hadrian: prosopographische Untersuchungen mit Einschluss der Jahres- und Provinzial-fasten der Statthalter*. Vestigia. Beiträge zur alten Geschichte Bd. 13 (Munich 1970)
Eck, W.	'Beförderungskritirien innerhalb der senatorischen Laufbahn dargestellt an der Zeit von 69 bis 138 n. Chr.', ANRW II, 1 (1974), 158–228
Fitz, J.	'Auszeichnungen der Praefekten der Alae Milliariae', *Klio* 52 (1970), 99–106
Gabelmann, H.	'Die Typen der römischen Grabstelen am Rhein', *Bonner Jahrbücher* 172 (1972), 65–140
Gabelmann, H.	'Römische Grabmonumente mit Reiterkampfszenen im Rheingebiet', *Bonner Jahrbücher* 173 (1973), 132–200
Gordon, A.E.	'Quintus Veranius, Consul AD 49', *Univ. of California Publications in Classical Archaeology* 2 no. 5 (1952), 231–352. Appendix 2. Triumphal Honors and Statues and other Official Honorary Statues set up in Rome during the Empire
Harmand, J.	*L'Armée et le Soldat à Rome de 107 à 50 avant notre ère* (Paris 1967)
Hofmann, H.	'Römische Militärgrabsteine der Donauländer', *Sonderschriften des Österreichischen Archäologischen Instituts in Wien* 5 (Vienna 1905)
Holder, P.A.	*Studies in the Auxilia of the Roman Army from Augustus to Trajan* (British Archaeological Reports S 70, Oxford 1980).
Jahn, O.	'Die Lauersforter Phalerae', *Fest-Programm zu Winckelmanns Geburtstage am 9 December 1860. Herausgegeben vom Vorstände des Vereins von*

Select Bibliography

Altertumsfreunden in den Rheinlanden (Bonn 1860)

Mann, J.C.   'A Note on the Numeri', *Hermes* 82 (1954), 501–506

Mann, J.C.   'The Development of Auxiliary and Fleet Diplomas', *Epigraphische Studien* 9 (1972), 233–241

Mann, J.C.   'Duces and Comites in the 4th. Century', in ed. D. Johnston, *The Saxon Shore* (CBA Research Report no. 18. London 1977), 11–15

Matz, F.   'Die Lauersforter Phalerae', *Winckelmannsprogramm der archäologischen Gesselschaft zu Berlin* 92 (1932), 2–41

Maxfield, V.A.   *The Dona Militaria of the Roman Army*. Unpublished Durham Ph.D. thesis (1972)

Nagy, T.   'Die Auszeichnungen des P. Besius Betuinianus und das Problem der Dona Militaria zu Trajans Zeitalter', *Acta Antiqua Academiae Scientiarum Hungaricae* 16 (1968), 289–295

Nagy, T.   'Les Dona Militaria de M. Macrinius Avitus Catonius Vindex', *Hommages à M. Renard* (1968), 536–546

Pflaum, H.-G.   *Les Procurateurs Équestres sous le Haut-Empire romain* (Paris 1950)

Pflaum, H.-G.   *Les Carrières procuratoriennes équestres sous le Haut-Empire Romain* (Paris 1960)

Radnóti, A.   'Zur Auszeichnung "torquata" und "bis torquata" der Auxiliartruppen', *Germania* 39 (1961), 458–461

Ritterling, E.   *Fasti des römischen Deutschlands unter dem Prinzipat* (Vienna 1932)

Ritterling, E.   'Legio', Pauly-Wissowa, *Real-Encyclopädie der classichen Altertumswissenschaft* XII col. 1211–1829

Robinson, H.R.   *The Armour of Imperial Rome* (London 1975)

Roxan, M.M.   *The Auxilia of the Roman Army raised in the Iberian Peninsula*. Unpublished London Ph.D. thesis (1973)

Roxan, M.M.   *Roman Military Diplomas 1954–1977*. London Institute of Archaeology Occasional Papers no. 2 (London 1978)

Saddington, D.B.   'The Development of the Roman Auxiliary Forces from Augustus to Trajan', ANRW II 1 (1974), 176–201

Speidel, M.   'The Captor of Decebalus: a new Inscription from Philippi', *Journal of Roman Studies* 60 (1970), 142–153

Starr, C.G.   *The Roman Imperial Navy 31 BC–AD 324* (New York 1941)

Stein, E.   *Die kaiserlichen Beamten und Truppenkorper im römischen Deutschland unter dem Prinzipat* (Vienna 1932)

Steiner, P.   'Die Dona Militaria', *Bonner Jahrbücher* 114/115 (1905), 1–98

Syme, R.   *The Roman Revolution* (Oxford 1939)

Versnel, H.S.   *Triumphus: an Enquiry into the Origin, Development and Meaning of the Roman Triumph* (Leiden 1970)

Walbank, F.   *A Historical Commentary on Polybius* (Oxford 1957–1967)

Watson, G.R.   *The Roman Soldier* (London 1969)

INDEX

Index

Index